Creating the Big
Game

Coach John W. Heisman in his coaching prime. (Photo courtesy of the Sports Information Department, University of Pennsylvania.)

Creating the Big Game

John W. Heisman and the Invention of American Football

Wiley Lee Umphlett

CONTRIBUTIONS TO THE
STUDY OF POPULAR CULTURE,
NUMBER 34

GREENWOOD PRESS
Westport, Connecticut • London

Library of Congress Cataloging-in-Publication Data

Umphlett, Wiley Lee.
   Creating the big game : John W. Heisman and the invention of
American football / Wiley Lee Umphlett.
      p.   cm. — (Contributions to the study of popular culture,
ISSN 0198–9871 ; no. 34)
   Includes bibliographical references and index.
   ISBN 0–313–28404–0
   1. Heisman, John W. (John William), 1869–1936.   2. Football—
United States—Coaches—Biography.   3. Football—United States—
History.   I. Title.   II. Series.
GV939.H38U46   1992
796.332′092—dc20
   [B]   92–10087

British Library Cataloguing in Publication Data is available.

Library of Congress Catalog Card Number: 92–10087
ISBN: 0–313–28404–0
ISSN: 0198–9871

First published in 1992

Greenwood Press, 88 Post Road West, Westport, CT 06881
An imprint of Greenwood Publishing Group, Inc.

Printed in the United States of America

The paper used in this book complies with the
Permanent Paper Standard issued by the National
Information Standards Organization (Z39.48–1984).

10 9 8 7 6 5 4 3 2 1

Copyright Acknowledgments

The author and publisher gratefully acknowledge Strode Publishers/
Circle Book Service for permission to quote from *Ramblin' Wreck: A Story
of Georgia Tech Football*, © 1973 by Al Thomy.

Every reasonable effort has been made to trace the owners of copyright
materials in this book, but in some instances this has proven impossible.
The author and publisher will be glad to receive information leading to
more complete acknowledgments in subsequent printings of the book and
in the meantime extend their apologies for any omissions.

This book is dedicated to the pioneers of American football. Their vision and commitment not only helped create the "Big Game" but also resulted in what John Heisman himself hailed as a "great game."

Contents

Acknowledgments   ix

Introduction: In Search of a Man and His Game   xi

1. Young Heisman and the Origins of His Game (1869–1891)   1

2. Coach Heisman, Football Missionary: The Game Spreads
   (1892–1903)   29

3. Heisman and the Coming of the Forward Pass (1904–1911)   79

4. Heisman and the Shaping of the Modern Game (1912–1919)   117

5. Heisman and Football's Golden Age: The Big Game Goes
   National (1920–1927)   159

6. The Inception of the Heisman Trophy: Memorializing the
   Coach, the Player, and Their Game (1928–1936)   213

   Conclusion: The Heisman Legacy   247

   Appendix: John W. Heisman's Coaching Record, 1892–1927   255

   Bibliography   257

   Index   263

Acknowledgments

Upon John Heisman's death in 1936 sportswriter Joe Williams remarked in the *New York World-Telegram* that the old coach's "collection of records and documents was amazing, and it is to be hoped his survivors will see that they are placed in sympathetic hands." Having first conceived of this book as a biography, I had planned to gain access to at least part of this important source material, particularly after learning that it had fallen into the "sympathetic hands" of Coach Heisman's relatives. Unfortunately, all of my requests for permission to review this collection were never acknowledged. Compelled to work from records secured from any cooperative source I was fortunate enough to locate, I revised my plans and set out to write what is essentially a biocultural study. In this light, I have attempted to reveal how an inspired and dynamic personality, through his varied contributions to the development of a national game, helped create one of this country's most cherished public rituals—the Big Game. Any error in fact concerning John Heisman's life and career, then, may be attributable to my reliance on whatever seemingly relevant information I could uncover, no matter how insignificant.

Fortunately, John Heisman was a prolific writer, and wherever possible I have tried to capitalize on the body of his writings that appeared in periodicals, newspapers, and student publications. His strong public image and natural rapport with the media made him the subject of numerous articles and feature stories over the years, another major source on which I have depended.

For access to most of this information I am indebted to the schools where

Coach Heisman played and coached, as these institutions were most gracious in responding to my numerous requests. In particular, thanks are extended to Martha Mitchell, the Brown University archivist; Maryellen C. Kaminsky, archival specialist at the University of Pennsylvania; Roland M. Baumann, archivist at Oberlin College; President William V. Muse of the University of Akron (formerly Buchtel College), who personally saw to it that material about Heisman's brief but significant tenure there was sent to my attention; David J. Rosenblatt of the Auburn University archives department; Dennis Taylor, archivist at Clemson University, and Bob Bradley, former sports information director there; Nancy V. Gauss, Anne Bartlow, and Denise Winkler of Georgia Tech's archives and records department; Dr. Eugene Griessman, director of Georgia Tech's national media relations (a Heisman authority in his own right); David W. Kraeuter, public services director of the Miller Library at Washington and Jefferson College; and the team of Barbara Sheffert, Nancy Boothe, and Anthony Narkin of the Woodson Research Center at Rice University.

I am also grateful to Mrs. Marty Kinnear of Phoenix, Arizona, a former resident of John Heisman's spiritual hometown of Titusville, Pennsylvania, who got me started in the right direction. Other helpful Titusville contacts were the Benson Memorial Library director Barbara Auchtor and research specialist J. D. Waychoff.

Thanks also go to Bernadette M. Beglane, promotions director at the Downtown Athletic Club of New York City, and Margaret McNulty of the National Football Foundation and Hall of Fame.

Closer to home, I benefitted immensely from the prompt attention of the University of West Florida library staff to my numerous requests for books and articles secured through the interlibrary loan system. It was the word-processing expertise of Lauren Booth, Patricia M. Salem, and Cheryl Phelps, however, that helped ease the burden of refining my material and organizing my manuscript into its final form. Without their help this project would have presented me with a most formidable editing task. My special thanks to them for helping me formulate this complex and fascinating story of a "man and his game."

Introduction
In Search of a Man and His Game

Lack of recognition has epitomized the football heritage of John William Heisman. Ever since his death in 1936 and the resultant naming of the Heisman Trophy in tribute to his many athletic accomplishments and contributions to the development of intercollegiate football, the identity of Heisman-the-man appears to have been increasingly obscured by the popular reception of the trophy itself. Indeed, in developing into something of a public relations media event for the organization that sponsors the award annually, the Heisman Trophy soon evolved into an image more directly associated with the player who is presented with it each year than with the person who originally inspired it. Consequently, the passing years have revealed that the public in general and the winners of the trophy in particular possess little or no knowledge about the person whom it honors. Mike Garrett, the University of Southern California halfback who won the Heisman in 1965, was actually echoing the sentiments of many other recipients before and since when he rather pointedly remarked: "The award's wonderful. But who's Heisman?"

One of the primary reasons for such anonymity is that during his lifetime Heisman posed as a man of many faces. Educated in law, he tried his hand at such varied callings as acting, writing, teaching, real estate, and business, although he found his greatest success in coaching athletics. Consequently, the personal idiosyncrasies, even the contradictions attendant to his multifarious professional interests and private pursuits, have served to obscure the dominant features of his personality, resulting in a diffused, enigmatic, mostly misunderstood image of the man. Not only was he an intensely private person, but on occasion he could be highly volatile and even melodramatic in his dealings with the press, the public, and his players. He was a scholarly type, but one who preferred a life of physical action to one of monastic contemplation. Although he was essentially a sincere, highly sensitive person in his personal dealings, he could also be severe, even bitterly vindictive when he chose to be. As a part-time actor who performed in summer stock, he apparently allowed his histrionic side to have center stage in creating a public persona that often contradicted itself.

John Heisman, then, was a many-faceted individual who was an extremely complex, elusive figure, but nonetheless still fascinating in the diversity of his personal makeup. He characteristically professed a single-minded devotion to the proper development of a sport that started out as a simple game played by schoolboys and young college men but that he helped evolve into a national ritual that enthralls a huge segment of the American population each fall. Like many of the mercurial running backs he coached, Heisman was continually changing his course of direction, testing the resistance before him to discover the best way to achieve any personal goal he may have set for himself. And like many of the linemen he coached, Heisman was sufficiently stubborn to hold his ground if he knew such a reaction was necessary to bring about a proper result. As a naturally success-oriented person who took his cue from the fabulous go-getter types that big business and industry spawned during the formative years of his life, Heisman and the corporate nature of football were truly made for each other, as his overall coaching success bears out.

From a humanistic perspective, the story of John Heisman is really the story of American football. The fact that his life (1869–1936) directly paralleled the evolution of intercollegiate football makes him a convenient point of reference for recognizing significant events in the complex history of the game. Because Heisman coached at eight different schools of varying missions in every part of the country except the far West, and because his coaching career spanned some of the most momentous years in American history, he is an appropriate figure to relate to not only the growth of intercollegiate athletics but also the growth of American higher education. His public involvement also connects him with important political, economic, and social developments that had an impact on American society and sports during his day. These culturally significant factors govern the form and shape this book ultimately takes.

My underlying purpose here, then, is not so much biographical as it is biocultural, revealing how the strength of one man's personality and the sociocultural background of his time affected the emergence of an indigenous American public ritual—the Big Game. In the process, this book tries to do more than just cover the highlights of Heisman's life and his personal contributions to the development of American football. It also discusses other influential coaches' contributions while tracing the game's sixty-year (c. 1880–1940) expansion into a national sport.

On yet another level, this book is the story of how college football developed into the complex, problematic, and highly structured big business that it is today. Whether for good or bad, John Heisman himself played an unwitting role in this development, mainly through his emphasis on the worth of winning and his understanding of the coach's role as that of an uncompromising autocrat. In the long run, Heisman's football inventiveness may have been overshadowed by more heralded coaching figures like Walter Camp, Amos Alonzo Stagg, and Glenn Warner, but the innovations he introduced were of such consequence that the game as we know it today might not have come about had it not been for the concerted efforts of this far-sighted man and his contemporaries of kindred spirit.

If for no other reason, though, John Heisman-the-football-coach should be remembered as the foremost proponent of the forward pass, a lone voice at first but one whose relentless, tireless efforts finally resulted in acceptance of the game's most revolutionary feature since Walter Camp's proposal of the scrimmage line in 1880. Considering how much a part of the game the forward pass has become, we would find it difficult today to realize how strongly opposed to its adoption certain factions were in Heisman's day. In championing its cause, Heisman was as much a competitor off the field as he was on it, and he exercised a visionary quality in his quest to open up the game that few coaches ever had. At the time of Heisman's death in 1936, sports columnist Joe Williams, a personal acquaintance, observed:

> Heisman was a football institution. He knew the game back in the days of the flying wedge and he knew it in its current razzle-dazzle form. It isn't too much to say he grew up with the game.
> Heisman coached football all over the country. For 36 years he was tinkering with the offense and experimenting with the defense. Football was practically his life's work.... He never lost his enthusiasm for the game, and he never grew old mentally....
> Even back in the Stone Age of football, Heisman's mind ran to innovations which are now so much a fixed part of the modern scheme.... He had vision, and he could see that football in due course would become more and more open in technique.[1]

The acuteness of Heisman's creative vision was such that he could see more clearly than most of his peers in diagnosing the ills of the game and prescribing cures for them. In this respect, he was the right person in the right place at the right time, for he possessed the necessary obstinacy to stick to his convictions in carrying out what he knew had to be done to save football from itself.

Nevertheless, in his desire and eagerness to experiment and improvise to find ways to open up the game and help eliminate its questionable elements, Heisman was often accused of deception and underhanded stratagems, and for this reason he was the most misunderstood of our more-successful football coaches. The most positive defense of Heisman's special role in the development of intercollegiate football was written by old-school sports reporter and football historian L. F. "Fuzzy" Woodruff in 1928 after Heisman had retired from coaching:

I'm inclined to believe after a careful study of Heisman's record and a careful study of the times in which he developed his football teams that the just historian will reach the inevitable conclusion that Heisman never did anything that it wasn't customary for his rivals to do. Sometimes he had to fight fire with fire and he always fought. . . .

I know there are men who will take exceptions to these paragraphs, but they are written in the hope that future football generations may have a correct idea of a gentleman much abused.[2]

If this book can help substantiate Woodruff's position by giving the reader "a correct idea of a gentleman much abused," as well as fill in the gaps in the life of an important figure as it relates to the development of a major American sport, it will have succeeded in its primary intent. Actually, as his life reveals it, the reputations of Heisman-the-man and of Heisman-the-football-coach are inseparable and say a great deal about his important role in helping "invent" the game that became his lifelong passion.

NOTES

1. Joe Williams, "Heisman Knew Football," column in *New York World-Telegram*, October 1936.

2. L.F. "Fuzzy" Woodruff, *History of Southern Football* Vol I (Atlanta, Ga.: Georgia Southern, 1928), 143.

1

Young Heisman and the Origins of His Game (1869–1891)

The years after the Civil War when the continent was only partly explored were the halcyon days of the Go-Getters. They went in search of what others had never imagined was there to get. The Go-Getters made something out of nothing, they brought meat out of the desert, found oil in the rocks, and brought light to millions. They discovered new resources, and where there seemed none to be discovered, they invented new ways of profiting from others who were trying to invent and to discover.

—Daniel J. Boorstin,
The Americans: The Democratic Experience (1974)

The danger to college football, as in anything else, lies in the failure to know the origins of the game and the people responsible for its growth and maturity.

—Jack Whitaker,
Foreword to John T. Brady, *The Heisman: A Symbol of Excellence* (1984)

THE "GREENING" OF A FOOTBALL COACH (1869–1886)

The world John William Heisman was born into was the fiercely competitive world of the cattle, railroad, and oil barons, a world that saw the rise of big business and the advent of the corporation. In short, it was an era dominated and controlled economically by rugged individuals known popularly as go-getters. A peculiarly American breed, these were men who found ways to get rich by capitalizing on every opportunity that came their way, often from the unexpected windfalls of a rapidly developing country still searching for its identity.

For a number of years, the town in which young John Heisman grew up was a microcosm of this dynamic age in American history. Fittingly enough, one of the premier go-getters who played a significant role in contributing to the town's pervasive dynamism was a figure of soon-to-be legendary proportions—John D. Rockefeller.

In the late summer of 1859, when oil was first discovered there, Titusville, Pennsylvania, was nothing more than a tiny rural village of some four hundred souls nestled in the wooded foothills in the northwestern part of the state. In just a few years, though, the town and its environs were transformed into a bustling, sprawling community overrun with thousands of opportunistic, get-rich-quick speculators common to a frontier boomtown. By 1863, in fact, Titusville was no longer the picture of a tranquil, idyllic village-town that would become so much a part of American lore. A London newspaper correspondent described the area at this time as a place where "derricks stand as thick as trees in a forest.... Derricks throng the low marshy bottomland, derricks congregate on the sloping banks, derricks even climb the precipitous face of the cliffs, establishing a foothold wherever a ledge of rock projects or a recess exists."[1]

Helping perpetuate the dynamic transformation of the area were countless success stories like the one about a poor Methodist minister from Cleveland Ohio, Van Vleek, who was having a tough time supplying the basic needs of his family. While employed by a contractor to negotiate the right of way for the construction of the Oil Creek railroad, Van Vleek encountered an obstinate farmer who refused to give up his land. The minister borrowed money to buy the farm at a moderate price, and a short time later oil was discovered on the property. Van Vleek then sold out for a profit of more than $100,000, a tidy sum of money in those days.[2]

Only about a hundred miles away from Titusville, the city of Cleveland was both inundated and impressed by such stories of the opportunities to get rich in the burgeoning Pennsylvania town to the east. When oil had first been discovered in Titusville, Rockefeller was a young man of barely twenty but was a Cleveland businessman-industrialist well on his way to amassing his fabulous wealth. Aware of the growing demand for rock oil to fuel kerosene lamps for illumination purposes, Rockefeller employed his unique organizational sense to full advantage and exploited the Titusville oil strike to such an extent that ultimately he came up with the most efficient way to turn rock oil into a highly marketable commodity at home and abroad.

It was not until the Civil War, however, when the railroads initially connected Cleveland to the oil fields, that Rockefeller first bought into the numerous refineries that began springing up along the tracks. By war's end he was able to buy out a partner and, in true go-getter fashion, start to forge his own destiny. In fact, by the late 1860s, the future billionaire was well on the way to monopolizing the oil market, having survived economic depression and the overproduction of his competitors by craftily playing the railroads one against the other. Rockefeller had helped his cause even more by growing his own timber and setting up his own cooperage plants to manufacture the barrels that would hold his product. It was during the expansion of this latter enterprise that the Heisman name would become permanently associated with the town of Titusville.

Of old German stock, John Michael Heisman and his wife, Sarah, had settled in Cleveland to raise a family and build a better future for themselves.[3] A cooper by trade, the senior Heisman, upon hearing stories of the fabulous happenings in Titusville, promptly moved his family there and started up a lucrative business manufacturing barrels for the oil industry.[4] Although John the younger had been born in Cleveland in 1869, his adolescence was to become so intimately involved with the Pennsylvania boomtown that thereafter he would identify with it as his spiritual place of origin. Furthermore, during the future coach's growing-up years in the 1870s and 1880s, something of the commercial fever and atmosphere of the 1860s still lingered and must have had a vivid, lasting influence on the personal makeup of an ambitious and impressionable youth. As such, he was probably looking ahead to the time and the opportunity to make his way in the world, after the manner of the popular Horatio Alger go-getter type of juvenile fiction.

Although information is scarce about this early part of Heisman's life, we do know that during his high-school years he was highly motivated to achieve in both athletics and academics. Indeed, throughout his entire coaching career, his evaluation of the worth of a good education inculcated in him the persistent desire to impress upon his players the goal of academic excellence. A nephew, William Lee Heisman, once recalled a locker-room incident that exemplified his uncle's impatience with any player who thought playing football was more important than getting an education:

My uncle came busting through the door and went over to this guy and said, "Red, you can't play today because you haven't got your grades." The player looked up at my uncle and said, "Coach, don't you know that the sportswriters call this toe on my right foot the million-dollar toe?" My uncle snapped right back quick and said, "Yeah, but what good is it if you only have a fifteen-cent head?"[5]

As the outstanding student of his graduating class of 1887, young Heisman had been captain of the baseball team, a champion gymnast, and, in spite of his slight size, a member of the football teams of 1884, 1885, and 1886. But of all sports it was the game of football, then still in its developmental stages, that made such an indelible impression on him that it would later change the direction of his life. Heisman's own story relates that it had been the inspired purchase of a ten-cent rules book that had motivated him to begin a serious study of the game as well as beginning a lifelong love affair with it. The thing that had prompted his procurement of the rules book was the discovery that the American version of football actually allowed a player to run with the ball. Until several eastern college players returned home on vacation and demonstrated this innovation, John and his teammates at Titusville High had been playing soccer style. The ball-carrying show put on by the college men was a revelation: "Then and there the old game lost its savor. From that moment nothing of football which did not permit running with the ball appealed to me."[6] But in the long run, Heisman's fascination with the rules and strategies of the game and how they might be modified to benefit both participants and spectators would inspire him to come up with some of football's most daring innovations as well as to compel him to take on a self-appointed role as guardian of the game's ultimate destiny.

In 1984, the city of Titusville, in observing the 125th anniversary of the "Birthplace of the Oil Industry," dedicated an athletic field to Coach Heisman's memory. In attendance were William Lee Heisman and his son, who were both featured speakers during the ceremonies. At one point in his speech, the elder Heisman made a significant observation about the influence of the Titusville environment on his uncle: "The process of the greening of a football [coach] began in Titusville," he said. "Titusville, you have the same hills and turf that John Heisman walked. He honed his skills here."[7] And these were skills that were competitive not only in a strictly athletic sense but also in a self-motivated, success-oriented manner.

A basic contention of this book is that John Heisman's lifelong interest in athletics, particularly the game of football, was honed to a considerable degree during his youth by the predominantly capitalistic and commercial ambiance that Titusville had inherited from its boom days. Within this goal-oriented side of the American belief that success in work and material acquisition is in itself a sign of God's favor and therefore a kind of religious experience, John Heisman and the game of football discovered themselves. Consequently, after the American version of the game started to evolve, it demanded the leadership of empathetic go-getter types like John Heisman to see that the game kept to its course in order to realize its true destiny. As a naturally symbolic contest inspired by the nineteenth-century passion for land acquisition and the expansion of business and industry, football would evolve from these roots to find its fullest expression in twentieth-century technology.

If the game of American football can be categorized as *the* corporate game, as indeed it has been,[8] its natural origins and gradual development from a British-style game into today's purely American version of corporately structured play stem from the era of the doggedly acquisitive capitalists—the John D. Rockefellers and others of his ilk, who, in letting nothing stand in their way to achieve the goal and rewards of material success, inspired the prototypical leadership model for the expanding corporate world of their day. Their strategies for success had a dominant influence on university men of the eastern educational establishment, men of individualistic mold and bold determination who were ultimately responsible for football's development into a purely American game, which, as the years passed, became increasingly businesslike, corporate, and even technological in nature. As substantiated in numerous sources, the growth of team sports in the late nineteenth century resulted in large part from the intensely competitive commercial development and industrial expansion of that era.

John Heisman would become a part of this intensely competitive environment, as it was expressing itself in the developing eastern athletic establishment when he arrived on the Brown University campus in the fall of 1887 and later at the University of Pennsylvania. He was naturally conditioned to this competitive milieu. Indeed, the special training in self-aggrandizement he had acquired during his early years in Titusville would affect all of his relationships for the rest of his life, whether of an athletic, business, or interpersonal nature. As the rise of organized sports coincided with the expansion of business and industry in late nineteenth-century America, so Heisman's life would correlate directly with the development of football in America. Accordingly, this future legend of American sport would live to see his beloved game evolve through various distinct phases over a fifty-year period to become very much like the game we see played today. He himself would play an intimate part in this evolutionary process, not only by dreaming up unique innovations to help refine the game's rough places but also by stubbornly championing many changes that contributed to transforming football into the highly sophisticated spectacle it is today. As Gene Griessman observed: "Heisman, perhaps more than any other, moved football into the modern era through his innovations, which opened up the game, through his emphasis on strength of character in coaches and players, and through his organizational and public relations flair."[9]

THE ORIGINS OF THE GAME (1869–1890s)

Appropriately, Heisman's life parallelled the birth and development of American football in amazingly precise stages. This is why we need to examine what had transpired in the development of American football up to the time when young John Heisman started playing his version of the game in the 1880s.

Almost as though it were a harbinger of things to come, Heisman's birth on October 23, 1869, preceded by only two weeks an event that came to be officially recognized as the first intercollegiate football match ever played.[10] But the match itself, scheduled between Rutgers and Princeton on November 6 in New Brunswick, New Jersey, was a wild and woolly affair whose style of play would hardly be recognized as the kind of football we have come to know today. With each side composed of twenty-five players, this contest would seem to today's spectator to be nothing more than an all-out, unstructured free-for-all. Actually, the rules in effect then were loosely adopted from British football (soccer), in which both teams had agreed that the ball could only be advanced by kicking it or striking it with the hands or fists. The first side to propel six goals between two stationary posts at either end of the field was to be declared the winner of the match. Under these rules, Rutgers, which had the home-field advantage, went on to win, 6–4. This was an inconsequential outcome at the time, but with this confrontation the seed for the evolution of American intercollegiate football had been planted.[11]

It was during the 1870s that trends toward the transformation of both soccer and rugby into American football began in earnest. In 1870, Columbia fielded a team, and by 1872 both Harvard and Yale, perennial leaders in the development of intercollegiate athletics, were playing the game as it then existed, although the Harvard Crimson's modified version of soccer-rugby had greater import for the future of football. In this respect, a confrontation of even greater significance than the Rutgers–Princeton game of 1869 was the 1874 match between Harvard and McGill University of Montreal.

Until this pivotal encounter, American football had continued to be dominated by variations of British-style soccer in which the main way to score was by kicking. The contest between McGill and Harvard featured the McGill team's rugby-style football, which allowed a player to run with the ball, and Harvard's "Boston-game" interpretation of football. This was a variant of soccer, with the lone exception that, as in rugby, a player could pick up the ball at any time and run with it. Actually, the major difference between the two styles of play lay in McGill's use of rugby's scrummage or scrum, a rather crude means of putting the ball back in play after play had been halted by a player being tackled, by an out-of-bounds play, or by some other on-field incident. The problem with the scrum was its ineffectiveness in starting up play again, as a tangled knot of opposing players often struggled for several minutes before finally succeeding at their task. Even then a team's possession of the ball was more often determined by pure chance than by any special skill or strategy.[12]

Surprisingly, of two matches played between these schools, one according to McGill's rules and the other according to Harvard's, the Crimson won the first and tied the second. And in spite of the confusing aspects of the scrum, the American team instinctively realized that the rugby style of play had a lot to offer. Clearly, something highly individualistic about the running, passing, and tackling elements of rugby appealed strongly to the American approach to interpreting the self-expressive aspects of football. Actually, Harvard's stubborn resistance to playing by soccer rules while championing its own version of rugby was a significant step toward the development of an American-style game, for Harvard's leadership in athletics at this time was widely influential.

The very next year, Harvard and Yale, having been rivals in the first intercollegiate sport of rowing since the 1850s and in baseball since the 1860s, proposed to play each other in football for the first time. But because there was no standing agreement as to whether soccer or rugby rules should govern play, student representatives from the two schools met in Springfield, Massachusetts, in October 1875 to make plans for the match. What resulted was a number of concessions to the rules of each system of play, with Harvard's preference for rugby prevailing. Running with the ball, the scrum, lateral passing, tackling, and fifteen players on a side would now be allowed. Such a game was made to order for the Crimson, of course, and when the match was played that November before some two thousand onlookers in New Haven, Harvard won handily, 4 goals to 0. The Crimson's success at winning through the predominantly rugby style of play, though, provided the impetus for other schools to start switching to this system. As a result, 1875—the year of the first Harvard–Yale match—was the last year in which soccer elements were a part of American collegiate football, although other sections of the country were slow to adapt to any sudden innovations. (For example, see Heisman's description of the soccer style of football he played as late as the 1880s in Titusville, p. 14).

While Harvard won the initial match in this long-standing series (one to grow so venerable over the years that it would be affectionately referred to as The Game), Yale began to dominate the ensuing matches in such impressive fashion during the 1880s and into the 1890s that Crimson fans could just about concede victory to the Blue every time the annual game rolled around. In fact, over a thirty-three-year span, Yale defeated Harvard twenty-nine times.[13] Yale enjoyed national dominance, too. When the Helms Hall of Fame Foundation started naming an annual football champion in 1883, the Blue won the title nine times from 1883 through 1900. (From 1883 until the advent of the Associated Press's ranking of top teams in 1936, the Helms national champion was considered official by most football observers.)

One reason advanced for Yale's lopsided edge in the Harvard series during this time—and one quite germane to a basic premise of this work—is that the New Haven school professed and practiced a different philosophical approach to how football should be played. Harvard, with its more aristocratic traditions, as well as its British understanding of sport as an end in itself, viewed athletic endeavor as a gentlemanly diversion. On the other hand, Yale, with a student body recruited mainly from the plebeian ranks of the nouveau riche, looked upon sport, particularly football, as a way to indoctrinate its participants in an all-winning philosophy based on the capitalistic precepts of the day. After all, weren't the go-getters themselves now sending their sons to Yale to learn how to advance the cause of capitalism? Essentially, the Harvard–Yale series, as it was played during the last quarter of the nineteenth century, represented a clash in values in which Yale, because of its sensitivity to the realities of a changing world, always held the upper hand. (Even the way in which athletics were controlled at these institutions was markedly different. Whereas Harvard assigned faculty committees to oversee athletic programs, Yale placed such control mainly in the hands of its students.)

During the post–Civil War period, American values were being tempered by the spread of industry and big business and the colleges were coming more under their influence than that of the church and the established aristocracy. The game of football began to reflect this trend in both its organization and its style of play. With this development, of course, the seeds of professionalism in college athletics were first planted, in particular at institutions like Yale—if only imperceptibly at first.

There was a paradox in the British sporting tradition that Harvard subscribed to, stemming from the fact that even though the British considered the code of gentlemanly involvement in athletics an essential part of a young man's schooling, they contributed many sports innovations that were purely capitalistic or corporate in nature. Not the least of these was the practice of molding individual wills to a common goal by emphasizing the gains, as well as profits, to be made from planning ahead through teamwork and training. As a result, the coach came to play an increasingly prominent role in the management of such a system.

That the capitalistic belief in management control, fine-tuned organization, and the will to win should be essential to the successful makeup of any football team was emphatically demonstrated in Yale's preparation for the Harvard match of the very next year. Eugene Baker, captain of Yale's 1876 team, was still smarting from the loss to the Crimson when he brought his men together that fall to begin training for the upcoming Harvard match. Thoroughly grounded in the rules of rugby, Baker drilled his men relentlessly in such basic elements of the game as running, lateral passing, and tackling. But what was more apparent in his practice drills was his insistence on self-discipline, team play, and a determined will to win—all qualities of the pervasive capitalistic system. Baker's coaching tactics and his players' hard work ultimately paid off, as Yale went on to outplay the more experienced but conservatively prepared Harvard team, winning the second game of the series 1 goal to 0.

But an even bigger payoff for the development of intercollegiate football in the years ahead was the legacy Gene Baker left behind as the prototypical coach who professed both a solid game plan and a positive philosophy of winning. Professionally appointed coaches of future years, such as John Heisman, owe a great debt to the pioneering efforts of dedicated player-coaches like Baker, who was among the first to realize that bringing out the best in his players is the football coach's primary goal in the process of producing a winning team.

Of course, in Baker's day the game truly belonged to the students. There were no paid coaches and even graduate advisers had yet to make an appearance. In a student-controlled athletic system like Yale's, for example, football teams elected a captain at the conclusion of the season to organize and lead the next year's team, as Gene Baker had done. Respecting his responsibilities, the captain was actually the prototype of the professional coach, soon to make an appearance. He organized training procedures and practice sessions, selected the players who would start a game, and made important decisions during a game. The student manager, forerunner of the athletic director, handled the administrative side of things, such as scheduling games and accounting for finances.

Even with the general acceptance of rugby as the model for American football, though, disagreement persisted over such matters as the number of players to make up a team (eleven was beginning to win favor over fifteen) and a uniform system of scoring, by both running (touchdown) and kicking (goal).[14] Following the first Harvard–Yale game in 1876, the American Intercollegiate Football Association was formed, composed of Columbia, Harvard, Princeton, and Yale. This organization instituted several significant developments in addition to the acceptance of the English rugby style of play. The old round rubber soccer-style ball was replaced by rugby's oval, leather-covered one. The length of the game was fixed at two forty-five minute halves, and the size of the field at 140-by-70 yards. Provisions were also made for a championship game to be played on Thanksgiving Day, an innovation that would become one of the most popular traditions in intercollegiate sports and, as such, a prelude to the advent of the publicly recognized ritual known as the Big Game.

However, the most far-reaching innovations that would ultimately transform the derivative features of rugby into a truly American game originated with a shrewdly imaginative player-coach from Yale named Walter Chauncey Camp. He had been a star athlete in prep school, and as a freshman at Yale was good enough to play on Gene Baker's team, which had defeated Harvard in 1876. A physical fitness devotee, young Camp had little difficulty adapting to Baker's strict training system. So versatile an athlete was he, as well as a leader and overachiever in virtually everything he undertook, that Camp could easily have served as the model for Gilbert Patten's Frank Merriwell, the fictional athletic hero from Yale who was popular with juvenile readers during the late 1890s and the early twentieth century.

From a coaching standpoint, Camp subscribed to Baker's formula for organizational efficiency. In staying on without pay after graduation to direct the football fortunes of the Yale varsity each fall while he worked toward the eventual presidency of the New Haven Clock Company, he developed into the ideal combination of the corporate man and the go-getter type. In his zeal for efficiency and organization, Camp epitomized the code of the successful businessman in action. He hated to lose, always planned to win, and, in order to achieve this end, subscribed to a social Darwinist code that involved Yale players in a tough survival-of-the-fittest training program.[15]

Although he never officially performed as "head" coach at Yale, Camp was certainly the dominant figure in control and the one to whom Yale captains and athletic leaders looked for counsel and coaching direction. Even after his coaching days, Camp's dedication to the game of football, as evidenced by his attendance at every football rules convention from 1878 until his death in 1925, would earn him the well-deserved title "Father of American Football." But if this title honored the fruits of Camp's efforts, the mission of John Heisman in a later day would transcend that of Walter Camp through his role as a zealous overseer of the proper development of the game, as his fight to legalize the forward pass was to bear out.

Naturally, to the management-minded Camp the game of rugby came across as a loose and generally unstructured affair, moving him to propose a series of revolutionary rule changes. Although his initial proposal (limiting teams to eleven players rather than fifteen) at his first meeting of the American Intercollegiate Football Association in 1878 was voted down, with dogged persistence he returned the following year with the same proposal, among others. (Because Baker's model 1876 team had played so well with just eleven players, Camp was convinced that this number would be the most practical makeup of a team.)

However, it wasn't until 1880 that he presented his most revolutionary departure from the rugby rules—a scrimmage system for getting the ball into play, one that would allow the offensive team to plan more strategic maneuvers than could be achieved with rugby's scrum and its disorderly mass of interlocked bodies. Camp's argument obviously impressed the members of the association, as they voted unanimously to accept the change. The die was now cast, for with the adoption of Camp's scrimmage system, American football was born. Concerning the organizational significance of this innovation, John Heisman himself commented in later years: "Walter Camp's scrimmage plan gave the ball into the possession of the center, and he alone could put it into play with a snapback. This control of the ball made it possible for the offensive team to plan plays in advance, and the use of signals by the quarterback made for better team play."[16] A rational way to plan plays in advance was the key breakthrough in Camp's scrimmage system, of course, demanding strict management control as well as providing for countless strategic possibilities. Indeed, it was a breakthrough whose strategic repercussions are still being felt today.

At that same 1880 meeting, agreement was also reached on again changing the dimensions of the field—they were further reduced to 110-by-53 yards—and the number of players on a team was finally set at eleven rather than fifteen. Although there were various interpretations as to how the eleven players should line up, it was again Camp who produced the standard formation that won most favor and eventually gave rise to the names of the positions, mainly due to their stations: seven linemen, a quarterback, two halfbacks, and one fullback.[17]

Although Camp's revisions were monumental in their overall impact, they would eventually lead to other necessary changes. For example, Camp soon discovered, to his dismay, that his scrimmage system created an unexpected situation that allowed one team to dominate the action by maintaining unlimited possession of the ball. The undesirable result was that long, uneventful stretches of offensive maneuvering occurred, thus permitting the team in possession to keep the ball away from an opponent at will. In 1880, for example, Princeton and Yale played their infamous "block" game in which each team managed to keep the ball away from the other and by so doing, provided the spectators with probably the most boring football game ever played. (Another rule that extended indefinite possession of the ball was the "safety," which allowed a team to retreat behind the goal line and retain possession on the 25-yard line. Camp countered this maneuver in 1883 by penalizing teams one point for possession of the ball behind their own goal.) However, it was not long before the indomitable Camp came up with a brilliant solution to this problem: a system of downs, which permitted the team in possession of the ball three attempts to advance the ball five yards, or turn the ball over to the opposing team. In 1882, this proposal was adopted by the association. With the advent of 5-yard stripes that same year, the football field suddenly took on its "gridiron" appearance, as well as one of its most descriptive metaphors.

Among Walter Camp's other significant contributions during this time was a numerical scoring system, which was adopted in 1884: a field goal by drop kick counted 5 points (the emphasis was still on kicking, even though the running game had become dominant); a touchdown, 4 points; a goal after touchdown, 2 points; and a safety, 2 points (as reevaluated from the preceding year's 1 point). He also advocated permitting tackling below the waist (low tackling was at that time illegal), proposed penalties for jumping offside and for delay of game, and argued for a neutral zone between scrimmage lines to deter impulsive fighting.[18]

Unfortunately, Camp's constructive contributions to improving the style of play in American football, particularly his innovations in tackling and blocking procedures, helped transform the game from an open game of reverses, laterals, and end-around plays into a more closed style of play that lasted from 1884 on into the 1890s. The result was an offense that concentrated power at the point of attack as the most reliable way to move the ball down the field. Due to the overriding desire to win, this led to tactical innovations that added to the increasing brutality of the game.

The science of tackling was always a major concern of John Heisman during his coaching years. Even after he had retired, he wrote about how rule changes governing tackling converted the game into a more closed offensive style during the 1880s, resulting in even more on-field violence. As Heisman described the early years of football tackling techniques, "tackling below the waist was taboo. You could leap upon the runner's shoulders. You could fetch him down with a strangle hold. You could put a head-lock on him. But you were penalized and put down as a dirty player if you tackled him below the waist."

Soon tackling around the neck was ruled out, and Heisman went on to describe the results of the Rules Committee's 1888 decision to allow tackling as low as the knees, and how this ruling made it easier for a light man to bring down a big man, with the upshot being that the ball carrier began to charge low behind a protective wall of blockers, often hurdling the line feet-first with devastating impact.[19]

Also during this time, the offensive technique of "guarding the runner" or interference—what Camp called "the keynote of the American game"— began to evolve into a concerted attack, with blockers escorting the runner in front as well as on either side. (In this early developmental stage of American football, innovations seemed to crop up practically overnight, mainly because the existing rules were in such a state of flux that experimentation became a matter of course.)

Almost as an inevitable consequence, the V-formation or wedge attack soon appeared, in which the ball carrier was protected by a tightly knit phalanx of blockers preceding him. In 1884, when Princeton first pulled off its so-called V trick against the University of Pennsylvania, it shocked the football world. But by the 1890s, this system of momentum attack had evolved into the notorious "flying wedge," an offensive style that, due to its natural tendency toward steam-roller brutality, did more to undermine public sympathy for football than any other tactic. Invented by Harvard's football adviser Lorin DeLand, who, interestingly, had never played football, this tactic first made its appearance in the 1892 Harvard–Yale game. Heisman has described the flying wedge's awesome advent:

> Yale's first glimpse of this new bruising machine was had early in the game. Two lines of Harvard men, five in a line, fell back 20 yards along either boundary of the field. Trafford of Harvard was standing over the ball in the conventional position of a center man. . . .
> Blithely, Trafford waved his arm and the two lines of his teammates started running toward him in Indian files. By the time they had reached him their momentum was terrific. Trafford scooped up the ball, thereby putting it in play, stepped back between the two leading runners, the two lines instantly converging, and ran within this flying V with Yale men being hurled hither and yon like spray from the prow of a battleship.[20]

The negative side of football, considerably heightened by the monster of mass momentum DeLand had created, grew steadily worse in the eyes of the game's critics.

In its day Heisman felt that the highly feared flying wedge tactic was "quite as startling and unique as is the forward pass of today." Part of this fear emanated from the early method of getting a game underway:

> Today we start the game with a kick-off, but in those days it was a fake kick, the center merely touching the ball to his toe and then tossing it back to a team-mate who ran with it while the rest of the team gave him what interference it could.
> In the flying wedge, however, nine of the players of the team withdrew about 20

yards from mid-field and at a signal those nine, in two lanes, started simultaneously and at full speed, converging on a point indicated by the ball. By the time they arrived at the ball, they had worked up a stupendous mass momentum, and the interference they gave for the runner was something wonderful to behold, and terrible to stop.

The following year, as Heisman related, Coach George Woodruff at Penn came up with his unique version of the wedge—a tactic he called the "flying interference," which could be utilized every down his team had possession. Before the ball was snapped, the tackle and end swung back together to come around to the positions of the other tackle and end. As the ball went into play, the blocking at the point of attack was doubly reinforced. Like the flying wedge, Woodruff's strategy proved so unstoppable that the Rules Committee outlawed both it and the wedge "in order to preserve the proper balance between offense and defense."[21]

Although the last quarter of the nineteenth century was a testing time for college football, the game was growing rapidly in popularity as an intercollegiate sport. And in spite of the game's brutal aspects, football was generally defended as a builder of character, manhood, and teamwork—all qualities considered essential to perpetuating the American way by helping produce what many considered to be the ideal man, the virile, take-charge leader of men who stood in marked contrast to the effete, scholarly type.

The real measure of football's popularity was revealed in the number of schools in other areas of the country beginning to launch programs. In the 1870s, the University of Virginia, Washington and Lee, and the Virginia Military Institute (VMI) became the first schools in the South to play football, just as Michigan was in the Midwest. The Michigan Wolverines even dared to travel East as early as 1881 to play the likes of Harvard, Princeton, and Yale in what were the first intersectional matchups. In the early 1880s other midwestern schools such as Minnesota, Purdue, Indiana, and Notre Dame had also jumped on the football bandwagon, and during this time even the West Coast teams of the University of California, the University of Southern California (USC), and the University of Washington had initiated interclass play, resulting in intercollegiate matches in the 1890s. Perhaps due to their more conservative systems, the service academies did not start playing football until 1890 with the advent of the first Army–Navy game, won by the Navy Midshipmen, 24–0. Attendance at games was increasing, too. Whereas in 1883 some ten thousand spectators had watched the Harvard–Yale game in New York, eight years later forty thousand saw Princeton and Yale square off.

THE GAME DURING HEISMAN'S COLLEGE DAYS (1887–1891)

Such was the ever-expanding but still embryonic state of American football that John Heisman encountered during his playing days at Brown and Penn during the period 1887–1891. As a protean game still striving to define itself, it emphasized brawn as opposed to speed and skill at the playing positions, and as such was a kind of survival contest in which a participant's physical endurance was put to the ultimate test. According to Heisman, however, something was clearly lacking in the style of play practiced during his high school days at Titusville, which "was only a species of Association football [soccer]. Of rules we observed few, having few. Signals we had none—needed none, wanted none. We butted the ball, punched it, elbowed it and kicked it." In the meantime,

Yale, Harvard, Princeton and several other Eastern colleges were playing Walter Camp rules, still very much a mystery to us of the inland schools. . . .

We were having the times of our lives assaulting a round, black rubber ball up and down expansive fields. We had fifteen men on a side and in the game that we played, the ball belonged to him or them strong enough and fleet enough to take it.

If we had regret, or if we harbored a single longing for the game as played at Yale and Harvard, it was that they could carry the ball, and under our so-called rules we could not. There was not one among us who, with the soaring ball within our reach did not long to gather it to his chest and go galloping down the field to glory.[22]

While Heisman's natural affinity for even this early form of football is apparent in these passages, his father's reaction to game play, like that of many observers during this time, was considerably less enthusiastic, calling it "bestial," even refusing to watch his son's high school games. And as the game of football evolved into the kind governed by "Walter Camp rules," the brutality would increase, and with it a growing crescendo of protest.

Yet even during those uncertain, primeval days of football's genesis, Heisman's analytical mind, which like Camp's was attracted to the intellectual and strategic side of the game, recognized numerous deficiencies in the way football was being played. As one of the pioneer football coaches, Heisman would help remedy many of these deficiencies.

By the time Heisman entered Brown as a seventeen-year-old freshman in 1887, the school had been engaging in football for a number of years, but the game had not really caught on to the extent it had at many other New England schools. Part of the reason for this slow acceptance could be attributed to Brown's generally conservative position in controlling student participation in extracurricular activities. Established by the Baptists of America at Warren in 1764 as Rhode Island College, this seventh-oldest institution of higher learning in the United States was essentially following the educational precedent that had been set by other denominations such as the Presbyterians at Princeton, the Congregationalists at Harvard and Yale, and the Episcopalians at William and Mary. Probably because of the Baptists' stricter policies governing student behavior, athletics made little headway until long after the college had moved to Providence in 1770 and been renamed Brown University in 1804 in honor of a prominent benefactor. By the time of Heisman's matriculation, the city of Providence had developed into a thriving commercial center, one whose spiritually conservative roots were juxtaposed with a materialistically progressive side that had been evolving since the middle of the nineteenth century.

It was not until the 1850s that organized athletics first came into being at Brown. But the annual interclass football game between the freshmen and sophomores (a long-standing student tradition at other eastern schools as well) soon grew so wild (on-field fighting had become more popular than playing) that the university president had it stopped in 1862. It was not until four years later that the event was renewed. By this time, baseball had become the more popular team sport, which by 1874 had achieved varsity status.

Accordingly, a university historian recorded that during the 1860s and 1870s, "social and athletic activities played an increasingly important part" in the life of Brown students.[23] And in spite of the school's inauspicious beginnings in intercollegiate football during the period 1878–1886, the Brown Bruins went on in later years to establish a proud reputation in the game, producing four championship teams (among them the first team from the East invited to play in the Rose Bowl in 1916) as well as players and coaches of the stature of Tuss McLaughry, Fritz Pollard, Wallace Wade, Rip Engle, Joe Paterno, and, of course, John Heisman.

Why young Heisman chose Brown over more popular schools or those closer to home is not clear. Perhaps his concerned parents picked the strictly governed school for him, or it could have been that he himself wanted to attend a school that played the eastern style of football, where he might have a better chance of making the team despite his slight size. But the fact that Brown had adopted an elective system of broad studies, allowing him to enroll in a two-year course in law (an increasingly popular subject at the time) could have been a significant reason. At any rate, the Brown historian observes that as a result of the elective system, a new type of student was enrolling during the 1880s, students who displayed a "semi-professional enthusiasm for some one line of study."[24] This description applied aptly to an eager, ambitious young man like John Heisman, for in two years he would transfer to the University of Pennsylvania to complete work on a bachelor's degree in law.

However, as his reminiscences reveal, Heisman caught his first glimpse of Brown's College Hill with his love of football more intact than any attraction to academics. He was "seventeen and football mad," he tells us, and after missing his train connection at Albany—where he had engaged in an impromptu football game—he finally made it to Providence and the campus of Brown University. But what impressed him more than anything else was a game of football in progress:

On one side were freshmen who had caught their trains and had arrived in good order and according to schedule. Opposed to them were town boys.

And as I stood there watching all this magnificence, Luck tapped me. *One of the freshmen had to quit.*

Well, I was the nearest to the spokesman for the college boys and as I was the first person he saw and did not look as if the rigors of the game would ruin me, although I weighed only 144 pounds, he asked me whether I wanted to play.

Now I had left Titusville clad in a manner warranted not to fetch the blush of embarrassment to my home town. I was wearing a handsome and stylish (Titusville) suit—black, as I recall it. On the numerous trains which had fetched me to Providence, I had frequently been at some pains to brush and fleck the coal particles and lint from those elegant trousers and that carefully tailored coat that I might arrive among the swells of the campus unashamed.

With an alacrity which must have startled them, I leaped into the fray. I don't know how long we played, nor who won, nor what nor how many rules I broke.

The game ended. I had one thoroughly black eye and a freely bleeding nose. That suit, that gallant effort of Titusville's best tailor, was an unqualified ruin. But I was happy. *I had run with the ball.*[25]

In addition to revealing his intense passion for football as it was played in his youth, the style and tone of this passage suggest another side of John Heisman—an occasionally somewhat pompous use of language that always colored his personal manner, especially when relating to a group or an audience, in particular, his players. Robert B. Wallace aptly observes, in that part of his history of Georgia Tech that tells of Heisman's coaching tenure there: "Like his speech, Heisman's writings were full of involved satirical sentences that reflected his obsession with the dramatic." Perhaps it was his penchant for Shakespearean declamation in the grand theatrical style that inspired his manner. And although he spoke with a strident, somewhat nasal voice, he always used perfect, if obviously overblown, diction. Wallace recounts the occasion of Heisman defining a football to his players, as "a prolate spheroid—that is, an elongated sphere—in which the outer leather casing is drawn tightly over a somewhat smaller rubber tubing."[26] Nevertheless, such inflated language must have had a real inspirational impact on his players, for Heisman's overall coaching record certainly speaks for itself.

As far as participating in varsity football at Brown, though, his opportunities were not as fortunate as they had been in the pickup game. The school discontinued intercollegiate football during 1887 and 1888 in favor of informal club teams whose games were not officially recognized. Even so, Heisman reports that he took part in these games, with the same degree of enthusiasm he had displayed back in Titusville. However, the claim that he also played varsity baseball at Brown is not as easily substantiated, for the records during these years do not list him in the lineups.[27]

Ironically, Brown renewed intercollegiate football in 1889, the same year that Heisman transferred to the University of Pennsylvania, and one wonders if the Penn Quakers' intercollegiate program, which had been ongoing since the 1870s, might have motivated the athletically minded Heisman to move to the Philadelphia school. However, a more practical factor that probably affected his decision was Penn's reputation as one of a growing legion of schools that offered a Bachelor of Laws degree and the specialized training needed to enter an increasingly lucrative profession. Penn, in fact, was a pioneer in the field of law training, having first established a program in 1790.

Daniel Boorstin has commented that the expansion of law schools in America was directly related to the demands on the legal profession during this time, due mainly to the promising new careers afforded by a rapidly developing country: "In the mid-nineteenth century, with the settlement of the West, founding of new states, the building of canals and railroads, and the construction of modern industry, peculiarly American opportunities for the legal profession called into being American law schools."[28]

There was also a significant change in the philosophical and pedagogical approaches to legal education, involving a refutation of traditional principles of legal education in favor of the more scientific case method, with its attention to nuances of fact and the ability to manipulate details. In short, the world that the Go-Getters had created had itself created an attendant, necessary sphere of opportunity. And young men of John Heisman's bent—intelligent, ambitious, imbued with a natural flair for negotiation and public relations— saw the legal profession as a golden opportunity to get ahead. Ironically for Heisman, though, a markedly different career prospect loomed just down the road.

In Heisman's student days, the University of Pennsylvania was a growing urban institution, whose humble origins dated from the Reverend George Whitefield's Charity School, established in 1740. Actually, the prime instigator for building a university of a new order was Philadelphia's own Benjamin Franklin. His "Proposals Relating to the Education of Youth in Pennsylvania" led to the eventual transformation of Whitefield's School into Franklin's Academy in 1749, the actual forerunner of the university itself. In his time, Franklin's educational philosophy was considered unique in advocating that the best education was that which was "most useful and ornamental." Franklin was also sensitive to the role of athletics in the educational process, stressing "that to keep [students] in Health, and to strengthen and render active their Bodies, they be frequently exercised in Running, Leaping, Wrestling, and Swimming, etc." To be sure, John Heisman, as both an educator and athletic coach, would have agreed with Franklin's practical ideas on how a university should be run.

The Penn campus that Heisman first saw in 1889 was in the midst of its first real physical expansion and enrollment growth under the capable leadership of Dr. William Pepper, who had become provost of the university in 1881. Relocated from the city proper to the west bank of the Schuylkill River in 1872, the university finally had the room it needed to grow into a nationally recognized center of learning during the 1880s and on into the 1890s.

But not only was Penn growing in academic stature during this time, its football program was on the verge of becoming an Ivy League power in the 1890s, one that would compete for supremacy with the Big Three of Harvard, Yale, and Princeton. Like other ambitious athletic programs of the day, Penn's was becoming more professionally oriented and less student controlled. In addition, Penn authorities were evidently well aware at this time of football's image-building power. In 1887, the school participated in a precedent-setting event by playing Rutgers in the first indoor football game in New York's old Madison Square Garden. Penn won, 13–10, and played in the Garden a number of times thereafter.

That John Heisman would even consider playing football at Penn, particularly as a lineman, was a testimonial in itself to the young man's competitive zeal and fortitude. Weighing only about 150 pounds at the time, he confessed to a fear that his larger teammates playing on either side of him in the line might fall on him and cause a disabling injury.[29]

But play he did, fighting his way up from the scrubs to make the varsity team as a center in 1890. The coaches had been so impressed with his determined style of play as a scrub that he was taken along to New York for the Thanksgiving game with Columbia, which was won by Penn, 24–0. Although that 1889 team was mediocre at best, compiling a 7–6 record, the next two years of Heisman's varsity playing days saw the Quakers rack up twenty-two wins against only five losses. Penn's golden era on the gridiron was at hand.

In fact, the year Heisman departed, George Woodruff assumed the coaching reins at Penn, and during his tenure (1892–1901) the Quakers had their greatest period of continued success, and were one of the most successful teams in the history of college football. During the years 1894–1897, Penn won an astounding fifty-five of fifty-six games, losing only to Lafayette in 1896 by the close score of 6–4.

Theorizing that the strongest defense depended on a strong offense that concentrated power at the point of attack, Woodruff ran his team from a basic T-formation but with a number of innovative maneuvers. When the Rules Committee abolished his flying interference, he came up with the revolutionary "guards back" formation against Princeton in 1894. In Heisman's account of its inception, Woodruff made his dramatic reply to the Rules Committee the first time Penn received the ball:

"Guards back—right," shouted Carl Williams, Penn's quarterback.

The huge guards . . . dropped back beside Williams. They stood in close tandem formation. I remember that a curious quiet came over the field. The players had ceased chattering. Williams' voice was sharp and clear.

He clapped his hands, received the ball and slapped it into the arms of the rear guard. The leading guard plunged forward, his ball-carrying mate at his heels. Behind the second guard came the whole Penn backfield. . . .

You have, doubtless, seen circus performers dive through a paper-covered hoop. Well, that describes it. First one side of Princeton's line was assaulted and then the other. And Penn won 12–0.[30]

According to Heisman, "the football-playing world began talking guards back" at once. As an early example of the pulling guard who pulls out of his line position to become an open-field blocker, this was a tactic that made for many more play options, of course. Unfortunately, by the time of one of Penn's and the game's greatest players, T. Truxton Hare, a four-time All-American at guard (1897–1900), the guards back formation had been abolished by the Rules Committee. Heisman contended that Hare was the "only guard worthy of being paired with [William "Pudge"] Heffelfinger." Although linemen of that day were small by today's standards (averaging 170 pounds, with most under 6 feet tall), ball carrying was not limited to backs. In fact, anyone on the field could run with the ball, particularly linemen, whose size made them a formidable force in momentum formations. In this capacity, Heisman declared that there had never been a player superior to Princeton's Hector Cowan: "I have seen him plunge on for 10 and 15 yards, the ball clamped to his ribs and three and four earnest young athletes struggling to fetch him down. . . . I saw the man gain more than 300 yards against Penn in 1889."[31]

A teammate of Amos Alonzo Stagg and Pudge Heffelfinger at Yale, George Woodruff, who had been a Phi Beta Kappa student as well as an athlete, was a master strategist, subscribing to a strong kicking game and the element of surprise. Long before the advent of the forward pass, he devised a procedure that was nearly its equal in intent—a quarterback quick kick, actually the forerunner of the on-side kick because at that time the ball could be recovered down field by the quarterback and any other back stationed behind him. The result was usually a substantial gain.[32]

In an era when the ends normally played wide to force a runner out of bounds, Woodruff had them move in close to the tackles for a more direct shot at the ball carrier, or what he termed a "smashing" defense. His 1897 team, considered by many to have been his best, is said by some to have attempted the first place kick for a field goal, rather than the more popular drop-kick method at the time. (The place kick was successful against a Harvard team that Penn defeated, 15–6.) Actually, George Woodruff was the first of a long line of innovative "professional" coaches whose fearless experimentation would have a lasting impact on the game of football. During his own coaching career, John Heisman would pay his respects to Woodruff through many references to his achievements, including making sure that Woodruff's innovations were properly attributed to Woodruff rather than to Heisman. According to Heisman, George Woodruff was the perfect coach whose methods were never questionable.

Two notable events during Heisman's playing days at Penn attest to his bold determination to succeed as a football player. During the 1890 Penn–Penn State game, the aggressive Heisman, playing a roving center position on defense to avoid hazardous contact, saw his chance to block a punt attempt by a Penn State back named Atherton. To accomplish this, he leaped high over the line:

The ball left Atherton's foot while I was at the top of my leap. My hands were there to block it but that ball came directly between them and smashed the Heisman nose. From the center of my face the ball rebounded wildly and, half blinded, I gave chase.

So did Atherton; presently I saw him dive. At what should he dive except the ball? So I dived too and clutched something hard and round. Out of what I fondly believed to be the ball came bitter complaint:

"Hey, what the hell you trying to do?"

It was Atherton's head.

The ball? Oh, it had gone bounding down the field and one of my teammates . . . had fallen on it for a touchdown.[33]

Some stories have it that the result of Heisman's reckless foray was a slightly flattened nose that altered his appearance for the rest of his life. To Heisman it had all been worth it, though, for the Quakers won, 20–0.

The other event occurred the following season when he decided to try out at end, an unfamiliar position to him. And even though he was competing with ten other candidates, Heisman eventually beat out all of them for the starting job. Typically, once his mind was made up to go for a particular goal, he would allow nothing to stand in his way until he had achieved it. It was a trait that would characterize this athletic go-getter's personal dealings throughout his life. Heisman's own version of how he made the starting position reflects this determination:

It was not until mid-October that I felt that I had the inside track. Just before the Lehigh game our head coach said to me:

"Heisman, I believe you're the best man I've got for left end but nobody else seems to think so. Nevertheless I'm coach and I'm sending you in against Lehigh today. Son, you and I stand or fall on what you do today. Get in there, boy. Play football."

I think that I'd have fought a battery of buzz-saws barehanded after that.[34]

In that same Lehigh game, Heisman witnessed a situation that brought about the important ruling that time cannot expire until the ball becomes dead. Penn's Pop Thayer had kicked a field goal just as time ran out, but the Lehigh captain contended that the goal should not count because time had expired. Nevertheless, the referee ruled that the play would count, even though there was nothing in the rules book governing such a situation. That winter, though, the Rules Committee, realizing the logic of a dead ball ruling for this situation, adopted the following rule: "Time shall not be called for the end of a period until the ball is dead."[35]

Many of Heisman's teammates during his years at Penn would later gain prominence in business, politics, and athletic affairs. One of them, Harry Mackey, who played tackle for three years and went on to become mayor of Philadelphia, acknowledged that John Heisman's lack of size was compensated for by his knowledge of the game: "We always considered that Johnny Heisman knew more football than he could play," he said. "He was very light, but he knew every trick of the game as well as the fundamentals."[36]

Coached by Elwood O. Wagenhurst, the Penn teams of Heisman's day were competitive, but they always had problems with Princeton and Yale—the closest match they had with either of these two perennial powers was a 6–0 loss to Princeton in 1890. Nevertheless, one of Heisman's prized possessions from those years was a gold watch that was presented to him for playing the best defensive game of any of his teammates in a Princeton game.

During his years at Penn, Heisman also played baseball, participated in activities of the law school, and cultivated a reputation as a prodigious devourer of pancakes, becoming one of the leading members of the school's "Pancake Club," whose members vied for the championship at periodically scheduled "eat-offs."

But of all the memories of his time at Penn, Heisman's fondest were those of his football playing days. Despite that time's barbaric style of play, his innate love of and pride in the game in its primitive form always shine through whenever he discusses it. The following excerpts from a piece Heisman wrote about how the game was played during his college days reveal both his special feeling and the extent to which the game has changed since that time:

The time of the playing halves of a game in those days was 45 minutes, not 30 minutes, as now. Furthermore, the game was not divided into quarters, as now, so there is today a rest period we never had in the old days. Players of my time had to be real iron men, because we played two games a week—Wednesdays and Saturdays.

Once a game started, a player could not leave unless he actually was hurt, or, at least, pleaded injury. Accordingly, whenever the captain wanted to put a fresh player into action, he whispered, "Get your arm hurt, or something." In one game my captain whispered to me, "Get your neck broke, Heisman."

We wore jerseys and shorts of great variety. We had no helmets or pads of any kind; in fact, one who wore home-made pads was regarded as a sissy. Hair was the only head protection we knew, and in preparation for football we would let it grow from the first of June. Many college men of that day, especially divinity and medical students, permitted beards to grow. Often they were referred to as "Gorillas . . . ."

We didn't have many sweaters in those days, but we all wore snug fitting canvas jackets over our jerseys. You see, the tackling in that day wasn't clean-cut and around the legs as it is today. All too often it was wild, haphazard clutching with the hands, and when runners wore loose garments they were often stopped by a defensive player grabbing a handful of loose clothing. Some players wore pants, or jackets, of black horsehair. When you made a fumbling grab, you lost your fingernails.[37]

As far as a game uniform was concerned at this time, Princeton led the way in fashion innovations. In 1877, for example, its players showed up wearing laced canvas jackets called smocks, which other players soon took to wearing, as Heisman mentions. The smock remained in vogue until 1902, when wearing just the jersey itself came into acceptance. Because of the orange and black striped sleeves and stockings that the Princeton players also wore, someone commented that they looked like tigers, and as a result the first nickname for a college team was born. When "moleskin" pants were introduced in 1888 (canvas pants had been fashionable since 1878), soon to be followed by cleated shoes in 1890 along with the rubber nose guard, the standard uniform for play during this era was set. Helmets did not come in until 1896, when the increasing rough play demanded such protection, but many players still refused to wear them. Prior to this innovation, as Heisman observes, players either let their hair grow long or they wore skull caps. [38]

His pride in the punting skills of the early players is expressed in this next quote from the same piece:

We practiced every afternoon as players do now, but as we had no forward pass in the game then, we put in large chunks of time on sprinting and getting down field under punts. As a result of this, I have no hesitation in saying our punting of those bygone years was decidedly better than what we witness today. [39]

In support of Heisman's claim about the quality of his day's punters, one of his teammates at Penn, Harry "Pop" Thayer, was surely in the legendary class with his ability to boot a ball seventy to seventy-five yards, as Heisman attests:

Once, just before we were to play Rutgers in old Madison Square Garden, we advised the caretaker of the place to remove the huge and probably costly chandelier which hung high in the arched roof.

"Why?" he demanded. "What are you going to do—shoot at the lights? Or do the boys climb into the rafters when they get warmed up?"

We explained about Pop Thayer's kicking—or tried to.

"Gwan," he scoffed. "Do you know how high those lights are? Don't be foolish."

"Show him, Pop," I said, tossing Thayer a tight ball.

Pop took a little hitch and then threw his foot against the ball. There was a horrid smash above us and a rain of broken glass descended.

Before Thayer could get off another kick, the caretaker readily conceded to the Penn players' request. [40]

Heisman further revealed his awareness of the early game's peculiarities as he rationalized the upright stance of linemen during his college football days:

Nearly all linemen, as a rule, lined up squarely against those who played the same position on the opposing team. They didn't crouch or squat or play low. They mostly stood bolt upright and fought it out with each other hammer and tongs, tooth and nail, fist and feet. Fact is, you didn't stand much chance of making the line those days unless you were a good wrestler and fair boxer.[41]

Actually, the fighting or boxing posture of linemen was due to there being no neutral zone to separate opposing linemen at this time. But Heisman notes that even professional boxers could be taken aback by the brutal experience of playing football:

Once at Penn . . . one of the coaches appeared on the field with a couple of hard-bodied heavyweights who, he explained, were prizefighters who had conceived the bright idea that it would help them get into condition if they tried a bit of football. In fifteen minutes one of the boxers had to quit. "It's too rough," said he. "In the ring you've got a chance to see it coming. In this game—well, anybody who gives much time to football's a damned fool."[42]

In this last quote, Heisman's fascination with the primitive playing style of that era is again revealed:

In the old days, players of one side were permitted to grab hold of their runners anywhere they could and push, pull or yank them along in any direction that would make the ball advance. Sometimes two enemy tacklers would be clinging to the runner's legs, and trying to hold him back, while several team-mates of the runner had hold of his arms, head, hair or wherever they could attach themselves, and were pulling him in the other direction. I still wonder how some of the ball carriers escaped dismemberment.

Some backs had leather straps, like valise handles, sewed or riveted on the shoulders of their jackets and on the hips of their trousers, so as to offer good handholds for their team-mates.[43]

Needless to say, officials of that day had their hands full trying to keep the on-field action under control. In 1883, each team was assigned an umpire, but the referee could overrule them. Because of extensive arguing between teams, the two umpires were eliminated the following year and only the referee was allowed to officiate. The 1885 season introduced rule changes under which a player could be ejected from the game for a first fighting offense, and teams were now subject to a five-yard penalty for being offside. By 1887, two officials were back on the field: a referee to make on-field decisions concerning progress of the ball and an umpire to watch for fighting violations. Even so, some players still managed to make a practice of deceiving the officials. Observe the tactics of Princeton's Sport Donnelly, whom Heisman called the best end in football in 1889:

Sport's favorite method was to taunt and badger his opponent until that unfortunate lad, unable to bear more goading, would take a wild swing at his tormentor's head. And Donnelly was forever timing it so that the umpire would be one of the spectators of the attempted assault. Of course the offending youth would be banished and Sport would be left to bedevil somebody else.[44]

What then was it about his day's openly wild and violently aggressive game of football that so obsessed young John Heisman? To endure the daily drudgery of practice drills and to stand up to the brutality of actual game play were tests of manhood that many young men of his day either relished or merely condoned, for the game had become the kind of experience in which playing for enjoyment was subservient to winning. But to Heisman the player, football was more than just an initiation ritual or rite of passage. The game appealed to him much as it eventually would to the nation at large, as something derivative of the American spirit itself—an intense, all-consuming physical experience designed to challenge and prove one's manly worth as a winner or a bona fide go-getter, no matter how formidable the obstacles that lay in the way toward a goal. To players of Heisman's bent, then, undergoing such an experience was the real enjoyment and satisfaction derived from playing football.

Looking back from a nostalgic perspective, Heisman could always make the questionable elements of the game he loved seem appealing, even though football, as a result of its deteriorating public image toward the end of the last century, was headed for dire straits. In fact, had it not been for the dedicated and untiring efforts of bold, inventive men like John Heisman during football's trying times, the game would surely have died.

But Heisman's own good old days of rough and tumble college football were soon to be a thing of the past. Armed with his coveted law degree, the ambitious twenty-two-year-old go-getter departed from Penn and the world of college football in the spring of 1892, setting forth in search of a career in the legal profession. Or so he thought. In twenty-eight years, following successful coaching tenures at five different schools, during which time American football achieved its modern form, John Heisman would return triumphantly as the head football coach of his alma mater.

NOTES

1. J. Stanley Clark, *The Oil Century: From the Drake Well to the Conservation Era* (Norman: University of Oklahoma Press, 1958), 52–53.

2. Ibid., 55.

3. An interesting genealogical oddity concerning the Heisman name has to do with the family's supposed baronial ancestry. It seems John Heisman's great-grandfather was Baron von Bogart, who disinherited his son following the latter's marriage to a peasant girl from Alsace-Lorraine. Undaunted, the son adopted his wife's maiden name of Heisman, and it was their son who immigrated to America where the name Heisman started out on a new life of its own. Because of his German ancestry, Heisman started out with the given names Johann Wilhelm at his birth in 1869, but they were soon Americanized. He had two brothers, Daniel and Michael.

4. Through an outlet with Rockefeller's Standard Oil Company, the business soon grew prosperous enough for J. M. Heisman to employ around thirty-five workers.

5. Quoted in "Titusville's Tribute to John W. Heisman," an occasional pamphlet dated July 18, 1984.

6. John W. Heisman, "Signals," *Collier's*, October 6, 1928, 12. (Incidentally, the rules book that caught young Heisman's fancy was probably that in the "Dime Library" series published by Beadle and Co. of New York. Henry Chadwick had authored the first such booklet on baseball rules in the 1860s.)

7. Jon Sherman, "Titusville Pays Tribute to John Heisman," *The Titusville Herald*, September 1, 1984, 3, 10.

8. For example, observe the comments of Michael Novak in *The Joy of Sports* (New York: Basic Books, 1976), 76:

Football dramatizes, on a well-defined grid, the psychic contest in which those who work for corporations are engaged. In various places in the corporate network, we push ahead, we "run for daylight." Phalanxes of bureaucracies block everything we try to do. Football exemplifies the strategies, the tactics, the crushing disappointments and the explosive "scores" that constitute our working lives. Football more than baseball has become the mythic form most illuminative of the way we live. It is the liturgy of a bureaucratic world.

9. Gene Griessman, "The Coach," in *The Heisman: A Symbol of Excellence* by John T. Brady (New York: Atheneum, 1984), 20.

10. Heisman's life span also approximated another, more momentous development—the Land Grant Act of 1862, which set in motion the inevitable democratization of higher education in America. Heisman's coaching tenures at eight schools of varying missions in different parts of the country reflect the impact of this transformation from 1892–1927. The role football played in this movement has been duly noted by Michael Oriard: "Football and the American college developed together in the nineteenth century, producing a university system unique in the world. Although many continue to talk about college football as if it were an appendage to the university, it is in fact deeply imbedded in the university's very tissue." Michael Oriard, "On the Current Status of Sports Fiction," *Arete: The Journal of Sport Literature* 1 (Fall 1983): 10.

11. A rematch was played one week later at Princeton in which the Tigers were victorious, 8–0. Actually, the inception of these matches grew out of a long-standing rivalry among the students over a cannon on the Princeton campus that had been used in the Revolution. When Rutgers' periodic raids to seize the cannon became impractical, a football series was proposed in lieu of the tradition.

Actually, the students themselves, who were initially in control of their athletic ventures, should be accorded the lion's share of credit for the perpetuation of early football in this country. They would eventually relinquish control to faculty committees and alumni governing boards, but had it not been for their stubborn persistence in the face of dogmatic school authority and tumultuous public outcry against the game's brutal aspects, football may never have come into its own.

12. For a precise description of the rugby scrum see John Durant and Les Etter, *Highlights of College Football* (New York: Hastings House, 1970), 30.

13. See Allen L. Sack, "Yale 29—Harvard 4: The Professionalization of College Football," *Quest* 19 (January 1973): 24–34. Yale's football dominance during this time

is graphically reflected in the fact that between 1872 and 1909 its teams won 324 games, lost only seventeen, and tied eight. Many of these teams went undefeated.

14. Durant and Etter note that the Harvard–McGill matches of 1874 first established a system of scoring from which later systems evolved: "At each end of the field were goal posts connected by crossbars; when a player running with the ball made a touchdown he was given the privilege of a free kick for a possible goal; the touchdown itself did not count in the score" (*Highlights*, 29). However, the group that met at Springfield in 1875 "voted that touchdowns should count in the scoring, not goals alone, as the British rules prescribed, and a match would be decided by a majority of touchdowns" (*Highlights*, 41).

15. See Donald W. Calhoun, *Sport, Culture, and Personality*, 2nd ed. (Champaign, Ill.: Human Kinetics, 1987), 51–52. Nevertheless, in emphasizing brains over brawn Camp saw the real challenge of football as deriving from "its practically unlimited field of tactical development. The fascinating study of new movements and combinations is never exhausted." John Heisman would have concurred with this observation, which appeared in the book on football that Camp and Lorin DeLand coauthored in 1896. Quoted by Harford Powel, Jr. in *Walter Camp: An Authorized Biography* (Freeport, N.Y.: Books for Libraries, 1970, reprint of 1926 ed.), 77.

16. Quoted in John McCallum, *Ivy League Football Since 1872* (New York: Stein and Day, 1977), 30. McCallum also notes that according to the rules of that day, a scrimmage would take place "when the holder of the ball . . . puts it down on the ground in front of him and puts it in play . . . by snapping it back with his foot [a maneuver known then as "heeling"]." At first players used their hands to stay the ball, but by 1890, due mainly to the advent of close formation play and the possibility of interference, they were using their hands to snap the ball to a backfield man.

17. When the seven linemen were drawn in closer together, their positions fronted those of the backs whose stations resembled the modern T-formation. Hence, as Durant and Etter contend, this resulted in discarding the rugby names for new ones to describe line positions:

The "rushers" or "forwards" of Rugby became "linemen." The outside men on the line, originally known as the "end rushers," became "end men" and finally "ends" and the players alongside them, formerly known as the "next to ends," were called "tacklers" because they made more tackles than the other linemen. The two men on either side of the center who protected, or guarded him against a mauling by the opposing linemen (there was no neutral zone between the scrimmage lines) were called "guards."

The Rugby terms for the backs continued to be used. The quarterback was closest to the line and handled the heeled ball. The two halfbacks stood about halfway between him and the fullback, who played deepest and was back of the others (Durant and Etter, *Highlights*, 46).

18. In addition, Camp supposedly originated the All-America team selections, which first appeared in 1889. Speculation is that Camp first collaborated on this endeavor with Caspar Whitney, a popular journalist of that day. At any rate, Camp was soon making his own annual selections for *Collier's* magazine, a practice he continued until his death in 1925. Sportswriter Grantland Rice carried on this feature through 1947, after which a board of college coaches chose the selections until the magazine's demise.

19. John W. Heisman, "Hold 'em!" *Collier's*, October 27, 1928, 12.

20. John W. Heisman, "The Thundering Herd," *Collier's*, October 13, 1928, 13. Another variation of the wedge was the "turtleback," invented by Amos Alonzo Stagg

in 1891 when he was coaching at Springfield College. Since the rules required only one man on the line, Stagg moved his entire offensive line into the backfield except the center, who sufficed as the lone lineman. The backfield then formed an oval (turtleback) to surround and protect the ball carrier. The turtleback represented momentum play at its most absurd.

21. Frank Menke, *Encyclopedia of Sports* (New York: A. S. Barnes, 1953), 356–57. After the 1893 season, all mass momentum formations were outlawed, and the token kick to start a game was abolished. From then on a kickoff had to travel at least ten yards.

22. Heisman, "Signals," 12.

23. Walter C. Bronson. *The History of Brown University, 1764–1914* (Providence, R.I.: Brown University Press, 1914), 375. Socializing with the opposite sex was a rare experience at this time, as the Women's College did not open until 1892 (renamed Pembroke College in 1928).

24. Ibid., 415.

25. Heisman, "Signals," 12–13.

26. Robert B. Wallace, *Dress Her in White and Gold: A Biography of Georgia Tech* (Atlanta: Georgia Tech Foundation, 1969), 56, 57.

27. Substantiated by a letter, dated February 8, 1988, from Martha L. Mitchell, university archivist, Brown University Library. Playing football was a much more serious matter, though. Observe Heisman's reaction to Brown's not fielding a varsity football team: "I was all but irreparably crushed . . . to learn that from a football standpoint I had chosen my college badly. Brown had played such a rotten game during the several preceding seasons that the authorities had decided, in defense of the fair name of the college, to abandon intercollegiate competition." (Heisman, "Signals," 13). Apparently, even in those early days of competition the honor of the school's name was an important issue in whether to take a chance on winning or losing in athletic ventures.

28. Daniel J. Boorstin, *The Americans: The Democratic Experience* (New York: Vintage Books, 1974), 62.

29. Heisman's relatively small frame was naturally come by: "Heisman's father was a short, erect man—about five-four—who, when he walked down the street, was said to look seven-foot tall." Griessman, "The Coach," 21. Clearly, this latter characteristic would come through in the younger Heisman's undaunted playing and coaching styles. However, most players of Heisman's day were small by today's standards, with the average weight around 165 pounds. In the case of certain players, size had little to do with playing ability as, for example, Yale's intensely aggressive little end, Frank Hinkey.

30. Heisman, "The Thundering Herd," 60.

31. Ibid., 13.

32. To those who credited Heisman with inventing the on-side kick, he declined the honor and gave the credit to Woodruff, who, he says, brought it out around 1893. "As he played it then, and as many teams played it for years afterwards, the kick was made by the quarterback, standing in the usual position, and the regular backs—all on-side—were the ones deputed to recover it." John W. Heisman, "Inventions in Football," *The Baseball Magazine*, October 1908, 41.

33. John W. Heisman, "Hold 'em!" 12.

34. Ibid., 13.

35. John W. Heisman, "Rules Rush In," *Collier's*, November 10, 1928, 13.

36. "Report Heisman is Picked as New Penn Football Coach," Philadelphia *Evening Bulletin*, January 1920: 22.

37. Menke, *Encyclopedia of Sports*, 356.

38. Concerning his on-field dress when he first went out for football at Penn, Heisman wrote that he had

reported for football valiantly equipped with moleskin pants and a canvas jacket of my own manufacture. If they had no other virtue, they fitted. They were not padded. Padding was scorned in those days. Nose guards and helmets had not been invented. Wood-fiber thigh protectors I invented, but not until 1905, while I was coaching at Georgia Tech. I wore no stockings. I never wore them on the field. When I went south to coach, in 1895, I carried the bare-legs idea with me and my Auburn squad adopted it. So, later, did Clemson and Georgia Tech. It's cooler, that's all. (Heisman, "Signals," 13).

39. Menke, 356.

40. John W. Heisman, "Fast and Loose," *Collier's*, November 20, 1928, 15.

41. Menke, 356.

42. Heisman, "Fast and Loose," 15.

43. Menke, 356.

44. Heisman, "Hold 'em!" 13.

2

Coach Heisman, Football Missionary: The Game Spreads (1892–1903)

The passion feeding football in western Pennsylvania was the passion of chargers and hitters who gloried in their endurance of pain and punishment. There is a strain of masochism in the western Pennsylvania character, almost a need to absorb punishment in order to prove oneself.

—Michael Novak,
The Joy of Sports (1976)

American football, with its violent element, fit well into the American mentality which demanded manliness and the virile features of society. The perceived function of football as a facilitator of manly qualities was a potent force in making the sport a featured activity on most college campuses.

—Ronald A. Smith,
Sports and Freedom: The Rise of Big-Time College Athletics (1988)

PIONEERING THE GAME IN THE MIDWEST—HEISMAN AT OBERLIN AND BUCHTEL (1892–1894)

The western Pennsylvania football heritage, which is said to be compounded in part of a characteristic passion for glorying in the "endurance of pain and punishment," evidently instilled in John Heisman the necessary fortitude to withstand one of the more unnerving experiences of his collegiate years. While still at the University of Pennsylvania, he reportedly suffered a freak accident that would ultimately force him into changing his plans for a law career. According to one source, during the 1891 game with Princeton in the new (1890) Madison Square Garden, Heisman somehow came in contact with an outlet for the galvanic lighting system used in those days. His eyes became so impaired following the encounter that the team physician warned him to rest them for a satisfactory period of time or suffer irreparable damage.[1] But by the time he was preparing to try his hand at law in the spring of 1892, his eyes still had not cleared up.

Another version of this story relates, somewhat ambiguously, that Heisman was about to open a law office in Cleveland when his eyes suddenly went bad on him:

He was unable to read a line, go to a theater, or engage actively in any pursuit of pleasure. It was a trying time indeed, but by patience and dogged determination that has characterized his whole life, he finally won out with his eyes whole, but not strong enough to stand the heavy reading necessary in his chosen profession.[2]

Whatever the source of Heisman's eye problem, we do know that he took to wearing glasses at this time, and after forsaking his Cleveland law office applied for the coaching job at the local Western Reserve University. Although at the time the profession of coaching athletics was in its infancy, to Heisman it seemed the natural thing to do, mainly because of the challenge it presented to his enterprising nature. But for some reason he was turned down by the Western Reserve officials. Thus, one of the most successful coaching careers in college football history started out on a painful and ironic note.

Reports of how Heisman came to coach at nearby Oberlin College differ. One says he was recommended for the position by Walter Camp himself.[3] Another, from the viewpoint of an Oberlin player, describes his inauspicious arrival in the early 1890s:

Jack Heisman appeared on the football field one day, bespectacled, stoop-shouldered and with a dejected, hands-in-pockets kind of air that made us believe him when he told us that Western Reserve had the day before declined to accept his offer to coach the football team. And I shall always remember how that afternoon he revealed to us a knowledge of the game that resulted in his engagement as pioneer coach in Northern Ohio, and how we trounced Reserve that season.[4]

Regardless of which source is more reliable, Oberlin is where John Heisman officially started out on his long coaching career in the fall of 1892.

One of the most remarkable histories in the annals of American educational institutions is that of Oberlin College. Established in 1833, it became the first coeducational school in the world when four women were accepted into a full course of studies in 1837. (This came about in spite of those who predicted immoral consequences resulting from mixing the sexes in the classroom.) Oberlin was also among the first institutions to admit blacks, and prior to the Civil War the school attracted a number of Abolitionist proponents. Situated in a quiet town of stately homes and shady streets in Heisman's day, the school prided itself on its liberal educational views as well as its strong academic tradition, which have continued to this day. Fittingly, Heisman arrived on the scene at the very time when football, in spite of sporadic faculty protest, was finally getting underway. Soccer had been played as early as the 1860s, but baseball was the most popular sport at Oberlin, although a varsity team was not fielded until 1880. Then, in the fall of the very next year, some entering freshmen from the East introduced the rugby game, setting the stage in northern Ohio for the emergence of American-style football by the early 1890s.

Students from the East, like those who attended Oberlin, may have helped spread the game of football to other areas of the country, but it was really "the outstanding eastern players [who] were the game's missionaries." One source has aptly observed: "As soon as they graduated they were in great demand as coaches everywhere, and they went out and taught the game, often at colleges that had never seen football. Besides teaching the basic principles of football, they also instituted the rigid training rules and discipline which had been instilled in them back East."[5] Heisman, of course, was one of these football "missionaries"—one whose coaching style was to enjoy immediate success everywhere he went in his early coaching years.

Just two years before Heisman's arrival at Oberlin, a student committee had convinced the Oberlin faculty (the most formidable obstacle to organizing athletic programs during football's early days) that intercollegiate football would be of great value to the school, and an experimental game was scheduled with Adelbert College. Somewhat prophetically, the *Oberlin Review* (November 11, 1890) editorialized: "The athletics of a college owe their very existence to competition, competition not only among the college classes but to a much greater extent with other colleges."[6] However, intercollegiate football at Oberlin was delayed another year when a blizzard unfortunately intervened, and the match had to be cancelled.

But football at Oberlin was not to be denied, and in 1891 the school's first intercollegiate schedule of five games was played, resulting in two victories and three defeats. One of the losses was by a 26–6 score to the University of Michigan, the football pioneer of the Midwest. But in their initial venture into intercollegiate competition the Oberlin men had given a good account of themselves in spite of their lack of experience. Better days lay just ahead.

In the fall of 1892, John Heisman not only started coaching football at Oberlin, he also enrolled in a postgraduate art course, which made him eligible to play as well as coach—a common practice at that time. (Also a laissez-faire attitude toward eligibility rules for participation in athletics prevailed, with each college setting its own rules governing the eligibility of graduate students, freshmen, and other student categories.) Heisman immediately set to work building one of the most successful teams in Oberlin's history. By season's end the team was undefeated (7–0) and rated with Minnesota and Purdue as one of the three strongest teams west of the Alleghenies.

Persuaded now that coaching was a worthy calling, Heisman attributed much of his early success to tactics he learned from studying the play of the great Yale lineman Pudge Heffelfinger. An exceptionally big man for his day at 6 feet 4 inches tall and weighing over two hundred pounds, Heffelfinger, football's first pulling guard, had made a lasting impression on Heisman from his days at Penn: "I too have played against Heffelfinger. The black and blue bruises his shoulders left upon me and the dents I had from his hips and knees have gone long since but the memory of them will be with me always. As an interfering guard the game has never seen his equal. One learned much watching Heff. One learned even more by playing him."[7]

If a big man like Heffelfinger could come out of the line and lead interference for his backs, Heisman reasoned that two reasonably sized guards could pull off the same feat. Thus he concluded that his

first job at Oberlin was to find two speedy guards. I found them and made my experiment on Ohio State. . . . When those two "big" guards of mine, followed by the entire backfield, assaulted the Ohio State flanks little remained to do except to count the score. We won 40 to 0. We played Ohio State later in the season and won again 50 to 0. That's what came of studying Heffelfinger.[8]

As a result of Heisman's scientific coaching methods, the 1892 Oberlin team scored a total of 262 points to its opponents' 30. But overshadowing the two big wins over Ohio State was a 24–22 win over Michigan, highlighted by a 95-yard run by Oberlin halfback C. W. "Fred" Savage. The Michigan Wolverines had been playing football since the 1870s, so a victory over them was something to be dearly savored by any midwestern team.

Actually, the first intercollegiate game in the Midwest was played in Chicago in 1879 between Michigan and Racine College of Wisconsin. The match had been played rugby style, with the Wolverines coming out on top. Due mainly to lack of competition in the region during the 1880s, Michigan persisted in playing eastern teams whenever it could, as mentioned earlier. But its first victory over one of these perennial powers did not come until 1894, when the Wolverines downed Cornell, 12–4. By then, intraregional rivalries had begun to develop between Michigan and other athletically ambitious schools like Chicago, Indiana, Ohio State, Illinois, Purdue, and Minnesota.

That Oberlin had managed to defeat two of these schools in its initial year of competition was a tremendous accomplishment for John Heisman. It soon became clear that the disciplined, carefully planned strategies of a scientific coach like Heisman provided the formula for building a winning team. His system also began to impress upon critics and supporters alike the importance of rugged conditioning in maintaining the essential things every good football team should have—endurance, discipline, and precision teamwork.

That coaching was a learning process for John Heisman at this time, though, is attested to by Heisman himself as the most severe critic of his own coaching methods. Oberlin was playing Case in 1892 and leading comfortably by three touchdowns at the half when young Coach Heisman took it upon himself to tell his men how good they were:

"Play as you have been playing," I said fat-headedly, "and everything will be beautiful."

Alas. Those words went to my players' heads. They played that second half as though nothing of any importance depended upon what happened. Case scored one touchdown and very nearly another. I was never gladder in my life to hear the timekeeper's whistle ending the game.

It was a lesson to Heisman, and in the same article he said that thereafter he never told his teams how good they were but instead dished out criticism even when they played at their best. However, he was careful not to undermine the spirit of his players. As he put it, "You have to know what you're talking about and, even more important, your men must know too. And you have to know to whom you're talking."[9] These last comments reveal a great deal not only about Heisman's coaching methods but his off-field posture as well. In all his dealings with the public, he always impressed people that he knew for sure what he was talking about. But he also made certain he knew his audience and what it expected to hear from him.

Another factor in Heisman's early success was the quality of players he found at Oberlin. The captain of his first team was Carl Williams, a quarterback rated among the school's greatest players. On Heisman's recommendation he later transferred to Penn where he played for two years and was named to Camp's All-America team as a senior. (The future physician would eventually become head football coach at Penn from 1902 to 1907, compiling an overall winning record and two undefeated seasons.) Obviously, the Midwest was producing its fair share of capable football players whose proper cultivation merely awaited the discerning eye of a knowledgeable coach.

From the very start of his coaching career Heisman displayed a natural genius for innovation. At Oberlin, finding himself in a receptive environment for experimentation, he devised his own variation of the day's popular wedge-style offense. In his own words, it was

a smaller, secondary V which was to form when the primary wedge was destroyed. We used it first against Western Reserve University and the dividends it paid were huge. With Fred Savage . . . carrying the ball this secondary wedge had its premiere and Fred scurried 55 yards for a score and something new had appeared beneath the October sun.[10]

When Oberlin went on to win the game, 38–8, the Western Reserve folks must have rued the day they let John Heisman get away.

Incidentally, this was also the first football game attended by Heisman's father, whose earlier distaste for the game mirrored the prevailing attitude of the game's many critics. As Heisman expressed his father's attitude toward football:

It was brutal. It was a waste of time. It should be prohibited. But I caught Father in a weak moment when I went to Oberlin to coach. After an evening's argument, and much to my surprise, he was at the field on the following afternoon prepared to see what all the nonsense was about. He had decided that inasmuch as I had rejected the practice of law and had dedicated my life to the game, there must be something to football.

After watching the Oberlin team warm up, the elder Heisman approached his son with questions about whom he thought might win:

"What's the matter with you?" I demanded. "You're not a football fan, are you? What do you care who wins?"

"Oh, nothing," he said. "But I don't like this partiality. I'd like to see the big fellows licked."

A few minutes later my brother came to me. "Say," he said, "if you ain't pretty sure you're going to take this game you'd better let me head Dad off."

"Dad? What's he doing now?"

"Oh, nothing except walking up and down in front of Western Reserve's cheering section waving hundred-dollar bills and daring them to back their team," sighed my brother.[11]

Other innovations Heisman tried at Oberlin included a double pass play, with the tackle coming out of the line to hand the ball off to a halfback in a variation of what was then the forerunner of the reverse play. Another was a signal system that operated through the use of series plays. When the team lined up, the quarterback called a single number which meant that the next six plays were to be run off in sequence, as previously rehearsed, without further signals until that series had been complete. The idea, of course, was to get the jump on the other team. As a result, Oberlin enjoyed some success with this plan that first year of Heisman's tenure.[12]

One of Heisman's favorite trick plays came about accidentally in a game played in 1892. His center, in the process of hiking, realized that the quarterback was not in position to receive the ball, so the center wisely held on to it. The other backs, thinking that the ball had already been hiked, started in motion, drawing the defense away from the ball. In the meantime the Oberlin right end had enough presence of mind to take the ball from center and waltz to an easy touchdown. Heisman reported that he used this play successfully for ten years, claiming it to be his best trick play. But the rules eventually doomed it through demanding that the center hike the ball at once.

Heisman's most significant contribution at Oberlin occurred upon his return there in 1894 after coaching a year at Buchtel. Until that time no one had ever heard of a man playing any different position on defense from what he played on offense; if he was a halfback on offense that's what he played on defense, and that ended it. But in that year . . . I became impressed with the senselessness of my left halfback, a very fast but light man, battering himself to pieces helping to repel the heavy onslaughts while my fullback—a big, strong, husky fellow stood away back practically doing nothing for nearly all the time that opponents had the ball. So I put the little fellow at fullback's place and rested him up whenever we lost the ball, and had my fullback come up close and help back up the line.[13]

Heisman's plan proved to be so popular that other teams were soon doing basically the same thing. This maneuver would ultimately demand that the quarterback, usually the lightest man on the team, be the deepest man back on defense, such a station carrying the designation of "safety man."

In February, 1893, Heisman suddenly accepted a position as director of athletics at Buchtel College (now the University of Akron), located less than fifty miles south of Cleveland. Athletics had not been faring well at the Akron school, and when news of Heisman's coaching success at Oberlin spread to the Buchtel campus, the students, with the administration's approval, hired the young coach as their "physical director," with duties to consist mainly of coaching the football and baseball teams. It was the promise of an annual salary that convinced Heisman to take the job. At Oberlin he had received no regular pay, having gotten only token remuneration by random passing of the hat at games, while at Buchtel he was to be paid the munificent sum of $750 a year.

Heisman's spirited arrival on campus, as such an event would prove to be throughout his coaching career, had an immediate impact on the students' morale: "The coming of Mr. Heisman made the year 1893 a most significant one. The first thing to be done was the building of a baseball cage, toward the construction of which the boys had promised to raise four hundred dollars. . . . To hasten the work, the men of the College, under Heisman's direction, put on the shingles."[14] As a result, the money was subsequently raised and the job completed.

But Coach Heisman did not find his task of building an athletic program at Buchtel an easy one. Years later, he commented on the problem of his coaching days at the Akron school: "Athletics, as I remember matters, was a very difficult thing at Buchtel at that time." With only a little over a hundred male students, most of whom were working their way through college, Buchtel had difficulty in attracting a sufficient number of athletes to even field a team. "Under the circumstances," said Heisman, "I fancy we really did well enough."[15]

In spite of his contractual agreement with Buchtel in 1893, Heisman somehow managed to maintain his athletic ties with Oberlin that same year. He himself has revealed that in 1893 he coached the Oberlin football team on its westward trip, in which both Chicago and Illinois were defeated. Because of his previous year's success and familiarity with the players, it could have been that Oberlin obtained special permission to use him in a coaching capacity.

Oberlin's successful westward trip was a pivotal event in Heisman's young career, in that the extremely rough play the team encountered in these two games started him to thinking of ways to open up game strategy and help alleviate the brutal elements of the mass momentum offense, which was so prominent in the early 1890s. The infamous wedge formation that had originated at Harvard in 1892 and evolved into Penn's flying interference offense quickly found its way to the Midwest. But Heisman's coaching experiences would soon lead him to conclude that "the human frame is unequal to the wedge."[16] As we have seen, he had fashioned his own version of the wedge his first year at Oberlin, but after a few games he began to dwell more and more on ways to protect his players from their opponents' increasingly vicious onslaughts. One of his original methods was to fight fire with fire. For example, just before the 1893 game with Chicago, he gave the players his mandatory pep talk: "Don't stall around to see what they have. Jump in on them at the whistle. Bam! Like that. Don't let them get set. Charge, charge, charge. Start charging at the kickoff and keep it up."[17]

However, as the toll on his players continued to rise, Heisman began to realize that, in general, "counterattacks were as menacing to life and limb as the mass offensives."[18] In one of his most vivid accounts, he drew on Oberlin's 1893 westward trip to describe the physical mayhem that could result from the mass momentum offense:

Surely few coaches have had a more impressive array of mass play casualties than I had at Oberlin in 1893. Even such men as I was able to impress into service were bandaged almost beyond recognition. Football was a serious occupation. A team played at least twice a week and maybe more. It used up men.

On Saturday my Oberlin men overcame Alonzo Stagg's mighty Chicago squad, 33 to 12, and were reduced to crutches, canes, splints and yards of plaster thereby. On the following Monday we staggered off the field at Champaign, Ill., the very groggy victors over [the] University of Illinois team, 34 to 24.

On the trip home, Heisman noted that there was hardly any one of his players who "did not have his head bandaged and his face court-plastered."[19]

Although Heisman was recounting this story many years later, he realized at the time that something had to be done to eliminate the game's brutality or football would soon sound its own death knell. A visiting Frenchman who had viewed the Harvard–Penn game in 1893 provided a graphic contemporary description of the game's extreme roughness in an essay on American manners. He concluded that American football is a "fearful game":

The roughness with which the opposing players seize the bearer of the ball is impossible to imagine. He is grasped by the middle of the body, by the head, by the legs, by the feet. He rolls over and his assailants roll with him. As they fight for the ball, the two sides come to the rescue, and fall into a heap of twenty-two bodies tumbling on top of one another, like an inextricable knot of serpents with human heads. This heap writhes on the ground and tugs at itself. One sees faces, hair, backs, or legs appearing in a monstrous and agitated melee. Then this murderous knot unravels itself and the ball, thrown by the most agile, bounds away and is again followed with the same fury.

Often, after one of those frenzied entanglements, one of the combatants remains on the field motionless, incapable of rising, so hard has he been hit.[20]

By this time, too, a chorus of domestic criticism directed toward such irresponsible violence was rising in an even more acrimonious vein, as we shall see.

Heisman's record at Buchtel, while not as sensational as his previous year's accomplishment at Oberlin had been, did result in his winning five out of seven football games, in which his opponents were outscored 276–82. He also produced the state's best college baseball team. His innovations continued, too, with most of these designed to correct recognizable defects in game procedures. One of them led to the first use of the center snap, at least as Heisman would later recall the event:

As far as I know, I was the first coach to change the method of passing the ball from center to quarter. At the time we were following the current mode. The center would place one end of the ball on the ground. On the other end he'd place his hand. He'd press down smartly and, at the same time, draw his hand back. The result was that the ball would, when released, snap off the ground and backward. It was up to the quarterback to grab it.

At Buchtel, Heisman recalled in this same article that his quarterback was too tall to receive the ball this way. He suggested that the center "throw the ball up to him." It worked and "within the season all the colleges were using this method of transferring the ball."[21]

Following the invention of the scrimmage line in 1880, the direct relationship between the center and the quarterback compelled teams to start utilizing some kind of signal system to get a play off and running. Heisman has told us of one way tried by the early teams:

The quarterback usually asked for the ball by scratching the hard-working center's leg, which was quite all right as long as the leg scratching was done by your own quarterback.

I was the victim of a foul scratch while playing center for Penn. . . . Instead of passing the ball with my foot I was following the example of our regular center, and putting it into play with one hand. Thus intent I did not notice the hand of my long-armed opponent center circle my leg. But I felt his scratch—and passed the ball. That pass cost us five yards.[22]

Actually, Heisman's earliest experience with signals, as he tells us in this same article (p.13), had been that of the spoken code method employed by the club teams at Brown. This system consisted of a series of short sentences uttered by the quarterback, each one alerting the players to the type play they were expected to execute. For example, "Line up, Brown" meant left tackle through right tackle; "Charge hard now" meant left end around right; "Hit 'em hard, bullies" meant left half around his own end; and so on.

It was during the latter part of his years at Penn, though, that things began to get a little more sophisticated. According to Heisman:

Cornell was perhaps the first of the colleges to deviate from this spoken code, Glenn Warner tells me. The Cornell quarterback might chatter his head off but the actual signals were his gestures and the movements of his legs. . . .

Elwood O. Wagenhurst, captain of Princeton in 1887, came to Penn three years later as head coach and almost at once he concocted the first considerable variation in the favored signal system of that time. It was simple too, sending none of us to the hospital with brain fever. All that we had to do was to note carefully the first word of every sentence uttered by the quarterback.

If that first word ended with "Y," our right half was to carry the ball around left end—if he could. If that first word concluded with a "K," it was up to our left to lay down his life, if necessary, for Alma Mater.[23]

Although the Buchtel faculty tolerated football, faculty opposition to it was growing, mainly because of the increasing number of serious injuries, even deaths, that were occurring wherever football was being played. To many, Heisman's professional style of coaching, with its strong emphasis on playing to win as opposed to the amateur notion of participating in a sport purely for the physical good to be gained from it, did not sit well. In fact, the faculty even wrote Heisman a letter to this effect, and it probably led to his departure after the 1894 baseball season.[24]

From such contrasting attitudes toward athletics—his own and those of academia—a conflict emanated that Heisman (as well as many other coaches) would confront from time to time for the rest of his career: a conflict involving the role of athletics and its proper relationship to the academic mission. By his own convictions, as we have seen, Heisman always placed academics far ahead of athletics. But he was never hesitant to remind the critics of sports that football played an important educational role in developing a young man's moral character as well as contributing to his healthy mental outlook. Many of Heisman's ideas about this relationship, which were in the formative stage at this time, would find full expression in his 1922 book, *Principles of Football*. With his greatest success on the gridiron behind him by the time of its publication, Heisman had formulated a coaching philosophy that was uniquely his own.

Even though Heisman left Buchtel before the 1894 football season to return to Oberlin, some Buchtel players recruited him as player-coach in 1894 for a game with Ohio State. It was to be played as part of a football tournament involving several other Ohio schools at the state fairgrounds in Columbus. As Buchtel's only game of the 1894 season (actually the game was played September 1 before the school year got underway), it afforded Heisman's critics considerable insight into his contention that disciplined training and inspirational leadership were equally important in building the proper winning attitude in football players and that they were stronger men for having had these experiences. Heisman, of course, recognized that the match with Ohio State was an opportunity not only to put his team on public display, but to showcase his coaching tactics as well. So to prepare for what was tantamount to an exhibition game, he drove his players through a rigorous training program at a summer camp near Akron. The outcome of the game has been reconstructed from a letter Heisman wrote to a Buchtel official in later years: "After playing two twenty-minute halves in burning heat, and the score deadlocked at six points apiece, the teams took a ten-minute rest and then started a 'sudden death' overtime period." Heisman, who was playing quarterback, drove his team to Ohio State's four-yard line. Following a short, inspirational talk, he directed a play in which the fullback, who had been given the ball, was literally pulled across the goal line. According to Heisman, "We all went through together, just like the water of a mill dam when the dam goes out."[25] Questionable tactics notwithstanding, Buchtel had won, 12–6, the only time in its football history that the school would defeat Ohio State.

Other than his satisfying role in helping win this game, there was another, more intimate, reason for John Heisman to maintain his ties with Buchtel. It was there that he became involved in his first serious romance. According to his nephew, W. Lee Heisman, the young coach had courted a Buchtel coed from Wisconsin named Edith Maora Cole, but when she discovered she had a tubercular condition, they had decided not to marry. (In those days, tuberculosis was considered an incurable disease.) Although they drifted apart when Heisman's coaching pursuits took him south in 1895, they would eventually marry in the 1920s, following Heisman's divorce from his first wife in 1919.[26] As one singularly devoted to the things of a man's world, Heisman, like most men of his day, assumed a somewhat Victorian attitude toward the opposite sex and affairs of the heart. Consequently, we know very little of his intimate relationships with or personal attitudes toward the women with whom he came in contact.

In spite of the growing criticism of football and those like Heisman who were either daring or foolhardy enough to coach it, an appreciative audience for the game was now springing up everywhere it appeared. One of the reasons for this reception was the expanding urbanization of that day, which had created, in effect, a captive audience hungry for the emotional outlet that sports afforded. Accordingly, as the popularity of professional baseball and intercollegiate sports increased, the daily newspapers of large cities were beginning to devote more space to sporting activities to satisfy the demanding tastes of an ever-expanding audience. Not only were the results of significant sporting events being reported, but those who covered these events were beginning to express their own opinions about the participants, coaches, and personalities involved in such activities, recognizing that their readers might also have personal preferences for the background or human interest side of sports. For example, a reporter for the *Akron Beacon* in 1893 assessed Heisman's brief tenure at Buchtel as follows: "J. W. Heisman, the coach, has met with great success. He is an all-round athlete, and has that requisite of a successful coach—firmness. He has certainly done wonders in putting the team in shape." (Quotation is from Heisman's privately printed pamphlet, c. 1900, to promote his coaching qualifications. See below, note 27.) In other words, those who reported athletic events had begun to take on something of an editorial posture, reminding readers of the reasons for athletic success (and failure) and as a result helping to mold their attitudes toward sports. The day of the daily sports columnist who would play a key role in creating the cult of athletic hero worship was near at hand.

As far as his relationship with the press was concerned, the charismatic Heisman and the American newspaper were made for each other. In working to establish his coaching persona, he quickly grew sensitive to the power of the press to make or break the public image of an athletic team and also, by extension, its coach. As his career developed, Heisman himself would take on the role of a sports commentator. Prime examples of his unique ability in this area were the pieces he wrote for Atlanta newspapers and school publications while coaching at Georgia Tech and ultimately the personal reminiscences of his career published in *Collier's* weekly during the late 1920s. Even though he was not always on the best of terms with reporters in later years, Heisman continued to be a popular personality who attracted the press everywhere he coached. Even after he returned to Oberlin in 1894 and compiled a rather mediocre 4–3–1 record (two of the losses were in close games with Michigan and Penn State), news coverage about the young coach was still generous and commendatory. *The Oberlin News* commented in 1894: "Much praise is due to Heisman. He has made Oberlin football a synonym for good football." *The Oberlin College Review* had even higher praise, flatly stating: "We have the best coach in the West."[27] By the time Heisman left Oberlin in 1895 at the age of twenty-five, he had laid the foundation for his public image as a football coach. In this respect he had blazed a trail for other media-minded coaches to follow—notably Knute Rockne.

THE EASTERN GAME (1892–1894)

But what had been going on in the East during the three years after Heisman had departed Penn and the eastern gridiron wars? In 1892, the Yale Bulldogs continued to dominate the larger football scene, extending their unbeaten, untied, and unscored-on string to twenty-seven straight games. (The string had begun with a last game win over Princeton in 1890.) Sparked by the indomitable Frank Hinkey at end and coached by former Yale back Billy Bull, the Yale Blue, at 13–0, was declared national champion.

Harvard, with only a 6–0 loss to Yale, was runner-up in 1892. (The loss occurred in the infamous flying wedge game.) The Harvard Crimson featured the outstanding play of Marshall "Ma" Newell at tackle and William Henry Lewis at center. Newell was the first of only four men to make the All-America team four times (the others were Yale's Pudge Heffelfinger and Frank Hinkey and Penn's Truxton Hare), while Lewis, who had formerly played at Amherst, was the first black All-American.

In 1892, Heisman's alma mater was also in the thick of things, as new coach George Woodruff brought Penn to the fore with only a loss to Yale marring its record. Beating Princeton for the first time was a real boon, but a major reason for Penn's success was Woodruff's offensive strategy and effective use of the quick kick, as discussed earlier. Due to the lax eligibility rules of that day, he also had a number of graduate and professional school students playing for him, which naturally rankled a number of his opponents who lacked such experienced players.

In 1893, Yale's unbeaten shutout string reached thirty-five games, but the unscored-on record ended in the 14–6 win over Penn. However, Princeton (11–0) was named national champion when it hung a 6–0 shutout on Yale to end the Bulldogs' unbeaten streak.

With the flying wedge and V attack outlawed for the season of 1894, mass interference formations took over, and, as we have seen, Woodruff's Penn Quakers led the way here, compiling a 12–0 record. Nevertheless, Yale (16–0) won the national championship. This was also the year that playing time was cut to two thirty-five-minute halves, and a linesman was added to the crew of officials to keep track of time.

THE RISE OF MIDWESTERN FOOTBALL IN THE 1890s

During Heisman's three years at Oberlin and Buchtel, America was in the process of becoming a country where economic progress was something of a religion and urbanization its prophet and prime motivator in an increasingly materialistic culture. It was an era that separated a newer, more confident America from an older, more conservative and culturally isolated America. Growing cities like Cleveland and Akron, where Heisman periodically lived and coached during this time, epitomized what was happening in a sociocultural sense to the America of the 1890s. Through expansive industrialization the larger midwestern cities were attracting thousands of people from the outlying rural areas, as well as multitudes of immigrants from European countries to the job opportunities that these industrial centers had to offer. Cleveland, a veritable melting pot of foreign nationals, had profited from the industrializing efforts of prototypical go-getters like Rocke-feller and politician Mark Hanna, so that by the 1890s this city had established itself as a leading steel, oil, railway, and manufacturing center. During this same time, Akron, with the advent of the automobile just around the corner and the attendant growth of the rubber industry, was on the verge of be-coming a thriving boomtown as the country's tire-manufacturing center.

But it was the colossus of the Midwest, Chicago, that projected more dynamically than any other place at this time both the raw power that had energized the region and all the cultural inconsistencies and contradictions of the American experience. Although the railroad and telegraph had spanned the land by this time and brought the country closer together in a commu-nications sense (these advances would help spread the cause of sports through access to mass travel and quicker circulation of media information through on-site reporting), an ingrained provincialism kept the economic concerns of rural America far removed from the capitalistic priorities of industrialized urban society. And even while the United States was challenging England for first place in the world manufacturing marketplace, a persistent and pervasive hierarchy of social sectionalism divided the "haves" and the "have-nots." Whereas Chicago investors had made fortunes in wheat, meat packing, iron, and the railroad, it had been Civil War profiteering and the influx of immigrant labor that helped them maintain that wealth. Naturally, in such a milieu, corruption, political and otherwise, was bound to thrive. If Chicago was something of a living microcosm for all this, as Carl Sandburg would soon express so vividly in his poetry, it was also the cultural center of the Midwest, no matter how crude the city might have appeared on the surface.

Perhaps the World's Columbian Exposition held in Chicago in 1893, when Heisman was coaching at Buchtel, represented better than anything else the marvelous heights that the city had risen to, in both a cultural and a mater-ialistic sense. To commemorate the four hundredth anniversary of Columbus' discovery of the New World, Chicago had carved a symbolic testimonial to progress out of six hundred acres of waterfront swampland—a paradoxical and miraculous feat. The exposition served as a showcase not only for the achievements of Chicago itself but for those of the age.

That Chicago was a fitting location for a fair of international scope was attested to by the fact that in the year the Exposition opened, the city had gained a population exceeding one million, over two-thirds of which were foreign-born. In this kind of environment the acquisitive nature of capitalism was being continually tempered by the challenge of the adjacent frontier lands awaiting development. Contradictory forces continued to flourish, such as the vested interests of capital versus those of labor, the advantages of the wealthy over the squalor of the impoverished, and the attractions of high culture as contrasted with the low-life elements of the city. In keeping with these dichotomies, the view from the fair's giant ferris wheel included that of the University of Chicago's new campus. There, the city's inherent conflict between culture and vulgarism would find a fitting parallel in the clash between academics and athletics, particularly in the aggrandizing game of football as it was taking form at the university during the 1890s under the leadership of its dynamic, progressive president William Rainey Harper and its innovative new coach Amos Alonzo Stagg—one of John Heisman's truly great contemporaries.

A former Yale football player under advisory coach Walter Camp in the 1880s and one of Camp's first All-America picks at end, Stagg came to Chicago in 1892 after a short coaching stint at Springfield College (1890–1891).[28] Football was to be a unique sport at the brand new Chicago institution in that, unlike other schools, the University of Chicago and football would grow up together. For a football coach, Stagg's situation was unique, too, in that he held faculty rank as "director of physical culture." He had been specifically hired by Rainey to put Chicago on the gridiron map.

But Stagg found rough going in the beginning of his tenure due to the problems most coaches of that day (and many since) encountered: lack of funding, facilities, and equipment, as well as lack of faculty support. Although John D. Rockefeller had bequeathed a large sum of money to help the University get started, apparently none of it found its way to the athletic department. Stagg himself wrote about the problem of faculty opposition during those early years under President Harper:

For all his advanced views on physical training and his keen sense of advertising values, Dr. Harper shared the prevailing faculty fear of over-stressing competitive athletics as a public show.

"It is not the function of the university to provide at great cost spectacular entertainment for enormous crowds of people," he read into the constitution, so to speak, of the school.[29]

Nevertheless, Stagg's unflagging faith in the future of football was as strong as his own Christian faith and the city of Chicago's staunch belief in its own destiny. Thus it was not long before he was consistently turning out winning teams that attracted a loyal following. Indeed, the University of Chicago Maroon supporters soon found themselves with plenty to cheer about, as in over forty years of coaching at Chicago, Stagg would see four of his Maroon teams go undefeated and twelve of them lose only one game in a season. Stagg's best team was the 1905 undefeated squad that beat strong Michigan and Wisconsin teams and was declared national champion.

Also during the 1890s, Stagg appeared to be contributing more than anyone else to the strategic development of football, including his pioneering contemporaries, John Heisman and Glenn Warner. If there was controversy later on as to who first introduced a particular innovation, the reason for dispute was simply, as Stagg himself put it, that "credit often went astray in the '90s for new plays, due to the inadequate reporting and the lack of contact between the sport of one region with that of another."[30] It was an era when pioneering coaches of kindred spirit and a real feel for the game could come up with similar innovative techniques within a season or two of each other (perhaps even a few weeks) and never know who had been first.

For example, while Heisman was experimenting with his version of the mass momentum formations in the early 1890s, Stagg was doing the same thing at Springfield. He would ultimately receive credit for originating the first of such formations, the "ends back" formation, which in stationing linemen in the backfield looked ahead to formations such as Glenn Warner's double wingback attack. Heisman himself later admitted his debt to Stagg: "The business of pulling linemen back and giving them the ball was not at all new. . . . As early as 1891 Stagg, in his first year as a coach, utilized his ends as runners with the ball at Springfield. He ran them like halfbacks and I copied his theory and carried it along for years."[31] At about the same time, Stagg came up with a criss-cross play featuring deceptive handoffs, including a hidden-ball maneuver. Also during this period he invented a tactic he called the "Whoa Back" play, which was the forerunner of the fullback spinner play, only in this formation the quarterback was the one who spun around to make or take a handoff. Other mass interference formations considered to have originated with Stagg were the fanciful "turtle-back" in 1891 and the "tackles back" in 1894.

Stagg's innovations continued unabated over the decade. In 1894 he implemented a backward or lateral pass on the kickoff, and supposedly the center snap, which, as previously noted, Heisman claims to have invented at Buchtel in 1893. By 1896, Stagg was directing his punter to take a direct snap from center. Stagg's version of the on-side kickoff appeared in 1894, as did his modification of the quarterback's stance in the basic T-formation from that of a squatting position to one of a semistanding stance to receive the center snap as today's quarterbacks do.

As some of the Maroons' early games were played indoors in the old Chicago Coliseum, Stagg introduced the offensive huddle in 1896 to combat the noise level. This was long before the huddle would become an outdoor fixture, although Glenn Warner used it against John Heisman's Auburn team the same year. (See p. 52.) It was also the year he implemented his version of the quick kick, and a year later Chicago tried one of the first place kicks from scrimmage instead of a drop kick, although Penn claimed to have used it first that same year.

During this time Stagg's fertile mind was also busy originating defensive innovations. In 1890 he was utilizing a 7–2–2 defense when most teams were still relying on a nine-man line, and by 1898 he was pulling his center back to function as a linebacker to assist the regular defensive backs. Numerous other later contributions that Stagg made to the game were mostly in the area of offensive strategy, which will be described later. Many of his contributions had nothing to do with football strategy but rather with college sports traditions, such as the idea of awarding players letters (school emblems) as rewards for athletic achievement. Hence the term *letterman* that applies to a player who has played a sufficient amount of time to earn his letter.

The main point to consider here concerning the development of football in the 1890s is that its uncertain status continually invited innovation to give the game needed stability. In this vein, Stagg and Heisman were two seminal minds who were clearly in the right places at the right time, regardless of who received credit for being first at any one thing. Both men believed in the power of inspirational leadership in coaching, although they had somewhat different approaches to what leadership was all about. Stagg, who had studied for the ministry at Yale, decided early on against a career in the pulpit, feeling that he could minister more effectively to young men as a football coach. In fact, when he took on the head coaching position at Chicago, he declared that "it will give me such a fine chance to do Christian work among the boys who are sure to have the most influence. Win the athletes of any college for Christ, and you will have the strongest working element attainable in college life."[32] Appropriately enough, he proudly expressed in his 1927 autobiography that all his coaching years up to that time had been a form of ministering for Jesus Christ.

While John Heisman never professed Stagg's evangelical faith, he was no less dedicated to teaching his players about the worth of their commitment to an ideal. In fact, if Heisman had a personal religion (his formal church allegiance was Episcopalian), it was expressed in his belief that the strong inner desire of an individual to work toward a goal was the key to success at whatever task one undertook. For as we have seen, his personal formula for success was inherited from the go-getter philosophy of the American industrialist and businessman. That there was something akin to a religious experience concerning the varsity athlete's dedication to all-round individual excellence had always been an essential part of traditional college athletics with roots in England's Victorian concept of the "muscular Christian." But by the 1890s, with the advent of professional coaches like Heisman and Stagg and the competitive standards they established, this experience had developed into an idealized socialization process in American intercollegiate athletics, of which the varsity athlete was the exemplar. Although considerable social change has impacted on college athletics over the years, the code of character building and religious identification through sports involvement is still very much with us today, expressing itself through such active organizations as the Fellowship of Christian Athletes and Athletes in Action.

With such a dedicated and highly respected coach as Amos Alonzo Stagg continually refining and actively promoting the game, football quickly became a natural attraction to sports fans not only in the Chicago area but also throughout the Midwest. By 1895, the game had such a large following in the region that a number of schools came together to form one of college football's first leagues—what was then called the Western Conference, whose seven charter members were actually the nucleus of an organization that would soon become popularly known as the Big Ten. Officially recognized as the Intercollegiate Conference of Faculty Representatives, this organization attempted to establish a semblance of order and ethical standards throughout its membership by agreeing to a uniform set of rules governing play and eligibility. By acting collectively, the Western Conference pioneered the first effective system for controlling athletic standards. Chicago was one of its first powers, along with Michigan and Wisconsin, winner of the first conference championship in 1896.

If there were any who doubted the ability of midwestern teams to compete on an even par with the eastern powers, all doubts would have been erased had they been among the ten thousand people who witnessed the Penn–Chicago game in Philadelphia on October 29, 1898. Having gone undefeated the previous season and riding the crest of nine straight victories prior to the Chicago game, the Quakers were considered the best in the land at the time. But the determined Stagg had his team fully prepared for Coach George Woodruff's team and at halftime the Maroons led the mighty Quakers, 6–5. Nevertheless, the more experienced Penn team came back in the second half to win, 23–11, much to the relief of the hometown fans. Even so, eastern gridiron observers had been impressed with the level of competition that Coach Stagg's team had demonstrated. Clearly, with a degree of parity now beginning to set in, football was on the verge of becoming a national sport.

SOUTHERN FOOTBALL IN THE 1890s

By the mid-1890s, football was also establishing itself in other parts of the country other than the East and Midwest. Organizational efforts were especially evident among the southern schools during these years. While flagship institutions like the University of Virginia and the University of North Carolina had gotten an earlier start, the schools in the deep South, particularly in the Gulf states, didn't get football programs underway until the 1890s, and then in a very limited way. What was essential to the growth of the game in this region was recruitment of the so-called missionary coaches through whom the Midwest had so ably profited, particularly in their practical ability to teach promising candidates the basic playing skills of the game. According to some reports, the first game in the region was played in 1890 between Vanderbilt and the University of Nashville, which Vandy won, 46–0. Harry Thornton, one of Heisman's teammates at Penn, became the first full-time coach in the South when Vanderbilt paid him $400 a year for his services.

Even though the noble militaristic side of football appealed strongly to the southern desire to identify itself with a winning cause, especially after the bitter defeat of the Civil War, it would be years before the South would be capable of successfully competing with the teams of the East and Midwest. In 1890, for example, the University of Virginia had suffered a humiliating 115–0 defeat at the hands of Princeton, even though the Virginia Cavaliers were supposedly in the vanguard of southern football at this time.

By the fall of 1892, schools in the states of Tennessee, Mississippi, and Louisiana had also started playing football. But because an athletics governing body for the region was still several years away, player eligibility was difficult to control, as it had been in all areas of the country. Too often, faculty, coaches, and even nonstudents or tramp athletes called ringers, who sold their services, wound up playing. Since high school football in the South was virtually unheard of at this time except in Virginia and Tennessee, most football candidates' introduction to the game did not come until college. Like elsewhere, the style of play favored brute force over speed and quickness, with the flying wedge holding forth at those schools that had learned about it. Like elsewhere, too, injuries were rampant, and at many schools only those students who had secured parental permission could play football.

Practically from the start, southern schools that fielded teams began to point toward a big-game finale with a rival institution on Thanksgiving Day, as northern schools had been doing. So it soon became their practice to schedule games with a number of prep schools and athletic clubs in October as preliminary warm-ups for the tougher games along the way toward the big, climactic November match. Some of the South's biggest rivalries grew out of this practice as, for example, the Auburn–Georgia game, which for a number of years was played on Thanksgiving Day in Atlanta. Even extending beyond the "Turkey Day" tradition, rivalries of all sorts would soon start springing up, matchups that were considered to be social as well as athletic events. As football historian John McCallum has put it: "Down in Southeast territory, college football long ago became a geographical, historical, or social event—sometimes all three. The fans down there have always had somebody they especially love to see whomped. There are all kinds of rivalries: intrastate, border, crosstown and personal—all commonly classed as 'natural' rivalries."[33] During John Heisman's twenty-five years coaching at three southern schools—Auburn, Clemson, and Georgia Tech (1895–1919)—football took on one of its major distinguishing characteristics as a sport: a strong sense of place and deep pride as expressed through the gridiron fortunes of a particular school.

By the close of the 1920s, when the South had finally put itself on the national football map, one game played during this time vividly exemplified what football had come to mean to this part of the country. The year was 1929, and the event was the dedication of Sanford Stadium at Athens, Georgia, where Yale had come down to play the University of Georgia. By this time, intersectional games were common and they sparked considerable national interest. In this matchup, the southern exposure proved a little too much for the Yale team and its great back Albie Booth, as the Yale Blue wilted in the heat and lost, 15–0. Amid all the celebrating that followed, no one caught the spirit of the occasion more aptly than did *New York Sun* reporter George Trevor: "Football provides an escape valve for that adventurous urge; that martial ardor, which despite an outward appearance of languor is the heritage of every son of Dixie. Northerners may have originated the American version of rugby, but the game is in the blood down here in the Deep South, and they play it for blood."[34]

That football was in the southern blood was made evident on December 22, 1894, when Dr. William L. Dudley, a Vanderbilt dean, met in Atlanta with university representatives from Alabama, Auburn, Georgia, Georgia Tech, North Carolina, and Sewanee (the University of the South) to found a new athletic conference. Because a number of abuses had infiltrated college athletics in the South, chairman Dudley's avowed purpose in establishing an association of schools that participated in organized sports was "to develop, regulate, and purify intercollegiate athletics . . . in the South."[35] The new conference, of which these schools became the charter members, was called the Southern Intercollegiate Athletic Association (SIAA). It would eventually become so large and unwieldy that in 1920 it broke up into the Southern Conference, which in turn fragmented into the Southeastern (1932) and Atlantic Coast (1953) conferences, comprised of the region's largest schools.

With the establishment of the SIAA, nearly all the major southern colleges started playing football. This paved the way for the arrival of professional or paid coaches as well as more stringent interinstitutional control of player eligibility. Accordingly, concerns in this latter problematic area during Auburn's 1894 football season precipitated the search for a knowledgeable coach who could project an authoritative image to enforce strict standards.

HEISMAN'S AUBURN YEARS (1895–1899)

The fact that John Heisman had done rather well in coaching against a number of reputable Midwest teams during his time at Oberlin and Buchtel undoubtedly caught the eye of the people at the Agricultural and Mechanical College of Alabama (now Auburn) when the school became a charter member of the SIAA. In seeking him out as the Auburn coach, they reasoned that someone with proven credentials in coaching the game of football was exactly what was needed if they were to compete successfully against the caliber of teams in the league. (In three years of participating in football the Auburn record stood at a mediocre 6–6–1.) But how and why John Heisman finally decided to come to this school located some fifty miles east of Montgomery in an attractive but somewhat isolated village called Auburn is a story in itself.

Although he had grown up in a relatively small town, Titusville was not the usual tranquil American town, for reasons discussed in chapter 1. Having gone on to live in growing metropolitan areas such as Providence, Philadelphia, Cleveland, and Akron, John Heisman, during this early phase of his career, had been assimilating a variety of cosmopolitan experiences in addition to the go-getter influence of his youth. As a bona fide city man of urbane manners and interests, he undoubtedly thought of himself as a man of the world.

In spite of his basically urban background, the real reason for Heisman's decision to coach at Auburn was probably the challenge it presented him to "spread the gospel" of football in what was then virgin territory. Having been in the vanguard of football's key developmental years in the East as a player and then as a coach during the game's spread to the Midwest, the young, idealistic Heisman undoubtedly welcomed the opportunity that the South presented him to further the cause of his game, particularly at an athletically ambitious school like Auburn.

As an early land-grant college created by the Morrill Act of 1862, the school had a great deal to prove about itself—particularly, it needed to create an identity. Originally known as the East Alabama Male College, a Methodist liberal arts school dating from the 1850s, the college fell on hard times after the Civil War and deeded its property to the state of Alabama in 1872 for the establishment of a land-grant institution. The provisions of the Morrill Act stipulated that the curriculum of land-grant schools must consist mainly of agricultural and mechanical studies. Military tactics also had a significant place, with the traditional liberal arts playing more of a secondary role. Because of its emphasis on the practical side of education, such an institution of higher learning was made to order for this part of the South at the time, with its need to catch up with the more industrialized areas of the country.

But in spite of federal support, Auburn's early days were a time of financial struggle, characterized by occasional clashes between the faculty members who professed the agricultural and mechanical side of the curriculum and those who supported the traditional liberal arts as being essential to the proper mission of a university. To some, such a conflict would be never ending, but by 1885 the school's financial difficulties were alleviated to a large extent when the state legislature allocated funds to support agricultural research. Fortunately, it was a time when southern legislators were beginning to consider scientific education more seriously, and because of this attitude the school began to receive more support over the years. Today Auburn is widely known for its contributions to research and development in both agriculture and technology, but in John Heisman's day it was a school much like himself, still searching to establish an appropriate identity. Over a five-year coaching tenure at Auburn, Heisman's achievements on the football field would go a long way in helping to establish the school's long-standing athletic reputation as well as a name for himself. A concomitant result was a strong sense of community identity for the school. By 1899, Heisman's last year there, the institution's name had been changed from the Agricultural and Mechanical College of Alabama to Alabama Polytechnic Institute, but the place name eventually grew so popular that in 1960 the state legislature approved the name of Auburn University.

Prior to Heisman's arrival, the football team had gone through four coaches, each lasting no longer than a year. (There had been two appointments in the year 1893 alone.) The first, Dr. George Petrie, a history professor who had volunteered to coach the team in his spare time, had the distinction of also being the first coach of the oldest football rivalry in this part of the country, the Auburn–Georgia series, whose initial match was played in Atlanta in 1892 and won by Auburn, 10–0.

With a Princeton man (F. M. Hall) at the helm in 1894, though, Auburn thought it might have come up with the right person for the job of football mentor, but the only bright spot during the season was a record-setting 94–0 win over Georgia Tech. (At the time, the rules allowed the scoring team to get the ball right back on the ensuing kickoff, thus affording Auburn the opportunity to dominate possession in this match.) Over a four-game schedule, losses were to Vanderbilt, 20–4, and most disappointingly, to Georgia, 10–8, and Alabama, 18–0. This latter defeat was the first after two previous victories. The loss was particularly bitter because of two ringers the officials allowed to play even after Auburn had challenged their eligibility. These ringers went on to figure prominently in the game's final score, and helped fire up a heated rivalry that has lasted to this day. The upshot of the 1894 season, though, was that Auburn was now in the market for a new coach, one well versed in all the intricacies of the game. This qualification was particularly necessary due to the game's ever-changing rules and the attendant skills that players needed to keep abreast of to perform successfully. Thus, a man of John Heisman's proven capabilities appeared to be the answer to Auburn's immediate coaching needs.

Displaying his usual bold determination and infectious enthusiasm, Heisman boldly started out in 1895 to build a competitive football team at Auburn. Uncharacteristically, though, his first match ended up in a close 9–6 loss to Vanderbilt on a muddy field in Nashville. More prophetic of Heisman's future coaching style was his origination and use of a hidden-ball play in this game. With Vanderbilt leading 9–0 in the second half, Heisman relates that the Auburn team lined up in a revolving wedge, containing their quarterback, Reynolds Tichenor, with the ball:

The moment the milling started, Tichenor stuffed the ball under the front of his jersey. The mass around him disintegrated, the players scurrying to wide and varied parts of the field and with them went the Vanderbilt men who had industriously been trying to break up the wedge. Only Tichenor remained and he, apparently, was out of the play. He was on one knee, busy at tying his shoe lace.

But when the Vanderbilt team was as widely spread as his own, Tichenor arose and nonchalantly catfooted down the field for a deceitful touchdown.[36]

The play was soon to be outlawed, but the story of its origin at Auburn is worth retelling. In a bull session with some of his players, Heisman casually remarked, "You know, boys, I had a kid ask me once if it was against the rules to hide the ball. I don't see anything against it, but I honestly don't see how you could work a trick like that." This started everyone to thinking, and "once it was established that the ball could be easily and quickly concealed [under a jersey], they set up a formation to cover up the trick and draw opponents away from Tichenor so he could get free."[37] Auburn had a chance to win the Vanderbilt game when the Tigers moved the ball to the 2-yard line with two minutes to play. But the referee called the game "on account of darkness," even though a contemporary account reported that the sun had not yet set. Heisman's irate reaction was the first of many run-ins he would have with southern officials.

Later that season, the hidden-ball play is supposed to have also worked against Georgia, but there is no official record of its use. At any rate, Glenn "Pop" Warner, who was the Georgia coach, carried the same play with him to his next coaching appointment at Cornell, where in 1898 he was mistakenly credited with having invented it.[38] Heisman was obsessed, it seems, with inventing ways to hide the football. Even when he was at Georgia Tech, one of his players, Al Loeb, reported that Heisman "had players wear leather patches in the shape of footballs on the front of their jerseys, and opponents mistook them for the real thing and tackled the wrong guys."[39]

Auburn's 1895 season consisted of only three scheduled games, but with wins over rivals Alabama, 48–0, and Georgia, 16–6, Heisman's first season had ended auspiciously. Student reaction to Heisman's first year as head coach was positively reported in the school newspaper, *The Orange and Blue*: "As long as Heisman wishes to sign an Auburn contract, he may do it. Before he had been here a week, he had gained the love, admiration and confidence of every member of the faculty as well as the boys." (Quotation is from Heisman's promotional pamphlet.) The reason Heisman was so well liked was due to more than just his winning ways on the gridiron. He quickly became a respected member of the Auburn community, teaching classes in oratory (always a forte of his) and even trying his hand at acting in local play productions, an activity he would become increasingly involved in during his free time.

Earlier that year an event of monumental import for the future of football had occurred in Atlanta while Heisman was watching two other teams play. One of the first coaches to "scout" an opponent, Heisman was taking in the North Carolina–Georgia game when he witnessed the first use of the forward pass. Although such a play was then illegal, he immediately realized the impact that this innovation could have on opening up the game. With time running out and neither side having scored, the Carolina team found itself backed up to the goal line and its fullback preparing to punt. Heisman recounted the outcome:

But instead of punting straight into the leaping bodies of these on-rushing Georgians [the fullback] ran a few mincing steps to the right. Raising the ball to his shoulder he tossed it.

Luck was with the boy. The ball was caught by a North Carolinian.

Now as we today know forward passes it was not much. It traveled a few yards, and laterally as well as forward. It may have appeared to the spectators that it had been knocked from that fullback's hands.

At any rate that lad who caught it ran 70 yards for a touchdown!

Georgia was stunned, not quite realizing what had happened there beneath North Carolina's goal. But Glenn Warner, then coaching Georgia, had not missed a moment of it. And neither had I. I had been standing not more than eight yards from North Carolina's fullback.

I had seen the first forward pass in football. It was illegal, of course. Already Warner was storming at the referee. But the referee had not seen the North Carolina lad, goaded to desperation, toss the ball. And he refused to recall the ball. A touchdown had been made and a touchdown it remained.[40]

Heisman had long realized that the closed style of play created by the mass momentum tactics was "killing the game as well as the players," as he noted in his article about the illegal forward pass. From that time on, his crusade to get the Rules Committee to adopt the forward pass became a personal obsession. But it would not be until 1906 that his efforts came to fruition. Walter Camp, as an influential member of the committee, maintained a strongly conservative position. As a result, he was fearful of what the adoption of the forward pass would do to the basic nature of the game. In the long run, only the stubborn persistence of a man like John Heisman would ultimately turn his head.

It didn't take long for football to spread and entrench itself in the Deep South. During most of the 1890s, Virginia and North Carolina were the premier teams of the entire South, but by the middle of the decade the signs of change were in the air. In 1895, Virginia had barely defeated Vanderbilt, 6–4, for the SIAA championship. But in 1896, North Carolina was finally beaten (24–16) by a team from the Deep South–Glenn Warner's Georgia Bulldogs. At Auburn, Heisman's second year was upbeat, with convincing wins over Mercer (46–0), Georgia Tech (40–0), and Sewanee (38–6). Only a narrow 12–6 loss to Georgia kept the Tigers from an undefeated four-game schedule.

It was also in the Georgia game that Heisman met his match as far as the introduction of innovative play by a coaching opponent was concerned. Glenn Warner, who as a player had learned his football at Cornell and whose coaching career would be as far-ranging as Heisman's, went on to become one of the creative geniuses of the game. (His many significant contributions to football will be discussed later.) In the game with Auburn, played on Thanksgiving Day in Atlanta before a crowd of eight thousand spectators, Warner had his players prepare their plays out of a huddle, the first time such a procedure had ever taken place on an outdoor football field. This innovation proved to be so confusing to the Auburn players that they had a difficult time setting their defense, and it had a great deal to do with their defeat in this game. Ever the student of the game and willing to try anything new, Heisman must have learned a lot from this experience. In fact, before his tenure at Auburn was over, he had devised his own unique system for starting up a play from scrimmage:

At Alabama Poly I had my quarterback use the word "hike" when he was ready to receive the ball, and the word became popular for that office. It served us variously. For example, our opponents, hearing the quarterback's "hike," would charge, but presently we adopted a trick of trapping them by not putting the ball into play at the sound "hike" but waiting a couple of seconds. Naturally we won many off-side penalties.

Feeling that this procedure was an example of bad sportsmanship, Heisman wrote Walter Camp about it, and a rule was adopted forbidding a team to intentionally draw an opponent offside.[41]

With the limited material Heisman initially found at Auburn, he felt compelled to come up with as much deception as he could (hence, the hidden-ball play). Another deceptive play Heisman used at Auburn, one that would have wide-ranging impact, he claimed to have literally dreamed up. "I dreamed many plays, but this was the only dream of mine that ever worked," he declared:

The dream was too vivid to ignore. So we tried it on the scrubs. The quarterback simply gave the ball to, say, the right end while the latter was on the dead run. The right halfback and fullback galloped in front of the left halfback, who stood still until the right end passed him.

Then he took the ball from the right end and went through center with the quarterback preceding him. They found nobody there. My dream had produced a touchdown in its first trial. That play, virtually the forerunner of all delayed bucks, served me for fifteen years and with it my teams gained thousands of yards.[42]

But it was Heisman's unique brand of inspirational leadership that got the most results, commanding his players to give their all on the field of play. Edwin Pope has observed how Heisman "railed and snorted in practice, imploring players to do their all for God, Country, Auburn, and Heisman. Before each game he made squadsmen take a nonshirk, nonflinch oath."[43] In 1897, with Auburn reputed to have its lightest team and its first six-game schedule, Heisman knew he had to muster all the resources at his command.

The first two games of the season resulted in relatively easy wins over Mercer (26–0) and the University of Nashville (14–4), but the match with the University of the South at Sewanee, Tennessee, proved to be an altogether different matter. Having split two previous games with Auburn,

Sewanee was on the verge of becoming a recognized southern football power. While Vanderbilt was considered Sewanee's natural rival, a rivalry of sorts had also been developing between Auburn and the Sewanee Purple. In twelve games played between 1893 and 1931, Auburn always found the Purple a tough foe, with the Tigers managing only four wins, while two games ended in ties in this series. This rivalry can be attributed to the controversial incidents that seemed to always occur when these two teams played each other. In 1893, a tying Sewanee touchdown was allowed to stand after fans had interfered with Auburn players so that the Purple could score. Officials awarded Sewanee a 2-point conversion for a 16–14 win over Auburn, whose players had left the field in protest. The 1897 game, although it ended as a 0–0 tie, was not without its share of controversy, once again due to questionable officiating. When the regular officials for the game failed to show up (a common occurrence in those days), the Sewanee coach and an injured Auburn player agreed to officiate, with the natural result that each man exhibited undue favoritism toward his own team. By the second half there had been so much disagreement over questionable decisions that the match had to be called early "on account of darkness." Considering the state of flux in which the game of football found itself during the 1880s–1890s and the rate at which rule changes were implemented, it is not surprising that up-to-date, well-informed officials were so hard to come by at this time. By 1894, the crew of officials consisted of an umpire, referee, and linesman. They were usually men who had played the game, but who found it difficult to keep abreast of the latest rules developments. Although this was a problem that undoubtedly irked Heisman no little, it was one that would loom even larger in his final years at Auburn.

But there were other concerns of greater consequence to the future of football. On the day after the Auburn–Sewanee game—October 31, 1897—a tragedy occurred on the gridiron that came close to putting an end to football in the South. In the second half of the Georgia–Virginia game, played in Atlanta, the Georgia fullback, Richard Von Gammon, suffered severe injuries and died the following morning. After a hard-driving smash into the Virginia line, Von Gammon fell unconscious during the ensuing pileup of players. Doctors on hand diagnosed his case as a severe concussion, and although he was rushed to the hospital Von Gammon never recovered consciousness. Virginia went on to win the game, 17–4. When word of the Georgia player's death got out, a huge cry against football was raised all over the South. Most schools, including Auburn, cancelled the remaining games on their schedules. John Heisman's worst fears about the future of football, due primarily to its failure to open up the game, seemed about to come true.

The fate of football, at least in Georgia, appeared to lie in the hands of the state legislature, which after considerable debate voted to abolish the game as a collegiate sport. The governor vetoed the bill, however. What helped sway his mind was a letter to the trustees of the university from the mother of the deceased student. Because of her son's deep love of the game, Mrs. Von Gammon expressed her desire that football not be abolished. Rather, she felt that if schools—particularly the University of Georgia— would continue playing the game, it would be a kind of memorial to her son.

Although repercussions from Von Gammon's untimely death were still in the air by the time the 1898 season rolled around, most southern schools were gearing up to field teams as usual. For Auburn the three games that had been cancelled after the Georgia player's death were carried over to make up the 1898 schedule. The games had all been set for November, so Heisman and his players had a lot of time to prepare for them. Their efforts paid off, too, as they defeated Georgia Tech, 29–4, and their big rival of the time, Georgia, 18–17. The Tigers lost to a powerful North Carolina Tar Heel team, 24–0, as the Tar Heels went on to win the Southern championship that year.

The victory over Georgia was not without controversy, however, as once again shoddy officiating figured in the game's outcome. (By now, Heisman had to conclude that poor officiating was getting to be as much of a problem as brutal playing tactics.) This time, though, the judgment of the officials favored Auburn. After falling behind at the half, 13–4, Heisman directed his big fullback, George Mitcham, to start pounding at the line, a strategy that soon resulted in three touchdowns and the score in Auburn's favor, 18– 13. Nevertheless, Georgia came back to score a touchdown, only to miss the extra-point try. Although the Georgia players tried to convince the officials that Auburn had been offside on the play, they were overruled. With the score at 18–17 and eight minutes still left in the game, the Georgia team walked off the field in protest.

Heisman had to make the most of this game's fortuitous outcome because the next year he was involved in two games in which officiating figured more prominently against him than ever before. One of these games, the last of the season with Sewanee, may have actually helped him make up his mind to secure another coaching position. In 1898, the Sewanee Purple was a team on the rise, defeating its big rival and the dominant power of the region, Vanderbilt, 19–4. That same year, the ambitious Vanderbilt team ventured north to engage in one of the Deep South's first intersectional clashes, only to lose to the University of Cincinnati, 10–0. While Sewanee was on the verge of making a strong impact in the southern region, a national football reputation for the South still lay some years in the future.

The season of 1899, John Heisman's last at Auburn, promised to be his best. He had finally built a team of veteran players who obviously responded to his flair for no-nonsense, aggressive leadership. The Auburn attack in 1899 featured a cadre of hard-running backs led by Captain Arthur Feagin, Franklin Bivings, and Ed Huguley. Heisman, in fact, began the tradition of great running backs at Auburn. That year also brought significant changes in football's scoring system: touchdowns were now worth 5 points instead of 4; extra points after touchdowns became 1 point instead of 2; but field goals, which were still nearly always drop-kicked, were still worth 5 points. Clearly, though, the running game was about to catch up with the kicking game.

Playing a five-game schedule, Auburn blew out its first three opponents: Georgia Tech, 63–0; the Montgomery Athletic Club, 41–0; and Clemson, 34–0. (This game may have alerted Clemson, another athletically ambitious school, that John Heisman would be a good choice as their next coach.) But what happened in the next two games undoubtedly convinced Heisman that southern officials were out to get both him and his Auburn team and that it might be time to depart from the Alabama school.

Typically, the Georgia game, played in Atlanta on November 18, turned out to be another hard-fought contest. But with only thirty seconds left in the game and Auburn leading, 11–6, the umpire, Mr. Rowbotham, called the match "on account of darkness," a major reason many games were never finished in those days. However, not only did Rowbotham call the match, he also declared that because the game had not been completed, the final score should stand at 0–0. An incensed Heisman, feeling that he had again been victimized by an official, protested the outcome to the SIAA. It was not until a year later that the executive committee of the Association ruled in Auburn's favor, with the final score reverting back to 11–6. This reversal was unusual for the time, because an official's final decision was usually never questioned. But there was even more controversy to come in the next game, the outcome of which was to be debated long after it was played.

The Auburn game with Sewanee would decide who played North Carolina for the Southern championship. Because Sewanee's Purple from the mountains of Tennessee were unbeaten at the time, there was much ballyhoo over this match to be played Thanksgiving Day in Montgomery. One of the reasons for the hoopla was Sewanee had fielded the South's first notable football power in 1899. Not only were the Purple unscored on in ten consecutive contests, they had recently returned from a road trip on which they had defeated five big schools in six days (Texas, Texas A&M, Tulane, LSU, and Ole Miss).

But by the day of the Auburn game, either Sewanee's luck had run out or its players were just plain worn out from so much traveling, for Heisman's team was soon running circles around them. At one point, after Auburn had advanced the ball to Sewanee's 10-yard line, the Purple took over on downs and punted, but Auburn was not to be denied. After three straight plays, the ball wound up on Sewanee's 10-yard line, from which point Auburn scored. But the referee called the play back, indicating that the whistle had blown before the touchdown was made. Undaunted, Auburn came right back for a touchdown, the first score against Sewanee that year.

Things looked bad for Sewanee when minutes later the speedy Ed Huguley broke loose for a 50-yard touchdown. Once again the referee ruled against the score, this time without even an explanation. After Sewanee got the ball, they launched their first determined drive, which resulted in a score.

Auburn countered with another big run by Huguley, who later scored, but the point after was missed, making the score 10–5, Auburn's favor. Fuzzy Woodruff described how the game ended:

Darkness was beginning to fall. Simpkins' powerful toe sent the ball to Auburn's 5-yard line and Auburn fumbled. Sewanee recovered, and it looked like a game of football.

Three times the Sewanee backs hit the Auburn line, and in all three trials they didn't advance the ball a foot. The ball went over and Auburn heaved a sigh of relief.

On the first play, the ball was given to Huguley. Ed fumbled but Dan Martin of Auburn fell on the ball.

Again enter the referee.

For some reason, never explained until this good day, he gave the ball to Sewanee on Auburn's 1-yard line. Simpkins went over for the touchdown and kicked goal. The score was 11–10, and Sewanee had won the game.[44]

Something of a charmed team that year, Sewanee went on in the very next game to win its first Southern championship, defeating North Carolina in Atlanta, 5–0. Needless to say, Sewanee's success did little to pacify John Heisman, who was thoroughly outraged at the questionable work of the officials, particularly after having endured the absurd ruling that altered the score of the Georgia game played earlier. Little wonder, then, that the pros and cons of Sewanee's fortunate win over Auburn continued to be debated by football fans for a long time afterwards. The vagaries leading to the game's outcome even compelled Heisman to state his case in a lengthy letter to the sporting editor of a Birmingham newspaper on December 4, 1899: "I think we completely outplayed Sewanee from start to finish, both offensively and defensively; and it was only the outrageous work of the officials that made it possible for Sewanee to score at all. I think the work of both officials was, by all odds, the worst I ever saw, and I don't mind proclaiming it from the housetops." Heisman went on to point out that he had no intention of lodging a protest, although umpire William P. Taylor, a boys' school headmaster, had willfully made a series of poor decisions that countered whatever chances Auburn had of winning the game. (Heisman characteristically labeled the man's actions as "meddling interposition.") Heisman appeared to be more concerned about the umpire's decisions contributing to "bad blood" between the two schools, rather than about making an official protest, as the close of his letter indicated.[45]

The very next day Taylor came back with an embittered rebuttal in a lengthy letter of his own. His argument appeared to stem from the unfounded contention that the Auburn team was poorly coached and had been resorting to unfair tactics on the playing field. To Taylor, Heisman was not a coach, but a "would-be actor of character parts." He wrote:

The plain truth of the matter is that Coach Heisman has proved a failure in producing winning teams at Auburn; he wishes to retain his position as football coach and hopes to be retained also as professor of elocution and oratory. Is it not most likely that he must keep in Auburn's good graces by ascribing his defeats to the officials?[46]

Clearly, Heisman's letter had struck a sensitive nerve in Taylor, and he was striking back any way he could, lashing out in particular at the man's professional abilities as both a coach and an actor—one of the earliest attempts, it would appear, to discredit a sporting figure by referring to him as an entertainer. Nevertheless, Taylor's diatribe served mainly to undermine his own weak argument, particularly when he naively remarked that the public cared little for the finer technical points of the game and that Heisman was guilty of corrupting his athletes.

What Taylor had done now, of course, was to pour more oil on the fire, and Heisman, drawing on his best debating skills, came right back at him in another letter on December 8:

What on earth has my capacity or incapacity as an actor to do with Mr. Taylor's rank football decisions on Thursday last? I charge him with transgressing his powers as umpire in ordering play to be resumed, and he answers, "You are a very bad actor." I state that it is the referee's business to judge of fair catches, and his reply is that the Auburn team was poorly coached. . . . Have I then proved such an ignominious failure as a coach? I suppose I ought to begin to worry. Singular, though, that I have coached for eight years in succession, and the last five of them at Auburn. People don't usually re-engage failures. Strange that I have never failed to get two or three offers each year, and already have them for next season.[47]

And so, John Heisman, with clearly the stronger case in this overdrawn matter, had the last word. With the 1899 season now history, it was time to turn his attention to other, more important concerns. Like that mentioned in his letter of securing another coaching position, something that had been in the back of his mind for some time. But now, after the public debate with umpire Taylor, the goal of proving himself elsewhere had become an even more pressing matter. If he had an honorable way out of his Auburn commitment, it was primarily because the school was unable to meet his demands for a higher salary.

Actually, Heisman had come to feel very much at home at Auburn. Evidence is he enjoyed a good relationship with the administration and faculty as well as his players. In later life, thinking back on his Auburn years, he observed: "I never had a team at Auburn that I did not love, nor did I have one quarrel with any player during the whole five years. . . . There is not one man who ever played with me during those five years that is not still my very warm friend."[48] But Heisman had been compelled to supplement his income by teaching classes in elocution and oratory and by acting in stock productions during the summer in Atlanta and other area locations. How he got into acting should make an interesting story in itself, but this surprising side of the man appears to have been kept pretty much to himself. Perhaps teaching elocution aroused in him a natural inclination toward histrionic expression, for such patterns cropped up frequently in his speech and writings. And although he was somewhat reserved by nature, there was a decided theatrical bent to his public posture.

The comments of one of Heisman's Auburn players, Walter R. Shafer, who was a fullback on the 1895 team, provide a clue to Heisman's motivation for a higher salary. As though to counter any future attacks on his coaching qualifications by someone like the "meddling" William Taylor, Heisman had a personal brochure printed while he was at Clemson. In it he cited numerous references by his former players and positive comments of the press concerning his growing reputation as a successful coach. Shafer's remarks in this document appear to substantiate the fact that Heisman's eventual move to Clemson was financially motivated: "Mr. J. W. Heisman is a thoroughly cultured gentleman in every sense of the word. As a football coach his work is incessant, careful, painstaking and, above all, honest. . . . That my old team is unable to employ him is a source of sincere regret; our inability, financially, and that alone being the cause."[49]

But there was another, perhaps more personal reason for Heisman's decision to cast his lot with Clemson. An "Auburn connection" was already there in the person of Walter Merritt Riggs, a professor of engineering who had been at Auburn before Heisman's arrival in 1895. While at Auburn, Riggs had been introduced to football and had immediately fallen in love with the game. Upon his arrival at Clemson in 1895, it was at Riggs's urging that Clemson fielded its first football team the following year. In fact, Riggs, who would go on to become president of the college, was himself the school's first coach, leading the team to wins over Furman and Wofford, while losing to South Carolina by a close score in what was to become one of the South's longest-standing rivalries. Riggs even brought with him Auburn's nickname of "Tigers" and the school's colors of orange and dark blue. Others who coached during the years before Heisman arrived were also Auburn men, but together with Riggs they had a combined record of only nine wins against eight losses. So when Auburn defeated Clemson, 34–0, in 1899, the ambitious Riggs, who headed the Clemson Athletic Association, realized that if his athletically minded school was ever to field a first-rate football team, then John Heisman would be the man to get the job done. A significant reason for the ready acceptance of football by many southern schools was that academicians like Riggs were staunchly in favor of participation in football as a true test of manhood, and ambitious coaches like Heisman supported this outlook.

THE NATIONAL GAME (1895–1899)

While Heisman was at Auburn, his alma mater, the University of Pennsylvania, continued to win big under the redoubtable George Woodruff, fashioning a 14–0 season in 1895 on the way to a national championship. In the process, the Quakers had edged out another tough Yale team that had only two ties to mar its record. Actually, Penn was into its great winning streak at this time, one that after thirty-four games would finally be broken in 1896 by Lafayette, 6–4. That year Princeton survived a scoreless tie against this same strong Lafayette team to win the national crown. But in 1897, Penn, with what many think was its greatest team, rolled to a 15–0 season and the national championship. This was also the year that the Quakers were supposed to have made the first-ever field goal from a place kick. The fact that the ball was now more of a prolate spheroid in shape helped make for a better goal-kicking game.

By 1898, Woodruff had his Penn team working on another string of victories, this one ending at thirty-one, when Harvard beat the Quakers for the national title. The Crimson would repeat in 1899 as they began to make the most of their day in the sun. In the Midwest, Michigan (11–0) won its first Western Conference crown, while a Chicago back named Clarence Hershberger became the first man who was not from the East to make Walter Camp's All-America team. In selecting his dream team, Camp was now finding it increasingly difficult to ignore the accomplishments of players from other parts of the country.

The 1880s and 1890s had seen the first heroic figures emerge from the game, mostly in the East. Much of the public adulation of these players resulted from the newspapers' glorified descriptions of their achievements on the playing field as well as the increasing popularity of Camp's annual All-America selections. As we have seen, Camp had a wealth of material to choose from in the East, particularly in a day when linemen could steal the show running with the ball as Pudge Heffelfinger, Frank Hinkey, Ma Newell, and Truxton Hare often did. There was even a brother troupe during this era—the six Poes who played at Princeton between 1889 and 1900. Of the three who were All-Americans—Arthur, Edgar, and John—Arthur was the most outstanding because of his ability at both running and kicking.

Although during this period the game was still primitive in a number of respects, kicking was given top priority, and some great kickers came forth to meet the challenge. One of the greatest was Princeton's Alex Moffat (1882–1884), who as a drop-kicker made thirty-two field goals in fifteen games, including six in one match against Penn in 1882. To John Heisman such players were "giants," in that they played at a time when "individual genius stood out more prominently . . . because the mass play was the customary ground-gainer."[50] His admiration extended to Alex Moffatt, of course:

Here was a youth with wings on his heels. He could stop dead from a hard run and in that same moment boot the ball, frequently 65 yards. No trouble at all. No fiddling for stance or shifting of feet. Either of Alex's feet could send the ball 50, 60, 70 yards. Against Harvard in 1883 he drop-kicked four field goals—two with the right foot and two with the left.[51]

Toward the end of the 1890s, another giant appeared in the unlikely person of an Australian playing for Wisconsin in the Western Conference. Primarily because of his prodigious drop-kicking and punting ability, Pat O'Dea led the Badgers to two consecutive conference championships in 1896 and 1897. Having perfected the spiral punt, he averaged an astounding sixty to eighty yards a kick on most attempts. Consistent and accurate, his dropkicks were almost always good from up to fifty yards out. Surely, here was one player from another part of the country that Walter Camp could not readily ignore, and when the Badgers came east in 1899 to face Yale, Camp got a firsthand look as O'Dea put on another eye-popping display of his kicking prowess.

Harvard closed out the 1890s by winning the national championship with a 10–0–1 record, as only Yale had held the Crimson to a 0–0 tie. Also in 1899, there were signs of things to come upon Glenn Warner's arrival at a small Indian school in Pennsylvania called Carlisle. He displayed his naturally innovative side in the 45–0 win over Columbia by having his linemen position themselves in a three-point crouching stance. The standing pugilistic posture of linemen would soon be a thing of the past.

HEISMAN'S CLEMSON YEARS (1900–1903)

So it was that 1900 saw the coach that many called the best in the South come to Clemson for an undisclosed salary, which was probably in the range of $1,000 annually when the usual baseball coaching responsibilities are taken into consideration. (Before the day of specialization, as we have seen in Heisman's other coaching tenures, a football coach's duties usually included every sport in its season.)

Although he was earning more money than he ever had before, Heisman must have thought himself in a world even more isolated than Auburn had been when he first arrived in the Clemson community. Located in a rural area near Greenville in the northwest part of South Carolina, Clemson, like Auburn, was a land-grant institution with one notable difference from the Alabama school. Its student body was strictly military in makeup, a situation that was to play into Heisman's hands, for it undoubtedly accounted for Clemson's fierce competitive spirit, the quality that Heisman found so essential to building a successful football team. (With some modifications, Clemson would remain primarily a military school until 1955.)

The school itself had opened its doors in 1893 to 446 students. But as the pet project of then Governor "Pitchfork Ben" Tillman and philanthropist Thomas G. Clemson, the school was born out of controversy, mainly about the kind of role it should play in comparison to the other state-supported school, the flagship University of South Carolina at Columbia. Tillman and his supporters ultimately won out over the opposing forces, contending that Clemson was founded to "give practical education at such a slight cost that any boy in South Carolina, if only he be diligent, shall be able to attain it."[52] The day of practical education had arrived in the South, and naturally South Carolina was as ready for it as Alabama had been with the establishment of its own land-grant college.

Just as he had at Auburn, John Heisman found the student athletes at Clemson much to his liking—green but eager and receptive to his rugged training methods and strict disciplinary measures. It was this mutual relationship that became the chief ingredient in accomplishing what southern football authority Fuzzy Woodruff described as "the sudden and sensational rise of Clemson from a little school whose football teams had never been heard of before, to become a football machine of the very first power."[53]

As he had done elsewhere, Heisman quickly established his coaching presence at Clemson. Indeed the very first game played in 1900, a 64–0 pasting of Davidson, started Clemson on its first undefeated, untied football season, a feat that would not be equaled at Clemson until 1947 by Coach Frank Howard. But even though Heisman's team went on that year to shut out Wofford (21–0), South Carolina (51–0), and Alabama (35–0) and to down Virginia Polytechnic Institute (VPI), 12–5, it was the big win over Georgia that made everyone sit up and take notice. The game was played November 10 in Athens, and after Heisman turned loose his fleet-footed runners with their deceptive line bucks and power-primed end runs, the Bulldogs ultimately found themselves on the short end of a devastating 39–5 score. The convincing win demonstrated that Heisman had brought with him his natural propensity for innovation as well as his genius for strategy, which often bordered on trickery. Winning football had finally arrived at Clemson, and local supporters were obviously ready for it.

Heisman's achievement in capturing an SIAA championship in his first year at Clemson was best summed up by the press. After the South Carolina game, the *Columbia State* reported: "The greatness of Clemson's game lay in the play of scientific football. Never before have so many new formations been put into play." The *Atlanta Journal* was even more lavish with its praise: "Clemson has the strongest team in the South. Heisman has taught them to play like lightening. In one year Clemson has risen to sublime heights in football." (Quotes are from Heisman's privately printed pamphlet.) True to Walter Riggs's expectations, John Heisman had gotten the job done, but in much quicker fashion than Riggs had ever dreamed he would. The results should not have been too surprising, though, because everywhere he had gone in his young career, Heisman had established his formidable coaching presence in the very first year.

In 1901, though, there was something of a falling off, with a tie and a loss over a five-game schedule. But following the opening game stalemate with Tennessee (6–6), Clemson amassed the greatest point total in its football history against Guilford, 122–0, even though the game was called after thirty minutes of play for obvious reasons. The Clemson Tigers continued to flex their muscles in convincing wins over Georgia (29–5) and perennial power, North Carolina (22–10), with their only loss that year to troublesome VPI, 17–11. But having compiled a scintillating 9–1–1 record after two years, Heisman realized that his veteran players were primed for the 1902 season, one that would turn out to be another one of his better efforts. After a close opening victory over N.C. State (11–5), his team pounded Georgia Tech, 44–5, a defeat so embarrassing that it must have started the Atlanta school to thinking it needed a coach on the order of a John Heisman.

Then the inspired strategy that Heisman pulled off in the Furman game, which was played at nearby Greenville, proved once again that he had not lost his touch for improvising. Fond of employing the lateral pass in practically any situation, Heisman appeared to have hit on the ultimate lateral tactic in this game. The moment he spied an oak tree that "stood on the 50-yard line well inside the boundary," he had a "beautiful idea" for a play, which, after he explained it to his players, came off as follows:

We had worked the ball nearly to mid-field. The oak was on our right and slightly ahead of us. We started what appeared to be a short end run toward the tree. Maxwell, our quarterback, slipped the ball to Pollitzer, left half, and Pollitzer darted off in a curving end run just inside of the oak, thereby drawing Furman's left and secondary defense down to that threatened area.

But Sitton, my left end, had sped off past Pollitzer and behind and past the tree. And there he was, alone, uncovered. Polly, safe behind strong interference, flipped the ball laterally to Sitton, who ran 40 yards for a touchdown.[54]

Relying on this play twice more that afternoon, Clemson won the game, 28–0.

Heisman's ingenuity for devising deceptive plays was apparently limitless, and he made a practice, it seems, of trying out something different in virtually every game at this time. Many opposing coaches, aware that the man made use of everything in the book, had to conclude, often too late, that he also pulled off a lot of things that were not in the book. However, a later Clemson coach, C. R. "Bob" Williams, who had coached against Heisman while at South Carolina, said that it was fruitless to scout any of Heisman's games because he rarely used the same trick over again.

Sometimes, though, the Heisman brand of deception might even take place off-field, as in the case of a comic episode that could possibly have contributed to the lopsided Georgia Tech defeat mentioned above. The story has gone down as another version of the classic situation of country bumpkin winning out over city slicker. When the train with the Clemson contingent had arrived in Atlanta the day before the game, the Tech supporters made it a special point to entertain their opponents in royal fashion. Marveling at the ease with which they were able to get the Clemson players to sneak out that night, the Tech boosters seized the opportunity to keep them out late, drinking and carousing, thus setting the stage for a sure gambling bet on Tech to win. Considering the disastrous results of the game, though, the Tech supporters had to wonder at the hardiness of the Clemson men in winning so handily after enduring a night of debauchery. That is, until they discovered that Coach Heisman had sent a bunch of country boys ahead to Atlanta with the team's equipment the night before the game while keeping his varsity players at Lula, Georgia, a small town some miles from Atlanta.

Perhaps looking ahead to both Georgia and Auburn was the reason Clemson was upset by South Carolina that year, 12–6, their only loss, and a painful one. The defeat obviously taught Heisman a lesson in game preparation, though, for his team went on to a second SIAA championship by shutting out their remaining foes: Georgia, 36–0 (clearly, Clemson had the Bulldogs' number in those days); Auburn, 16–0; and Tennessee, 11–0.

The Auburn game had to have been the one Heisman was more concerned about prior to the South Carolina game, for it would mark the first time he had faced his old school since his departure. Played at Auburn, the emotional aura of this setting alone could have presented some real problems for Heisman. Although Auburn put up a good battle, Heisman's predilection for trick plays was evident throughout the game as he employed the double pass (that day's term for the reverse play) on several occasions and the quarterback on-side kick a number of times, resulting in three touchdowns and an extra point. In shutting out Auburn, Clemson had held them to just thirty yards. Obviously, Heisman's soft spot for Auburn did not extend to competition on the football field.

It was in the Tennessee game, the last of the season, that a feat occurred which, according to Heisman, turned out to be the longest punt ever executed, a 109-yard boot by Tennessee's Toots Douglas on a field then 110 yards in length. In recording the event, Heisman noted that the game was played in a full-scale blizzard:

Toots was a great natural punter to begin with. But on this memorable day his powerful kicking foot gave the ball to the winds and the combination broke all records.

Johnny Maxwell, Clemson's safety man, was fifty yards behind our line. His face filled with amusement and snow, Johnny watched the ball fly high and wide above his head. And then he joined the chase. It fell to earth I know not where but presently it halted on our one-yard line, where Johnny fell on it and on him twenty-one of his playmates. Clemson won with two touchdowns but the talk that night was all of Toots Douglas' 109-yard wallop.[55]

The unexpected loss to South Carolina earlier that season resulted in an unfortunate encounter between the students and supporters of both schools, one that could have ended in tragedy had cooler heads not prevailed. The game was played at the State Fairgrounds in Columbia during Fair Week, a tradition that would continue until 1960. But the outcome of this game revealed the staunchly partisan posture that southern football supporters had taken by this time concerning their favorite teams.

Favored to beat the Gamecocks for the fifth straight time, Clemson found itself the victim of a major upset by game's end, 12–6. The worst was yet to be, however, when that night following a South Carolina victory parade, the Clemson cadets and Carolina students confronted each other in a potential brawl involving firearms. Violence was finally averted when police, faculty, and a joint committee of students negotiated a settlement.[56] The emotional aura of this incident had run so high, however, that Carolina athletic officials were moved to break off football relations with Clemson, and the series between the two schools was not resumed until 1909. Clearly, Southerners had begun to take their football seriously.

As to Heisman's reaction to all this furor we have no information, probably because the incident did not directly involve his players. Concerning his attitude toward how barbarous the field of play itself had become, though, he undoubtedly took a dim view of any situation that would provoke the students and supporters of opposing teams into a kind of open war among themselves. One thing he surely realized at this time, though, was that intrastate football rivalries in the South had become a serious business.

The year 1903, Heisman's last at Clemson, was a momentous one in his personal life for several reasons. His team had now developed into an annual contender for the SIAA championship, one openly feared by the other schools in the league as well as others outside it; in October, following his first serious courtship since his Buchtel days, he was married; and in the first game of the season his team hung such a devastating defeat on Georgia Tech that football supporters in Atlanta started a campaign to obtain the Clemson coach as their own.

The surprising thing about the outcome of the Georgia Tech game is that this was the year that the Techs thought they at last had a real chance to win. They heard that Vedder Sitton, the star back for Clemson (and a future major league baseball player), had been injured and would not play. This news was highly encouraging to the Tech ranks because Sitton had been the player chiefly responsible for their humiliating defeat of the previous year. Now once again there was heavy betting on Tech to win the match. But the ever-resourceful Heisman came up with a dependable substitute for his incapacitated back, and even though the game was played on a muddy field, the Tigers came through with a resounding 73–0 victory. Disgruntled Tech supporters now knew beyond a shadow of a doubt whom they wanted as their next coach, as the drive to recruit Heisman doubled in intensity.

In its next game Clemson once again took the measure of Georgia, this time by a score of 29–0. Along with the Georgia Tech backers, there were probably many Bulldog supporters wondering what it would take to secure the coaching services of the redoubtable Heisman who, in less than ten years in the South, had built such a strong reputation for himself.

But there were areas other than coaching in which John Heisman had been active since arriving in the South. It was during his Clemson years that he met, courted, and married Evelyn McCollum Cox, an attractive widow who was one of the featured actresses in a summer stock company with which Heisman had become associated and in which he occasionally took part in plays that were staged in the area. Concerning Heisman's sideline as an actor, Al Thomy has commented:

> As he was born to the game of football, [Heisman] also was born to the theater. Many coaches have acted. Knute Rockne was adept in playing parts. But Heisman was a professional actor and a lawyer and a coach, a deadly combination. . . .
> He was proud of his acting. But a writer-friend, commenting on this facet of his personality, put it succinctly. "John Heisman," wrote Fuzzy Woodruff, "is a great coach and a terrible thespian."[57]

Although Heisman's ability as an actor was subject to question and even ridicule, his real-life side at this time was evidently appealing enough to Evelyn Cox for their relationship to be consummated in marriage on October 24, 1903, one day after the groom's thirty-fourth birthday. Like the wives of most coaches, though, the new Mrs. Heisman soon realized that her new role would be primarily that of a "football widow." Heisman now found himself a father, too, for a twelve-year-old stepson came with the marriage.

The remaining games of the 1903 season saw Clemson defeat N.C. State, 24–0; lose to North Carolina, 11–6; shut out Davidson, 24–0—the team's fourth whitewash effort of the season; and vie with a strong Cumberland team for the SIAA championship.

Played in Montgomery on Thanksgiving Day, the match with Cumberland, a small college located at Lebanon, Tennessee, that had earlier defeated powerful Vanderbilt, turned out to be a thriller when Clemson made a great second-half comeback. During the first half, Clemson was never really in the game due mainly to the formidable line play of the Bridges brothers—giants in their day at 6 feet 4 inches—and a big center named "Red" Smith, who was all over the field backing up the Cumberland line on defense. Clemson had been outweighed before, but certainly not like this. As one reporter who witnessed the game put it: "The Clemson players seemed mere dwarfs as they lined up for the kickoff. To the crowd on the sidelines it didn't seem that Heisman's charges could possibly do more than give a gallant account of themselves in a losing battle."[58]

And as expected, by the end of the first half Cumberland, having forced the Tigers into a defensive game, found itself ahead by a comfortable 11–0 score. So by now the main question on the minds of most onlookers was just how large the final Cumberland point total was going to be. But the never-say-die Heisman evidently charged up his players with another of his patented pep talks. For at the start of the second half, Maxwell, the Clemson quarterback, took the kickoff behind his goal and following perfect interference, ran the length of the field for a touchdown. After the goal was kicked, the score stood at 11–6, and Clemson was back in the game.

By this time, too, the brothers Bridges were tiring, and toward the end, with darkness descending, Heisman saw his chance to exploit a weakness in the Cumberland defense: run the ball where the ubiquitous Red Smith wasn't. So the next time Sitton started out on one of his slashing end runs, at the last second he tossed the ball back to the fullback who charged straight ahead over center (where Smith would have been except that he was zeroing in on the elusive Sitton) and went all the way for a tying touchdown. All that now remained between Clemson and the SIAA championship was an extra point. But the kick was missed, and the game ended in an 11–11 tie. Fittingly, the next monumental meeting between Heisman and a Cumberland team would be Georgia Tech's classic runaway game in 1916.

With feelers now starting to come his way from Atlanta, this disappointing outcome must have prompted Heisman to seriously consider whether or not to cast his lot with Georgia Tech. Although he had been coaching now for nearly ten years in the South and had even captured two SIAA championships at Clemson, Heisman was now looking to locate where he could achieve even more recognition. He had built his reputation on taking the most unlikely material and molding it into a smooth-running football machine. Accordingly, the stamina and dedication of his players were established facts. Game reports, in fact, revealed that Heisman took only a half dozen substitutes with him on road trips, and one of his players, J. A. "Pee Wee" Forsythe, a tackle, probably held the endurance record for his day for playing every minute of every Clemson game during 1901–1903. If he could produce championship teams with inferior material, what was he capable of doing with superior players?

Perhaps over the long run, then, the thinness in the ranks of his country-boy players had been the thing that was holding Heisman back from true greatness. What he really needed was more players coming out of high school who were already knowledgeable of the game's finer points instead of the green candidates he had been training from scratch. One of Heisman's classic stories concerning the naïveté of his players occurred at Auburn when one of his country boys reported for football and admitted he had never seen a football game before:

"That's all right," I said after sizing him up and recognizing the possibilities he represented. "When you come upon something you don't understand, just ask me."

Presently he came to me and said: "Mr. Heisman, I've been hearing the fellows talking about the first half and the second half and what's puzzling me is, how many halves do you have in this game anyway?"[59]

With Virginia and Tennessee as model states, football had helped build up the high-school sports system in the South, and finally it was beginning to spread. Heisman could possibly have realized that moving to a metropolitan area like Atlanta would be a step in the right direction as far as recruiting more quality material was concerned.

Then, too, at this point in his young coaching career, Heisman knew he was at a crossroads. College football, in spite of its problems, was becoming an integral force in the American sporting scene, and because of his intense love of the game, he undoubtedly wanted to be where he could do the most good in helping promote it. In seeing to it that he was sought out for the right place at the right time, Heisman was his own best press agent. As sportswriter Joe Williams noted, Heisman was never "suffocatingly modest,"[60] and whenever he put pen to paper, he was not only extolling the accomplishments of the school where he was coaching but those of John Heisman as well. For example, in 1903, he identified the qualifications of a winning coach—knowledge of the game, teaching ability, inspirational leadership, maintenance of physical conditioning, and knowing the capability of his players:

In the light of these required qualifications, it is small wonder that successful coaches—i.e., those who can consistently turn out winning teams year after year no matter what the obstacles and conditions—are few and far between, and when found it is equally small wonder that they command salaries practically without limit.

At Clemson we have a style of football play radically different from any other on earth. Its notoriety and the fear and admiration of it have spread throughout the length and breadth of the entire Southern world of football and even further.... Three wonderfully successful seasons of "Heisman Football" have served to establish the system as Clemson's traditional policy of play.[61]

With "Heisman Football" now a marketable product, its progenitor's intent was to promote his commodity in true go-getter fashion—that is, to use its salability to enhance his own professional reputation. The promotional pamphlet Heisman had put together earlier was clearly in this vein, and one of the more noteworthy endorsements it contained was that of Walter Riggs, president of the Clemson Athletic Association and then vice-president of the SIAA. He expressed the following sentiments about the inventor of Heisman Football:

In my opinion [John Heisman] is the best football coach in the South or, indeed, in the whole country. His strategy is of the highest order, and as a predictor of opponent's [sic] movements and an ingenious deviser of modes of defense he is a wonder. His systems of play are classic, far above anything encountered in the South. Rapid and varied movements, ability to keep opponents always guessing, and a desire on the part of his men to risk all to win—these qualities have made his coaching well-nigh phenomenal. As a disciplinarian I have never seen his equal; he commands and receives, with cheerful compliance, absolute obedience. We hope that no college will be able to take him from us.[62]

But Riggs's hope that his charismatic coach would stay on at Clemson was to no avail, as Georgia Tech ultimately succeeded in luring Heisman to Atlanta for the then princely sum of $2,000 per year plus 30 percent of the net gate receipts for both baseball and football. (Heisman's salary during his final year at Clemson was reputed to be $1,800.) Heisman's contention that "successful coaches . . . command salaries practically without limit" had been put to the test in his negotiations with Tech, as the sterling 19–3–2 record he had compiled at Clemson as well as the one-sided defeats his teams had administered to the Tech team provided sufficient leverage to secure the lucrative contract.

There were other positive points Heisman must have considered in moving to Tech. Having played many of his matches in Atlanta since his Auburn days, he was well-enough acquainted with the city to realize that urban life afforded numerous cultural advantages. Also the fact that he now had a family—a wife along with a stepson—to support made taking any available opportunity to supplement his income more mandatory. His wife also had family ties with Cherokee County, Georgia, north of Atlanta. In a sense, then, the move was a kind of homecoming for Evelyn Heisman. So the chance to associate with still another athletically ambitious school, but one in a fast-growing metropolitan area, had to be naturally appealing to Heisman. And for someone of his cosmopolitan bent, the city was the natural place to be, the place where momentous things were happening during this time in the country's history.

Nevertheless, it had not been easy for Georgia Tech to recruit Heisman. In fact, had it not been for the campaign efforts of a Tech alumnus and current faculty member named Frank Turner, Heisman might have stayed on at Clemson or taken another more financially rewarding position, which was really what he was after at this point in his career. In fact, Lyman Hall, the president of Georgia Tech, had not made the coaching job seem altogether enticing in his meeting and correspondence with Heisman, for in his letter of November 12, 1903 offering the job, he was somewhat noncommittal and even careless enough to misspell the prospective coach's name.

Clearly it was time for someone with the drive of a Frank Turner to step in and take action, and according to Georgia Tech historian Robert Wallace that is precisely what happened. After convincing the faculty and student body that Tech should get into big-time athletics, Turner spearheaded a fund drive to recruit Heisman as their head football coach:

The success of the fund drive helped Turner convince Heisman to leave Clemson for Tech after President Hall's lukewarm letter had failed to excite the coach about the school's coaching vacancy. Before the contract was signed, Turner—who eventually became the first graduate manager of athletics—had to make a couple of trips to South Carolina to talk to Heisman and convince him that the floundering athletic program was a challenge he couldn't resist.[63]

Turner's dogged efforts paid off, even though Heisman, ever the one for dramatics, did not wire his acceptance until the day after President Hall's specified deadline of November 25, 1903. Upon hearing the news, Tech students were so elated that during their Thanksgiving Day game with South Carolina they strung up an intimidating banner proclaiming, "TECH GETS HEISMAN FOR 1904." The Heisman era at Georgia Tech had gotten off on a typically theatrical note even before the star of the show had come on stage.

THE NATIONAL SCENE (1900–1903)

As it had been throughout the 1890s, the overall mood of the country at the turn of the century was one compounded of boundless energy and supreme confidence. The brief but decisive Spanish-American War of 1898 had turned in America's favor, producing a cadre of honored military heroes and the undeniable feeling among most Americans that the American way was the best way; indeed to many, America's way was God's way. That America was divinely blessed was attested to by the country's soaring economic progress resulting from the expansion and productivity of business and industry during the last quarter of the nineteenth century as well as the numerous technological advances of the day—in particular, the revolutionary inventions that were transforming the life-styles of the American people.

Although it still had a long way to go as a practical tool, the telephone was becoming fairly well entrenched by the start of the new century, a significant step toward drawing the country closer together. The capability of controlling electrical energy now made it possible to expand opportunities and services in the areas of home life, entertainment, business and industry, and even sporting events, primarily through more efficient power sources. The motor car was also becoming an adjunct to American social life, and in Heisman's last year at Clemson, the first continental crossing of the United States by automobile was accomplished. In the same year came the incorporation of the Ford Motor Company, whose mass production methods would transform the country both socially and economically. That same year also saw the most world-shaking achievement of all—the first flight of the Wright brothers and the birth of air travel, the repercussions of which are still being felt today.

It was a fabulous time to be alive, provided one had the wherewithal to maintain a comfortable level of living. Whatever the ills of society at large—and there were many—the American political philosophy referred to as Progressivism existed to make things right. Or so most everyone thought. Although the predominantly agrarian South of Heisman's day had its share of economic and social problems, its isolation made it seem fairly immune to many of the problematic issues that had affected urban areas—dire poverty, mounting labor concerns, the influx of immigrants, and the suffrage question, to name some of the more pervasive. But in a country of over sixty million people of which seven million were black (most of whom resided in the South), it would not be until the second half of the century that the nation's social conscience would fully awaken. In this earlier time, America was a country where social responsibility was held in check by a simplistic philosophy of life that emphasized the intrinsic worth of the individual and one's special capabilities for achieving success, no matter what the circumstances of one's background. It was thought that every American had the potential to realize the rewards of the American Dream. Therefore, anyone could get ahead in life if he but tried.

Having become part of the ideology of the American public school system, this socialization process was most dramatically exemplified in intercollegiate athletics and the coaching philosophies of men like Amos Alonzo Stagg and John Heisman. They saw individual success in sports as the measure of a man's worth off the field as well as on. Even black athletes had begun to prove the supposed validity of this outlook during the 1890s through their limited but quality performances on eastern football teams. Denied participation on the segregated southern college teams, some outstanding players migrated to the North to realize their full potential. As noted earlier, one of them was William Henry Lewis, who went to Amherst and later Harvard, where he was named the center on Walter Camp's All-America teams in 1892 and 1893. (In the early 1900s Lewis was an assistant football coach at Harvard, probably the first black man in the history of intercollegiate athletics to fill such a position.) Soon after the establishment of black institutions in the South with their industrial training missions, these schools started fielding their own teams. But from a national perspective the day of the black athlete would not come into its own until the 1960s. The black athletes of this later day would succeed to a degree that people around the turn of the century would never have dreamed possible.

That sports were becoming a social force in American life was affirmed by Vice-President Theodore Roosevelt (soon to be president upon the assassination of William McKinley in 1901), in word as well as deed. Athletically active himself, Roosevelt saw the college athletic field as a necessary training ground for the youth of this country who would become its future leaders. The outspoken enemy of any negative force, foreign or domestic, that sought to undermine the American way, Roosevelt stood up for the virtues of what he termed the "strenuous life," which he made public in a notable speech in 1899. Its summation was highly prophetic:

> The twentieth century looms before us big with the fate of many nations. If we stand idly by, if we seek merely swollen, slothful ease, and ignoble peace, if we shrink from the hard contests where men must win at hazard of their lives and at the risk of all they hold dear, then the bolder and stronger peoples will pass us by and will win for themselves the domination of the world. Let us therefore boldly face the life of strife, resolute to do our duty well and manfully. . . . Above all, let us shrink from no strife, moral or physical, within or without the nation, provided we are certain that the strife is justified; for it is only through strife, through hard and dangerous endeavor, that we shall ultimately win the goal of true national greatness.[64]

It was a social philosophy that could easily have emanated from the football field, which had greatly inspired Roosevelt, a Harvard man, in the choice of many of his metaphors. It was the kind of philosophy, too, that John Heisman certainly subscribed to. Even though the game of football was in serious trouble during the 1890s and the early part of the twentieth century, both Heisman and Roosevelt, as proponents of the "strenuous life," would eventually play significant roles in saving the game from itself. During the early years of the new century, Heisman, as one of football's most active promoters, would build toward his greatest success as a football coach and become an "ardent admirer and supporter of Teddy Roosevelt and the Bull Moose party."[65] Roosevelt, as a supporter of football and of Heisman's push to make the forward pass an integral part of the game, was naturally sensitive to whatever changes the game needed to open it up and free itself from the inherent brutality that had characterized intercollegiate football from its inception.

THE NATIONAL GAME (1900–1903)

Since 1893, which had been the roughest year in intercollegiate competition up to that time, various rule changes had been implemented to lessen the game's rougher aspects, as we have seen. But other important steps toward eliminating mass interference plays occurred in 1896, when rules were introduced that commanded five men to be on the line of scrimmage and that an offensive player could not take more than one step without coming to a full stop before the ball was put in play. Another rule in the same vein was established in 1902, stipulating that seven men had to be on the offensive line between the 25-yard lines; and in 1903, any back who first handled the ball could run forward with it as long as he was five yards from the center. This change supplanted the old rule dictating that a quarterback could not run with the ball until another player touched it. In spite of all these rule changes, though, the game was still terribly rough by any standard, and football's survival was in jeopardy in the years just ahead.

That college football was still growing in popularity around the turn of the century, though, was confirmed by the ever-increasing attendance at popular matchups. Played as the last game of the year for the first time, the Yale–Harvard game of 1900 determined the national championship (won by Yale, as usual) and attracted over twenty thousand spectators. It was only natural, then, that by 1903, Harvard dedicated a significant monument to its own overall gridiron success—the largest reinforced steel and concrete stadium in the world at the time. Seating close to sixty thousand, the Harvard Stadium was America's first football coliseum, presaging the day of big-time college football that would take the nation by storm in just a few years. By 1914, both Yale and Princeton had their own stadiums, but the Yale Bowl outdid them all at this time with its seating capacity of seventy-five thousand.

It was estimated that by 1896 approximately five thousand school and college football games were being played across the country on Thanksgiving Day, not only attesting to football's growing popularity but revealing that such events had been elevated to glamorous social spectacles that could be attended by males and females alike. The epitome of the Thanksgiving Day game as social event was the game played in New York City, usually between Princeton and Yale, with area socialites in prominent attendance among the forty thousand spectators at the Polo Grounds. Big-game football weekends provided women with a grand opportunity to show off the fashionable finery of the day and to be around men in a socially acceptable sphere of activity. The popular conception of the sophisticated, independent woman known as the Gibson Girl was rapidly becoming a fact of life at this time. (John Heisman himself had dared to marry an actress, the kind of woman who a generation before would have been socially unacceptable, and in many circles still was.) Also with college alumni rolls swelling across the nation, many schools recognized that athletic events like big-game football rivalries represented a way not only to keep in touch with alumni but to gain their financial support. The times were ripe for football's expansion, and as a significant social attraction, the game had begun to vie with vaudeville and the theater as a popular source of entertainment. With a ready-made audience awaiting, the main thing college football coaches had to do now to hold their followers' interest and support was produce a winner. Under this kind of pressure, increased professionalization of the game was inevitable.

While Heisman was enjoying his success at Clemson there were some big winners coming to the fore in the Midwest. In 1900, physician Dr. Henry Williams left Penn, where he had been a devotee of George Woodruff, and went to Minnesota, where he devised the tackle-back formation and won the Western Conference title with an unbeaten record that included two ties.

Just two years later in 1902, Nebraska wound up unbeaten, untied, and unscored on in ten games, while Amos Alonzo Stagg was experimenting with the unbalanced line at Chicago with great success.

But during the period 1901–1905, the coach at the University of Michigan named Fielding Yost overshadowed the accomplishments of practically everyone else. Having coached successfully at Kansas before arriving at Michigan, Yost had performed as a tramp athlete when he "transferred" from West Virginia to Lafayette in 1896 to play against the Penn dynasty. In one of that day's biggest upsets, Lafayette defeated the Quakers, 6–4. At Michigan, in the first five years of the 1900s, Yost produced a dynasty of teams that compiled an astounding 55–0–1 record, scoring 2,821 points to only 40 for their opposition. Because the 1901–1905 teams averaged more than 560 points a season they earned the apt epithet of "point a minute." Yost's 1901 and 1902 teams would be the first from outside the East to win national championships. Stressing speed over brawn to wear down an opponent (heretofore brute force had been a trademark of Midwestern teams), Yost, an intense, straitlaced man, picked up the nickname "Hurry Up" by training his men to start up a play even before the opposing team had recovered from the previous play. Made to order for this kind of attack was a powerful, fleet-footed All-American halfback named Willie Heston, who in his four years of play scored an astounding ninety-three touchdowns, still a national record.

Although the official records reveal that the January 1, 1916 contest between Brown and Washington State was the first game to be played in the Rose Bowl series, Yost's great 1901 Michigan team had been invited to Pasadena to play Stanford on January 1, 1902, in what was actually the prototypical game for the Rose Bowl. Sponsored by the Tournament of Roses Association and played before over eight thousand spectators, this game undoubtedly provided the group with the seminal idea for an annual affair, in spite of Stanford's embarrassing 49–0 loss to the team from the Midwest. (The game turned out to be so one-sided that it was called at the request of Stanford with ten minutes still left to be played.)

In 1903, Princeton was recognized as national champion, but Minnesota had helped out Princeton's cause by tying Michigan, 6–6, thus ending the Wolverines' twenty-nine-game winning streak. This was also the game that started these two teams playing for the Little Brown Jug, one of the more popular traditions that grew out of this era of increased rivalries in college football. However, the precedent for one of football's greatest traditions— the post-season bowl game—was the most significant introduced during this period. Although it took some years for the concept to catch on, the early years of the Rose Bowl saw only the strong teams of the East and Midwest receiving invitations to play. As football powers, the teams of the Far West, Southwest, and South were yet to have their day in the sun. As far as John Heisman was concerned, though, his move to Georgia Tech presented him a ripe opportunity to see to it that the South would have its day—although not as soon as he would have liked.

NOTES

1. See Gene Griessman, "The Coach," in *The Heisman: A Symbol of Excellence* by John T. Brady (New York: Atheneum, 1984), 21.
2. "Who's He and Why?" (Heisman profile in Georgia Tech student magazine) *The Yellow Jacket* (March 1913): 418–21.
3. See J. H. Nichols, "50 Years of Football," *Oberlin Alumni Magazine* (1941).
4. David P. Simpson, "Historical Sketches of Athletics at Oberlin," *Oberlin Alumni Magazine* 10, no. 6 (March 1914): 161–62.
5. John Durant and Les Etter, *Highlights of College Football* (New York: Hastings House, 1970), 72. Yale and Princeton produced most of these "missionary" coaches, but Harvard and Penn turned out their share, too. That the East was still showing the way in training innovations was evidenced by the contributions of Harvard's captain Arthur Cumnock in 1890, which included the startup of spring practice, stressing calisthenics for warming up, the use of a tackle dummy, and the invention of the nose guard, as ineffectual as it may have been.
6. Quoted in Nichols, "50 Years of Football."
7. John W. Heisman, "The Thundering Herd," *Collier's*, October 13, 1928, 13.
8. Ibid., 59.
9. John W. Heisman, "Between Halves," *Collier's*, November 17, 1928, 18.
10. Heisman, "The Thundering Herd," 13.
11. John W. Heisman, "Look Sharp Now!" *Collier's*, November 3, 1928, 19.
12. John W. Heisman, "Signals," *Collier's*, October 6, 1928, 31.
13. John W. Heisman, "Inventions in Football," *The Baseball Magazine* 1, no. 6 (October 1908): 40–42.
14. A. I. Spanton, ed. *Fifty Years of Buchtel, 1870–1920* (Akron, Ohio: Buchtel Alumni Association, 1922), 244.
15. Ibid., 247.
16. Heisman, "The Thundering Herd," 13.
17. Heisman, "Hold 'em!" *Collier's*, October 27, 1928, 50.
18. Ibid.
19. Heisman, "The Thundering Herd," 13.
20. See Charles J. P. Bourget, "Poet Beyond the Sea," in *This Was America*, ed. Oscar Handlin (New York: Harper and Row, 1964), 370–83.
21. John W. Heisman, "Fast and Loose," *Collier's*, October 20, 1928, 54.
22. Heisman, "Signals," 31.
23. Ibid., 13, 31.
24. The letter, dated February 23, 1894, read in part: "The main object should not be to win in the contests in which the clubs may participate, but to minister to the physical development of those engaged in the exercise." We can well imagine Heisman's indignation at receiving what amounted to a pointed criticism of himself and his coaching methods. See Spanton, *Fifty Years of Buchtel*, 246.
25. George W. Knepper, *New Lamps for Old* (Akron, Ohio: University of Akron

Centennial, 1970), 71. Centennial publication on the one-hundredth anniversary of the University of Akron.

26. See Griessman, "The Coach," 27.

27. Heisman would eventually make use of such laudatory comments in a promotional pamphlet he had printed to publicize his qualifications as a coach: "Announcement of Mr. John W. Heisman, Football and Baseball Coach," seven-page pamphlet, privately printed, from the early 1900s. That Oberlin still thinks highly of its first football coach is attested to by the establishment in 1978 of the John Heisman Club, an organization of alumni and supporters whose aim is to keep both the academic and athletic programs as strong as possible through the recruitment of scholar athletes.

28. This would place Stagg at Springfield during the same time that another inventive spirit was on hand, Dr. James Naismith of the local YMCA, who came up with basketball as an indoor sport to be played during the winter months. It would go on to rival, but not outdo, football as a popular intercollegiate sport.

29. Quoted in Allison Danzig, *Oh, How They Played the Game* (New York: Macmillan, 1971), 29.

30. Ibid., 37.

31. Heisman, "The Thundering Herd," 13.

32. Richard J. Storr, *Harper's University: The Beginnings* (Chicago: University of Chicago Press, 1966), 179.

33. John McCallum, *Southeastern Conference Football* (New York: Scribners, 1980), 4.

34. Bob Gutkowski, ed., *The College Game* (Indianapolis: Bobbs-Merrill, 1974), 60.

35. McCallum, *Southeastern Conference Football*, 31.

36. John W. Heisman, "Rules Rush In," *Collier's*, 10 November 1928, 42.

37. Edwin Pope, *Football's Greatest Coaches* (Atlanta, Ga.: Tupper and Love, 1956), 122–23.

38. Although he was unsure of the dates that Warner used the hidden-ball trick at Carlisle, Heisman recorded his own use of it in an apologetic manner in later years:

The hidden-ball trick which the Carlisle Indians played successfully on Harvard about 1898 or 1899 first originated with me, I believe; though I take no great pride in the matter as I used the play but one year, coming to the conclusion that it was a play open to question from the standpoint of pure and clean sportsmanship. (Heisman, "Inventions in Football," 41.) [Actually, Warner used the play as late as 1903 against Harvard.]

39. See Al Thomy, *The Ramblin' Wreck: A Story of Georgia Tech Football* (Huntsville, Ala.: Strode Publishers, 1973), 42.

40. John W. Heisman, "Fast and Loose," *Collier's*, October 20, 1928, 14.

41. Heisman, "Signals," 31.

42. Heisman, "The Thundering Herd," 60.

43. Pope, *Football's Greatest Coaches*, 122.

44. L. F. "Fuzzy" Woodruff, *History of Southern Football*, vol. 1 (Atlanta, Ga.: Georgia Southern, 1928), 100–101.

45. Heisman's letter appeared in the *Birmingham Age-Herald*, December 4, 1899.

46. Taylor's reply appeared in the *Birmingham Age-Herald*, December 5, 1899.

47. Heisman rebutted in the *Birmingham Age-Herald*, December 8, 1899.

48. Griessman, "The Coach," 24.

49. "Announcement of Mr. John W. Heisman," privately printed pamphlet.

50. Heisman, "The Thundering Herd," 13.

51. Heisman, "Fast and Loose," 15.

52. Wright Bryan, *Clemson: An Informal History of the University, 1889–1979* (Columbia, S.C.: R. L. Bryan Co., 1979), 38.

53. Woodruff, *History of Southern Football*, Vol I, 103.

54. Heisman, "The Thundering Herd," 59.

55. John W. Heisman, "Hero Stuff," *Collier's*, November 2, 1929, 18.

56. For a full account of this incident, see Bryan, *Clemson: An Informal History*, 76–77.

57. Thomy, *The Ramblin' Wreck*, 35.

58. Woodruff, *History of Southern Football*, Vol I, 152.

59. Heisman, "The Thundering Herd," 60.

60. Joe Williams, "Heisman Knew Football," *New York World-Telegram*, October 1936.

61. Quoted in Joe Sherman, *Clemson Tigers: A History of Clemson Football* (Columbia, S.C.: R. L. Bryan Co., 1976), 8–9.

62. This quote, dated July 2, 1902, is from Heisman's privately printed pamphlet cited at note 49, above.

63. Robert B. Wallace, *Dress Her in White and Gold: A Biography of Georgia Tech* (Atlanta: Georgia Tech Foundation, 1969), 51.

64. Quoted in Oliver Jensen, ed., *The Nineties* (New York: American Heritage, 1967), 84.

65. "Who's He and Why?" 418–21.

3

Heisman and the Coming of the Forward Pass (1904–1911)

Heisman's worth was never better displayed than when he left a college. He departed from Auburn and pretty soon Auburn's football glory went glimmering. He departed from Clemson in 1903 and from the minute of his departure Clemson dwindled as a football power. He came to Georgia Tech the next year and Tech promptly arose from a team of tertiary importance in a football way, to a football power that must be reckoned with and finally to a position of undisputed domination in the Southern section.

—L. F. "Fuzzy" Woodruff,
History of Southern Football (1928)

The addition of Tech's first full-time football coach, John Heisman, the erudite, creative, colorful genius of the sport, was probably the move that made more impression on the outside world than any other appointment in the history of the school.

—Robert B. Wallace, Jr.,
Dress Her in White and Gold: A Biography of Georgia Tech (1969)

HEISMAN AT GEORGIA TECH (1904–1905)

Although his Auburn and Clemson teams had played numerous times there, John Heisman probably never gave a passing thought to the notion that one day he would actually be living in Atlanta. Affording a variety of cultural attractions, Atlanta also presented a great many acting opportunities for both himself and his wife. And because of his own natural desire to write, he realized that such a cosmopolitan city could provide numerous opportunities for publishing. So it was that in February, 1904, Heisman and his new bride moved into a house on Ponce de Leon Avenue in one of the city's more respectable neighborhoods near the Tech campus. Evelyn's son, Carlisle Cox, came with them, of course, and although the boy had disapproved of his mother's marriage in the beginning, the new father, or "Cousin Jack" as he was referred to by his young charge, soon won the boy over.

The Atlanta that John Heisman and his family settled in at this time was a city that had literally risen from the ashes of the Civil War, as only forty years before, General Sherman's troops had left the city in smoking ruins. By 1900, however, the population had grown to ninety thousand, and by the time of Heisman's departure some twenty years later, Atlanta's population would have nearly doubled in size. With the expansion of the railroad system throughout the South, Atlanta, by virtue of its strategic location, was destined to become a major railroad hub as well as a financial center and distribution point for the Southeast. And, naturally, its centrality as a railroad city was one reason a large number of college football games were scheduled there during this time.

Work had recently begun on another dynamic symbol of the new South, the Candler Building at the corner of Peachtree and Houston streets. When it was completed in 1906 its seventeen stories of skyscraper opulence were a graphic advertisement for Atlanta's resurgence as a city. Asa G. Candler, for whom the building was named, was something of a symbol himself. Having acquired the rights to a soft-drink formula, he had established the Coca-Cola Company in 1892, through which he soon parlayed his modest investment into a fabulous fortune. In promoting the soft drink that would become a national habit, another go-getter of the day had made his mark, and the name Candler soon became part of the Atlanta heritage.

At the time of Heisman's arrival, the history of the school known popularly as Georgia Tech had been a brief one. Established in 1885 by legislative act, the Georgia School of Technology had had a difficult time coming into being, due mainly to the University of Georgia's desire to have the proposed technological school made an integral part of its own campus in Athens. Like the states of Alabama and South Carolina, Georgia placed a high premium on technological education as a key factor in helping build the new South. Nathaniel Harris, a Macon attorney, had actually won a seat in the state legislature campaigning for the establishment of a state-supported technological school. Because of his diligent work toward this end during the early 1880s, it is Harris who deserves most of the credit for the eventual establishment of Georgia Tech. The University of Georgia, with its well-entrenched departments of physics, chemistry, and agriculture, believed it had a natural right to absorb the new school into its own operations. And although various cities and towns throughout the state put in their bids for the school, Athens had more reason to fight against having a state-supported school established in another area, especially in the fast-growing city of

Atlanta, which would create more competition for legislative funding support.

Nonetheless, by 1887, Atlanta had won out as the locale for the school, and nine acres of land in what was then the outskirts of the city were acquired for the startup of the Georgia School of Technology. The matriculation of its first class commenced in October, 1888. (Not until 1948 was the name changed to the Georgia Institute of Technology.) Although in the beginning it was organized and administered as a branch of the University of Georgia, the school soon evolved into an increasingly autonomous entity deserving a separate identity and separate funding. Indeed, by the time of Heisman's arrival in 1904, political relations with Athens had become steadily more competitive as the upstart Atlanta school had grown in size and reputation. It was a situation that helped fire the natural athletic rivalry between the two schools, particularly on the gridiron. But Georgia failed to beat Georgia Tech in six tries following Heisman's appointment, and it was not until 1910 that the Bulldogs recorded their first win over a Tech team. During John Heisman's tenure as coach the Atlanta school would put itself on the map, both as a school and as a football power.

Actually, had it not been for the energy and determination of one man, football might have taken a long time to catch on at Georgia Tech. In 1893, Captain Leonard Wood, a medical officer at nearby Fort McPherson, had enrolled in a course at the Atlanta school—not necessarily to broaden himself but rather for the express purpose of playing football. The 1892 team, the school's first, had lost all its games, so Wood figured he was the man destined to set the true course for Tech football. Having earned an M.D. degree at Harvard in 1884, he was familiar with the eastern style of play, while as a professional military man he had served successfully in the West as an Indian fighter. Apparently, the rugged military flavor of football appealed to the action-oriented nature of Leonard Wood.

As Tech's first football captain and its first unofficial coach, Wood challenged the University of Georgia to a match in 1893. To his everlasting fame among Tech supporters, he produced a decisive 28–6 win over the Athens team. However, Wood's military career soon sent him on to other ventures— the irrepressible Wood eventually became a founder of Teddy Roosevelt's Rough Riders, Army Chief of Staff, and even a presidential candidate in 1920—and Tech's football program foundered. Before Heisman's arrival, in fact, Tech had compiled a dismally poor record of only eight wins in forty-five games after eleven years of competition. Only the unbeaten 1901 team with its 4–0–1 season had enjoyed any success.

Realizing that to build a winning football team at Georgia Tech would be no easy task, John Heisman went right to work in his usual no-nonsense manner to create a winning environment. As the school lacked a playing field, he first set his sights on securing one, recognizing, of course, that the

clause in his contract giving him 30 percent of the gate would not amount
to very much without a home field to play on. Even after obtaining a seven-
year lease on a parcel of land from a local real estate company, Heisman did
not see his plan to construct an athletic complex for both football and baseball
taking shape until the winter of 1905. To clear the leased land of stumps
and undergrowth, he had the city put to work a large group of convicts,
while the Tech students themselves were sufficiently inspired to build a
wooden grandstand along the steep bank that flanked the field as well as a
fence to enclose the entire area. The low-lying field, which was then referred
to as the Flats, formed part of what was to become the present-day Bobby
Dodd Stadium. By the time the 1905 baseball season opened, Tech athletes
found themselves with a brand-new diamond and gridiron awaiting play.

Heisman's baseball teams at Tech were as well-coached as his football
teams; the 1906 team, led by pitcher Ed LaFitte, who would wind up in the
Majors, won the Southern championship with a 14–3 record. Tech would
also capture the 1909 baseball championship.

As he had done in all his previous appointments, Heisman made his presence known among both students and players right from the start. He was
now a bona fide professional coach, highly motivated to achieve the goal of
competitive excellence in his own inimitable way. In holding to his football
conditioning theories, he put his men through fast-paced practices, even
requiring them to run extra laps that a manager was appointed to keep a
record of. One of his later players recalled:

There was nothing easy about a Heisman practice. At the time there was a 40-
foot hill right behind the athletic offices, and there were two trenches, about waist
high. We'd run up one trench, make a circle, and come down the other one until we
were exhausted.

Heisman demanded few calisthenics. Mostly it was running up and down that hill
and scrimmages, about two hours of scrimmaging and dummy drills.[1]

He also enforced strict training rules that some of his players later said
were actually a reflection of the man's own peculiar prejudices. They were
ordered to take only cold showers after practice with warm showers permitted
only after a game. As far as the training table was concerned, Heisman
forbade the consumption of pastry, coffee, pork, veal, cabbage, hot bread,
nuts, and apples mainly because, as his players recalled, these things disagreed with Heisman himself, and, of course, he considered his players as
extensions of himself. The water allowance on the practice field was strictly
rationed, and meat, usually roast beef, was served practically raw on the
assumption that such half-cooked fare would make his men tougher. One of
Georgia Tech's early football players, who ironically was on Turner's committee that actively sought out Heisman as the school's first full-time coach,
later observed: "I never really liked him too much. He was too rough and

too demanding. But, being realistic about it, the football process was new, and I imagine it needed a coach like Heisman."[2]

In terms of on-field success, this latter surmise proved correct, as Heisman's regimented coaching style paid off with an 8–1–1 record chalked up by his first Tech team in 1904. Highlights of the season included wins over the University of Florida (77–0), just then starting out playing the game; Tennessee (2–0); Georgia (23–6); and Cumberland (18–0). But the match with Heisman's previous school, Clemson, ended in an 11–11 tie while his other southern school, Auburn, with new coach Mike Donahue at the helm, shut him out, 12–0.

The Tennessee contest on October 22 of that year was a grueling affair in which Heisman's disciplined training was the determining factor. After a scoreless first half, Tech drove to the Volunteer 3-yard line, where it gave up the ball on downs. After two futile shots at the line, Tennessee dropped back to punt, but the kick was blocked and recovered by the Volunteers behind the goal for a Tech safety, the only points of the game.

Since Tech had never beaten Auburn, supporters had hoped that Heisman would come up with a victory his first time out. But not only did Tech lose, the game marked the first time in Heisman's football career that a team of his did not make a single first down. One questionable feature of this game that gave the Tech team problems was Donahue's "hike" play, in which a big lineman, as the ball carrier, was dragged or pushed along by a backfield man for whatever first-down yardage was needed. (This tactic would soon be declared illegal.) In spite of Heisman's nearly miraculous success in beginning anew at a different school, the Auburn match revealed that there was a human side to the man's coaching. In effect, there was still plenty of work ahead to get Georgia Tech up to the competitive level of schools like Auburn and Clemson, whose gridiron reputation Heisman had played such a big role in building. Tech supporters in the meantime would learn to cultivate a degree of patience in awaiting their team's day in the sun.

Another bizarre incident involving a Heisman team occurred that year in the game against Georgia, which was played in Atlanta's Piedmont Park. (All of Tech's 1904 home games were scheduled there while Heisman planned for his new campus athletic complex.) At one point in the game, the Georgia punter dropped back behind his goal line to punt, but his kick struck the goalpost and the ball bounded back over the fence behind him. As there was then no rule to cover the situation, the ensuing confusion was not resolved until, following a wild melee, a Tech player leaped over the fence and retrieved the ball for a touchdown!

But if John Heisman had been the reigning master of southern football during his tenures at Auburn and Clemson, he would soon be overshadowed by the accomplishments of two new professional coaches who arrived on the southern scene in 1904: Vanderbilt's Dan McGugin, who had been a lineman at Michigan under Fielding Yost; and Auburn's Mike Donahue, a Yale man.

The two coaches had distinctly contrasting styles of play. Donahue instituted a conservative, eastern approach to the game while McGugin, in line with his midwestern background, took a more open tact, particularly on offense. Along with Heisman, both coaches would help put southern football on the map.

These two coaches and their schools, as well as his old nemesis Sewanee, would give Heisman his biggest headaches during his Tech tenure. Although he would lose only twenty-nine games in sixteen years at Tech, ten of these losses would be to Auburn's Donahue while Tech would lose three of the five games it played against Vanderbilt and McGugin. And in spite of Heisman's overall success at Tech (102 wins from 1904 to 1919), it was soon clear that Auburn's Donahue had Heisman's number, as over the stretch of 1906–1914, Tech won only one match with the Auburn Tigers, losing eight in a row, while three matches with Vanderbilt during this time (1906, 1907, and 1910) resulted in lopsided losses. (Actually, Vanderbilt was the dominant team in the South at this time, regularly winning the SIAA championship.) During these years, five of eight matches would be lost to Sewanee. Thus, eighteen out of Tech's twenty-nine losses would be to just three schools. The losses to Vanderbilt Heisman could readily attribute to the quality players produced by Tennessee's superior secondary/preparatory school system, but the reason for his lack of success against his former school Auburn must have weighed heavily on his mind.

Nevertheless, without either Auburn or Vanderbilt on the 1905 schedule, Heisman's Tech team, which was apparently inspired, too, by at last beginning play on its new home field, turned in an undefeated season of 6–0–1 but conceded the SIAA championship to powerful Vanderbilt. A satisfying 17–10 win over Clemson came early in the season, this after the Tigers, in a brilliant goal-line stand, held Tech for three downs within inches of the goal. (This was the first game in which Chip Robert appeared. Weighing less than 150 pounds, the fleet-footed halfback would become one of Tech's all-time greats.) Other big wins came over Alabama (12–5); Cumberland (15–0), now starting to wane as a southern power; Tennessee (45–0), and Georgia (46–0). The only blemish on the 1905 record was an 18–18 tie with Sewanee, but considering Heisman's poor luck with the Purple a tie had to be something of a moral victory.

The Alabama game turned out to be one of Heisman's most rewarding victories of his early years at Tech. In spite of the brilliant play of Auxford Burks, the Crimson Tide's great back, Tech hung on to win, 12–5. The overworked Burks, who appeared to bear the entire brunt of Alabama's offense, collapsed during the second half and had to be carried off the field. In the Cumberland match, the Tennesseans ran the ball up and down the field throughout the game but made numerous mistakes on which Heisman readily capitalized. One of Heisman's prime dictums, of course, was to make the most of an opponent's errors, and this game served him well in this respect. The decisive victory over Tennessee was the result of plain old-fashioned, pile-driving football. But the game with that other perennially troublesome Tennessee school, Sewanee, saw an entirely different approach that exemplified the exciting possibilities of open-style football. After Tech scored first, the Purple tied it up on a 50-yard run, but Heisman's team took the lead again after a long drive. The score was tied at the half, 12–12, when Sewanee scored on another long run, this one for forty-five yards. Sewanee grabbed the lead for the first time in the second half on a drive of its own, only to have Tech come up with a scoring run of fifty yards to ensure the final 18–18 tie. For the first time, Georgia Tech had made a good showing against this always tough opponent. The lopsided win over Georgia was highlighted by two sensational runs by Tech players, one of ninety-five yards and the other the entire length of the field.

In spite of their success, Tech players knew that a lot of hard work lay ahead under their demanding new coach if they were to develop into the kind of team he envisioned. Although from a national perspective football had considerable public image problems by this time, Heisman had never lost his enthusiasm for the game. Indeed, if anything, his dedication to football had waxed even stronger as its problems proliferated.

THE NATIONAL GAME (1904–1905)

Although certain rule changes were enacted in 1904 to help alleviate the game's brutal aspects, they actually had little impact overall. To counter mass momentum play, the entire field was now covered with five-yard squares to govern the ruling that the first man to receive the ball from the center had to be five yards behind the line before running forward. Six men were now stationed on the line, and the field goal was reduced in value from 5 to 4 points. Significantly enough, this marked the first time that a touchdown was worth more than a field goal.

In spite of its critics, football continued to grow in popularity. Penn, with its 12–0, unscored-on record, was considered the national champion. The team was coached by Dr. Carl Williams, who succeeded George Woodruff in 1902 and who had been one of Heisman's star backs at Oberlin. This team featured the stellar defensive play of its All-American captain, Bob Torrey, whose playing style heralded the arrival of the roving center. In the Midwest, Michigan continued its winning ways under Fielding Yost with an 11–0 record. The Michigan Wolverines fielded a huge—for that time—line, anchored by Adolf "Germany" Schulz, a 245-pound All-American center, while the backfield showcased Willie Heston, a not-necessarily fast but lighting-quick runner, who as a senior brought his touchdown total for his career to an incredible ninety-three.

Meanwhile at Chicago, Amos Alonzo Stagg was still experimenting with various training and strategic innovations that other coaches would soon adopt, such as devising a charging sled for linemen to use in practice and initiating the backfield shift and the quarterback "keeper" play. Minnesota, under Dr. Henry Williams, turned in a perfect 13–0 season and was considered by many to be the national champion, while Nebraska's twenty-seven-game winning streak came to an end at the hands of Colorado, 6–0. As regional pride helped rivalries increase in intensity, the popularity of the game increased as well.

The year 1905 saw the Chicago–Michigan game that was played in Chicago determine the national champion and attract the largest crowd (25,791) to see a football game in the Midwest up to that time. Still a recognized power, even without the great Willie Heston, Michigan lost on a safety, 2–0, in an exciting, fiercely contested match that even found Walter Camp in attendance. His presence was further testimony to the fact that midwestern football had arrived. Back east, though, the Harvard–Yale game, won by the Yale Bulldogs, 6–0, attracted forty-three thousand fans, the largest football crowd anywhere up to that time.

THE FORWARD PASS WARS (1904–1906)

Rumblings from various quarters over the apparent disregard for player safety continued, however. Although the innovative Glenn Warner introduced the use of fiber-constructed shoulder and thigh pads during this time, deaths and injuries continued to mount. (Heisman also claimed to have invented "thigh protectors" at this same time, as discussed in note 38 of Chapter 1.) In 1904, twenty-one players had been reported killed and over two hundred injured, and a year later twenty-three deaths were recorded along with an astronomical number of debilitating injuries. For all the changes enacted since the 1890s by the Intercollegiate Rules Committee to help rid the game of its inherent brutality, playing football continued to be a barbaric experience in which a player risked life and limb on the field of competition.

Ironically, at a time when football was enduring its most severe criticism, its popular image was at a high peak, as attested to by the reception of Gilbert Patten's stories about super athlete Frank Merriwell and his exploits at Yale, and a veritable deluge of other fiction series for juveniles in which college athletics were prominent. Magazine stories for adults and popular plays of the contemporary New York stage such as George Ade's *The College Widow* (1904) and Rida Johnson Young's *Brown of Harvard* (1906), whose central action revolved around football, also extended the game's popularity. And, of course, game attendance was building unabated.

Nevertheless, since 1893, the most serious attacks on football had been generated by muckraker journalism, which kept appearing in reputable journals like *Nation*, *Harper's*, and *McClure's*, as well as respected newspapers such as the *New York Times*. One of the most vociferous voices during this time was that of Edward L. Godkin, who soundly denounced football because, in his view, "it undermined scholarship, scared away potential students, and attracted depraved elements of society."[3] By 1905, the sound and fury had reached such a pitch that a University of Chicago professor was moved to attack football as "a social obsession—a boy-killing, education-prostituting, gladiatorial sport. It teaches virility and courage, but so does war. I do not know what should take its place, but the new game should not require the services of a physician, the maintenance of a hospital, and the celebration of funerals."[4] For some schools the "new game" was rugby, which California and Stanford wound up substituting for football during the years 1906–1914. (These two perennially athletically minded schools would eventually relent and produce powerful football teams in the 1920s.) During this same time Columbia discontinued football as did Northwestern, although for only two years. Some members of the Western Conference (Big Ten) conceded by cutting their schedules in half. Clearly, the antifootball movement was becoming national in scope.

But it was Henry Beech Needham's two-part condemnation of football serialized in *McClure's* in 1905 that spurred President Theodore Roosevelt into taking remedial action. Roosevelt, an avowed supporter of intercollegiate football, summoned representatives from Harvard, Yale, and Princeton to meet with him in October 1905 to discuss how to eliminate the game's rough elements. As a Harvard man himself, Roosevelt was undoubtedly fearful that the school's president, Charles W. Eliot, a confirmed opponent of the game, would take steps to abolish it and do away with one of the President's prized systems for nurturing manhood. While Eliot's public stand denounced football as not only brutal but overly commercial, Roosevelt's attitude toward the abuses that had corrupted the worth of college football was always constructively expressed, as in his Harvard Union address, delivered on February 23, 1907, a year after the legalization of the forward pass. Because preparatory schools had been "able to keep football clean," Roosevelt contended that colleges should be able to follow suit in order to justify the continuation of this "manly sport":

We cannot afford to turn out of college men who shrink from physical effort or from a little physical pain. In any republic courage is a prime necessity for the average citizen if he is to be a good citizen, and he needs physical courage no less than moral courage. . . . Athletics are good, especially in their rougher forms, because they tend to develop such courage. They are good also because they encourage a true democratic spirit.[5]

Even though the upshot of his White House meeting did little more than inform the public that there really were some concerned individuals interested in reforming football's unethical side, Roosevelt's remedial posture would help inspire concerned coaches like John Heisman and set the stage for important later meetings on a national scale. These meetings would be de-

signed to review the rules and enact new ones, with the intent to do away
with football's overly brutal elements. Despite the problems football was
facing, many educators were beginning to accept football as an integral part
of campus life by this time, choosing

to compromise their views or even to revel in the new prominence their institutions
enjoyed each fall. Emerging from the gray decades of the late 1800s into an era of
larger student bodies and increased public interest in higher education, it was easy
to conclude that football was somehow responsible, if only partially so. And despite
the outraged cries of a few, one could agree with a certain validity (as some still do)
that the sport contributed much to college life.[6]

As a result, two opposing camps concerning the future of football had
formed: those who sought ways to keep football a part of college life and
those who would do away with it altogether. One person who was influential
enough to help resolve the game's problems was Walter Camp, whose long-
time membership on the Intercollegiate Rules Committee had ensured his
role as caretaker of the game's healthy development and expansion. Having
attended President Roosevelt's White House meeting, he had expressed his
sincere interest in developing a cleaner game. As one observer put it, however,
Camp was an "able diplomat [who] deftly steered football around the shoals
of public criticism and intercollegiate squabbles without hampering its phenomenal growth."[7] In short, Camp's relationship with the game he had
nourished from its beginnings had become increasingly conservative as he
grew older. He was therefore opposed to any radical rule changes, in particular the proposal of what some referred to as the "dream-like" forward
pass, although in some quarters its adoption was gaining momentum.

Ever since the day in Atlanta in 1895 when Auburn coach John Heisman
had witnessed the startling results of an illegal forward pass and immediately
realized its merits and possibilities in helping to open up the game, he had
been its champion. But it was not until 1903, while he was still at Clemson,
that he started actively campaigning for adoption of the forward pass, securing the support of many worthy contemporaries. Among those who supported Heisman's radical proposal were Navy coach Paul Dashiell, former
Penn standout John Bell, Amos Alonzo Stagg, and then Clemson coach Eddie
Cochems. In advocating adoption of the forward pass, Heisman wrote directly to the keeper of the rules, Walter Camp himself. As Heisman reflected:

Remembering the desperate fling of that tired boy from North Carolina I wrote
to Walter Camp, chairman of the Rules Committee. Here was a way to open up the
game we loved too much to see proscribed. The forward pass would scatter the mob.
With the forward pass speed would supplant bull strength. Lighter, faster men would
succeed the beefy giants whose crushing weight maimed or killed their opponents.

But after writing, Heisman disclosed that he "got no reply from Mr. Camp." So in spite of "a great hue and cry," the old mass plays resulted in longer "casualty lists," prompting another letter to Camp, but

again he was silent. However, he must have been pondering it because, in 1905, at a meeting of the Rules Committee he spread before the members the forward pass plan with his own excellent restrictions thereof.

The forward pass had been legalized. American football had come over the line which divides the modern game from the old. Whether it was my contribution to football or Camp's is, perhaps, immaterial. Football had been saved from itself.[8]

However, general acceptance of the forward pass did not come about as readily or promptly as Heisman would have us believe. (Not until 1906 was the forward pass finally legalized, and then only after long and arduous debate in a series of significant meetings.) In fact, had it not been for the mounting public pressure brought to bear on the college football establishment to come up with ways to open up the game, the forward pass as a part of football strategy might have been delayed indefinitely. Camp and his followers, who were at first simply too protective and conservative to wholeheartedly endorse anything as radical as the forward pass, eventually yielded to the inevitable.

Accordingly, the meetings that followed Teddy Roosevelt's original entreaty served to keep the key issues before a concerned public who, by now, fully expected some kind of remedial action to be taken. The most auspicious of these gatherings was the national convention of football-playing schools held in New York on December 28, 1905 (the meeting to which Heisman was referring above).[9] With delegates from nearly seventy schools all over the country attending—some determined to abolish the game, others to save it through reform—agreement was finally reached to form a new committee charged to negotiate with Walter Camp's existing Rules Committee and develop necessary resolutions. After considerable behind-the-scenes maneuvering, a master committee (The Intercollegiate Athletic Association) was ultimately organized, which by 1910 would evolve into the National Collegiate Athletic Association (NCAA). Relatively weak in its beginnings, this organization would grow in power over the years as an autocratic interpreter of the rules, particularly as member institutions began to subscribe to more parochial interpretations in lieu of their previous collective outlooks.

The major charges of the original committee were to develop and enforce rules of play and eligibility and to oversee their general administration. A concurrent development of the 1905 convention was the acknowledgment that the academic authorities, whether they liked it or not, were responsible for the integrity of their respective programs. (Unfortunately, this charge would result in a lack of collective purpose and continuing abuses, as each institution sought to either ignore their problems or resolve them as school authorities saw fit.) Since each geographical section of the country had representation on the committee, delegates were asked to submit their personal recommendations for bringing about the desired results. The suggestions of the Washington and Jefferson College delegation are typical of those presented at large: that rules be enacted to encourage the development of playing skills that would help create a more open game, such as requiring ten yards in three downs and adopting some variation of the forward pass; that rough and brutal playing be eliminated by penalizing a guilty player through his dismissal from the game for the rest of the half; and that eligibility rules hold the duration of a player's career to four years and bar professional athletes from play.[10]

While a series of meetings over the next several months were scheduled to discuss the implications of such recommendations and produce rule changes that would help improve the game, the delegates usually wound up in fierce debate and lack of consensus over what was needed to achieve this end. Nevertheless, by the spring of 1906, the committee finally came forth with some significant revisions. Linemen could no longer drop back on offense, since at least six men had to be on the line. There would now be four officials (a referee, two umpires, and a linesman) on the field to help control the game's progress; playing time was reduced to sixty minutes; hurdling and mass momentum plays were strictly prohibited; a neutral zone was established between opposing lines; and a team on the offense would have to gain ten yards in three downs to retain possession of the ball.

Most significantly, the controversial forward pass was legalized, but with the following restrictions (for which Walter Camp was primarily responsible): If an attempted pass fell incomplete on first and second down, a 15-yard penalty would result, and if incomplete on third down, the passing team would lose possession regardless of who recovered the ball. Even passes that had been touched but not caught could be recovered by either side. Also, the ball had to be thrown to only an end or a back from at least five yards behind the line of scrimmage, and it had to cross the line five yards to the right or left of the spot where the ball was put in play.

In spite of these revolutionary changes, the season of 1906 would see teams use the forward pass sparingly, if at all. For most teams, there was simply too much risk involved to even attempt a pass, so teams usually relied on it only as a last resort. Nevertheless, there were sporadic reports of success with this newly acquired offensive weapon, particularly in the Midwest where coaches were more prone to innovate. As to who was the first to use the forward pass, claims vary. Wesleyan University completed a pass against Yale on October 3, 1906 for an 18-yard gain, while Marietta College of Ohio passed for 47 yards and a touchdown against Ohio University about the same time. (As early as December, 1905, prior to the legalization of the forward pass, two Kansas colleges, Fairmont and Washburn, played a game in which they experimented with the uses of the forward pass.)

However, it would appear that the most valid claim to the first official use of the forward pass is that of St. Louis University, which successfully completed a pass in early September 1906 against Carroll College of Waukesha, Wisconsin. The St. Louis coach, Eddie Cochems, was, along with Heisman, among the few who had long recognized the potential of the forward pass and had been preparing for its advent. In Cochems' own words:

> Of course we developed the pass first, at St. Louis University. I first conceived the idea immediately on getting the official football guide of 1906. . . . In 1905, as coach at Clemson College, John Heisman (whose place I took when he went to Georgia Tech) and I talked over the possibility of having the Rules Committee permit the use of the forward pass. . . .
>
> I took the team [St. Louis] to Lake Beulah, north of Chicago, in July, 1906, for the sole purpose of studying and developing the pass.[11]

That Cochems was ahead of his time in realizing what could be done with this new offensive weapon was attested to by a contemporary sportswriter. Ed Wray of the *St. Louis Post-Dispatch* described the reaction of a referee who worked one of Cochems' games in 1906:

> The St. Louis style of pass differs entirely from that in use in the East. There the ball is thrown high in the air and the runner who is to catch it is protected by several of his teammates forming an interference for him. The St. Louis players shoot the ball hard and accurately to the man who is to receive it and the latter is not protected. With the high pass, protection is necessary. . . . The fast throw by St. Louis enables the receiving player to dodge the opposing players, and it struck me as being all but perfect.[12]

At 11–0, St. Louis was even in the running for the national championship in 1906, but yielded the title to a more reputable school, Princeton, which finished its season at 9–0–1.

Although the forward pass was now legal, it would not be until some years later that its full potential would be universally acknowledged—most dramatically in the 1913 Notre Dame–Army game. In the meantime, most coaches, particularly those in the East, were reluctant to employ this newfangled device, apparently fearful that it would either backfire on them or that it would turn the game into an aerial circus, undermining what they considered to be the true nature of football.

HEISMAN, THE FORWARD PASS, AND THE QUICK SHIFT (1906)

Although John Heisman had to be highly pleased with the news of the forward pass's acceptance, the date of his first use of it is open to conjecture. But use it he did in the very first year it was legalized. In fact, in the 1906 game with Auburn in Atlanta, the forward pass figured in yet another of those controversial plays that seemed to dog Heisman everywhere he went.

Called on to punt during the first half, Tech kicker W. S. "Lobster" Brown sliced the ball off his foot directly up in the air. It came down into the hands of a Tech player who, in a moment of inspired improvisation, threw a touchdown pass to halfback Chip Robert. With nothing in the rules against it, the referee allowed the play to stand. Later, Robert scooped up a blocked Auburn punt and ran it in for a touchdown. The final score was 11–0, marking the first time ever that Georgia Tech had defeated Auburn.

But even with the forward pass at his disposal, Heisman produced a rather lackluster 5–3–1 season in 1906. Other wins were over Davidson (4–0), thanks to Lobster Brown's 40-yard field goal, and Georgia (17–0), while the match with surprising Maryville of Tennessee resulted in a 6–6 tie. Losses were to Sewanee, as usual (16–0); to Clemson (10–0), a Thanksgiving Day game in which the Tigers finally tried their first forward pass; and to powerful Vanderbilt (37–6). The Georgia win featured the stellar play of Chip Robert, particularly his timely pass receptions that set up two touchdowns.

The game with the Vanderbilt Commodores was played on a stormy day, alternately raining and snowing, and the only bright spot in the embarrassing loss occurred when Chip Robert recovered a muffed punt attempt behind Vandy's goal line for Tech's only score. In planning to kick the coveted extra point, Heisman pulled off a ruse that was yet another example of his knack for skirting the rules. He sent a substitute into the game who was wearing a raincoat to keep the football he was carrying dry. When Vanderbilt protested, Heisman countered the referee: "All that the rules say is that the game be played with the prolate spheroid specified in the rules. Well, here's a prolate spheroid, the twin of the one we've just made a touchdown with. How about it?" Finding nothing in the book to refute Heisman's contention, the referee allowed the punt to be kicked with the fresh ball. But today, as Heisman indicated, "the referee decides when a new ball shall be taken into the game, and not the coach."[13]

Although Tech never came close to winning the game, its supporters, having wagered large sums of money on its team to at least score in the match, wound up winning in a big monetary way, this being a time when open gambling on sporting events was not under close surveillance as it is today. Accordingly, the 1906 game with Clemson saw Tech supporters at a fever pitch of gambling frenzy. Taking any odds the Clemson backers offered, Atlanta wagerers were sure they would be in complete command of this match. But (according to Fuzzy Woodruff) Tech's 10–0 defeat "came close to bankrupting Atlanta."[14]

After having tied Sewanee the previous year, Tech reverted to its old ways in the loss to the Purple. Nevertheless, the game was notable for the first appearance of Heisman's soon to be notorious "jump shift," which he would use in ensuing years with considerable success. A contemporary reporter, as Woodruff notes, questioned the legality of the innovation "that was later to revolutionize football attack and defense in the South":

"That's a neat trick of Heisman's," says the chronicler, "in making a fake move just before the ball is snapped."

He then explained that as he saw the play, Heisman caused his team to shift in order to have the other team charge too soon and be penalized for being offside.[15]

According to Heisman, though, the "quick shift," as he referred to it, occurs "when a team, after seemingly assuming a settled position or formation, rapidly shifts one or more of its men to new positions, and then shoots the ball into play immediately after those men have come to a stop in their shifting movement." The most important advantage of the quick shift formation, according to Heisman, it that it affords a team

a great variety of differing formations while the ball, coming back so soon after the strange formation has been assumed, allows opponents no time in which to "size-up" that it is different from the others; or, if some of the defensive players should be quick enough to note the change, they have no time to notify their comrades thereof nor to confer with each other as to the best way to meet it.[16]

Ironically, years later, the venerable Amos Alonzo Stagg, who himself had been a pioneer of such tactics, criticized Heisman's quick shift tactics as a reintroduction of the momentum principle that gave his team an unfair advantage and "violated the spirit of the rules."[17] Nevertheless, during the 1920s many teams would come up with variations of the shift formations developed at both Georgia Tech and Minnesota, as we shall see. Heisman would continue to experiment with his shift offensive during the time that his pet project—the forward pass—had been finally approved, with both developments attesting to his perennial obsession with innovation.

THE FORWARD PASS AND THE NATIONAL GAME (1906)

The upshot of that first year of the forward pass was that while its adoption did help open up the game, it had little impact on bringing about a decrease in the injury and death tolls. Clearly, there were still a number of strategic problems to be dealt with in football. But from a tactical point of view, the coming of the forward pass functioned as an on-field equalizer in that it afforded small schools more of an opportunity to compete on equal footing with larger schools. For example, during the first years of its use of the forward pass, St. Louis University won all its games, scoring 402 points to 11 for its opponents, even defeating Midwest power Iowa, 39–0. In the South, schools on the order of Davidson clearly benefited from the new rule when, for example, it beat Georgia, 15–0, by effectively employing a short pass over the middle of the line. Surprisingly, high schools began implementing the forward pass as soon as the rule appeared, and as a result it was not long before players skilled in the special proficiencies that the new rule required began filtering into the college ranks.

Other than Heisman and Cochems, others who were quick to make the most of the forward pass and its strategic possibilities were, as expected, Amos Alonzo Stagg and Glenn Warner. At Chicago, the ever-inventive Stagg, who always seemed to be ahead of his time, began to experiment with what today would be known as a play-action pass. In such a play the quarterback had the options of faking to a back running toward the line and then throwing to an end, or pitching to a halfback who could then roll out to pass to an end or halfback, or throwing directly to either an end in close or to an end flanked wide. With a coach like Stagg the natural opportunities the new rule afforded were unlimited.

Warner's inventiveness also extended to areas other than that of utilizing the forward pass. As noted, John Heisman had already experienced a sampling of this man's creative tactics in the 1895 Auburn–Georgia game. But when Warner took on the challenge of coaching at a small Indian school called Carlisle in 1899, his talent for innovation began to assert itself in earnest.

As an agricultural and mechanical college situated on a former Army installation in Pennsylvania, the school had been set up to teach trade skills to the disenfranchised American Indian. When football was introduced as a varsity sport, eligible students, of whom there were only about 250 on the undergraduate level, took to it with unexcelled enthusiasm. Their zeal for the game inspired Warner to schedule road games against some of the toughest opponents in the country. This was the main reason he was continually compelled to come up with new approaches to playing style and game strategy. For example, in 1899 he instructed his linemen to use a crouching start. This resulted not only in a quicker play start but better blocking leverage. Anticipating Heisman's quick shift, Warner also implemented a modified shift formation by having his linemen move a step or two either to the right or the left before the ball was snapped.

In 1903, Warner even resurrected the old hidden-ball trick that Heisman had concocted. During the game against Harvard with the Crimson ahead, 6–0, Carlisle took the second half kickoff and after withdrawing into a wedge near their goal line, one of the players stuffed the ball under the back of a teammate's jersey. Using their helmets as improvised "footballs," the Carlisle players proceeded to divert the Harvard defense while the designated ball carrier ran the length of the field to score unmolested. (The touchdown wasn't declared official until a teammate rushed up, pulled the ball out of the jersey, and touched it to the ground, a required ritual in those days.) Such Heisman-like deception was not enough to help the Carlisle cause, though, as Harvard went on to win the close contest, 12–11.

The fact of the matter is, Carlisle played everybody tough in those days without much recourse to deception. After going on to coach three years at Cornell, his alma mater, Warner returned to Carlisle in 1907 and turned out one of his best teams, a team that in eleven games lost only to Princeton to warrant high national ranking. Warner's Carlisle teams were characterized by a competitive ardor that grew out of the Indians' strong sense of pride in their race and the opportunity that football offered to compete with the white man on an equal footing. The Indians' ability to beat white men at their own game was never more dramatically projected than through the stirring efforts of Warner's Carlisle football teams in their heyday. And no team of their day made more effective use of the forward pass than did Carlisle, as a number of outstanding teams discovered. Villanova, Penn, Harvard, Minnesota, and Chicago were all victims of Warner's deployment of the pass in 1907.

At this time, too, the Carlisle coach must have been looking ahead to the advent of the single-wingback formation, one of his major contributions to the game. Capitalizing on a rule that allowed an offensive man to be stationed outside and behind an end, provided there were six men on the line, Warner came up with a new kind of power attack that provided additional interference for the ball carrier. But more glory days lay ahead for the Carlisle Indians, mainly because of the future exploits of a player who made his first appearance in 1907, a player many would acclaim as the greatest all-around football player ever: Jim Thorpe.

RINGERS ON THE SOUTHERN SCENE (1907–1908)

In the meantime, Heisman, now fully acclimated to his Atlanta environs, had high hopes for his 1907 team. But, as so often happens in the fortunes of football, Heisman's expectations were not to be realized. In this, his fourth season, Tech supporters had been confidently looking to a possible Southern championship, especially after two warmup opponents were demolished by the combined score of 123–0. But a close 6–4 win over Tennessee revealed that against frontline competition Tech's Yellow Jackets had some serious problems in getting their attack on course. In fact, Tech's victory had really resulted from a lucky break. At one point in the first half, a Tech back fumbled and Tennessee recovered near its goal line. Dropping back behind his own goal to punt, the Tennessee kicker's foot missed the ball completely and a Tech player jumped on the loose ball for the only touchdown of the game. The Vols managed to kick a 4-point field goal in the second half, but by then it was too late to pull the game out.

Next came Heisman's growing nemesis, Auburn, and this time the Tech team was not to be so lucky. Although the overall quality of Heisman's players was superior to that of Donahue's, the Auburn team had always presented something of a psychological problem to Tech, and this meeting proved to be no exception. Actually, in preparing for this match Heisman's game plan was complicated by another concern: a natural tendency to look past Auburn to the game with big rival Georgia the very next week.

Tied at the half, 6–6, the Auburn game could easily have ended with that score intact, except that toward the end of the contest, Tech elected to throw a desperation pass from midfield. It was intercepted and returned for a touchdown, making the final score 12–6, in favor of Auburn. It must have been difficult for Heisman to realize how the revolutionary innovation for which he had campaigned so long and hard could work against him so tellingly in this painful loss. But being the natural competitor that he was, it is likely that Heisman would have readily acknowledged that, in relying on the forward pass, a coach had to live or die by whatever breaks or misfortunes came his way.

The year 1907 was declared the "Ringer Season" in many quarters, and the events leading up to the Georgia match the following Saturday show the term was aptly coined. Mainly due to Vanderbilt's growing domination, a number of Southern schools desirous of competing on a more equal footing with the Commodores had taken to recruiting tramp athletes or ringers, as they were referred to then. Heisman's own pet term for the tramp athlete was "boilermaker." These were football players who traveled the college circuit offering their talents to any school that would have them for a price. (Other eligibility concerns at this time had to do with controlling the participation of freshmen, graduate, special or transfer students, and even alumni.) In promoting the Georgia game, the Atlanta papers had set the stage for a battle royal by openly charging the Bulldogs of professionalism due to their alleged recruitment of ringers. Although local reporters had demanded an official announcement of the starting lineup from Georgia authorities so that the players' eligibility could be verified, the actual lineup was not revealed until just before the opening kickoff, when a Georgia official furnished the referee with a list of starters. Thus the scene was set for a grudge match with repercussions transcending the game's outcome.

Yellow Jacket fortunes appeared bleak at the very start when Chip Robert, Tech's multitalented halfback, dislocated his shoulder on the runback of the kickoff and was forced to leave the game. Following this blow, the match settled into a defensive struggle with each side waiting for the other to make a mistake. It finally came when overly aggressive Georgia players tackled a Tech man who had signaled for the fair catch of a punt. The ensuing penalty resulted in a free kick from placement, for 4 points. Then after a 45-yard touchdown pass in the second half, Heisman's team took a commanding 10–0 lead. Georgia managed to score after a Tech kick was blocked, making the final score 10–6. Ringers or no, Heisman had won four straight over his big intrastate rival, and Bulldog morale was now at a very low ebb indeed.

In addition to the pressures on its players stemming from charges of professionalism, Georgia's poor team play in this game was supposedly related to gambling. According to Fuzzy Woodruff, the Georgia supporters, having wagered thousands of dollars, had promised the Bulldog player who scored the first touchdown a large sum of money. Consequently, "individual jealousies" destroyed Georgia's teamwork.[18]

The aftermath of this game was a large-scale investigation of players' credentials who had suddenly and inexplicably shown up on southern campuses. Georgia, Alabama, Sewanee, and even Georgia Tech were among the schools open to suspicion of having used ringers in their games. With alumni numbers growing each year, many of these "professional" players had been recruited by overzealous boosters eager for their teams to compete on a more competitive basis, particularly with powerful Vanderbilt. Due to a steady stream of seasoned players coming in from Tennessee's prep schools, Vanderbilt, with little or no recruiting problems, had achieved the role of the team to beat each year in the SIAA. The Nashville team was also beginning to establish itself as a national power.

In 1906, Coach McGugin had taken the Commodores north to play his alma mater, powerful Michigan, and lost by the surprisingly close score of 10–4. That same season, Vanderbilt took on Glenn Warner's Carlisle Indians, the great barnstorming team with a reputation for winning on the road. But this time Vanderbilt shocked the football world by setting up a strong defense and winning, 4–0. With only one loss at 8–1, the Commodores finished in the running for the national championship, the first southern team to do so. With Vandy in the vanguard, southern football was starting to make a name for itself.

As far as charges of professionalism at Georgia Tech were concerned, though, Heisman appears to have run a program that, like those of other schools, took advantage of the lax recruiting regulations of that day. If institutions were expected to monitor their own programs, then abuses were bound to occur. But because of his strong views on the worth of an education to the student athlete, Heisman would not have taken kindly to the tramp athlete who was out primarily to play football rather than attend class. His own outlook on the problem of recruiting, which was summed up in an article he later wrote in 1928, sided with the players, justifying the system as a means to an end:

There are many lusty boys who could not get college training unless they traded their athletic cunning for jobs which defray the expense of tuition, board and lodging. And there have been a surprising number of these poor but strong youths who have by their postgraduate contributions to society justified their education. Society would have been the poorer had college athletics been purer.[19]

Ironically, as Heisman analyzed the situation, the problems of his own day appear to be not that much different from our own, particularly with regard to overzealous alumni and boosters eager to keep their school among the front-runners at any cost. Nevertheless, the fact that Georgia Tech was aboveboard in its recruiting practices was attested to in an article Heisman wrote in 1912 on the difficulties he encountered inducing athletes to come to the Atlanta school:

Many a time when I have been told by an athletic boy that he would like to come to Tech if we could only give him such or such financial assistance, and I have had to tell him that we could not and did not do that at Tech, he has bobbed up serenely at some other Southern college; after telling me in the most positive manner that he could not go to any college unless given financial aid. Well, that difficulty we shall never be able to overcome at Tech, for we couldn't do it if we would, and we wouldn't do it if we could.[20]

The problems, temptations, and pressures that recruiting presented to Heisman at Georgia Tech would continue until his departure following the 1919 season. In fact, they would pursue him throughout his coaching career.

After the resounding 54–0 defeat at the hands of Vanderbilt in 1907, Heisman must have been convinced that nothing less than a whole team of "boilermakers" would have succeeded against this increasingly formidable foe. Once again the forward pass had been a big factor in Tech's downfall. Other than problems with opponents who recruited ringers, it appeared that Heisman was now facing a potentially more problematic concern in trying to come up with a way to defend against the innovation he had ardently campaigned for as a way to improve the game.

Heisman most assuredly would prefer posterity to forget about the two other 1907 games in what would be his most mediocre (4–4) season at Tech: an 18–0 loss to Sewanee and a 6–5 squeaker defeat at the hands of Clemson. For the most part of ten years giant-killing Sewanee had been rampaging southern football fields, so Heisman had become reconciled to the Purple's winning ways. But to lose to Clemson in so close a match must have been a bitter pill to swallow.

One of the big surprises of the 1908 season—Louisiana State University's 10–2 win over Auburn—served notice that professionalism was a bigger problem in the South than most people had realized. Grantland Rice, beginning to make a name for himself at this time as a sports reporter for the *Nashville Tennesseean*, published a documented story charging the LSU football staff with using seven players who had been paid specifically to play football. LSU officials denied the charge, but Rice stuck to his guns, declaring that he could prove his contention. Although no investigation came about, LSU, which at 10–0 considered itself a contender for the Southern championship, had now lost its credibility, and Auburn went on to claim the crown that year. In just two years, in 1910, the National Collegiate Athletic Association would appear, and steps toward the regulation of player eligibility would begin in earnest. It would be some years, though, before this organization would become a powerful force in controlling the eligibility process.

Georgia Tech's 1908 season started off with easy wins over the usual "breather" opponents—the military prep and normal schools. Then in an extremely rough contest, Tech defeated Mississippi A&M (later, Mississippi State), 23–0. In this game Chip Robert was ejected for "unduly vigorous" play, as the euphemistic style of that day's sportswriters described his behavior. In another October match that featured Heisman's increasingly successful adaptation to the pass, Tech came from behind to defeat Alabama, 11–6. However, three straight losses followed to undermine the Yellow Jackets' title chances that year: to Tennessee (6–5), Auburn (44–0), and Sewanee (6–0). Tech had started off strong against Auburn, but once Coach Donahue's defensive strategy asserted itself, the Tech offense and defense both collapsed, particularly after Auburn halfback L. W. Hardage ran the second-half kickoff back 108 yards for a touchdown.

Nevertheless, the 1908 season closed out on a positive note for Heisman, with wins over Mercer (16–6) and Clemson (30–6). Not only was Tech's 6–3 record an improvement over the preceding season, it also boded well for the 1909 season and the elusive hunt for the Southern championship. On a grim note, the death of a VMI player in a game with Roanoke College that fall once again reminded the football world that, in spite of recent rule changes designed to open up tactics, the brutality of the game remained an ever-present problem.

THE COMING OF THE HAUGHTON SYSTEM (1908)

That football's changing style of play and coaching techniques, as well as the fact that it had ceased to be a student-controlled activity, had begun to reflect an instinctive corporate nature was borne out in 1908, with the appointment of Percy Haughton as head coach at Harvard. Haughton wasted no time in implementing an executive management style of coaching that soon came to be known as the Haughton System. It was a system, in fact, in which the coach was in complete control. Recognizing the game's expanding areas of specialization, Haughton was the first coach to hire assistants who functioned primarily as backfield, line, kicking, and even scouting specialists. As an innovator who took what he needed from other systems to mold his own, Haughton was an iron disciplinarian and perfectionist who sought to promote a winning psychology predicated on the strictest possible training schedule and diligent attention to the game's fundamentals.

In demanding the undivided allegiance of both his coaches and players, Haughton's game strategy was designed to wear down an opponent over the early stages of a match so his team could be in an advantageous position to ensure winning toward the end. Also, with no huddle to detract from his quick striking offense (similar to the way Heisman's Georgia Tech teams functioned at this time), Haughton advocated punting early during a series of downs to force a break. If it came, then his team was directed to revert immediately to a power or surprise play, depending on the on-field situation. Prophetically, the field goal played a prominent part in his system, although he viewed the forward pass as essentially a means to an end, the kind of play that would hopefully set up a scoring opportunity. In his strategic plan, a strong defense was as essential as a powerful offense, because continual pressure on an opponent's kicker could result in an offensive break. He scouted future opponents for both their strengths and weaknesses (again like Heisman) and developed defensive signals tailored to each opponent, which the center could call by numbers and signs.

The Haughton System resulted in Harvard's Golden Era (1908–1916), during which the Crimson won seventy-one games (including a streak of thirty-three without a loss), lost only seven, and tied five. Best of all, for Harvard supporters during this period, Haughton's teams lost only once to Yale. While his first team went undefeated, as did others later, Haughton rated his 1914 team with its unbeaten but twice-tied record 7–0–2 as his best because of its fighting, never-say-die spirit. To Haughton, football was a metaphor for war, a game essentially militaristic in nature in which the coach was the field general and the players his troops. (In a few short years, many gridiron warriors as well as Haughton himself would have the opportunity to translate their football experiences into the grim reality of the World War I battlefield.)

Like Heisman, Haughton had championed the intrinsic worth of the forward pass and was adamantly opposed to the original restrictions Walter Camp had placed on it. In the winter of 1909–1910, after the deaths of still more players had put football on the spot once again, Haughton competed outright with Camp for leadership of the new Rules Committee of the NCAA. He did this mainly by proposing changes to eliminate the existing restrictions on the forward pass, to adopt a fourth down, and to protect the pass receiver, who was then subject to defensive interference without penalty. Haughton also maintained that a player who had to leave a game ought to be allowed to return if healthy enough. Clearly, Percy Haughton proved himself a dynamic force in affecting football's future, both on the field and off.

Because John Heisman's coaching style also advocated military-style discipline, authoritarian rule of the coach, strategic innovation, and a winning philosophy derived from absolute player loyalty, he probably came closer to practicing the professional standards of Percy Haughton than any other coach of that day. Throughout their careers, too, both coaches maintained an aloofness from their players which stemmed from their strict attitude toward team discipline. Although Heisman's relationship with his players did not exactly command their love and affection, Haughton's was so demanding, particularly during practice, that some of his players confessed to actually hating the man. In action and deed Percy Haughton was truly the go-getter type from American business and industry made over into a football coach.

It was also in 1908 that Jim Thorpe's career moved into high gear, and for some time thereafter the back that many would hail as the greatest football player ever to suit up for a game helped keep the name of Carlisle in the limelight. (After the 1908 and 1909 seasons he left school, but he returned for the 1911 and 1912 campaigns.) At about 180 pounds, Thorpe was built for the game in a way most backs of his day were not. His style of play incorporated speed, elusiveness, and extraordinary strength. He was also very versatile, excelling in punting, drop kicking, passing, blocking, and tackling. In short, Jim Thorpe was a football coach's dream come true, and those coaches who saw or heard of his exploits on the gridiron, including John Heisman, must have fairly drooled at the thought of having him as a player. In another of the *Collier's* pieces written in 1929, Heisman reminisced on Thorpe's greatness as a player: "Jim was so good that he liked to amuse himself and his mates by telling an end or a tackle to get set because . . . he was coming that way in a moment. And he'd do it."[21] Although Thorpe never played for Heisman, the Tech coach would be fortunate enough to recruit one of Carlisle's most talented athletes during the Yellow Jackets' highly successful seasons of 1917 and 1918. Joe Guyon, whose contributions to the accomplishments of the Georgia Tech team will be recounted later, had already played several seasons at Carlisle when he transferred to Tech. But in those days there were no strict rules governing the eligibility of transfer athletes, as has been pointed out.

HEISMAN AND THE 1909 SEASON

By this time, John Heisman, at 39, had become a well-known and respected figure in the Atlanta area. Popular with the press and with area business leaders, he had forged an identity for his Tech teams that commanded strong allegiance from both the campus and Atlanta communities. In fact, a number of civic leaders were lending their full support to Heisman in his quest to build Georgia Tech into a national gridiron power. Among these were industrial and business captains George Adair, Lowry Arnold, Frank Holland, Robert T. Jones (father of Bobby Jones, the great golfer of the 1920s), Billy Oldknow, Joe Rhodes, and Marion Swann—all influential names in the building of Atlanta's modern image. They typified the new wave of successful industry and business men who made it a special point to become directly involved in community affairs.

Heisman himself was taking an active part in the community; in 1908 he was appointed athletic director of the Atlanta Athletic Club. Organizations like this, supported by private membership, were common to large cities throughout the South around the turn of the century, and many of them fielded athletic teams that competed with those of area colleges. Heisman's directorship of the Atlanta club not only substantiated his positive image in the community, it also provided him with another income source, evidently a perennial concern of this opportunistic son of Titusville, Pennsylvania's oil boom era. (This experience also prepared him for a role he would fill in his final years—athletic director of the Downtown Athletic Club of New York

City.) If there was a way to pick up some extra money, Heisman seemed always prepared to take advantage of any situation that came his way. Shortly, he would be dabbling in real estate.

As a coach, of course, Heisman had established a strong personal image among his players on the practice field. Normally attired in high turtleneck sweater and baseball cap with his ever-ready megaphone in hand, he struck a commanding figure as he drove his players through their drills. At 170 pounds, he had gained some weight since his playing days, but his 5 feet 10 inch frame didn't display an ounce of flab. To complement his militaristic physical bearing, Heisman's stridently demanding voice seemed to come from all directions at once. In 1913, during the heart of his Tech tenure, a student wrote in the school magazine a rather down-to-earth profile of his imperious locker-room and practice field manner. After complaining about his squad's slowness in suiting up and the team manager's oversights, Heisman urged his players to take the field:

> They are out with a whoop, and, from then on until well after dark, Tech Flats resound with the bark of the quarterback, the thud of falling bodies, and [the] stentorian tones of Coach Heisman. It is a rush from start to finish, hard, sweaty, grinding work with a relentless taskmaster, ever calling for better and more sustained effort. It all seems a mere jumble of motion and command, but at the end of the week Tech watches with pride the smooth piece of machinery that trots out on the gridiron, the result of weeks of preparation.[22]

Heisman's genius for turning out a "smooth piece of machinery" from raw, untried material endeared him to those supporters who looked upon him as a true symbol of Georgia Tech athletics and the formulation of a winning tradition. But because of his autocratic coaching posture not many of his players really took to him personally. They respected him, but that was about as far as the relationship between Heisman and most of his players went. This, of course, was the way he preferred to keep the relationship. Over the years, though, his attitude toward his players would deteriorate to the point of arrogance toward some and favoritism toward others, particularly during his final years at Rice and the waning of his coaching prowess. His later years at Tech were a time when his coaching system was at its peak, bringing his players' abilities to a national championship level.

The 1909 season loomed as another promising one for Tech's football fortunes, but once again, losses to Sewanee and Auburn burst Heisman's bubble. In fact, Sewanee, with its undefeated and untied record, would capture the Southern championship that year, overcoming the perennially tough obstacles of Vanderbilt and Auburn. An early 59–0 whipping of South Carolina had Tech supporters dreaming of a championship season, but in the very next game, Sewanee took advantage of Tech fumbling to deflate any hopes Tech fans might have had, 15–0. Later, the 8–0 defeat by Auburn sealed the Yellow Jackets' doom. It was another typical contest with the Tigers, with Tech playing as though it already knew defeat was eminent. Heisman must have been talking to himself by now about what he had to do to win over Sewanee and Auburn.

On the bright side of this 7–2 season, Tech won its last three games: Georgia (12–6), Mercer (35–0), and Clemson (29–3). Tennessee had been beaten in an earlier game, 29–0. The Georgia match saw Heisman up to his old tricks, this time at the very outset. Echoes of the hidden-ball play Pop Warner perpetrated against Harvard in 1903 were heard after a Tech player was tackled and the Bulldogs discovered that the man had been carrying his helmet to simulate a football while the real ball carrier had gone on to score. Even the officials had been fooled, and, as though to pacify their ruffled dignity as much as to help resolve the matter, they called the ball back to the point of the headgear tackle, penalizing Tech with a loss of down. Although football was moving away from such deceptive practices as variations on the old hidden-ball trick, Heisman evidently had difficulty resisting an occasional sly experiment of his own.

John Heisman's perennial obsession with football's rules and how they might be interpreted, modified, or even circumvented in order to win got him into some strange onfield predicaments at times, a number of which have been previously cited. But in 1928, he based one of his *Collier's* articles on such unexpected situations, some of which actually resulted in rule changes. Once, for example, when his Alabama Polytechnic (Auburn) team was playing Georgia Tech in the 1890s, a Tech punt that had traveled straight up in the air came down and was recovered by Tech following a mad scramble. But instead of awarding the ball to Auburn because Tech had failed to gain the necessary first-down yardage, the referee ruled a "free fumble" and thus granted Tech a first down. Heisman reacted indignantly:

"Free fumble," I roared. "Why, man, there hasn't been any such term since Noah played the game. There's nothing in the rules today about a free fumble. Tech kicked and Tech recovered. Also Tech had five yards to gain and hasn't made it. Poly touched the ball several times during the scramble, but we never had possession. It was never in our control. Therefore they've had it for the full number of downs and they haven't made their distance. Give us the ball."

Nevertheless, the referee ruled in Georgia Tech's favor. Heisman wasn't through, though. After writing to the Rules Committee, he saw his contention become part of the rules: "That when a fumbled ball is recovered by the team which fumbled, it counts as a down. Unless, of course, the required distance to first down is made in the excitement."[23]

Although his deceptive practices had been something of a trademark, Heisman went on in this piece to discuss how the rules had succeeded in banishing "hocus-pocus"—uniforms with leather handles (for pulling), feet-first hurdling by running backs, the hidden-ball variations and even disguised players hiding on the sidelines—from football. He concluded by defending the rulemakers for their efforts:

> I hear it said that the Rules Committee is forever doing its utmost to kill the game— smother it with rules. That criticism is unintelligent. These critics have it that the game is being ruled colorless, that the machine age in which we are living is making the game mechanical and that it develops no great heroes as it did in the days of Hinkey, Heffelfinger, Hare, Heston, DeWitt, Thorpe and Mahan. That, of course, is nonsense. The Rules Committee has compelled the development of team play.[24]

But 1909–1910 was still a far cry from Heisman's 1928 viewpoint, when, for all intents and purposes, football had been transformed into the modern game by the rulemakers.

A real boost to Heisman's coaching morale at this time came in the first appearance of Al Loeb at center, a player who would become one of the all-time Georgia Tech greats. Severely nearsighted and outweighed by all opponents he faced at his position, Loeb was a dramatic example of the rare player who excelled not so much through athletic ability as by an indomitable fighting spirit. He would figure prominently in Tech's next three seasons and, as a spirited little man, develop into one of Heisman's all-time favorite players.

THE NATIONAL GAME (1909–1910): MORE RULE CHANGES

Among the eastern teams, the 1909 Yale Bulldogs compiled a 10–0 record and once again captured the national championship. With All-American Ted Coy at fullback (six Yale players were named to that year's All-America team) and Coach Howard Jones, a stickler for the fundamentals of blocking and tackling, at the helm, the Bulldogs proved their championship caliber by going through the season unscored on.

In other areas of the country, Minnesota, on its way to the Western Conference title, enhanced its success with a flamboyant tactic soon to be nicknamed the "flea flicker" (a forward pass off a lateral). Notre Dame, inspired for the first time by the stirring strains of its great fight song, the "Victory March," defeated Michigan at last and went 7–0–1. Other undefeated season records were posted by Arkansas (7–0), Washington (7–0), Missouri (6–0–1), Harvard (8–1–0), and Penn State (5–0–1), as college football continued to infiltrate all areas of the country.

In the same year, there was another important change in scoring rules: The field goal was now valued at 3 points and has remained so ever since. But 1909 was also the year when matters of a more serious nature came to a head. In spite of the forward pass and relevant rule changes designed to lessen brutality, a total of eight college players were killed that fall, and the high injury count continued. As a result, the public outcry against football had begun to swell again.

Subsequently, early in 1910, the organization officially known for the first time as the National Collegiate Athletic Association held a series of meetings to produce yet another set of rules aimed at remedying football's propensity toward brutality and violence. This time, modification of the rules governing the forward pass loomed as the most formidable problem to deal with. Even though there were still those who wanted the forward pass abolished, stronger voices, such as that of Percy Haughton, advocated retaining this still-relatively-new tactic. Haughton wrote to fellow supporter Amos Alonzo Stagg that unless the forward pass was retained, football would die. And of course retention of the pass still had the unflagging support of John Heisman and his camp.

In early January, 1910, Walter Camp had written to Heisman concerning some suggested changes in the rules governing offensive formations, particularly those running out of a shift, the formation Heisman had helped pioneer. Camp's major recommendations to Heisman were to station the offensive backs at longer intervals behind the line and to make the required distance for a first down fifteen yards in three downs. At a meeting of SIAA representatives in Atlanta, Heisman had his players perform practical demonstrations of the changes Camp had proposed. However, he and his fellow members discovered in this experiment that backs would now be more disposed to running the ends than before, since their more distant stations behind the line made it easier to gain yardage that way. By now it was obvious to Heisman that Camp was looking for more conservative alternatives to the forward pass to open up the game. At any rate, Heisman soon wrote Camp a detailed letter of the results of his demonstrations, concluding that he and his representatives could see no real worth in Camp's suggestions.

To Heisman's way of thinking there were better ways to open up the game than to spread out offensive formations, and the forward pass was certainly one way that offered unlimited possibilities. So before the NCAA met that spring in New York, SIAA representatives, under Heisman's direction, came up with fourteen suggested modifications and rule changes of their own, of which the following were the most significant:

1. Remove practically all the penalties restricting offensive use of the forward pass.
2. Penalize a defensive player who interferes with an offensive player trying to catch a forward pass.
3. Require seven men to be on the line and all three of the backs (outside the quarterback) to be five yards apart.
4. Divide the game into quarters of even length with a rest period between each quarter.
5. Strictly enforce the penalty for piling on.

Other recommendations mainly had to do with safety factors such as the addition of a "new official to the game called Official Physician, who . . . shall have the power arbitrarily to stop the game at any time . . . in order to investigate the condition of any player." There were also several suggestions designed to monitor the health of players prior to participation, during practice, and during a game. The strangest of all the SIAA recommendations had to do with a new scoring system that would award a point for each 5-yard advance within the 25-yard line.[25]

While this last suggestion failed to gain any national support, the proposals as to the number of players on the line of scrimmage, dividing the game into quarters, and restricting piling on won a sufficient number of converts. But it was not until the May 13, 1910, NCAA meeting that the last of the important rule changes helping transform football into its modern prototype were announced.

Prior to this date, the following changes proposed by the SIAA and other representatives had already been adopted: A game was now to be played with four fifteen-minute quarters; a seven-man offensive line was mandated; interlocking interference was outlawed (as was the flying tackle); pushing or pulling of a ball carrier by his teammates was prohibited; and an on-side kick now had to travel at least twenty yards.

Curiously, though, nothing much had been done to change the rules governing the forward pass until the May 13 meeting when, much to the satisfaction of Heisman and others who saw the forward pass as the real solution to football's problems, some realistic rule changes were finally announced. Not only would there now be no penalty for an incomplete pass, the ball was to be brought back to the original line of scrimmage where play would be resumed. While the ball carrier would now be allowed to cross the line of scrimmage at any point, a pass could be thrown in any direction across the line. However, restrictions were also set forth, requiring that the ball be thrown from at least five yards behind the line and that a pass could not be completed for longer than twenty yards down field. But as the SIAA contingent and Percy Haughton had desired, defensive players were forbidden to make contact with a pass receiver before a reception. In line with Haughton's thinking, too, one other change would lead to a more open substitution system—a player who left the game in one quarter was permitted to return at the start of the next.

Innovative coaches across the country were quick to take advantage of the new rules. Now that a back could run in any direction after he received the ball from center, Amos Alonzo Stagg expanded on the possibilities of the quarterback option play in which the quarterback could either hand the ball off to another back, keep the ball and run with it, or throw a forward pass. The mandate for a seven-man line had both Harry Williams at Minnesota and John Heisman experimenting with the further possibilities of shift formations in which offensive players would move into new positions just before the ball was snapped, holding their stances long enough to satisfy the rule governing motion prior to the snap of the ball. Use of the shift was a successful tactic for any team who could perfect the required timing, since its success depended on hitting a point of attack before the defense could rise to the occasion. Heisman has described the similarities and differences between his and Williams's shifts: "Fundamentally the shifts were alike, but my backs at Georgia Tech took wholly different positions. The Tech backs lined up, upon the shift signal, in Indian file and at right angles to the rush line."[26] Not to be outdone in the move toward more advantageous blocking, Pop Warner concocted the Z-formation, which was actually another step toward the final unveiling of his single-wing attack.

Clearly, football had developed around the periodic introduction of rules designed to refine the game's rough spots and the reaction of enterprising coaches in developing innovations to extend the game's strategic possibilities within the rules' restrictions. Coaches like Stagg, Warner, Williams, and Heisman were among the most successful because they could always come up with imaginative ways to extend these possibilities.

THE NATIONAL SCENE (1910)

But if football was making progress in both refining and defining itself as a national game, there were important developments in other sociocultural areas that were evidence of not only progress but also tradition-breaking changes in the world of 1910—changes that in their way would contribute to making society more receptive to sports. Although the world moved at a much slower pace then, there were definite signs that life in America was on the verge of dramatic social transformation, primarily due to revolutionary technological breakthroughs. With more than two hundred thousand motor vehicles on the road at the beginning of the year, the automobile industry was on its way to becoming one of the nation's largest. (Heisman himself is reputed to have purchased one of the first cars in Atlanta, a Maxwell. It was said that Heisman had considerable difficulty in learning how to correlate its brakes and clutch.) Concomitantly, the success of the automobile industry led to commercial developments in other areas, such as a tremendous increase in the production of crude oil, the manufacture of rubber tires, and the proliferation of concrete roads. Even so, the railroad, with its three hundred thousand miles of track, still offered the most efficient mode of mass travel at this time and would continue to do so well into the century.

The nation at large was still undergoing its inevitable urbanization process, with Heisman's Atlanta becoming a prime example of this trend. The United States was now a country of some 90 million people, eight million of whom had immigrated to the country since 1900. But the more provincial United States still had a long way to go to overtake the British Empire as a world industrial and military power. Nevertheless, with the Germans and Japanese flexing their muscles for all the world to see, the unthinkable reality of a catastrophic world war lay just ahead, an event that would catapult America headlong into the status of a world power, whether it wanted to be or not.

As successor to Teddy Roosevelt, who as president had been mainly concerned with creating a conducive climate for the development of business and industry, William Howard Taft was naturally inclined toward maintaining the country's conservative values. In fact, among Taft's proudest achievements was being the first president to perform the ritual of throwing out a baseball to signify the beginning of the baseball season.

At this time, baseball was by far the most popular team sport, with sixteen professional teams playing to some seven million fans in 1910. (Football's day as a professional sport lay far in the future, although the college game was gaining momentum year by year.) Always the opportunist, John Heisman capitalized on the popularity of professional baseball by functioning as the president of the Atlanta Baseball Association from 1910 through 1914. Heisman, of course, was eminently qualified for the position, not only because of his management abilities, but also because he had turned out successful baseball teams everywhere he had coached, some of championship caliber. Football would always remain his first love, however, and as much as he liked the game of baseball it would only be of peripheral interest to him throughout his life.

As sports increased in popularity, the newspapers began allotting more space to them. This was particularly true with baseball, which, due to the expansion of the major leagues, was developing a strong following in the big cities of the Northeast and Midwest. Also of special interest during that day were the heavyweight boxing matches, which the papers treated with a great deal of ballyhoo. One in particular, the bout between Jack Johnson and Jim Jeffries, was promoted as the fight to decide the superiority of the "Great White Hope" (Jeffries) over the black man (Johnson). Staged in Reno, Nevada, on July 4, 1910, the fight disappointed supporters of the white cause when Johnson won in fifteen rounds of a scheduled forty-five-round match. The press, in its zeal to publicize the outcome of this event, played an unwitting role in precipitating racial violence in certain parts of the country. Even Atlanta, with its large black population, felt the shock tremors of this momentous sporting event.

By this time, newspapers were beginning to realize the power of sports as a social force. Sportswriters like Grantland Rice, who had demonstrated a flair for the investigative in exposing football professionalism at LSU in 1908, were becoming increasingly aware of their power to alert the public to problem areas. With an ever-expanding, ready-made audience awaiting, the sportswriter would come into his own by the 1920s. The versatile John Heisman, with two newspapers at his disposal in Atlanta (the *Constitution* and the *Journal*), would even try his hand at writing sports pieces. In addition, he turned out periodic articles for Tech's student magazine (*The Yellow Jacket*), but most of his sports publications were clearly of the inspirationally posturing type, written mainly to encourage both student and local support of Tech's athletic teams. In 1922, he would publish his well-received *Principles of Football*, a highly personalized explanation of his approach to coaching the game. His later pieces for *Collier's*, written in the late 1920s when he was out of coaching altogether, gave him free rein to say just about anything he wanted. Heisman's mind was a veritable compendium of football history and knowledge, and he had begun working on a history of the game just before he died in 1936. Had he lived to complete the book, it likely would have stood out as the definitive study of the origin and development of American football up until that time.

While vaudeville and the legitimate theater still provided the major sources of mass entertainment in 1910, the Hollywood movie was beginning to make inroads, attracting nationwide audiences of ten million people a week who willingly paid to sit in a darkened room and experience the novelty of viewing dreamlike figures moving around on a luminescent screen. Although the motion picture was still in an embryonic state as far as technical achievements and treatment of subject matter were concerned, sporting events became a popular attraction right from the beginning, particularly newsreel footage of sensational events like the Johnson–Jeffries fight. In a few short years, sports would provide the subject matter for a significant number of Hollywood's fantasized film stories. Sports also had an impact on entertainment modes closer to home, such as the piano (every parlor had one) and the windup phonograph, with an increased circulation of popular college fight songs (Georgia Tech's, like Notre Dame's, was among the most popular) and sports-related songs like "Take Me Out to the Ballgame" in sheet music and phonograph record form. As expressed through the forms of popular culture, sports were becoming an integral and acceptable part of American social life.

Another popular "sport" of the time was that of looking to the skies to follow the development of the airplane. Since its inauspicious appearance in 1903, the airplane was developing into more that just a novelty. With the advent of World War I just a few years away, air power would become a new, powerful force in planning military tactics. But in 1910 people were looking to the skies for yet another reason. It was the year of the return of Halley's Comet. And in spite of the prophets of doom who looked upon its coming as a harbinger of worldwide destruction, its arrival presaged a world that between 1910 and its next appearance in 1985 would change drastically, particularly in sociological and technological ways. The quarter-century of John Heisman's life that remained (1911–1936) would also witness considerable change. Naturally, the increasingly popular game he coached would undergo further changes indicative of the times that would produce them.

Although there were coaches who complained of the major rule changes introduced in 1910, it was soon apparent, particularly from the spectator's point of view, that the game would be much improved because of them.

Indeed, the popularity of football, which in spite of its image problems had never really waned, began to take on even more momentum as a spectator sport during this year. Alumni and other supporters began to demand the renovation and expansion of existing stadiums and the construction of new, gigantic facilities around the country. And because of the rule changes affecting the style of play, the game as we know it today was coming into its own as a socially acceptable sport around this time.

HEISMAN AND THE 1910 SEASON

From a coaching perspective, John Heisman was well prepared to take full advantage of the rule changes of 1910. After four games, with the Yellow Jackets at 4–0 and having scored 159 points to their opponents' 0, he had his players and followers burning with enthusiasm. But, unfortunately, three straight devastating losses ensued: 16–0 to Auburn, 23–0 to Vanderbilt, and 11–6 to Georgia, the first time a Heisman-coached team had lost to the Athens school.

In the Auburn game, played in the rain on a muddy field, miscues were highly instrumental in the outcome as the opportunistic Tigers converted key Tech fumbles into touchdowns. In the next match, Tech's misfortunes continued as Vanderbilt, destined to be SIAA champions once again at 7–0–1, shut out the Yellow Jackets. But losing to the powerful Commodores was not a great embarrassment at this time, as earlier that year they had enhanced the cause of southern football by holding Yale to a 0–0 tie in New Haven.

But then came the demoralizing loss to Georgia, which was largely attributable to the spectacular play of a running back who would become one of the Bulldogs' all-time greats and one of Tech's most formidable foes— Bob McWhorter. In fact, during the course of McWhorter's four-year career, Tech would not win one game against the Bulldogs. The 1910 game, witnessed by one of the largest crowds ever to congregate at Atlanta's Ponce de Leon Field, was rated even by area gamblers. Although Tech led at the half by 6–0, the Bulldogs, behind the hard, shifty running of McWhorter, came back in the second half to win, 11–6. The only bright spot for Heisman the rest of that disappointing 5–3 season was the expected season-ending victory over Clemson—this time, 34–0. Ever since his first season at Tech in 1904, Heisman's teams had been averaging no better than six wins per season. He knew he had to find ways to improve if Tech was ever to capture the coveted SIAA championship.

THE NATIONAL GAME (1910)

Nationally, Harvard was still making an impact, yielding only one touchdown all year and, with a 0–0 tie with Yale, going undefeated (8–0–1).

Another team in the East that enjoyed a successful season was Navy, which, except for a tie with Rutgers, was also unbeaten. In the Midwest, both Illinois and Pittsburgh, with undefeated seasons, were coming to the fore as powers to be reckoned with. In the West, Washington at 7–0 was still enjoying its unbeaten status under second-year coach Gil Dobie. (In fact, during his spectacular nine-year reign at Washington, Dobie's teams would remain unbeaten, an all-time record.) Regional pride had become a decisive factor in inspiring many schools to field teams that would soon be capable of competing with those of any other region in the country.

HEISMAN AND HIS "COLLEGE SPIRIT" GOSPEL (1911)

For Heisman, the disappointing letdown of the 1910 season was not easy to dismiss, and before the 1911 campaign got underway he took steps to avoid another lackluster season. He signed Pete Hauser, who had been an All-America fullback at Carlisle, as assistant coach, apparently hoping that Carlisle's winning ways would rub off on the Tech players. Heisman was also trying every ploy he could to instill in Tech's student body an inveterate interest in football, not only for moral support but to find a plan to help recruit more skilled, able-bodied players. As it was everywhere he had been, Heisman's coaching system depended on involving everyone he could in his recruiting plans, particularly those students who knew of talented athletes who could become candidates for the football team.

Accordingly, Heisman believed that the most important factor needed to generate success in athletics was plain, old-fashioned college spirit. It was an attitude that had originated in the 1890s with the eastern colleges who saw in football a way to bring the college community together. To remind students of the necessity to get behind their teams and be a part of the Tech community, Heisman helped establish the Tech Spirit Club, complete with membership buttons. It was actually a project designed to set a more positive tone for the 1911 season, since a serious dearth of experienced football material would follow graduation that spring. But writing in *The Yellow Jacket* in October of that year, Heisman maintained his positive outlook and reprimanded those slackers who were not taking the school spirit challenge seriously enough:

Fellows, college spirit makes fighting spirit on the football field. . . . If you can't play you can go down a couple of times a week at least and watch the practice and help swell the cheering. Learn the Tech yells, so that you know how to join in at the games. If for any reason you can't play yourself see if you can't get out some promising looking fellow who can. Take an interest in what the football men are doing. If they are eating or drinking things they should not, take the bull by the horns and go right up and tell them so. If reasoning with them doesn't do any good come and tell me about it. Yes, it's your business and your duty. That's the least you can do for the success of the team, seeing that you can't or don't come out and play yourself. If you are going to have the real, right college spirit this year you want to be man enough to take your stand and do your share to frown down on anything and everything that will work against the success of the team.[27]

Imagine a football coach of today resorting to such seemingly antiquated tactics to instill school spirit in students, and they in turn trying to keep a school's players from breaking training rules according to these suggestions. Yet in Heisman's day such cajolery was not too far-fetched, for as intercollegiate athletics grew less student centered, efforts to maintain involvement in the school community automatically devolved on athletic coaches. This responsibility also had the support of college authorities, since it relieved them of such pressures. Even today, many coaches feel compelled to get the student body behind their teams by using the most old-fashioned methods available—fiery speeches, pep rallies, and various promotional stunts. In athletics some things never go out of style, and in appealing directly to students, the Heisman method is still a viable means to encourage support to produce a winner.

Even with the 1911 season two-thirds over and Tech having lost yet another game to Auburn (11–6), the irrepressible Heisman issued still another call for players in *The Yellow Jacket*, this time a "Third and Last Call." Almost as though the season were just getting underway and he were out to recruit new material, Heisman presented his usual sales pitch on why a man should come out for football: First, for his "physical welfare"; next, for his "development of character"; and finally, to show his "college spirit."[28]

The season itself had started out in its usual promising fashion with convincing wins over Howard (28–0) and Tennessee (24–0). But then came a frustrating 0–0 tie with Alabama in a game that the Yellow Jackets were favored to win. It was one of those games in which neither team could do much once they were within sight of the goal. After the frustrating match was over, Heisman rationalized the tie by singling out the play of Alabama back Hargrove Vandergraaf as superior to everyone else. Never, he said, had he "seen a player so thoroughly imbued with the true spirit of football." Ironically, the spirit he had desired to see in his own players was more fully embodied in the play of an opponent, and he made sure they knew about it. Hardly one to give praise where it was due, particularly to his own players, Heisman was more prone to be critical than lavish with his praise; praising the play of an opponent was a way of alerting his players to their own weaknesses.[29]

In this same piece in *The Yellow Jacket*, Heisman went on to reveal why he was loathe to praise his players—he feared that telling them how good they were would spoil them. So he admonished the team's supporters to refrain from praising any player: "When a man is satisfied with himself in anything he will never improve further; he has reached the limit of his game and development. Don't you help him to become satisfied with himself."

After the next game against Auburn, Heisman probably concluded that never in his lifetime would he ever beat the Tigers. Even after gaining 246 yards from scrimmage to Auburn's meager 41 and amassing fourteen first downs to Auburn's three, Tech lost, 11–6. To make matters worse, Auburn's win was accomplished with Coach Donahue ill and his team having to rely on a makeshift lineup due to the illness of several key players. But two long scoring plays had done in Tech: a 102-yard return of an intercepted pass and a 75-yard punt return. With perennially tough Sewanee as his next opponent, Heisman surely figured that the fates were conspiring against him.

Nevertheless, Heisman's faith in college spirit was redeemed when the Yellow Jackets actually came through with a rare win over Sewanee by the convincing score of 23–0. The highlight of the game came when Tech's Homer Cook returned a punt forty-five yards for a touchdown. Supporters were so ecstatic over the victory that they predicted a new age for Georgia Tech football. But the new age was short-lived, as on the heels of the glorious Sewanee victory came another defeat at the hands of Georgia and the indomitable Bob McWhorter. With the ball at midfield in the closing moments and the game looking as though it would end in a scoreless tie, McWhorter suddenly burst off tackle and went all the way for the winning touchdown and a final score of 5–0. After the two disheartening losses to Auburn and Georgia, a 32–0 win over Clemson seemed anticlimactic as Heisman chalked up another 6–2–1 season.

The 1911 season marked the first appearance of a substitute lineman for Tech named William A. Alexander. Although he had served as captain of the scrub team, he seemed a most unlikely candidate for any kind of leadership role, due mainly to his extremely reticent nature. Nevertheless, he would ultimately spend a total of forty-four years at Tech—six as a student and player, eight as a math instructor and aide to Heisman, twenty-five as head coach after succeeding Heisman in 1920, and five as athletic director. Always at Heisman's elbow as an assistant coach, he obviously learned a great deal from his mentor. But as the first alumnus to coach at a southern school, his style was "a drastic change from the coaching of Heisman," according to one of Alexander's early players. "Aleck made you like the game of football, and it ceased to be a punishing grind. And instead of fiery orations by the eloquent Heisman, we were treated to low-key talks that relaxed our tensions before we went on the field."[30] Alexander, who coached from 1920 until 1945, when Bobby Dodd took over, led the Yellow Jackets to all four major bowls of the day, a feat that Georgia Tech was the first team to accomplish.

The 1911 season was hardly over when the relentless Heisman turned his attention to another source of gridiron talent—Tech's class games. These were intramural contests played between the various classes to determine a school champion in football. In addition to fostering school spirit, Heisman's underlying motive for promoting the worth of class games was to uncover additional football talent. In another of his articles in *The Yellow Jacket*, he praised this system, calling it

one of the biggest stepping stones toward ultimately making the Varsity that you can find; in proof of which you can look over our Varsity of this year and ask yourself the question where in the world would we have been this fall if a very large number of our Varsity players had not been largely developed by the class ball they played last winter?[31]

Always the opportunist, Heisman had turned to a proven source to help build his team for the 1912 season.

THE NATIONAL GAME (1911)

From a national perspective, the 1911 team of the year was Princeton, which went 8–0–2. The Tigers' coach, Bill Roper, was another unique study in the varied coaching styles that the increasingly professional side of the game was now attracting. An intensely emotional man, Roper fired up his players through spirited oratory that made them want to go out and "die" for Old Nassau. John Heisman naturally adulated this man's coaching manner because if any coach epitomized college spirit, it was Bill Roper.

Navy enjoyed an impressive 6–0–3 year, proving that the service academies could compete with the best. But the major event of the 1911 season was the return of Jim Thorpe after a two-year layoff. Demonstrating his worth in his inimitably dramatic fashion, he helped Carlisle beat Harvard with a 48-yard field goal, 18–15. At 11–1–0, Carlisle probably had the best team in the country but not, unfortunately, the prestige of Princeton. Elsewhere, Penn State (8–0–1) went undefeated while Washington (7–0) continued its winning ways.

At this point in his Georgia Tech tenure, John Heisman had seen the game of football weather severe storms of public protest and periods of doubt concerning its future role as an acceptable varsity sport. The major forces behind the trend toward football's long-term acceptability, of course, were its development into more of an open-ended game due to the adoption of the forward pass and the introduction of new tactical formations that lent themselves to a more wide-open style of play. Although the growing popularity of football since his arrival at Georgia Tech assured Heisman that the game had a bright future, one thing still concerned the ambitious coach more than anything else: his failure to lead Tech to the Southern championship. But the best days of the Heisman regime in Atlanta lay just ahead, an era that would result in an even-bigger prize than southern laurels—the first-ever national championship for a southern team.

NOTES

1. The player quoted was Bill Fincher, in Al Thomy, *The Ramblin' Wreck: A Story of Georgia Tech Football* (Huntsville, Ala.: Strode Publishers, 1973), 107.

2. Ibid., 32.

3. See John Hammond Moore, "Football's Ugly Decades, 1893–1913," *The Smithsonian Journal of History* 2 (Fall 1967): 49–68.

4. Ibid. 59.

5. Quoted by Allison Danzig in *Oh, How They Played the Game* (New York: Macmillan, 1971), 152–54.

6. Moore, "Football's Ugly Decades," 67.

7. John S. Watterson, "Inventing Modern Football," *American Heritage* 39, no. 6 (September/October 1988): 103–13.

8. John W. Heisman, "Fast and Loose," *Collier's*, October 20, 1918, 14–15.

9. It was Chancellor Henry MacCracken of New York University, with the support of Palmer Pierce of West Point, who convened the conference at the Murray Hill Hotel. It was attended by national representatives from the major football-playing schools of the day. Dr. Henry Williams of Minnesota, with the cooperation of Paul Dashiell of Navy, led the section on the forward pass.

10. For a detailed analysis of these suggestions, see David Scarborough, "Intercollegiate Athletics at Washington and Jefferson College: The Building of a Tradition" (Ph.D. diss., University of Pittsburgh, 1979), 36–37.

11. Quoted in Danzig, *Oh, How They Played*, 178.

12. Ibid., 182–83.

13. John W. Heisman, "Rules Rush In," *Collier's*, November 10, 1928, 12.

14. L. F. "Fuzzy" Woodruff, *History of Southern Football*, vol. 1 (Atlanta, Ga.: Georgia Southern, 1928), 196.

15. Ibid., 189.

16. John W. Heisman, *Principles of Football* (St. Louis: Sports Publishing Bureau, 1922), 267–73.

17. Quoted in Danzig, *Oh, How They Played*, 36.

18. See Woodruff, *History of Southern Football*, Vol. 1, 206.

19. John W. Heisman, "Their Weight in Gold," *Collier's*, November 24, 1928, 28.

20. John W. Heisman, "Our Athletic Outlook," *The Yellow Jacket* (October 1912): 77–78.

21. John W. Heisman, "Hero Stuff," *Collier's*, November 2, 1929, 73. Heisman once confessed to coveting a dream backfield composed of Thorpe, Willie Heston, and Red Grange.

22. "Who's He and Why?" *The Yellow Jacket* (March 1913): 418.

23. John W. Heisman, "Rules Rush In," *Collier's*, November 10, 1928, 12.

24. Ibid., 42.

25. John W. Heisman, "Suggestions As to Football Rule Changes for 1910," 2-page pamphlet (undated).

26. John W. Heisman, "The Thundering Herd," *Collier's*, October 13, 1928, 60.

27. John W. Heisman, "More About College Spirit," *The Yellow Jacket* (October 1911): 21.

28. John W. Heisman, "Are You Coming Out for Football? If Not, Why Not?" *The Yellow Jacket* (November 1911): 12.

29. John W. Heisman, "Our Football Team and Others," *The Yellow Jacket* (November 1912): 179–83.

30. Quoted in Thomy, *The Ramblin' Wreck*, 88.

31. John W. Heisman, "All Aboard for the Class Games," *The Yellow Jacket* (December 1911): 16.

4

Heisman and the Shaping of the Modern Game (1912–1919)

Armed with a marvelous invention, the forward pass, and chastened by President Theodore Roosevelt's stern admonitions . . . , football was no longer a simple campus diversion. . . . Football had moved from the province of the students to the hearts and pocketbooks of the old grads, who now made it a point to see that the old school kept up with other schools. Rivalries were born.

—Furman Bisher,
"Saturday's Child" in *The College Game* (1974)

In that intercollegiate sport and other extracurricular activities satisfied needs that were at least as important as involvement in intellectual activity or study to prepare for a professional career, athletic departments and student services became official concerns of educators. This triumph of anti-intellectual forces resulted in the creation of an operational structure that made possible the tremendous expansion of intercollegiate sport after 1920.

—Guy Lewis,
"Enterprise on the Campus: Developments in Intercollegiate Sport and Higher Education, 1875–1939" (1972)

SIGNIFICANT CHANGES IN THE GAME (1912)

The year 1912 can be considered a major point of demarcation in the development of American football—a time when the style of play began to look very nearly like that we know today. The major rule changes of that year were chiefly responsible for this transition. To the delight of John Heisman and other proponents of the forward pass, the rule restricting a pass to twenty yards had been abolished. The field was now one-hundred yards in length, with a ten-yard end zone at each end of the field. Accordingly, a forward pass caught in the end zone by the offense was to be ruled a touchdown instead of a touchback. To enhance the passing game the ball was trimmed down to afford a better grip. A touchdown was now worth 6 points, and the introduction of four downs in which to gain ten yards was instrumental in modifying offensive strategy. It had been forty-three years since that wild, primeval contest between Princeton and Rutgers was played, but as far as its on-field look was concerned, football was now fairly well set to project its modern image.

HEISMAN AND THE 1912 SEASON

Despite the new rule changes and the lifting of the restrictive limitations on the forward pass, Heisman looked toward the 1912 season with a degree of caution. The main reason for this outlook was the lack of suitable replacements for players who had graduated. But lack of experience and lack of talent were nothing compared to lack of grit, so he kept warning his players against yielding to what he called the quitter attitude: "Absolutely nothing can be done with a 'quitter,' and if there are too many of that kind on a team, you might as well say 'Good night,' and give it up for another year."[1]

Having built better-than-average football teams out of inferior material for years, Heisman was not about to tolerate a defeatist attitude among his players and supporters. In fact, a dominant factor of the coaching philosophy of John Heisman was that a positive outlook could be gleaned even from adversity:

Let's not get discouraged. Remember, I have had to face this proposition for years, and am quite undaunted by it. All I ask is that everyone of you look at the situation the same way I do, with complete realization of what a task we have before us, but yet with courage and determination to weather the storm, if such a thing is within the bounds of the possible.[2]

In order to keep his players properly motivated and updated on his football philosophy, Heisman, by this time, had begun to formulate a list of dos and don'ts about game play that he either posted in the locker room or periodically circulated among his players. Essentially, these pithy comments represented ways to avoid the psychological pitfalls Heisman had learned about the game at this point in his career. In his *Principles of Football* (1922) he enumerated them as "Heisman's Football Axioms." Following are some of his more characteristic and memorable maxims:

• Don't try to play without your head.
• Don't look toward where the play is going.

- Don't fumble; you might better have died when you were a little boy.
- Don't see how light you can hit, but how hard.
- Don't lose the game.
- Don't wait for opponents to come to you. Take the battle to them.
- Use your brain on both offense and defense all the time.
- Use your opponent up and yourself as well, till the game is won.
- You can't play superior football without brains.
- You can't fight like a man with less than 100 per cent loyalty and college spirit.
- You can't be a great player if you have the swell head.
- Never come on the field without your brains.[3]

Judging from their common theme, this sampling clearly demonstrates the high premium John Heisman placed on his players' intelligence as a contributing factor to successfully playing the game of football.

During the winter of 1912–1913, Heisman's football concerns were temporarily put on the back burner when he assumed coaching responsibilities for yet another sport at Tech. As basketball had been growing in popularity since its invention in the 1890s and Georgia Tech now had a "first-class basketball court," he issued a call for players to try out for a varsity team that fall; that is, for those students "who are not engaged with football." Class basketball had been played sporadically at Tech since the early part of the century, and in 1908–1909 the first varsity team took to the court, ingloriously losing five of six games. Clearly, the game of basketball was not taken very seriously at Tech until Heisman issued his call for the 1912–1913 season, when a more dedicated attitude to the sport became apparent. To instill fresh enthusiasm for basketball, he even referred to this campaign as "our first year at the game," concluding that "there is no reason that I can discern why we should not make a first-rate showing even in our first year."[4]

Even in taking up a fledgling sport he knew very little about, Heisman was able to project his natural flair for positive thinking. But the final record of this team, with wins over only Mercer and Clemson in eight games, was just slightly better than in 1908–1909. Not until the 1913–1914 season would Tech record its first winning basketball season, a 6–2 campaign highlighted by a win over Auburn, with losses only to Georgia.

The first football game of the 1912 season—October 5 against The Citadel at Charleston, South Carolina—proved to Heisman and his team just how potent a weapon the forward pass could be in the hands of an opponent that knew how to make the most of it. After "fifteen hours on a slow train," the stiff and cramped players found themselves more ready for bed than exploring the town on their arrival in Charleston. But the next morning they got their tour of the area, the highlight, according to Heisman, being Fort Sumter, where he led his contingent on a "brushup of our history." The scholarly side of John Heisman naturally came to the fore when his players had an opportunity to expand their intellectual horizons.

But in the football game that afternoon, his players soon learned something else of more immediate concern: The Citadel football team was no pushover. According to Heisman, one reason their opponent played them with such fierce intensity is that Tech came into the game highly rated. The newspapers by this time were well into their role of comparing the worth of opposing teams to help promote a game. As Heisman later reported:

> The papers said we were always four touchdowns better than Clemson, and Clemson was two better than Citadel, and so they feared we were going to be real rude about the way we would project our heads against their stomachs whenever we had the ball. . . .
> Their forward pass game was the best we have ever seen, and it was not until we were in the third quarter that our boys finally learned how to smother them up on this play, and then we made them fail on about eight out of ten.[5]

So in spite of The Citadel's "scintillating passing attack," as one reporter described it, Tech went on to win the game, 20–6. Pleased with the outcome, Heisman allowed his players to attend a local dance that night in their honor. But to keep them mindful of the real purpose of the trip, he called a team meeting punctually at the 10:00 P.M. curfew hour: "At the hotel . . . we all went up into one of the larger rooms, and we had a little 'pink tea.' Just what transpired there is not for everybody to know, but the result of it you all saw when we played Alabama on the 12th."[6]

In this latter game, Heisman turned the tables by installing a devastating passing attack of his own, and won, 20–3. With Homer Cook effectively demonstrating what he could do with the pass, Tech completely dominated the second half. But the key player of the game, according to Heisman, was little Al Loeb, whose fighting spirit he revered. Heisman later reminisced about Loeb's role in this game. The Tech team, out on the field first, watched in awe as the huge Alabama squad appeared. But Al Loeb was unimpressed:

> "Huh," he scoffed. "Well, fellows, we've seen them. Can't help seeing them. But they're going to FEEL us. Yessir. We gotta make them feel us the first time we meet. And they gotta feel as if somebody had slapped them with the grand stand. Understand? We gotta get mad. Listen; I'm so mad right now after seeing the drove of beef that I'd—Oh, hell, tell them to start this game so I'll have something soft to bite."[7]

According to Heisman, Loeb's speech inspired his teammates, and they went on to win, 20–3. The inspirational example of Al Loeb was enhanced by the fact that he played the entire game with two broken bones in his hand.

On the occasion of a big win, Heisman once again took the opportunity to remind the team's followers just what it takes to build a winning combination in modern football:

Playing old-style football perhaps [Alabama] would have beaten us. But what business has a team of featherweights like ours playing old-time football? None whatever. We have to play open formations with an extremely varied attack, and be pretty good at the forward pass game. I think we have shown that we can adapt ourselves to the times and to conditions.[8]

The essence of Heisman's football philosophy is contained in this last sentence, stressing that to be successful at football you have to adapt to change. Because the game had been evolving so rapidly, the most successful teams, Heisman would contend, were those who had sufficiently adapted to meet the challenges of the new rules.

Next came the University of Florida in a game played in Jacksonville, and after the Gators tied the game on a long pass, Tech went on to win it in the second half, 14–7. Once again the season's hopes were high, but then came a three-game stretch against formidable foes Auburn, Sewanee, and Georgia with the usual results. Against the Tigers of Auburn, Tech confronted a battering offensive attack in the 27–7 loss that featured an 80-yard run in the second half by Auburn's Kirk Newell. The game with Sewanee was much closer, but the Purple capitalized on a Tech miscue when one of its players scooped up a fumble and returned it for the only score of the game to win, 7–0.

Even though the Bulldogs' lineup still featured the incomparable Bob McWhorter, this was the year that Tech followers figured it could beat Georgia. Their reasoning was based on comparative scores of the teams' respective games against Alabama, Tech having decisively defeated the Tuscaloosa team while Georgia had barely eked out a last-second win. But once again McWhorter proved himself too tough to stop, and Tech went down, 20–0. Three games had resulted in three losses, and Heisman's championship hopes, as well as those of Tech's followers, were dashed again.

Heisman must have been convinced by now that the talent he had to choose from was decidedly inferior to that of his more competitive opponents, as Vanderbilt again captured the Southern championship. Since 1904, the Commodores and Sewanee had dominated the region, but now Auburn was coming to the fore. Even after Tech's expected Thanksgiving victory over Clemson (23–0), Heisman was probably wondering what else he had to do to attract the kind of talent he needed to compete successfully against the kingpins of the conference.

THE NATIONAL GAME (1912)

The national team of the year was undefeated Harvard (9–0), which under Percy Haughton was into the school's longest unbeaten streak. (Over a thirty-three game stretch the Crimson would win thirty games and tie three.) Many of these wins were achieved through the dropkicking skills of the fabulous

Charley Brickley, whose accuracy was unequaled within the 40-yard line. Other top teams of the year were Wisconsin (7–0), winner of the Western Conference, Notre Dame (7–0), Penn State (7–0), and Carlisle (12–1–1). Vanderbilt again made a strong pitch for the improved quality of southern football with a close 9–3 loss to Harvard, the only defeat on its schedule. At this time Heisman could well be envious of the Tennessee school and its coach, whose winning ways kept attracting high quality talent.

Penn State attributed a great deal of its success to copying the offensive style of Carlisle, as in 1912 Pop Warner produced a system that would have tremendous impact on offensive play—the single-wingback formation. Generating a power attack behind well-timed blocking, the single-wing had evolved from Warner's Z-formation. Now the key to a successful offense called for a versatile halfback who could do the things Jim Thorpe was so good at—running, kicking, and passing. Shortly, the sportswriters would be referring to such a player as a "triple-threat tailback." Many schools would soon be switching over to this kind of attack as their coaches became convinced of its potential, particularly when Warner first unveiled his new system and trounced Army, 27–6.

HEISMAN AND THE 1913 SEASON

During the off-season, Heisman attempted to impress on his football players the necessity of staying in shape. In the January 1913 issue of *The Yellow Jacket* he wrote a rather lengthy and didactic piece on the roles of sacrifice and perseverance in an athlete's quest for success in both athletics and academics. According to Heisman, the way to succeed in both areas was essentially the same:

Even if your ambition for athletic excellence be the stronger of the two, don't lose sight of the fact that at an engineering institution you have positively got to be a student before you can be an athlete; that no matter how talented you may be in an athletic way it will count for nothing and you will never get a chance to flash your gem "of purest ray serene," unless and until you have done some flashing (and not flushing) in the classroom.[9]

In addition to keeping his football players up to par, both academically and physically, Heisman had other concerns during the off-season. There was the brand new basketball team, whose entire eight-game schedule was to be played during the month of February. In describing the team's progress prior to the season, Heisman took a more realistic approach than he had the previous year: "Basketball teams cannot be made from the ground up in a single season any more than can football teams, and we will all have to be patient."[10] This turned out to be a prophetic observation, as the team won only two games.

However, Heisman was highly pleased with the way the class games in football and basketball had come off. In picking an All-Class football team, he even singled out certain players for special praise in *The Yellow Jacket* with the hope, of course, that these men would be coming out for the varsity in the fall.

By spring he had once again turned his attention to baseball, presenting a progress report in the May issue of *The Yellow Jacket*. Having won two previous baseball championships at Tech (1906 and 1909), Heisman always displayed more than just an incidental interest in the promise of a new season. (Also, in serving as president of the Atlanta Baseball Association, he kept an eye open for any talent that might be worthy of the professional ranks.) Praising the physical condition of the Tech baseball diamond, he used the opportunity to express pride in the entire athletic complex, the project he had initiated upon his arrival in 1904. Urging the students to help keep the area free of rocks and debris, Heisman made it clear that he was depending on their support to make it "the very finest field in the entire South."[11]

He was especially proud of another part of the sports complex—the newly proposed track—that would provide an excellent showcase for Georgia Tech's growing emphasis on all athletics. Heisman wrote glowingly: "It is going to be an "A" No. 1 track. Nothing in the South will come anywhere near touching it. Think of its proportions!"[12] An ulterior motive on Heisman's part, of course, was that the new track would not only help attract quality athletes but motivate his football players who didn't participate in other spring sports to take part in track and field activities and help keep themselves in shape.

That September Heisman presented his outlook for the football season. He was unusually optimistic, due mainly to the incoming athletes who had been recruited according to the college spirit system he had implemented the previous year. It was a system that would soon result in the best teams of his career. Accordingly, Heisman was quite lavish in bestowing praise on those who had helped out: "Our athletic outlook for this year is, in my honest opinion, brighter than it has ever been before in the history of athletics at Tech. . . . And for this state of affairs we have no one to thank but ourselves. . . . Never have I seen every man at a college put shoulder to the wheel the way nearly all have done at Tech during the past eight months to bring about this better state of affairs."

But lest anyone happen to get a big head from such praise, Heisman went on to remind his followers that they still had a lot of hard work ahead in helping build a solid football team: "Fellows, it takes cooperation and work to get material, and after that it takes more cooperation and much more work to weld it and make it win." It was a message directed to Tech supporters as well as players, for to Heisman's way of thinking they were *all* on the same team.

Just how seriously Heisman took his leadership role in alerting Tech sup-

porters to their special involvement in helping mold a first-rate team is reflected in the emotionally strong words he expressed toward the end of his
article. To Heisman, his athletes had taken a solemn pledge to uphold the
honor of their school:

And . . . every man who secretly does break [this] pledge is, and should be regarded,
as a *traitor* and an enemy to Tech and to her best interests. And when I say that I
mean that any Tech man who at any time sees or hears of an athlete breaking the
training pledge he has signed it is his patriotic and true *duty* to let the athletic
authorities know what he knows, in order that the whole barrel may not be spoiled
by that one rotten apple. When you keep silent under such circumstances you are
"aiding and abetting a felony" against your college laws, against your Alma Mater's
very life.[13]

The results of the 1913 campaign, in which Tech won seven of nine games,
underscored the effectiveness of Heisman's recruiting system. But in losing
once again to both Auburn and Georgia, he was again prompted in another
of his pieces in *The Yellow Jacket* to rationalize the losses as the result of Tech's
inferior material and injuries to key players. Undaunted, though, he emphasized the need not to let up in pointing toward the next season. Appropriately, with the world situation being what it was at that time, Heisman
chose a prophetic image to get across his main point:

I am here to tell every Tech man that [our opponents] are not going to be content
to stand in 1914 just where they stood this fall with regard to material. They are
going to work their heads off to get on, *on*—ever on and forward, ever building for
the future. It's like the battleship-building race between England and Germany. These
two nations are never content with what ships they *have*; they both realize they must
continue building and getting *more, more,* if they wish to at all hold their own with
rival nations.

Heisman closed out his "sermon" in an emotionally charged manner that
clearly revealed his special feel for football as something more than a mere
game. Rather, to him the game of football offered both participants and
supporters a challenging experience through which they could learn to cope
with the exigencies of life itself. Thus Heisman reminded both his players
and supporters of their concomitant roles: "Don't fumble! Don't get discouraged! Put drive in your offense! Organize, cooperate! Fight like wildcats
on defense! Every man hustle for material! This is the game of football; this
is the battle of life."[14]

Georgia Tech's 7–2 record in 1913 earned it a third-place ranking after
SIAA champion Auburn and runner-up Georgia. The Tigers (8–0), intro-
ducing their battle cry "War Eagle!" went on to dominate the region after
this season by winning twenty-two of their next twenty-three games—
twenty-one by shutouts. In so doing, Coach Mike Donahue fashioned one

of Auburn's greatest eras on the gridiron. As a championship contender for the first time, the Yellow Jackets had defeated a surprisingly tough Florida team, 13–3, and followed up this victory with its most convincing win ever over Sewanee, 33–0. Highlighted by Homer Cook's 80-yard touchdown run in the opening minutes, the Sewanee game started fans contemplating a championship season at last. But then came shutout losses to Auburn (20–0) and Georgia (14–0), which, of course, eliminated Tech from the championship picture.

Nevertheless, there were a few bright moments in the loss to Auburn. During the first half, the Yellow Jackets had held Donahue's team to a scoreless tie, but then the championship-bound Tigers poured it on in the second half. In the Georgia contest, Bob McWhorter once again proved too hot for Tech to handle as he scored both Bulldog touchdowns. For the Yellow Jackets the only pleasant thing to recall about this game was that it would be the last time they would have to face McWhorter. However, the 32–0 Thanksgiving Day win over Clemson enabled the Yellow Jackets to finish third in the conference and salvage some degree of satisfaction.

Although it resulted in a loss, the Georgia game that year did help bring about an important rule change in 1914 concerning the neutral zone between opposing lines: "the neutral zone may not be encroached upon *until* the ball is put in play." Before this rule came into effect, many teams had been shifting players through the neutral zone prior to starting a play. In the 1913 Georgia–Georgia Tech game, for example, the Bulldogs had some of their linemen doing this with advantageous results. According to Heisman, "Before our linemen could get back into position Georgia would put the ball in play, catch us out of position and charge all over us." Heisman then wrote a letter to Walter Camp, who saw to it that a rule was enacted banning all players from the neutral zone *until* the ball is put in play.[15]

During that season, too, an incident occurred that underscored the increasingly irascible nature of John Heisman at this time in his life. Sports editor Morgan Blake of the *Atlanta Journal* had drawn a favorable comparison between Tech's quarterback and a star player for Vanderbilt. Unbelievably, Heisman took offense at the former Nashville newsman and admonished him: "You must be careful not to make so many Nashville references. Remember, you are in Atlanta now!" Although football schools had grown fiercely proud of the regions they represented, Heisman's comment was certainly uncalled for.

In his forties by now, there were growing signs that he was not getting along with his wife as well as he did when they had first arrived in Atlanta. This situation was probably due to his increased involvement in numerous public relations roles as well as his time-consuming athletic endeavors. Never one to cultivate intimate friendships, though, Heisman at this time seemed more attracted to solitary pursuits in his spare time. As *The Yellow Jacket* reporter put it in his profile of Heisman cited earlier: "His particular pleasures are playing the phonograph . . . playing chess, and reading on biology, anthropology, archaeology, and kindred sciences. He hopes some day to have both the time and money to poke both his nose and walking-stick among the famous ruins of the world."[16]

If any athletic coach fitted the description of an intellectual, it was certainly John Heisman, though he was never one to exhibit a narrowly specialized interest in a scholarly subject. Clearly, he commanded a wide range of pursuits, and throughout his life his versatility and diversity of interests continued to amaze all those with whom he came in contact. Heisman's versatility extended to the athletic field where his natural ability to motivate his players inspired one of his star performers, Al Loeb, to call him an outright "genius. He could take minimums and make them into maximums. . . . He did that with me."[17] Along with a handful of other coaches of his day, Heisman helped bring an air of respectability to the game of football, not only due to his understanding of the game as a builder of manhood but because of his scholarly manner as well.

THE NATIONAL GAME (1913)

From a national perspective, football had now achieved such popularity that by October 1913 it was competing with the World Series for attention. With big-game matchups growing more prominent, even more spectacular intersectional pairings would soon be in the offing. Percy Haughton's Harvard team, led by All-American halfback Eddie Mahan and fullback Charley Brickley, went undefeated again (9–0) and won the national title. When the incomparable Brickley kicked five field goals in the Yale game, a mass mania developed around the art of drop kicking, as children as well as prep school and college players all over the country attempted to emulate Brickley's heroic feats. With the mass-circulated magazines and the newspaper sports pages becoming highly sensitized to their audience's growing reverence of sports heroes, Charley Brickley was a natural subject for feature story emphasis.

This was also the year that future power Ohio State was admitted to the prospering Western Conference, but Chicago, at 7–0, was the champion of the region. Still as inventive as ever, Coach Alonzo Stagg came up with the first instance of the Statue of Liberty play, resulting in a near score against Minnesota. Originally referred to as the Cherry Picker, the play received its ultimate name from the way an offensive back held the ball up as though to pass while another back retrieved it and took off on a run. The tactical vision of a coach like Stagg was still proving that the play possibilities of football were limitless.

The most startling achievement of 1913, though, was produced by a then little-known college in Indiana called Notre Dame. When it went east and defeated Army, 35–13, for the Cadets' only loss that year, the little Catholic school demonstrated the devastating potential of the forward pass, which even by this time was still a little-used weapon. Notre Dame would finish up the season undefeated at 7–0. The story has been frequently told of how quarterback Gus Dorais and end Knute Rockne practiced during the summer previous to the game by hooking up on a well-timed passing combination and then during the game that fall springing the results on unsuspecting West Point. Although the Irish led at the half by just 14–13, the combination of Dorais and Rockne picked up the pace in the second half to win easily. By the end of the game, Dorais had completed fourteen of seventeen passes for 243 yards, an astounding statistic for that day. To be sure, the modern day of the forward pass had now arrived. Rockne, who was to go on to even greater fame as a coach, later concluded that the Notre Dame win of 1913 was the first real demonstration of the advantages that the open style of play had over the traditional closed style.

John Heisman, an unsung hero in overseeing the triumph of the forward pass, undoubtedly envisioned what the shocking Notre Dame victory meant for college football. The age of giant stadiums, boosterism, and bowl game mania was now imminent with the demonstrable success of the forward pass and a more open style of play. In just a few years, the 1920s would showcase big-time football as a highly glamorous sporting spectacle that would attract millions through the turnstiles every fall. It is an ongoing social phenomenon that has changed very little since that time.

HEISMAN AND THE 1914 SEASON

In the spring of 1914, Heisman once again turned his attention to baseball, and with the turnout of "well over 100 applicants for places" he was highly optimistic about the team's prospects. But his review of the season's results in June revealed that the campaign had not lived up to expectations: "Candor compels the statement that the team was one of the most erratic in its performances I have ever seen." Clearly more concerned about what the football season held for Tech that fall, he again issued an appeal for athletes according to the recruiting system he had implemented.[18]

The 1914 football season at Tech, while not particularly noteworthy in terms of its 6–2 record, is notable because this was the year the Yellow Jackets started out on their fabulous thirty-three-game unbeaten streak, one that would peak with Heisman's 1917 national championship team. During this period his concerted recruiting tactics would finally begin to pay off as Tech assembled one of its greatest aggregations of football players ever.

Heisman's characteristic emphasis on defense resulted in four shutout wins in 1914—South Carolina (20–0), Mercer (105–0), Sewanee (20–0), and Georgia (7–0). Of these, the most treasured victories, of course, were those over Sewanee and Georgia. The Georgia win was the first in five years over the Bulldogs, as Heisman at last appeared to be gaining the upper hand over this old foe. But the lopsided win over Mercer served to underscore Heisman's propensity for running up the score whenever he had the opportunity. It was also a harbinger of things to come, since the classic runaway game with Cumberland was just two years away.

Other big wins that year were over VMI (28–7) and Clemson (26–6). Defeats were administered by a surprising Alabama team (13–0) and, as usual, by Auburn (14–0). But the Tigers would be the last team to beat the Yellow Jackets until Pitt would win in the sixth game of the 1918 season. The 1914 game with Auburn was fairly close throughout, but Tech fumbled at three critical moments, one resulting in a first-half touchdown. Not until the final quarter did the Tigers score their second touchdown, but by then it was too late for the Yellow Jackets to pull the game out. Incidentally, this was the game in which the South got its first view of players with numbered jerseys, a practice that received instant approval, particularly from the sportswriters. At first, numerals were worn only on the back of jerseys, and it was not until 1937 that they were required on both front and back. (Washington and Jefferson College, one of Heisman's future coaching assignments, is reported to have first worn numerals as early as 1908.) In spite of Auburn's claim, Tennessee with its 9–0 record was awarded the SIAA championship.

THE NATIONAL GAME (1914)

In 1914 American optimism was at a high point with the official opening of the Panama Canal, an achievement that ranks among the greatest engineering feats of all time. Ten years in coming, the Canal exemplified what could be accomplished through large-scale collective methods, a system of construction that would become one of the hallmarks of twentieth-century technology. Even the advent of dire political events in eastern Europe, which would eventually plunge the world into an unprecedented global conflict, could not diminish the feeling of intense nationalism that spread throughout the country following the canal's opening. Likewise, the sports world was caught up in patriotic fervor, and the game of football, as an example of goal-oriented collective techniques in its own right, was destined to increase in popularity during this time.

Fittingly enough, a military school was the team of the year, as Army turned out its first all-victorious team (9–0). Mindful of what had happened in the previous year's game with Notre Dame, the Cadets dismantled the Irish this time around, 20–7. Players on this team, along with All-American center John McEwan, who would go on to greater fame, were future Tennessee coach Bob Neyland and future military leaders James Van Fleet and Omar Bradley. If the game of football could be interpreted as a metaphor for war, as many did, it was certainly proving its worth at this time as a training ground for men of military bent.

In 1914, Coach Bob Zuppke was serving his second year of a record twenty-nine-year tenure at Illinois, leading his team to an undefeated season (7–0).

Pioneering the backfield I-formation, Zuppke was a highly enthusiastic coach who leaned toward a lot of razzle-dazzle in his attack, particularly precision-like lateral passes that appeared as though they should have been stopped long before they resulted in long yardage gains. Other specialties of Zuppke were the screen pass and the hook and lateral, in which a pass receiver curled back to make a pass reception and then passed off to a trailing player. In ten years he would showcase a halfback named Red Grange who would create his own kind of razzle-dazzle.

By this year, too, football in the Southwest (an area that would figure auspiciously in John Heisman's future) had begun to make an impression as the University of Texas Longhorns came up with eight wins and no losses. That the day of the giant stadium had finally arrived was celebrated on the occasion of the first game to be played in the seventy-five thousand-seat Yale Bowl. Embarrassingly enough the game resulted in a 36–0 defeat of the Blue by Percy Haughton's Harvard Crimson, who at 7–0–2 were again undefeated. (Characteristic of college football over the years is the fact that it has never been a respecter of any sentimental favorite to win a game commemorating a special occasion.)

Although John Heisman had been experimenting with an offensive shift for a number of years, other coaches around the country were more influential at this time in bringing this tactic to national attention. Foremost were Dr. Henry Williams at Minnesota, Alonzo Stagg at Chicago, and Jesse Harper at Notre Dame. One of Harper's players, Knute Rockne, would refine the Notre Dame shift to his own specifications when he became coach of the Irish in 1918.

While most students of the game would credit Williams as the originator of the shift, a strong case can be made for Stagg, who was said to have been experimenting with some form of the shift as early as 1903 or 1904. Regardless, the Minnesota version of the shift was apparently the most efficient to be implemented in its prototypical form, and its success influenced a number of other schools to take up this system of attack. Split-second timing among the movement of the linemen was the key to the success of Williams's system. The result was a confused defense being out-manned at the point of attack, particularly during an era before the Rules Committee ordered a one-second stop by all members of the offense prior to the snap of the ball.

By the time Notre Dame took up the shift under Jesse Harper (around 1913–1914 and later under his pupil Rockne), the emphasis was on the back-field shifting from the T-formation to a box formation. In such a move, the defense could never be sure if a run or a pass was in the offing. While Heisman credited Williams for his innovations in this area of the game, Rockne would identify Stagg as the real father of the shift because of his influential experimentation in the early part of the century. Regardless of which coach should receive credit, it was the utilization of an offensive shift, as well as the forward pass, that added an exciting new open dimension to football. This development paved the way for a multitude of formations to follow and the national acceptance of the game as a highly appealing spectator sport.

HEISMAN AND THE 1915 SEASON

The year 1915 would turn out to be Heisman's most successful football campaign since his arrival at Tech. But in turning his attention to baseball prospects that spring in one of his articles in *The Yellow Jacket*, he dwelled at some length on the unpleasant subject of why coaches now had to cut players unsuited for varsity play. It would be a "fine thing," he wrote, if a coach could work indefinitely with every player who came out.

> But that is not the province of the salaried varsity coach. He is paid, not to teach everybody in a college how to play ball, but to take vigorous hold of a few of those who have already reached a certain stage of proficiency and do the very best he can with this limited few in a very limited time by molding them into the strongest varsity, or *first*, team that he can. [19]

That college football had now reached a high level of professionalism was attested to by the motivation of the salaried varsity coach, to use Heisman's term, in selecting his players; coaches tried to mold the strongest varsity team or winning combination they could, developing recruiting and training systems like that utilized by Heisman in the selection of candidates for his football team. Such highly competitive systems can be taken as an indication of the growing pressure to win that all salaried coaches were starting to feel at this time.

By this time in his coaching career, though, Heisman had seen enough players come and go that he had developed his own strict personal standards regarding the qualities that constituted a good athlete and a successful football player. In his 1922 book, *Principles of Football*, the rational side of Heisman came up with the following valuations of football players' "natural qualifications"[20]: Athletic talent (25 percent), aggressiveness (20 percent), mentality (20 percent), speed (20 percent), and weight (15 percent). At this point in his coaching career, Heisman was at last able to recruit more players who had the desired qualities in the right percentage amounts. As a result, he was getting closer to turning out the strongest varsity he had yet produced.

That the quality of players at Tech had reached a high level was confirmed by the turnout for the 1915 team. Even though the number of candidates was not as great as in previous seasons, Heisman had determined that his system would work more efficiently with fewer players as long as they were of high quality. He observed in the October 1915 issue of *The Yellow Jacket* "that we shall this year keep the squad down to about 60 in an endeavor to concentrate the coaching on a smaller number of promising men rather than diffuse it over a large class."[21]

Also because the 1915 schedule, according to Heisman, was "a hard one, quite the toughest Tech [has] ever faced," and because there were "more good teams in the South . . . than ever before," he took steps to beef up his coaching staff. In addition to his immediate assistant Bill Alexander, he hired a coach to handle the scrub team. He also appointed a line coach, who had been an assistant at the University of Michigan and "had much experience from one end of the line to the other. . . . [He] will, I feel confident, prove a most capable director of the linemen."[22] By this time the corporate nature of football had begun to dictate specialized coaching assignments. As Percy Haughton had done at Harvard, so Heisman was taking the initiative to respond to this fast-developing aspect of the game, actually another sign of its growing professionalization. However, his characteristic optimism about the upcoming season was tempered by his usual note of caution as he warned students and supporters alike against the overconfidence that had preceded the shocking loss to Alabama in the previous season.

But with the anticipated completion of Tech's expanded athletic complex, Heisman had good cause to be enthusiastic about the Yellow Jackets' fortunes. In the article cited above, he boldly proclaimed the project as "the best athletic field in the entire south," one that would greatly enhance Tech's future athletic endeavors. In 1913, Atlanta businessman John W. Grant had donated $50,000 for the expansion of the stands that the students had originally designed and constructed upon Heisman's arrival in 1904. Grant stipulated that the new stadium be named the Hugh Inman Grant field in memory of his deceased son, and in ensuing years, the original stadium site, which originally seated fifty-six hundred, was periodically added on to until by 1925, it had a capacity of thirty thousand. (Today the stadium has been expanded to more than twice this capacity and renamed in honor of a later Tech coach, Bobby Dodd.)

Because of Grant's philanthropy the momentum for establishing giant stadiums in the South was put in motion, and the next several years saw the erection and expansion of football facilities throughout the region. In 1915, though, the act of donating private money for the improvement of an athletic complex was practically unheard of. So Heisman was highly moved by Grant's generosity: "I am certain that I echo the sentiment that pervades the heart of every Tech man, past, present and future, when I say that we are duly appreciative of Mr. Grant's benefactions, and that we will ever try to prove ourselves worthy of such a superb gift as Grant Field."[23]

As was still customary, Heisman had scheduled three October tuneup games, and the runaway matches with Mercer (52–0) and Transylvania (67–0) went according to plans. But the contest with Davidson turned out to be entirely different, for by the end of the first half Tech found itself on the short end of a 7–0 score. Everett Strupper, freshman safety man for Tech, had fumbled a first-quarter punt, and a Davidson player had scooped up the ball and run it in for a touchdown. Strupper would go on to become one of

Tech's greatest running backs, but his miscue was sufficient for Heisman to lash out at his players during halftime, inciting them to come back in the second half and win handily, 27–7.

On October 23, even the social distractions of New Orleans didn't seem to phase Strupper and fullback Tommy Spence as they led the Yellow Jackets to an easy 36–7 win over Louisiana State University (LSU). But Coach Heisman was not to be so fortunate during this game: After becoming involved in another of his patented arguments with the officials, he was escorted off the field by the police, much to the amusement of the partisan fans.

In the next game against the University of North Carolina, Strupper came into his own, running for two touchdowns as Tech defeated the Carolina Tar Heels, 23–3. The Yellow Jackets' rock-ribbed defense held Carolina to only one first down throughout the game. Even so, Heisman must have had an eye on the upcoming game with Alabama, which had become something of a vengeance match because of Tech's upset loss the previous year.

Once again, Everett Strupper came through, leading the Yellow Jackets to a convincing 21–7 victory. But it was Alabama that came up with the most sensational play of the day when the Tide's one-man gang, Bully Vandergraaf, started out on an end run with the entire Tech defense in hot pursuit. Stopping suddenly in his tracks, Vandergraaf fired the ball back across the field to a player who, with no defenders around him, dashed sixty yards for Alabama's only score of the day. Because of its natural tendency toward wide-open play, the pass, whether forward or lateral, was proving itself a formidable, if sometimes unpredictable, weapon.

With Heisman and his supporters now thinking toward possibly winning the Southern championship, Tech went into the Georgia game a heavy favorite. The fact that the game was played in a deluge undoubtedly had something to do with the disappointing 0–0 outcome. The fleet Yellow Jacket backs, having great difficulty with their footing, were kept bottled up; and, of course, in that day a passing game under such conditions was out of the question. But for the Bulldogs the situation proved ideal, as they set up a stubborn defense and turned loose a pile-driving fullback who at one point in the game had been the brunt of attack in moving the ball down to Tech's 10-yard line. At that point Heisman pulled one of his greatest defensive moves. He sent Canty Alexander, a defensive lineman, into the game to take the place of a tiring lineman the Georgia backs had been running all over. Known for his ferocious defensive manner in goal-line situations, Alexander wasted little time in proving his worth and the wisdom of Heisman's judgment as he personally stopped Georgia's line bucks four straight times.[24] It was a one-man defensive show, and instead of a defeat, Tech walked off the field with a tie and its undefeated string, now standing at nine games, still intact. Better yet, its shot at the Southern championship was still alive.

In the final game of that momentous season, which was played in Atlanta on Thanksgiving Day, Tech came away with a 7–0 win over Auburn, only the second time in the series that the Yellow Jackets had defeated the Tigers. Once again, Everett Strupper was the offensive star as he dashed for a 25-yard touchdown in the first half, a score that held up for the remainder of the game. The Tigers' most serious bid was halted on the 6-inch line.

With its 7–0–1 record, Heisman's 1915 team expected to be crowned SIAA champions. But Vanderbilt, although they had been beaten by Virginia, also entered a claim to the title. As a result no decision was ever made, which unfortunately was usually the case in those days when conference officials could not come up with a clear-cut winner. Heisman now realized that if he were ever to produce a championship team at Tech, then he had to put together a powerhouse that would decisively defeat all comers to win the championship outright. Accordingly, at this point in his coaching career John Heisman was building what would be his strongest team in his quest for a championship.

THE NATIONAL GAME (1915)

At the national level, Cornell claimed the championship by posting its first perfect season (9–0). Led by All-American quarterback Charley Barrett, the Big Red helped its cause in the year's biggest game by defeating All-American Eddie Mahan and his Harvard team, 10–0, and at the same time ending the Crimson's thirty-three-game unbeaten string.

With its football program now enduring its worst days, Pop Warner departed Carlisle this year and went to the University of Pittsburgh, where he turned in a surprising undefeated season (8–0) his first year. Compiling a string of thirty-one wins, Warner's Pitt teams never lost during the first three years of his tenure.

In other areas of the country, Nebraska, laying the foundation for an illustrious gridiron reputation, produced an all-victorious season (8–0) and extended its record since 1911 to 35–2–3. In the process the Huskers won the Missouri Valley Conference six straight times. But it was in this year's Notre Dame match that Nebraska won national recognition for the first time. Sparked by all-conference halfback Guy Chamberlain, the Huskers came back after trailing at the half, 13–7, to defeat the Irish, 20–19.

The University of Oklahoma also began to attract attention during this time, mainly due to its proficient passing attack, which was the main factor in producing a 10–0 season in 1915. Pioneering the option pass/run, the Sooners were unique for their day in that they averaged thirty passes a game.

The year 1915 was significant for football in the southwestern area, too, as the Southwest Conference was founded. It was composed of charter members Arkansas, Baylor, LSU (soon replaced by Rice, one of Heisman's future coaching stations), Oklahoma (replaced by Southern Methodist University), Oklahoma A&M (replaced by Texas Christian University), Southwestern (which soon dropped out), Texas, and Texas A&M. By this point in its forty-five-year history, college football had entrenched itself in every section of the country.

Other important developments saw the Rose Bowl, the prototype of all the annual bowl games, officially come into being, with Brown selected to face Washington State. Ironically, the Washington State Cougars were picked to play in this bowl game over Coach Gil Dobie's Washington Huskies, who at 7–0 had extended their amazing unbeaten streak. Although Brown featured the play of halfback Fritz Pollard, one of the first great black players, and future coach Wallace Wade, the Cougars won 14–0 before seven thousand fans in the rain. This was also the year when wearing numbered jerseys became standard practice. Signifying the growing need for an official to oversee downfield decisions and to keep a precise account of the time, the field judge became a permanent fixture in game officiating this year.

This era was propitious for the emergence of the black football player. Up until this time black athletes had a difficult time in gaining acceptance on the field of competition at predominantly white institutions. Following the sporadic success of football players like William Henry Lewis at Amherst and Harvard and halfback George Jewett, who played for Michigan in 1890, other black players began to find their way northward. By 1900, in fact, blacks playing at northern schools were no longer a novelty. Nevertheless, racial incidents persisted. Indeed, some schools, particularly those in the South, would not play a team that fielded black players, although there were seldom more than two on a squad. (Observe how Heisman's 1923 Washington and Jefferson team, which was scheduled to play a southern school, reacted to this problem, in chapter 5.)   To ensure increased opportunity and greater recognition and representation for their players, a number of black schools banded together in 1912 to form their own intercollegiate conference.

Due to inadequate training and poor facilities at racially segregated high schools, most black players came to college woefully lacking in game fundamentals. But the natural abilities and competitive instincts of athletes like Fritz Pollard and Princeton's Paul Robeson were exceptional enough to transcend the boundaries of race and belie the views of white supremacists.

Pollard, the first black running back named to Walter Camp's All-America team (1916), was a study in contrasts to Robeson. Whereas Pollard was small in stature and not much given to studious pursuits, Robeson entered Princeton (which traditionally had maintained all-white athletic programs) on an academic scholarship. A superb physical specimen, Robeson exhibited astonishing versatility as not only an end in football but also as a basketball star and world-class performer in track and field. He would go on to earn a Phi Beta Kappa key, perform as a leading operatic singer and actor, and become a controversial figure in the civil rights movement. The trail-blazing examples of Pollard and Robeson, each in his own way, would inspire many young blacks to follow in their footsteps even though the trail would prove a treacherous one, full of pitfalls for those daring enough to try to better their lot over the next several decades.

HEISMAN AND THE 1916 SEASON

With "some forty men [on hand] who possess undoubted football talent and who have been more or less well grounded in the theory of the game,"[25] Heisman approached the 1916 season with more than his usual share of optimism. Yet in beating perenially weak sister Mercer, 61–0, in the first game of the season, Heisman's charges, in spite of the lopsided score, never came close to the stride they would hit in the following week's game on October 7 against Cumberland. In that game, when the dust finally settled on Grant Field, the Yellow Jackets had rolled up the biggest point total in football history.

The game itself has been referred to as the funniest, strangest, most bizarre, if not the most mismatched football game ever played. According to Heisman in a 1928 *Collier's* article, his players had an ulterior motive in doing what they did:

"If you boys don't lick Cumberland by 50 points," said Bill Alexander, my assistant coach, "you ought to be whipped."

"If we score 100 will you set 'em up for the gang, Alex?" cried Strupper, one of our halfbacks.

"I'll set 'em up for the varsity scrubs and the frosh if you make it 200," grinned Alex.

Alex then left on a scouting trip. He must have felt faint when he read the newspapers. The score was Georgia Tech 222, Cumberland 0.[26]

The final score represented thirty-two touchdowns (the inspired Everett Strupper scored eight of them) and eighteen consecutive extra points in the first half alone (kicked by Jim Preas)—all are national records that still stand. While Georgia Tech recorded twenty first downs, Cumberland, unable to move the ball when it had possession, failed to register a single first down. Its biggest rushing gains were two 5-yard runs, while it managed to complete two of fifteen passes for fourteen yards (six of these were intercepted, five for touchdowns.) Not having to, Tech, of course, threw no passes and piled up a total of 501 rushing yards to −42 for Cumberland.

Once-proud Cumberland, in the process of disbanding football due to financial problems but eager to collect a $500 guarantee, showed up in Atlanta with a hastily recruited group of players, who were obviously not anticipating playing one of the strongest teams in the South. And as it turned out, the game was a total mismatch from beginning to end. By the end of the first quarter the Yellow Jackets found themselves ahead by 63–0, and the score was 126–0 at the half. At this juncture, the Cumberland players were undoubtedly ready to throw in the towel, for as Heisman humorously recalled the situation:

As you may suspect, Cumberland lost considerable interest in proceedings after Tech had scored her first hundred points and was inclined to let matters take whatever course they might. Among those enjoying it least were the Cumberland backs. All any one of them had to do to be subjected to a thorough going over was to receive the ball; and presently none of the Cumberland men appeared to care where the ball was—as long as it wasn't near them.

Once a Cumberland halfback found himself possessed of it. Instantly he was tackled so hard that he and the ball separated. It rolled toward the other halfback. One of Cumberland's ends yelled: "Fall on it, Pete, fall on it."

Pete looked at the fellow with infinite scorn. "Fall on it yourself—I didn't fumble it."[27]

Despite the overwhelming score at this point, though, Heisman was in no mood to show mercy as he told his charges during halftime: "Men, we're in front, but you never know what those Cumberland players have up their sleeves. So, in the second half, go out and hit 'em clean and hit 'em hard. Don't let up."[28]

Nevertheless, they did let up but just barely, adding another 96 points to their already momentous total, even though the final two quarters were cut to twelve and a half minutes each. In the third quarter when Strupper scored his seventh touchdown of the day for a 154–0 lead, Tech became the highest-scoring college football team of all time, surpassing Michigan's 153 point total against a practice opponent during Fielding Yost's tenure. By the end of the third quarter the score stood at 180–0, at which point the game should have been called, but the Yellow Jackets went on to pile up 42 more meaningless points. Naturally, most of the records set that day have stood the test of time: biggest score, greatest number of touchdowns and points after, highest score for a single quarter and half, most points kicked after touchdown by one player (Jim Preas established this record in the first half as three players divided the point-after chores in the second half, making twelve out of fourteen attempts), and greatest number of players scoring (twelve). Never having to punt, Tech gained over five-hundred yards in both punt and kickoff returns, with total all-purpose yards totaling 1,179.

Since the game was considered just another warmup contest that schools of that day were accustomed to scheduling, the Atlanta newspapers thought so little of the one-sided game that they devoted no more than a column of space to it. But later on, Heisman claimed he had a special reason for giving no quarter and instructing his players to amass all those points. He had a bone to pick with all the sportswriters who relied too much on football's statistics to make useless comparisons in publicizing teams and determining national rankings. So according to Heisman, the joke was on them. As he commented in the 1917 Tech yearbook,

> The writer has often contended that this habit on the part of sport writers of totaling up, from week's end to week's end, the number of points each team had amassed in its various games, and comparing them one with another, was a useless thing, for it means nothing whatever in the way of determining which is the better of an evenly grouped set of college teams. . . .
> Accordingly, in the Cumberland game the Jackets set all their sails to make a record run, and for the first time in our football career we turned loose all we had in the way of scoring stuff, and the result was a world's record of 222 points rolled up in 45 minutes of play. [The last quarter was called with five minutes to play.][29]

According to Gene Griessman there was actually another reason for Heisman's running up the score—a grudge. In a letter one of Heisman's players wrote:

> The reason for the high score was a grudge that existed between [Heisman] and Dan McGugin, who was the football coach at Vanderbilt. The year before, Vanderbilt played a rather weak schedule and ran up some high scores on weak teams. By this, he gained a lot of publicity and it got under coach's skin.[30]

Heisman also insisted that the opening game with Mercer, won by the Yellow Jackets, 61–0, was an experiment in which he wanted to see how much scoring his team could produce by running only through the middle of the line.

All experiments were off, though, when Heisman and his charges played the Davidson Wildcats on the following Saturday. As usual when they took on Tech, the Davidson players seemed to be at their inspired best, and at the half the score stood as a surprising scoreless tie. In the second half, though, Jim Senter, Everett Strupper, and Tommy Spence finally got on track, and the Yellow Jackets pulled out a hard-fought 9–0 win.

Another tough game was in store when Tech hosted North Carolina the following week. In this one, the "S" boys were not so fortunate. Strupper, who had scored on a 60-yard run to help lead the Yellow Jackets to a 10–0 advantage, was injured and had to leave the game. Next the hard-driving Senter broke his leg, and after Spence, an all-southern back, hurt his neck, Heisman realized that the depth of his team would be put to the test. At this point, the Tar Heels generated a successful drive to make the score 10–6. Then another drive stalled at the Tech 10-yard line, but a poor Yellow Jacket punt gave the ball right back to Carolina on the 15-yard line. A couple of plays later, the Tar Heels had a first down on the 5-yard line, but instead of running, the quarterback tried a pass, which fell incomplete. At that time, an incomplete pass over the goal line reverted back to the other team's possession. But for some reason the official became confused and awarded the ball to Carolina, only to see an irate Heisman charge out onto the field to straighten the matter out. Tech had won another game, but just barely.

Close matches had become the order of the day, and when Washington and Lee came to Atlanta on October 28, Tech found itself in another dogfight. The W&L Generals were one of the South's tougher teams, and defeat seemed likely early in the game as Tech's stage fright allowed W&L to penetrate to the 10-yard line. At this point, Heisman called on his old reliable, Canty Alexander, to stop the attack, and once again the feisty tackle rose to the occasion to help throw back four successive plays. But after Strupper's punt was blocked, Tech had to hold again, only to see Strupper's next punt also blocked, giving W&L possession on the 20-yard line. Following a fake line buck and end run, the ball wound up on the 2-yard line, from where the Generals scored to take the lead, 7–0.

It was beginning to look as though it would not be Tech's day, and Heisman could sense it. Especially after the Yellow Jackets moved the ball to the 15-yard line, where they tried a field goal with a drop kick, only to see the ball hit the upright, fall to the cross bar, dribble along it, and finally fall off on the wrong side. But during halftime, the Heisman "school spirit" magic apparently took hold again as the Tech men came back strong defensively, mustering enough offense to allow Strupper to pass for the tying score, and the game ended in a 7–7 tie. It was the second tie in his undefeated streak, but Heisman's men had shown they could hold up against the onslaught of a team considered by many to be their superior.

As though a premonition of things to come, Tech closed out the 1916 season with four convincing wins. After hammering Tulane, 45–0, the Yellow Jackets went against an Alabama team that at first appeared to have figured out how to stop Heisman's jump shift cold: move the defense with the offensive shift and wait for the play to develop. In spite of this maneuver, though, the Tech men had enough offense to win out in the end, 13–0.

Now the championship of the South depended on the outcome of the Tech–Georgia game, which was to be played on November 18 in Athens. Although both teams were unbeaten, Tech was the betting favorite. Because Georgia had scouted the Alabama game, Heisman fully expected the Bulldogs to come up with a similar defensive system to halt his jump shift. In order to counter their strategy, the wily coach directed his backs to move in the opposite direction from which the shift was normally meant to go. As a result, when the game was underway the Georgia defense became hopelessly confused, especially after it stopped shifting with the jump, only to see Tech return to its original system.

However, the turning point of the game came when Heisman sent in the ever-dependable Canty Alexander to shore up the defense after Georgia wound up with the ball on Tech's 5-yard line as the result of a poor punt. Playing his usual stubbornly determined role, Alexander managed to rally his teammates to hurl back the Bulldog attack four times in a row. After that, it was Katy bar the door, as Tommy Spence and Everett Strupper alternated in moving the ball down field for the first touchdown, eventually adding two more for a 21–0 victory.

With the Yellow Jackets blasting Auburn, 33–7, in their Thanksgiving Day classic, Georgia Tech finally won the SIAA championship uncontested. In accounting for its big win, the Yellow Jackets had put the game on ice in the second quarter by scoring three touchdowns. In going nineteen games without a loss, Tech had managed to beat Auburn two years in a row for the first time. But despite Tech's tremendous success in 1916 and the attendant jubilation of Heisman and his supporters over winning the Southern championship, the best was yet to come.

THE NATIONAL GAME (1916)

The national teams of the year were Pitt and Army, both undefeated, but Helms awarded Pitt (8–0) the championship. Pitt's Pop Warner, who by this time was tiring of the single-wingback with which he had enjoyed so much success, was starting to experiment with his inevitable variation—the double-wingback. The result was an offense characterized by a plethora of fakes and reverses that could be run to either side of the line, as well as increased passing possibilities because of the number of receivers available.

Led by All-American halfback Elmer Oliphant, unbeaten Army (9–0) defeated Notre Dame, 30–10. An all-round athlete, Oliphant came to West Point from Purdue where he had been a four-sport man. At West Point he also participated in boxing, swimming, and hockey, in addition to football. His six touchdowns and 45 points scored that year against Villanova still stand as West Point records.

One of the year's biggest upsets was engineered by up-and-coming Illinois coach Bob Zuppke as he concocted a way to stop the Minnesota shift and beat the Gophers, 14–9, to hand them their only loss of the season.

Yale, under its new coach Tad Jones, won all its games except the one against Brown as Fritz Pollard scored three times in the second half to down the Blue, 21–6. This was also the year of the Harvard game when Jones delivered his famous pep talk that started off: "You are now going out to play football against Harvard. Never again in your whole life will you do anything so important."[31] His words worked their magic as Yale beat the Crimson for the first time in seven years, 6–3.

With halfback Chic Harley at the helm, Ohio State went undefeated for the first time (7–0). He single-handedly beat Illinois (7–6) and Wisconsin (14–13) as he scored touchdowns and then kicked extra points to win both games for the Buckeyes.

This was the year, too, that the Pacific Coast Conference got underway with charter members California, Oregon, Oregon State, and Washington signing up. Stanford and Washington State would join the following year;

Idaho and Southern Cal in 1922; Montana in 1924; and UCLA in 1929. With another game in the revived Rose Bowl series to be played, football was now fairly well established in the West. In this year's match between Oregon and Penn, the Ducks of Oregon came out on top, 14–0. Future sports luminaries playing for Penn were quarterback Bert Bell, who would become commissioner of the National Football League, and tackle Lou Little, who would return to the Rose Bowl as coach of the Columbia Lions in 1934 and defeat Stanford in an upset, 7–0.

That some peculiar aspects of football's rules still needed overhauling in 1916 was attested to by an incident that decided the outcome of the Georgia–Auburn game. Played in Columbus, Georgia, where this matchup would continue to be scheduled until 1959, the close game was won by the Tigers, 3–0, when they kicked a 45-yard field goal that had been teed-up on a helmet! Although Georgia questioned the legality of the play, it was allowed to stand by the officials as just one more unexpected development the Rules Committee would have to look into.

HEISMAN AND THE 1917 SEASON

In climax to the unsettled European conditions of the past several years, in 1917 the United States was thrust into the war it had been trying to avoid but could no longer. The sinking of the British ocean liner *Lusitania* in May 1915 had brought the United States and Germany to the brink of war, but when German submarines sank three U.S. ships President Woodrow Wilson asked Congress in April 1917 to declare war. By May the conscription of men between the ages of twenty-one and thirty was underway. The impact on college football was immediate.

Ironically, preparation in the South for the 1917 season was more widespread than it had ever been before. Football was still growing in popularity year by year, and with many of the football-playing schools committed to enhancing their images, they were now putting more money into coach's salaries and athletic-support equipment. But dissension was dividing the member schools of the SIAA. It resulted from a quarrel over a proposed ruling that would require all athletes, mainly freshmen, to be in residence for a year before they could play. Most northern schools had made interinstitutional agreements restricting freshman eligibility, but in the South it was still a problem. To restrict the eligibility of freshmen would definitely hurt the smaller schools, for with fewer players to choose from they needed their freshmen athletes to help field a complete team.

But it was the call to arms that had begun to dominate everyone's thoughts, and particularly Georgia Tech football players' plans. Should they answer the call or stay in school? Since patriotic fervor characterized the reaction of most of these men, it wasn't long before nearby Camp Gordon was brimming over with former football players applying for officer candidate school. The game of football was thought by some to be a training ground for war, and those gladiators who had performed admirably on the gridiron were considered to be prime contenders for battle. Harvard coach Percy Haughton, who would serve as an Army officer, later wrote: "Football is a miniature war game played under somewhat more civilized rules of conduct, in which the team becomes the military force of the school or university it represents. Most of the combat principles of the Field Service Regulations of the U.S. Army are applicable to the modern game of football."[32] But those who marched off to war would quickly realize that the horrors of the battlefield itself greatly overshadowed the ephemeral skirmishes of the football field. An early casualty of the war was Georgia Tech's own Tommy Spence, who had trained as an aviator and was killed in Europe. As Tech's first athlete to die in combat, Spence's tragic death helped drive home the grim reality of the war.

However, Heisman had his own viewpoints about how a young man in college should cope with the temptation to volunteer, contending that a student could best serve his country by staying in school and awaiting his call. To back up his stand, the erudite coach quoted the duke of Wellington's famous line—the battle of Waterloo had been won on the playing fields of Eton and Harrow. Nevertheless, there were those who were critical of Heisman, charging that he was purposely trying to keep his players from joining the armed forces. These same critics were undoubtedly also aware of Heisman's Germanic origins. But Bill Fincher, one of the players on this 1917 team, called the basis for these charges "absurd" and "a lot of hogwash." Fincher went on to say: "I never heard Heisman say a word against volunteering. Fact is, after the 1917 season only three players did not go into service. I was rejected because I had only one eye. Another guy had a physical disability, and [Indian Joe] Guyon, oddly enough, was said to be an alien."[33]

Nevertheless, by the fall of 1917, Heisman had assembled a group of young men that for many years would be considered the greatest football team the South had ever produced. It won all nine of its games, seven of them by shutouts, scoring 491 points to the opposition's 17. In fact, over Tech's last five games for that year, the team averaged an astounding 72 points a game. What's more, not only did Georgia Tech win another SIAA championship, the team was declared national champion, the first southern team to claim the honor.

Much of Heisman's success that year can be attributed to the backfield he put together, consisting of quarterback Al Hill, halfbacks Everett Strupper (who had certainly proven his worth in previous campaigns), Indian Joe Guyon (a transfer from Carlisle), and fullback Judy Harlan. A strong case could be made for this group as the greatest backfield a southern school has ever assembled. The line was one of the best ever, too, with Cy Bell and Ray Ulrich at the ends, Bill "Big Six" Carpenter and Bill Fincher at tackles, Dan Whelchel and Ham Dowling at guards, and Pup Phillips at center. Of these players, Strupper and Carpenter were the first players from the Deep South to be named to a national All-America team in 1917. (With America at war in 1917, Walter Camp himself did not select his All-America team; and in 1918, he chose an All-Service team made up of players from military training camps.)

One of Heisman's favorite players, Bill Carpenter, performed with a sense of dedication that was hard to match. As Heisman wrote: "On three of Georgia Tech's greatest teams Bill Carpenter—Big Six—played right tackle in the manner that makes coaches believe that life is good. Even the coaches of the teams we walloped were given to saying that it was worth a beating to watch Bill."[34] Heisman then told how Carpenter was advised to quit football after suffering an internal injury during the 1916 season that resulted in the removal of one of his kidneys. So intent was he on playing the 1917 season, however, that he countered the opinions of his doctor, the Georgia Tech president, and even the governor of the state, who happened to be chairman of the board of trustees to whom Carpenter had made his last appeal to play. Upon hearing his case and realizing just how dedicated Carpenter was, the governor relented and allowed him to play, wishing "God and good luck" to be with him.

Surely one of the most colorful players Heisman ever coached was Indian Joe Guyon. An assistant coach for the Yellow Jacket team during this era was a personable fellow named Charley "Wahoo" Guyon, whom Heisman had hired from Carlisle. As a result, his brother Joe, who had been a star running back at Carlisle for several years, showed up on campus in 1917 ready to perform for the Yellow Jackets. And a formidable performer Guyon proved to be, as his play over the next two seasons attest. (He would go on to become one of the pioneer players in professional football.)

But Indian Joe was as notable for his wacky behavior as he was for his outstanding athletic performances. Teammate Judy Harlan in his later years offered some insights into Guyon's eccentric personality: "Once in a while the Indian would come out in Joe, such as the nights Heisman gave us a white football and had us working out under the lights. That's when Guyon would give out with the blood-curdling war whoops." And according to Harlan, Guyon was not above using a few old Indian tricks, either. Like the time in 1917 when he knocked out a W&L player by wearing an old horse collar shaped into a shoulder pad but reinforced with a little steel.[35]

A major reason for Heisman's 1917 success was that he now possessed the perfect material for executing the jump shift that he had been experimenting with for about a decade. Although some of today's football fans may think the I-formation and T-formation are of recent development, these later formations are really derivatives of a system like Heisman used during the 1917 season. As Al Thomy describes the 1917 Yellow Jacket attack,

First the Jackets lined up in the I, with Harlan, Guyon, and Strupper in a straight line behind Hill. Center Phillips stood erect, hands on hips, looking over his shoulder.

When he saw teammates in line, he bent over the ball, and that was the signal to shift to the T.

The shift barely preceded the snap of the ball—usually a direct snap to Strupper who went to his left or right behind the interference of three backs and two guards, a five-man convoy.[36]

According to New York sportswriter George Trevor, the Tech attack was something awesome to behold: "At the shift signal, the phalanx deployed with the startling suddenness of a Jeb Stuart cavalry raid."[37] But Heisman himself admitted to having difficulty in coming up with the proper signal system to get a shift play off and running:

At first the quarterback would set the shift . . . in motion by barking "Now" or "Shift" whereat all those required to "shift" would move with the rhythmic hop, step or skip to their new positions in so many synchronized counts. Then, at a new command, the ball would be snapped. To start my own shift we used "Now" but presently we found our opponents committing sabotage on our nice machinery by calling "Now" at frequent and disconcerting intervals.

Inasmuch as that situation demanded quick remedy I substituted a sight signal. My center would stand erect. All the other players would watch his head. The instant he started to bend forward, the shift would start. It worked beautifully and I am quite sure that many of our opponents never did unravel the mystery.[38]

The first to feel the sting of the Yellow Jacket attack in 1917 was not one team but two, as Tech took on both Wake Forest and Furman on the same day. There is no explanation as to why Heisman found himself having to face two teams on the same date, except that there must have been some kind of scheduling conflict and the Tech coach felt bound to honor his commitments. Or Heisman could actually have felt confident enough to take on these two teams on the same day, as talented as his players were. At any rate, Wake Forest fell 33–0 in the opening contest, and then Furman, against whom Heisman used only second-string players (with the exception of his quarterback Al Hill) went down, 25–0. Undefeated now in twenty-one straight contests, the 1917 Yellow Jackets were off and running toward regional honors. But it was the October 6 match, when Penn was scheduled to come south for the first time, that focused the national spotlight on Atlanta.

Until this time, southern teams had not fared well against northern opponents. Dan McGugin's Vanderbilt Commodores had given a good account of themselves in losing close matches to Michigan in 1906, 1907, and 1911. They had also come up with ties against Navy in 1907 and Yale in 1910. But only Virginia had turned in a win against a major northern school by pummeling Yale in 1915, 10–0.

Now it was Georgia Tech's turn to face a northern team, and ironically enough that team represented Coach Heisman's alma mater—a nationally ranked team that was heavily favored, mainly because it boasted four players of All-America caliber. These included quarterback Bert Bell and a pile-driving fullback named Howard Berry. It soon became obvious, however, that the Yellow Jackets had not paid much attention to the newspapers' predictions, as on the game's first play Everett Strupper streaked sixty-eight yards around left end for a touchdown. To the delight of ten thousand fans Heisman's jump shift was clicking on all cylinders that day, and by the half his men led, 20–0. In the meantime Penn's main offensive weapon, Berry, was stopped cold. By the end of the game Strupper had scored twice, Hill three times, and Judy Harlan, in his first varsity action, had intercepted a Bert Bell pass and had run it back seventy yards for a score. With Fincher making good on five extra points, the Yellow Jackets enjoyed a satisfying 41–0 victory. What's more, Heisman's team now found itself basking in the national limelight for the first time. After all the years of SIAA championship anticipation, on that memorable afternoon in Atlanta Tech supporters now had real cause to celebrate national aspirations.

It was in this same Penn game that Tech inherited its most colorful nickname. With the devastating defeat of the Quakers and the resultant national attention, Morgan Blake of the *Atlanta Journal* wrote of the "Golden Tornado attack" that had so handily beaten the northern visitors. The Golden Tornado tag soon gained favor with both the students and the public, and it didn't begin to fade from popularity until after the advent of Bobby Dodd's 1952 Sugar Bowl team.[39]

But Heisman knew only too well that a letdown could easily follow a big win, especially when the next opponent was a team that had always given the Yellow Jackets a rough time—Davidson. Accordingly, with their sensational back Buck Flowers running wild, the Wildcats of Davidson got off to a good start and even led for a while. But they soon fell to the Yellow Jackets' superior manpower as Tech went on to win, 32–10. Nevertheless, Davidson's point total was the highest that would be scored on Tech in a game that year.

After this test the flood gates were opened as the Yellow Jackets, led by Al Hill, overwhelmed one of the previous year's toughest teams, 63–0. Next, Vanderbilt suffered the worst football defeat in its history, 83–0. In this game the Tech backfield was so difficult to contain that it never failed to gain, and Bill Fincher kicked eleven out of eleven extra point attempts. As most onlookers found it hard to believe that a Dan McGugin team could be beaten so thoroughly, they had to concede that John Heisman had indeed put together a team of national championship caliber, a team that could defeat any it played.

When the once-heralded Carlisle team came to Atlanta on November 10, any doubt about Tech's potential as a national power was erased as the Yellow Jackets demolished the Indians, 98–0. The score could have been even higher except that the game had to be called in the final quarter when Carlisle ran out of substitutes. It was thought that the outcome of this game helped to close the doors of the proud Indian school, which during its brief career had so many grand and glorious accomplishments on the gridiron. But the times were now changing at too rapid a pace for a school like Carlisle to keep up with its more fortunate competitors.

Having earlier shut out Tulane, 48–0, Heisman's best team to date was looking to capture another Southern championship as Tech prepared to meet traditional foe Auburn. With Everett Strupper and Indian Joe Guyon well in command, the game, like all played that memorable season, wasn't even close. The Yellow Jackets won, 68–7, as Auburn endured one of its worst defeats ever.

Georgia Tech, of course, won the 1917 Southern championship, but in the previous week the Auburn Tigers had played a key role in helping the Yellow Jackets gain legitimate recognition for their first national championship. In a widely heralded matchup played in Montgomery, Alabama, Auburn had held national champion contender Ohio State and All-American Chic Harley to a 0–0 tie. Naturally, when Tech beat Auburn by 61 points the press had to recognize the Yellow Jackets as national champions, although Heisman had challenged Pop Warner's Pitt Panthers to a post-season match to determine the championship. Such contests were not readily organized in those days, and consequently the Pitt–Tech game wound up being scheduled for the regular 1918 season.

In addition to the national championship there were other honors for the Yellow Jackets in 1917: Besides Everett Strupper and Bill Carpenter being chosen for the first-team All-America, Joe Guyon and Al Hill were chosen for the second team, and six of Heisman's players were named to the all-southern team. Among them, of course, were Hill and Strupper who between them had scored forty-two touchdowns, and Bill Fincher who had kicked forty-nine extra points. To be sure, John Heisman had fashioned a scoring machine the likes of which would rarely be seen again, in the South or anywhere. Nevertheless, his own personal assessment of this team's success had more to do with his overall philosophy of football than it did with singling out various individuals for praise. As he wrote in the 1917 Georgia Tech yearbook:

In a system of play it's unfair to single out men too much for praise. To be sure we had our stars, as teams always must have; but the best part of a good football team's work is that it teaches a man his place in the scheme of things. It teaches him to subordinate himself to the rules that apply to all. It teaches him to give help to others by showing him how others will help him. . . .

The lesson is not only for this Fall's football, but for all of life and for all time to come—and for all of you. Ponder it.[40]

Once again, Heisman took the opportunity to express his understanding of success in football as an object lesson about success in life.

THE NATIONAL GAME (1917)

On the national scene, another successful team, in addition to Pitt (9–0) and Ohio State (8–0–1), was Texas A&M, who under first-year coach Dana X. Bible also went undefeated (8–0). Bible would enjoy many more successful years ahead. It being a war year, the Rose Bowl saw fit to fill its New Year's date with two military teams: the Army team from Fort Lewis against the Marines from Mare Island. The game was won by the Marines, 19–7.

With the Meuse–Argonne campaign in France having gotten underway right at the start of the 1918 football season, the city of Atlanta was naturally more interested in casualty lists than in football scores. (Something like 120,000 Americans would be killed in combat, many of them southern boys representing every state in the South.) A number of southern schools did not even field teams this year, including Alabama, Georgia, LSU, North Carolina, Tennessee, and Virginia; those teams that did play had abbreviated schedules. In the East, Cornell and Yale were conspicuously absent from area football schedules, and symbolically, the Army–Navy match was cancelled. Because of the lack of competition, other areas of the country, like the Southwest and the Pacific Coast, decided not to award a championship.

Writing at a point not far removed from these times, Fuzzy Woodruff, in his inimitable style, made some interesting comments about the football situation during the war years, not only in the South but across the country:

> Football is a game that demands mass support and feminine adulation to produce its color. There was nobody much who cared about seeing football games in the fall of 1918, and the fair sex was far more interested in men who wore Sam Browne belts than men who wore a letter on their sweaters.
>
> Then too, the football coach had disappeared. It was war time. Luxuries such as football coaches couldn't be afforded. Some of the coaches were hired by the government to stick around as athletic instructors but the salaries paid were meagre and the support given was decidedly limited.

Woodruff went on to show how schedule making had deteriorated as a result of all the colleges that had dropped football. In this void, military installations, practically all of which fielded football teams made up of former college stars, came to the rescue. "They would play anybody, anywhere, any time, and financial considerations didn't amount to anything."[41]

HEISMAN AND THE 1918 SEASON

Many coaches may have disappeared from the college scene at the time, as Woodruff points out (even Walter Camp had accepted an appointment as physical fitness director for the Navy Department), but John Heisman was still around, alive and well, and looking to play another season. In his late forties now, he was among the older active coaches, but there were continuing signs that things were not as amicable as they had been between the coach and his wife of fifteen years. So with his own private domestic war to wage, Heisman looked to the football campaign as a kind of buffer to ward off his problems at home. As a confirmed "football widow," though, Evelyn Heisman surely knew by now what her husband's real love was. Her loneliness was compounded by the fact that her son, Carlisle, was now gone. He had attended Georgia Tech, even played football under his stepfather, and although a scrub played sufficiently well to win his letter. (Clearly not taking the game as seriously as his illustrious coach, he labeled himself "The Eternal Scrub.") Joining up at the right time, Carlisle Cox went on to a distinguished military career.

With most football players, including his own, now gone into the service, Heisman had a hard time coming up with a competitive schedule. Joe Guyon was the sole holdover from the backfield that had demolished all their opponents of a year earlier. But on October 5, against traditional foe Clemson, Heisman unveiled another talented back in freshman Red Barron, whose running ability amazed the game crowd in a 28–0 win. Then the following week Tech overwhelmed Furman, 118–0. One of the main reasons for the lopsided score was halfback Buck Flowers, the same Davidson player who had given the Yellow Jackets such a tough time in the past but who had transferred to the Atlanta school. Since the SIAA had "no eligibility rules or disbarments for a football career" at the time, his eligibility was never questioned.[42] With Guyon, Barron, and Flowers in the lineup on November 9, Heisman and his team celebrated the signing of the Armistice two days early by lambasting N.C. State, 128–0.

When news of the Armistice was finally received, there was widespread, tumultuous celebration in Atlanta and throughout the country, as well as a deep feeling of relief that the conflict was over. No less a celebrant was John Heisman who, with the threat of the draft soon to be removed, looked to a return to prewar normalcy. But first there were other pressing matters to be taken care of, and after big wins over two Army camp teams, Tech approached its big game with Pitt, having averaged 84 unanswered points in its last five games. Signs looked good for a win over its northern foe.

But when Heisman took his Yellow Jackets to Pittsburgh's Forbes Field on November 23 to play Pop Warner's Panthers, he did not know at the time that he would be going up against the team of the year. The Panthers had a huge line in front of two All-American players in fullback Tank McLaren and halfback Tom Davies. All Tech had going for it were its three talented backs and its thirty-three-game unbeaten string. But these were not nearly enough as Pitt dominated the game from start to finish. Davies, who seemed to be all over the field that day, ran fifty yards for one touchdown, returned one punt fifty yards for another, then ran back another sixty yards for a score, and, to add insult to injury, threw two touchdown passes as Pitt won, 32–0. It was one of the blackest days in Heisman's coaching career, and now he could only wish that his

1917 team had played Pitt. While Joe Guyon had shown up well in a losing cause, Pop Warner called Red Barron, whose finest days still lay ahead, the "best half-back I've ever seen on Forbes Field."[43]

Even though the thirty-three-game unbeaten streak was now broken, Heisman still had a wagon-load of glowing statistics to savor. From late in 1914 through the fifth game of the 1918 campaign, his teams had scored 1,599 points for a 48.5 average per game, while holding opponents to a total of only 67 points, a mere 2.0 average per game. Twenty-one of the thirty-three games were shutouts, and no team had scored more than one touchdown in any game against the Yellow Jackets during that era. Truly, John Heisman had fashioned one of football's greatest dynasties.

After the loss to Pitt, Tech's immediate obligation was to beat Auburn on Thanksgiving and win another SIAA championship. And beat the Tigers they did, 41–0. Indian Joe Guyon closed out his career gloriously, scoring twice, once on a 25-yard pass from Flowers and then on a line plunge. The wet field conditions did not seem to bother the Yellow Jackets as they scored in every quarter to build up their final point total.

THE NATIONAL GAME (1918)

Although named national champion in 1918, Pitt saw its own winning streak, extending over a four-year period, come to an end. It came in a game with a service team, the Cleveland Naval Reserve, which, as expected, was made up of a considerable number of ex-college players. Former Georgia Tech back Judy Harlan was instrumental in the outcome of this game, as Al Thomy relates:

Harlan managed a bit of personal revenge when he served in the Navy at Cleveland during the 1918 season.

"We beat Pittsburgh 10–9," he says, "it was their only loss of the season. [Richard] Ducote kicked the winning field goal, and I intercepted a pass and returned it to midfield in the fourth quarter. I felt at least I had evened up some of the losses we had at Tech."[44]

Years later Tech would finally beat Pitt in the Sugar Bowl and Gator Bowl.

Because of the war, northern schools had begun to use freshman players for the first time, in contrast to the South where freshmen had always been eligible. Although playing abbreviated schedules, Michigan and Navy (under second-year coach Gil Dobie) turned out top teams. Other successful teams were Texas (9–0) and Virginia Tech (7–0). But for the future of football, from a national point of view, the most momentous, although unheralded, event of the year was the appointment of Knute Rockne as head coach of Notre Dame. As his career was soon to prove, he established himself as the model football coach whose success during his relatively brief tenure would become legendary.

Actually, a great deal of Rockne's coaching success can be attributed to the man's vibrant personality, which extended beyond the bounds of the football field. Whereas John Heisman could be crusty, even venomous in his dealings with players and public alike, Rockne conveyed a personable, human side that immediately won people over. Inclined to scholarship like Heisman (Rockne had been a chemistry professor who could quote the classics), the new Irish coach was more of a psychologist when it came to dealing with his players. Whereas Heisman had a manner that could rub a player the wrong way (as when he once publicly denounced Red Barron, who would earn a reputation as one of the South's greatest running backs, as a "flaming jackass" because of a defensive lapse), Rockne could be firm and yet understanding of any on- or off-field personal problems his players might be experiencing.

His handling of the talented but emotionally troubled George Gipp is a case in point. As a talented football player who could do everything the game demanded exceptionally well—run, pass, drop kick, and punt—Gipp required very little coaching. Yet he was somewhat lazy, even electing to forgo practice sessions occasionally, a problem that Rockne managed to handle quite tactfully. As a result, he got some superb performances out of the problematic Gipp. "A reputation as a martinet is invaluable to a coach," Rockne once said and then added, "providing he doesn't work at it too hard." For all his success as a coach, it would appear in retrospect that John Heisman did work consciously hard at being a disciplinarian. When Knute Rockne got his highly successful program underway at Notre Dame, Heisman, being the astute observer of the game that he was, undoubtedly marveled at and envied the tremendous success the man enjoyed, recognizing in him the necessary qualities a coach should possess in getting the most out of his players. At heart, the basic difference between the two coaches was in their personalities, for in their understanding of the game they had a lot in common.

After a 3–1–2 first year, Rockne would go on over his tragically shortened career to an amazing 105–12–5 record, a .881 percentage, which included five undefeated seasons. But his greatest contribution to the game itself was endowing it with more of a national image by helping to move it away from the control of the Eastern establishment. Naturally, the great teams he produced and with which he confronted any challenge from coast to coast were the major factor in this transition. Because of the thousands who had never seen the Notre Dame campus but became deep-dyed Irish fans anyway, college football took on even more of a popular image, a game not just reserved for the students and alumni but for the general public as well.

Due to the fact that the abbreviated schedules of that year had given the Rose Bowl organizers a limited picture of the strength of eastern teams, two service teams were again invited to play, this time the Great Lakes Navy team versus the Mare Island Marines. Led by a plucky back named George

Halas, the Navy team won, 17–0. Halas, who was named the outstanding player of the game, would go on to found the professional Chicago Bears. He, in fact, would become one of the early pioneers of professional football in the 1920s, a decade that saw a number of midwestern cities establish franchises, only to see many of them fold in the same year they were founded. It was an uncertain, highly experimental era for a professional sport that no one could have dreamed at the time would have such a glorious and prosperous future. Many of the early professional teams, which attracted college players like Jim Thorpe, Joe Guyon, and Pete Henry, originated as promotional ventures for the companies that supported them as, for example, the Decatur, Illinois, Staleys. Hired as the athletic director of the Staley Starch Company, George Halas, at twenty-two, began his professional sports career as player-coach of the Staleys.

THE NATIONAL SCENE (1919)

The year 1919, which was to be Heisman's last at Georgia Tech, was one of great prosperity in the South as it was in most areas of the land. In spite of the optimistic tenor that had pervaded the country at the close of the war, though, there were signs, both social and political, that America would never again be the same country it had been prior to the war. In January, one of Heisman's personal heroes, Theodore Roosevelt, died, and with him passed the spirit of an era. Following the Bolshevik Revolution of 1917, the threat of a Communist takeover generated periodic outbursts of Red hysteria around the country. While a death-dealing influenza epidemic had been raging throughout the country since 1918, sufficiently widespread to test the latest advances in medicine, there also sprang up rampant inflation, labor disputes, and occasional race riots, revealing that all was not well in the land, both economically and socially. Even continued technological advances, mainly in communications and transportation (the first nonstop trans-Atlantic flight was accomplished in 1919), were greeted with an air of suspicion in some quarters, an obvious reaction to the disenchantment with science that had grown out of the war itself. Other social developments like the Suffrage movement, which had been evolving since 1913, and Prohibition, which would result in the Eighteenth Amendment being finally ratified in 1919, would realize their fullest impact in the 1920s. But a social transformation had been set in motion, and America would never again have the complacent feeling and insular contentment it had enjoyed before the world-shaking events that occurred between 1914 and 1918.

The college campuses of 1919 were booming, as veterans returned to take up where they had left off. With many former football players back, too, the gridiron sport was poised to enjoy one of its most popular seasons. To meet spectator demands, Georgia Tech immediately realized it could use a stadium that would seat at least twenty-five thousand fans. On a wider front the practice of building stadiums or expanding those in existence was soon spreading all over the South, as most campuses of significant size looked for sufficient funding or perhaps even a philanthropist on the order of Atlanta's John W. Grant to help build a showpiece stadium. The day of football as a form of mass entertainment staged on a grand scale was fast approaching.

HEISMAN AND THE 1919 SEASON

As for Tech's football prospects for 1919, Heisman greeted Judy Harlan (back from military service), Ham Dowling, Bill Fincher, and Pup Phillips from the great 1917 team, and the backs Red Barron and Buck Flowers from the 1918 team. Thus he naturally felt he had the nucleus for another fine team. Nevertheless, something seemed to be missing in Heisman's usual enthusiasm, and once the season got underway, an uncharacteristic lack of intensity began to show. He began to spend more and more time away from the team, depending on assistant coach Alexander to take charge in his absence. Were the marital problems he was experiencing at home starting to weigh on his mind? Or was his atypical attitude due to the fact that after nearly sixteen years of coaching at Tech he was ready for a change?

At any rate, something that had occurred that spring may have had a lot to do with his dispirited frame of mind. It also pointed out what could result from the fierce rivalries that intercollegiate athletics had spawned by this time. The University of Georgia, which had not fielded a football team during the war years of 1917–1918, was ready to renew its gridiron series with Tech when a parade following a baseball game between the two schools in May 1919 aroused feelings of animosity that had been building for some time. Except for the years dominated by the great Bob McWhorter, Heisman's teams had pretty much had their own way with the Bulldogs, having built up a 7–4–1 advantage over the years, so the competition between the two schools remained intense. Furthermore, as Al Thomy points out:

Georgia men were somewhat resentful that Tech continued to field teams during the war years and, in fact, did win the national championship in 1917, not to mention the claiming of back-to-back Southern championships. Heisman made no apologies. He argued that wars should not stop the wheels of everyday life, and he denied discouraging his players from volunteering for service.

Judy Harlan backed up his coach's stand, saying that he volunteered in 1918 along with "just about the whole team" and Heisman said nothing to discourage him.[45]

It was during the student-sponsored victory parade in Athens that all these bad feelings came to a head. There was a series of comic exhibits in the parade that insinuated that Tech men had been slackers during the war years.

Tech officials, including athletic director Dr. J. B. Crenshaw, were outraged, and Crenshaw immediately took steps to break off all athletic relations with the University of Georgia. Heisman reacted as Thomy described, but the bitter feeling between the two schools would last for years, and the football series was not resumed until 1925. Such rivalries were not uncommon now in the South or, for that matter, in other areas of the country. During these years football's biggest intrastate rivalries began to develop, particularly between a state's two largest schools as, for example, LSU–Tulane, Texas–Texas A&M, and Indiana–Purdue. The growing obsession for winning was behind it all, of course, and great care was taken so that schedules could be arranged to accommodate a number of setup games at a season's beginning, leaving the important games for the end of the season, particularly the Big Game with an intrastate rival, usually scheduled as the final game of the season.

After opening up in 1919 against a service team it whipped 48–0, Georgia Tech went through its series of noncontenders, scoring three more shutouts in the process (Furman, 74–0; Wake Forest, 14–0; and Clemson, 28–0). On October 18 came the Yellow Jackets' first real test, against Vanderbilt in Atlanta. The Commodores had a superlative lineman in Josh Cody, but Tech still had its super back Buck Flowers, who scored three touchdowns that day on two punt returns and a long run, leading Tech to a surprisingly easy 20–0 win. It began to look as though Heisman had fashioned yet another powerhouse.

But then came another trip to Pittsburgh and another loss to the Pitt Panthers, this time by a closer score, 16–6. The outcome could have been worse, though, if Tech had not held Pitt on the 6-inch line in a remarkable goal-line stand. The following week, the Yellow Jackets got back in gear by overwhelming their old nemesis Davidson, 33–0, as Buck Flowers ran wild against his old teammates. But then on November 8 Tech was beaten by a southern opponent for the first time since 1914. The victor was Washington and Lee, which managed to kick a last-quarter field goal to win, 3–0.

Having lost two of his last three games, Heisman was thought by some to have lost his coaching touch as well. The players themselves must have sensed by now that some personal problem was eating at their coach, mainly due to his intermittent absences from the practice field. Even when he did show up, he seemed pressured into trying out plays that were so radically new they undermined team cohesiveness. Judy Harlan, in fact, felt that Tech lost the W&L game "because Heisman changed the offense completely during the week of the game and we didn't have a chance to learn it."[46]

Yet as the records reveal, John Heisman had one more surprising maneuver to introduce before he departed Atlanta. It occurred in the next-to-last game of the season, against Georgetown, when the first modern quick-kick in intercollegiate football is reported to have been officially pulled off. The Georgetown Hoyas, who had beaten Navy the week before, came into the game as openly confident as any team could be, and during the early stages of the game they had the Yellow Jackets backed up against their own goal line. Nevertheless, on an obvious punting down, Tech shifted into running formation with Buck Flowers prepared to receive the ball from center. Instead of running with it, he promptly drop-kicked a spiral that seemed to gather more energy as it soared over the surprised Hoya defenders. In fact, the ball did not come to rest until it had landed and rolled dead some eighty-five yards away! The play so completely shocked the Georgetown team that momentum fell Tech's way the rest of the day, resulting in a 27–0 win. The surprise element of the quick-kick would make it a forceful defensive weapon for many years to come, especially for those teams that employed the single-wingback formation.

In later years Flowers credited assistant coach Bill Alexander as having originally proposed the idea of the quick-kick. Flowers, who had honed his basic kicking skills during the two years he was at Davidson, soon caught Alexander's eye when he arrived on campus and, in addition to his running ability, demonstrated an uncanny knack for getting off a punt faster than anyone the assistant coach had ever seen. Everett Strupper, himself one of Tech's all-time backs, described Flowers' all-round abilities as follows:

He was a player without a weakness. . . . A specialist at the difficult business of kicking off, a punter of unequaled precision and consistency, a deadly drop-kicker within 35 yards, an amazing blocker for his inches and poundage, one of the hardest tacklers who ever hit me, a crack passer and an even better pass receiver, a master of knifing thrusts for a few necessary yards, a wizard in the open.[47]

The fact, too, that the quick-kick became a long-standing tradition during Alexander's coaching tenure underscores how instrumental he must have been in its development.

The win over Georgetown was to be Heisman's last at Tech. In spite of being favored by 2–1 odds over Auburn, the Yellow Jackets lost a tough game, 14–7, on Thanksgiving Day, and mistakes played a big part in the outcome. After staking his team to a 7–0 lead on a 42-yard pass play, Judy Harlan went back to punt from behind his own goal line in the second quarter. Sensing that his kick might be blocked by an on-charging Auburn lineman, Harlan deliberately stepped out of bounds to give Auburn a safety, which at this point in the game looked better than the touchdown that might have resulted. But, ironically enough, in the third quarter the Tigers scored on a 35-yard blocked punt play to take an 8–7 lead. The clincher and final insult came in the fourth period when Fatty Warren, the huge Auburn lineman, picked up a fumbled punt and lumbered forty-five yards for a score. Although undefeated W&L put in a claim for the championship, Auburn was declared 1919 champion. For Heisman the game with Auburn, played before the largest crowd ever to see a football game in the South up to that time (fifteen thousand), was a devastating loss, and it must have helped him make up his mind about something that had been bothering him for some time now.

Heisman and his wife had performed in summer stock together many times in the past, but their last act together was to outdo anything they had ever done before. Chip Robert, the former Tech athlete who had played under Heisman and who was now a key member of the school's athletic board, must have realized something was amiss when he received a Sunday morning telephone call from Heisman soon after the close of the football season. The call started out simply enough as an invitation to lunch, but then Heisman indicated he had something else to tell Robert and the members of the board, something about his continuing relationship with Georgia Tech. Sensing the seriousness in Heisman's tone of voice, Robert contacted the other members, who included noted Atlantans George Adair and Lowry Arnold, all of whom had been highly supportive of Heisman and his football program.

Lunch at the Heisman home went pleasantly enough, but soon afterwards Coach Heisman pulled off one of the most dramatic moments of his life when he arose from his chair to announce that he and his wife were in the process of getting a divorce. "There are no hard feelings, however," Heisman continued, "and I have agreed that wherever Mrs. Heisman wishes to live, I will live in another place. This will prevent any social embarrassment. If she decides to stay in Atlanta, I leave."[48]

After the initial shock had subsided, the board members, upon request, helped make an equitable division of some stocks and bonds between the two. Upon learning of Mrs. Heisman's decision to stay in Atlanta, they suddenly realized that they had lost their beloved coach and hastily departed, preparing to announce the startling news to the press.

If the University of Pennsylvania had made any overtures to Heisman to become its new head football coach at this time, a good job had been done in keeping the negotiations a secret. Nevertheless, something of this kind must have been going on behind the scenes, because early in 1920 John Heisman was in Philadelphia making plans to coach the Quakers that fall. The opportunity to coach in the East, particularly at his alma mater, was naturally very appealing to Heisman. Although football had begun to take on more of a national image, the East was still recognized as the hotbed of intercollegiate football. To coach at Penn presented Heisman a golden opportunity to add more laurels to his already illustrious career. His situation also pointed out the growing competition that existed among schools to recruit the services of a proven coach.

THE NATIONAL GAME (1919)

At Harvard, though, Percy Haughton had forsaken the gridiron to apply his management techniques to the world of business, and ex-Crimson player

Bob Fisher had become the new coach. Under his capable guidance things seemed to go on as they had before when the Crimson started out on a twenty-five-game winning streak. Rolling to a 9–0–1 record in 1919, Harvard, the premier team in the East and national champion once again, was invited to play in the Rose Bowl, where it topped Oregon, 7–6. With Texas A&M leading the way under Coach Dana Bible, the Southwest Conference was now coming to the fore. Bible and many of his players had served in the military in 1918 and, having become reunited in 1919, racked up a 10–0 record. An advocate of the fundamentals of blocking, tackling, and punting, along with a tough defense, Bible was sufficiently innovative to develop his own version of the popular shift formation of the time. It helped propel the Aggies to a series of eighteen unscored-on games.

Outstanding players who were nationally recognized during this time were Washington and Jefferson's Wilbur "Pete" Henry, the day's leading punt blocker, who at 230 pounds was considered huge for the time; Notre Dame's George Gipp, who contributed much to Knute Rockne's success in turning out his first undefeated team; and Chic Harley, who played in only one losing game at Ohio State, ironically his last, which was lost to Illinois on a field goal in the final seconds, 9–7. As a game controlled by the clock, football was developing a style of play that would extract the utmost drama from a competitive situation, often in the final minutes of play.

During this same year, Pennsylvania State University, an up-and-coming rival of Penn, started out on a thirty-game winning streak under Coach Hugo Bezdek, who had turned in successful tenures at Arkansas and Oregon. His consecutive victories at Penn State would extend to the 1922 season. The fact that Penn coach Robert C. Folwell had never defeated intrastate rival Pitt during his four-year tenure and had lost to upstart Penn State in 1919 contributed a great deal to the feeling among Quaker supporters that they needed a new coach and that the man for the job was John W. Heisman.

NOTES

1. John W. Heisman, "Our Athletic Outlook," *The Yellow Jacket* (October 1912): 85.

2. Ibid., 86–87.

3. John W. Heisman, *Principles of Football* (St. Louis, Mo.: Sports Publishing Bureau, 1922), 114–23.

4. Heisman, "Our Athletic Outlook," 80.

5. John W. Heisman, "Our Football Team and Others," *The Yellow Jacket* (November 1912): 176.

6. Ibid., 178.

7. John W. Heisman, "Hold 'em!" *Collier's*, October 27, 1928, 13.

8. Heisman, "Our Football Team and Others," 182.

9. John W. Heisman, "For Athletes During the Off-Season," *The Yellow Jacket* (January 1913): 306.

10. John W. Heisman, "Athletic Odds and Ends," *The Yellow Jacket* (February 1913): 368.

11. John W. Heisman, "Our Baseball Team," *The Yellow Jacket* (May 1913): 573.

12. Ibid., 576.

13. John W. Heisman, "Our Athletic Outlook for 1913," *The Yellow Jacket* (October 1913): 55–56.

14. John W. Heisman, "Review of the Football Season," *The Yellow Jacket* (December 1913): 172–73.

15. John W. Heisman, "Rules Rush In," *Collier's*, November 10, 1928, 13, 38.

16. "Who's He and Why?" *The Yellow Jacket* (March 1913): 421.

17. Gene Griessman, "The Coach," in *The Heisman: A Symbol of Excellence*, by John T. Brady (New York: Atheneum, 1984), 25–26.

18. John W. Heisman, "Review of the Baseball Season," *The Yellow Jacket* (June 1914): 470.

19. John W. Heisman, "Tech's Baseball Outlook," *The Yellow Jacket* (March 1915): 261.

20. Heisman, *Principles of Football*, 333–34.

21. John W. Heisman, "Football Again," *The Yellow Jacket* (October 1915): 35.

22. Ibid., 35.

23. Ibid., 33.

24. According to Heisman, Canty Alexander "was the kind of football player who resented the rule that a man may not go right on playing for his college after he has been graduated." See John W. Heisman, "Rough Humor," *Collier's*, (November 9, 1929, 48, for an amusing account of Alexander's supreme dedication to playing football.

25. John W. Heisman, "Athletics," *The Yellow Jacket* (February 1916): 260.

26. Heisman, "The Thundering Herd," *Collier's*, October 13, 1928, 60.

27. John W. Heisman, "Rough Humor," *Collier's*, November 9, 1929, 47.

28. See Griessman, "The Coach," 26.

29. Quoted in Al Thomy, *The Ramblin' Wreck: A Story of Georgia Tech Football* (Huntsville, Ala.: Strode Publishers, 1973), 56–57.

30. Griessman, "The Coach," 26.

31. Quoted in John McCallum, *Ivy League Football Since 1872* (New York: Stein and Day, 1977), 63.

32. Ibid., 61.

33. Thomy, *The Ramblin' Wreck*, 63.

34. John W. Heisman, "Here Are Men," *Collier's*, November 16, 1929, 44.

35. Thomy, *The Ramblin' Wreck*, 70, 72.

36. Ibid., 59.

37. Quoted in Griessman, "The Coach," 27.

38. John W. Heisman, "Signals," *Collier's*, October 6, 1928, 32.

39. John Heisman had his own story about the origin of Tech's most traditional nickname—the Yellow Jackets. In 1906 during a game with Davidson, two spectators were overheard (reputedly by Mrs. Heisman herself sitting nearby) to have said: "All the fellows fight a good game. They buzz around like yellow jackets. They actually swarm." Another version has it that the yellow jacket symbol first appeared in an *Atlanta Journal* cartoon on November 7, 1906, prior to the Georgia game. The drawing

depicted a Georgia player being attacked by a determined wasp-like creature with a caption that read: "Somebody's going to get stung."

40. Quoted in *The Blue Print*, the 1917 Georgia Tech yearbook.

41. L. F. "Fuzzy" Woodruff, *History of Southern Football*, vol. 2 (Atlanta, Ga.: Georgia Southern, 1928), 70.

42. Ibid., 74.

43. Ibid., 77.

44. Thomy, *The Ramblin' Wreck*, 72.

45. Ibid., 78–79.

46. Ibid., 64.

47. Ibid., 74.

48. Robert B. Wallace, *Dress Her in White and Gold: A Biography of Georgia Tech* (Atlanta, Ga.: Georgia Tech Foundation, 1969), 60.

5

Heisman and Football's Golden Age: The Big Game Goes National (1920–1927)

By World War I . . . American college football had weathered a severe crisis of criticism and self-doubt to become firmly entrenched on the campuses of every major college and university in the United States. Open but deliberate, still violent though controlled, football reflected the variety, the contradictions, and the polarities of American life.

—William J. Baker,
Sports in the Western World (1982)

Ode to John W. Heisman
They say you were a Cracker Jack
   Down there at Georgia Tech.
They're sorry you will not be back,
   But Penn is glad, by Heck!
Your Alma Mater sent for you
   To change her football style;
She wants to see the Red and Blue
   In winning togs awhile.
Beneath her student's cap and gown
   She'll wear your filial gift,
And proudly show the old home town
   Her famous Heisman shift.

—Philadelphia *Evening Bulletin*
(February 9, 1920)

HEISMAN AT PENN (1920)

Although he was into his fifties by now, John Heisman arrived at Penn armed with the same go-getter attitude that had characterized his young coaching days. The main difference at this point in his life was that his go-getter credentials were well documented. As a pioneer innovator as well as a mover and a shaker, he had produced winning teams everywhere he had coached, and during his sixteen years at Georgia Tech he had won more than one hundred games. Having captured a national championship with his great 1917 team, Heisman was a natural to take over the reins at Penn. By this time, too, Heisman, with the exception of Amos Alonzo Stagg who had coached one year longer, had the longest coaching tenure of any active football mentor.

His predecessor at Penn, Robert C. Folwell, had not done too badly—Folwell's tenure (1916–1919) actually produced a higher winning percentage (27–10–2) than Heisman's (16–10–2)—but there were a lot of alumni who remembered the glory days of the 1890s when George Woodruff was beating everyone in sight. Heisman, who played just before the Woodruff era, would be the man to lead the Quakers to the same heights, they reasoned. With the appointment of Heisman, they were sure the revitalization of the football program was near at hand.

Back in Atlanta, Tech supporters were mourning the unexpected departure of their longtime coach. Atlanta sportswriter Oscar Davis, perhaps unaware of all the facts surrounding Heisman's decision, rationalized in part:

Heisman raised Tech from the mists of athletic obscurity to the brightest place in the limelight, and Tech has always been grateful. But not until Tuesday did she realize just how much Heisman has meant to her and how keenly his loss would be felt. . . .

But Coach is gone and Tech can lose no time crying over spilt milk. Tech realizes too late that the proposition which Penn offered was a wonderful opportunity, the acknowledgement of greatness and the fulfillment of a life's work.[1]

Once the realization had finally sunk in that John Heisman was actually gone, most fans and supporters of the renowned coach would undoubtedly have agreed with Davis. But another Atlanta writer, Morgan Blake, had a more realistic approach to the reasons for Heisman's break with Tech and a better understanding of the basic nature of the man himself, though he, too, was apparently ignorant of Heisman's marital difficulties. The Philadelphia *Evening Ledger* for February 9, 1920, reported that Blake accused "the Tech authorities of being asleep at the switch in the Heisman situation. . . . No one thought he would leave, and therefore, when his contract ran out, nobody took any notice." Aware of the man's domineering, outspoken personality through previous encounters, Blake further substantiated his reason for Heisman's sudden departure:

[Heisman] is not an easy man to get close to, but after you do you might find many sterling characteristics. I had heard a lot detrimental to Coach Heisman before I came to Atlanta, but I am happy to say that as I grew to know him I realized the injustice that was done him. . . .

I cannot help but feel that the loss of Heisman to Tech was due to the belief by the Tech authorities that nothing could wean him away from the southern college.[2]

Rumors about Heisman's appointment at Penn had been circulating in Philadelphia long before the new coach's appointment was announced. Around the first of the year the Philadelphia *Evening Bulletin* reported: "No announcement has been made by any Penn official, but reports are being circulated among the students and the alumni that Heisman will be Robert C. Folwell's successor."[3] The incumbent coach did not take kindly to such talk, and in spite of the fact that Penn's football committee was openly favorable toward hiring the Tech coach, Folwell, ignoring mounting pressure, refused to resign until the committee's final choice was announced.

The *Bulletin* went on to note that the factors in Heisman's favor were too auspicious to overlook: his "phenomenal success" as a coach, his ability to "handle football men," his strong "personality" and reputation as a "disciplinarian," and, of course, his ongoing friendship with a number of Penn officials who had followed his career since his undergraduate days.

After twenty-eight years, many alumni saw Heisman's appointment as an example of history repeating itself, for when Heisman's coach, E. O. Wagenhurst, had been deposed in favor of George Woodruff, Penn had started out on its greatest period of gridiron success. As Woodruff had enjoyed tremendous results with his formidable guards back formation, so Heisman was expected to continue a winning tradition through implementing his highly successful jump shift offense at Penn. Upon accepting the Penn appointment, though, Heisman undoubtedly realized his work was cut out for him, for nowhere over his career had the alumni been as powerful. He would soon be experiencing the unaccustomed pressures of such an environment.

Nevertheless, in typical Heisman fashion he relished the challenge before him, and putting his well-honed public relations skills in action he hit the ground running. Accepting every banquet and speaking invitation that came his way, Heisman made the most of each opportunity, and as his popularity spread with every speech he soon had the most dubious outsiders lending the support he had already secured from the alumni and the students. One of the highlights of this promotional period was a luncheon hosted by football committee member Sidney Hutchinson, which had been organized for area newspapermen to get to know the new coach. As planned, Heisman came across in grand fashion, and the Philadelphia *Evening Bulletin* commented that the new coach's "heart-to-heart talk won their confidence." Ironically, his seemingly mellowed posture was in stark contrast to the way Atlanta newspapermen had remembered him. It was almost as though Heisman's divorce, coupled with his new location, had given him a fresh, new perspective on life.

In one of the first press interviews after his arrival, Heisman revealed that his attitude might also have mellowed toward his players and his system of coaching them. In fact the reporter was sufficiently impressed to label Heisman "a new type of coach": "Combined with his thoroughly human qualities of sympathy and kindliness for the members of his squad is the respect which his college-bred intellect commands. The day of the rough-necked 'bawl 'em out' coach is passing. Perhaps Professor John W. Heisman may be the first occupant of the chair of football at Penn."[4]

Although Heisman fully appreciated such an attitude in that he had always worked hard to lend dignity and respect to the image of the football coach, it was undoubtedly his distinguished appearance and professorial manner that had more to do with this impression than anything else. As this same reporter put it:

In appearance or conversation, one would scarcely pick him for what he is. Slightly above medium height, rather light in weight for the size of his frame, with gray hair and pleasant hazel eyes, he wears his eyeglasses on a silken cord, which gives him rather the appearance of the scholar.

His forcible manner of speaking, the firmness with which he expounds his convictions, shows the results of the training he received at the Penn law school. Although born in Cleveland he has spent so many years in the South that occasionally he lapses into a drawl and speaks of "over yonder."

The interview went on to allow "Professor" Heisman the opportunity to expound upon his philosophy of football, more specifically the kind of football he was planning to introduce at Penn. Much of it was familiar enough: "Football games are not won by taking unfair advantages of an opponent. Success in the game—the real science of it—is working out plays that keep within the rules, but which develop new methods." One of his methods was his jump system, which he described in his own ostentatious words as "based on perfect synchronization—a harmony of movement . . . capable of infinite permutations and combinations." But Heisman was somewhat cautious in relating his system to the Penn situation:

"I am firmly convinced that in football the best defense is a good offense. Penn has always been strong defensively. My job will be to mould a strong offensive. If we can keep that combination, I believe we will get results. But it remains to be seen just how far the football which I have used in the South will be applicable to conditions at Franklin Field."[5]

In spite of Heisman's ambivalent reference to "conditions at Franklin Field," his enthusiasm had the alumni, students, and supporters sufficiently inspired to wish that the 1920 season was already underway, even though the gridiron season was still some seven months away.

Franklin Field, about to undergo major renovation and expansion that would place it among the premier football stadiums in the country, was another attractive reason for Heisman to return to his alma mater. When work was completed, the stadium would seat over fifty thousand fans in a milieu of Italian Renaissance splendor. Actually, the Penn campus itself was indicative of Philadelphia's progress at this time, as an urban institution with more than seventy buildings crowded into an area a little larger than one hundred acres. After so many years in the South, Heisman must have been somewhat taken aback to find himself in a large cosmopolitan element once more, for Philadelphia at the beginning of the 1920s was a fast-growing metropolis, soon to be the third-largest in the United States after New York and Chicago.

Many significant changes on campus had transpired since Heisman had graduated in 1892. The twenty-year span since 1900 had seen the adoption of the dormitory system (including women's); the establishment of fraternities; and the construction of a number of buildings and laboratories, including a hospital and (to Heisman's delight) a gymnasium, training house, and Franklin Field. With the evolution of a variety of academic departments and establishment of a graduate school, enrollment had grown from less than a thousand in the late nineteenth century to well over ten thousand students by Heisman's return. Penn's burgeoning enrollment mirrored a prosperous middle class's newfound faith in higher education. In fact, between the years 1919 and 1928, college enrollment nationally would rise by a half million. By 1926, one out of every eight youths was in college, and with increased opportunities in the workplace, pursuing a college education became a practical decision, as a means of advancement. This was a trend that had been developing since Heisman's undergraduate days at Brown and Penn.

But the development Heisman found most attractive was that Penn students had now cultivated a more personally involved relationship with the campus than when he had been a student. This boded well for building a winning football tradition, and thinking back to the student support he had nurtured at Georgia Tech, he told his supporters:

I have a big job ahead of me, but I am going to try to get the whole spirit of the undergraduates into this attitude. It doesn't seem that college athletics fulfill their purpose if the habits of the football or baseball squad are carefully guarded while the rest of the students are left pretty much to themselves.[6]

THE NATIONAL SCENE (1920)

In 1920 a young writer named F. Scott Fitzgerald made a big splash with a revealing novel about campus life called *This Side of Paradise*. A postwar mood of cynicism and disenchantment had led to a "flaming youth" lifestyle among the younger generation, and as a consequence Heisman would see his school spirit theory put to a test in the more sophisticated atmosphere in which he now worked. It was a more complex time, too; one in which college life would become the center of various social movements, publicly reflected in student dress and behavior, including a more open relationship between the sexes. While many students found their social identity in the wilder aspects of fraternity parties, football rallies, and the new-found sexual freedom and mobility that the automobile offered, others turned their backs on these diversions to identify with worthier causes such as the exposure of social injustice or corruption in political office.

In spite of any cynical attitude toward the American system and the problems of postwar recession, though, the mood of the country during this time was generally optimistic. Business was booming, with new industries developing practically overnight—particularly those related to transportation, communications, and, with residential construction on the rise, home appliances. On the verge of the wildest spree in American history, the U.S. economy was inspired by the continuing technological revolution that had conditioned the American people to believe that anything was possible. Commercial air flights, which had been expanding since the end of the war, were now being scheduled to more places; the Indianapolis 500 was won in six hours at an astounding average of eighty-eight miles per hour; and the election of Warren G. Harding to the presidency was the first time that returns had ever been broadcast over the radio. Radio would soon have wide-ranging repercussions for organized sports, and the movies, though still silent, would produce a mythology all their own, one that would also impact on sports.

Naturally, such developments contributed to the upbeat tempo of the times—what many social analysts have referred to as a Jazz Age mentality after the frenzied style of music that had swept northward from the French Quarter of New Orleans. It was also an age of extremes, a time when the Eighteenth Amendment to the Constitution could prohibit the sale of alcoholic beverages but not stop their consumption, and the Nineteenth could grant women the right to vote while their social behavior was still proscribed. It was an atmosphere, too, in which middle-class prosperity could create a new kind of go-getter—the booster, one who promoted the interests of local business through salesmanship and advertising. As a result, the process of publicizing and making more goods and products available helped raise middle-class standards of living. Such a milieu in which mass communications played a significant role also created mass celebrity worship and a demand for celebrities, particularly cultural figures, movie stars, and athletes.

In keeping with the positive upswing of the country, football in the fall of 1920 was on the verge of achieving its greatest popularity. Something about the game was right for the times. It had been making tremendous strides in all phases, especially in developing player proficiency and coaching efficiency. Actually, these two areas had become closely interrelated, as highly accomplished players were now working with coaches well-versed in specialized areas of the game. What Fuzzy Woodruff said of the southern football situation in 1920 could also be applied to the country at large:

No longer was the football coach at a college an underpaid individual employed for a short term of instruction. He was an artist who gave his entire time and entire thought to the game and he was assisted by skilled specialists, men versed in line play, the technique of ends, backfield experts, accurate scouts and highly experienced trainers.[7]

HEISMAN AND THE 1920 SEASON

As a head coach with five assistant coaches, Heisman's situation at Penn exemplified big-time college football programs at this time. Heisman's prospects looked bright indeed, with a student body of over four thousand male undergraduates and an undefeated freshman team from the previous season from which to draw players. When the season finally got underway in late September, it appeared that Penn's investment in its native son's coaching system was going to pay huge dividends. The Quakers rolled to four consecutive shutout wins, defeating Delaware, 35–0; Bucknell, 7–0; Swarthmore, 21–0; and Lafayette, 7–0. Penn's supporters were all enthusiastic now, as the Heisman magic seemed ready to take the Quakers to even greater heights.

Ironically, it was the very next game, one involving a southern opponent, that started Heisman's men on a nosedive of four straight losses and an attendant loss of supporter confidence. The Keydets from Virginia Military Institute (VMI) came to town for what was supposed to be a practice game, but when the game was over they had rolled up 280 yards from scrimmage to Penn's meager 78 and a shocking final score of 27–7. Heisman and his followers were dumbfounded as they began to realize that Penn's success was not as much a certainty as they had thought. Still, they consoled themselves, the season was only half over. There were still five games left.

But over the next three games, shaky faith turned into outright doubt as the Quakers lost all three encounters, two of them to in-state rivals Penn State (28–7) and Pittsburgh in a heartbreaker (27–21). Old grads grumbled bitterly about the results of these contests, but the ensuing 44–7 defeat administered by Dartmouth had Heisman rationalizing to them that his was a young team and it would take some time before they became winners.

As though to underscore his posture on their future chances, the Quakers rose to the occasion in the last two games of the season to put down Columbia, 27–7, and Cornell, 28–0, the third time the Big Red of Cornell had been shut out by the Quakers since 1917. With the season ending on such a high note, Heisman was certain that his 6–4 record would assure his team's getting off to a solid start in 1921. He had not reckoned on the fact that the Big Red team, whom they had handled so easily, was on the verge of developing into a national powerhouse in 1921 under its redoubtable new coach, Gil Dobie.

THE NATIONAL GAME (1920)

Paradoxically, the year of Heisman's return to the East was the year that West Coast football came to the fore, in particular at the University of California as Andy Smith, a former Penn coach (1909–1912), installed his style of play there. For five years (1920–1924), Smith's so-called wonder teams remained unbeaten, winning forty-six games and tying four. As a dynasty, his teams would compare with those of Yale in its heyday, George Woodruff's Penn teams in the 1890s, those of Fielding Yost's Michigan years, Percy Haughton's Harvard teams that dominated the East prior to World War I, and Gil Dobie's Washington teams during the same time.

With a lineup that Smith had convinced to believe itself invincible, the Golden Bears of California was the first Far West team to be named national champion. In spite of their 9–0 record, the skeptics persisted until Cal decisively defeated Ohio State, the Western Conference champions, 28–0, in the Rose Bowl. The highlight of the game was All-American end Brick Muller's 60-yard pass for a touchdown off a backfield lateral. As the ultimate example of Minnesota's flea flicker, the play was significant enough for Muller to be named the game's most outstanding player.

On a sad note, 1920 saw the career of Notre Dame's great George Gipp come to a tragic close. More attracted to a life of partying and gambling than disciplining himself and hitting the books, Gipp practiced a life-style that probably contributed to his early demise. Although he began to show the effects of his dissolute life as the season progressed, he pulled himself together long enough to lead the Irish to its second consecutive unbeaten season at 9–0. Perhaps the 1920 Army game can be singled out as the one in which Gipp displayed his astonishing versatility more dramatically than he had in any other. Used primarily as a decoy due to his sickly condition, he still managed to gain 124 yards rushing, pass for 96, and run back kicks for 112 as Notre Dame beat the Cadets, 27–17.

Gipp played the remainder of the season injured, but missed the final game of the season against Michigan State when he was confined to the hospital with a strep throat infection. It still came as a terrible shock to football fans when Gipp died from pneumonia in mid-December. Although he had been named to Walter Camp's All-America team, his lasting monument—one that would become legendary over the years—was his supposed deathbed words to Coach Rockne, imploring his coach that, when the going got tough in some future game, Rockne should get the players to "win one just for the Gipper." Even though he established records at Notre Dame that would withstand the test of time, the greatest contribution of George Gipp was the legendary role he played in enriching the mythology of college football during this highly dramatic time of the game's development.

In the Southwest, Texas A&M's unscored-on streak finally came to an end on Thanksgiving Day against the Texas Longhorns as the Aggies lost, 7–3, before twenty thousand spectators in Austin. This Texas A&M—Texas matchup not only helped fire up a heated rivalry that still lives on but clearly demonstrated how receptive all areas of the country had grown toward the game of football. In fact, the time was approaching when the venerable East would relinquish its dominant hold on football, for after some fifty years of play the game was finally establishing itself as one that was truly national in scope. Not even Major League baseball could make such a claim at this time.

Still, many of the game's most renowned events and notable personalities awaited the decade's evolvement, a decade that would contribute even more glamour and luster to football's growing popular image. Actually, the game was developing into a form of mass entertainment that would soon be looked upon as a national industry. As the support of both the public and alumni swelled, the colleges and universities were increasingly compelled to commit their resources and allegiance to maintaining successful programs, feeling, of course, that by doing so their images would be positively enhanced in the eyes of the public and financial support would continue to come in bountiful amounts from the alumni.

Both institutional and regional pride were such that many schools, hungry for national recognition, had taken to scheduling annual intersectional matches. This was particularly true of southern schools, who at this time had more to gain in countering the South's "lost cause" image by establishing powerful gridiron teams and by hopefully claiming a national championship. A case in point was Georgia Tech, which under the low-keyed tutelage of Bill Alexander was winning as easily over its southern foes as it had under Heisman. To maintain a solid national reputation the school now looked to the East and Midwest for suitable opponents. The quest would eventually result in another national title in 1928. But football historian Fuzzy Woodruff questioned the reasoning of Tech and other southern schools for scheduling intersectional games at the time, particularly since Tech had met nothing but disaster on its trips to Pittsburgh:

The honest truth of the business was, I think, that Georgia Tech had perhaps—in a football way—outgrown its southern pantaloons. Tech took the position that it couldn't find sufficiently keen competition in the South to make the games interesting either for the players or the spectators. They had to go out to conquer new worlds or be conquered.

And as Tech was getting five times the newspaper space that the other teams were getting and five times the turnstile revenue, all the other southern colleges began making intersectional arrangements.[8]

As though to bear out Woodruff's thinking, Georgia Tech faced Penn State on October 29, 1921, at the Polo Grounds in New York and lost decisively, 28–7. Nevertheless, the football image of the South as a region of national powers was just a few scant years away.

But regardless of where regional strength lay at this time, football mania was taking firm root everywhere. With each fall came the attendant hoopla— whole weekends given over to revelry, featuring colorfully staged pageantry and inspirational pep-rally parades. It all culminated in the Big Game on Saturday when enthusiastic marching bands and pretty cheerleaders conspired to cheer their team on to victory. The celebrations took place before, during, and (if victorious) after a game. The highlight was the performance of a school's marching band on the field at halftime in front of capacity crowds titillated by the antics of student couples dressed in the latest fall fashions or faddish dress. Many spectators—students, alumni, and boosters alike—arrived on the scene by auto or private train, with their celebratory moods in full swing, as evidenced by those in various stages of inebriation. (The constraints of Prohibition never put a damper on the day's big football games, it seems.) It is a bacchanalian tradition that has continued to this day.

In this kind of manic atmosphere the pressure on a coach to produce a winner was mounting every year, particularly at institutions like Penn where tradition dictated that the good name of the school be raised high in all areas of endeavor. Accordingly, the other big schools of the region that extended northward from Penn to Cornell and Dartmouth were dutifully performing their roles in the scenario inspired by the gridiron mania of the 1920s. Naturally, every school wanted to play a winning role.

HEISMAN AND THE 1921 SEASON

Having now experienced the unique pressures of coaching in the East and hoping to avoid the mistakes of the 1920 campaign, Heisman, in looking confidently ahead to the promise of the upcoming season, called a meeting of his coaching staff in early April, 1921. Ostensibly, the main topic on the agenda was the status of his jump shift offense, which in its initial season had not come off as well as had been planned. As the press reported it, Penn's problems had been the result of overly cautious measures. In strictly interpreting the shift rule to assure staying within legal bounds, Heisman had seen his system lose much of its effectiveness. "When it was seen, however, that other colleges, notably Dartmouth, was [sic] running off a shift with lightning-like rapidity, without a kick from the officials or rules makers, Heisman did likewise, and the results in the Cornell game were a complete vindication of his 'glide play.' "[9] Dartmouth had overwhelmed the Quakers, 44–7, but in the last game of the 1920 season, Penn had easily downed Cornell, 28–0. So now Heisman and his coaches were in agreement that since the Rules Committee had not acted to change the existing restrictions governing the jump or glide shift, Penn should work to speed up its timing of the glide. In the upcoming season, the pressure was on Heisman to prove the worth of his shift system.

Heisman, of course, had never lost faith in the worth of his pet offense. At this April meeting to plan ways to improve it with his staff, he introduced his highly qualified coaches to the press: Bert Bell, backfield coach; Gus Ziegler, line coach; Izzy Lavigne, line coach; and Tom McNamara, scrub team coach. It was also rumored that Bill Hollenbeck, former All-American fullback and captain of Penn's 1908 championship team, would become Heisman's first assistant. To promote unity of purpose, Heisman tactfully complimented the group he hoped would help him perfect his shift and build a winner: "It was the first time I had a chance to meet several of my coaches, and let me tell you the football committee has picked out good ones. In the main the gathering was more to welcome these new men than anything else."[10]

Paradoxically, though, big-time football's growing emphasis on trained coaching specialists was starting to work against Heisman's natural instinct for autonomous, inspirational coaching. When Heisman said he had to have absolute control as head coach, he meant just that, for his greatest success had come when he enjoyed full autocratic powers. But he had now arrived at a point in his career when the coaching style pioneered by Harvard's Percy Haughton was becoming so pronounced that a head coach could no longer be as personally involved with his players on the field as he once was. Rather, a coach now learned of his players' capabilities, and not so much their individual personalities, indirectly through his assistant coaches' specialized assignments. It was a managerial style ultimately alien to Heisman. Over the course of the next several years, this highly compartmentalized way of coaching would contribute more than anything else to his decline and eventual demise as a successful coach.

Bolstered by his usually optimistic outlook, though, Heisman assembled his coaches and a squad of some thirty men in September for pre-season drills. Following a rugged but fruitful training camp, he felt even more positively about producing a big winner at his alma mater. With the season underway, Penn's prospects looked especially good as Heisman's plan for quickening the pace of his jump shift appeared to have gotten his players off on the right track. After their first five games the Quakers were undefeated, with only a 7–7 tie with Swarthmore spoiling an otherwise perfect record. Included in their wins were three shutouts: 89–0 over Delaware, 20–0 over Franklin and Marshall, and 7–0 over Gettysburg. In the big win over Delaware, Captain Rex Wray scored 33 points on four touchdowns and nine extra points, a Penn record. The Gettysburg game was considerably tougher, as the only score came when Poss Miller took the opening kickoff back eighty-five yards for a touchdown. But the most satisfying win of the first five games was the 21–7 victory over VMI. Not only did this win serve as payback for the previous year's defeat, but the decisive defeat of one of that day's southern powers served notice that Heisman's coaching methods were beginning to pay off.

Shockingly, though, the sweet taste of victory soon turned into the bitter ashes of defeat as the Quakers suffered two successive one-sided losses to intrastate rivals Pitt (28–0) and Lafayette (38–6). The latter team, coached by former Pitt player Jock Sutherland, was enjoying its finest season, also including among its victims Pitt and Fordham. Apparently having learned a great deal from Pop Warner's single-wingback offense at Pitt, Sutherland came up with a flawless team performance against the Penn defense, hardly ever having to resort to a forward pass. It was now clear to Heisman that his jump shift was not working as effectively as he and his coaches had so painstakingly planned.

Consequently, many supporters found it hard to understand how a school with an enrollment as large as Penn's could be outplayed by a much smaller school like Lafayette, jump shift notwithstanding. But Heisman knew that Lafayette's competitive spirit was akin to that of those small southern schools like Sewanee and Davidson who annually fielded teams that successfully took on more formidable foes. What was lacking at Penn, Heisman was soon to conclude, was this very quality—a strong sense of school spirit among its impatient supporters and a concerted will to win among his players, the kind of milieu he had come to take for granted at Georgia Tech.

His growing concern was confirmed by the final games in a disappointing 4–3–2 season. First came a 14–14 tie with Dartmouth in a game played at the Polo Grounds in New York. The Dartmouth game could have wound up in defeat except that, with fifty seconds left to play, Rex Wray ran twenty-five yards to tie the game on one of Heisman's patented hidden-ball plays. Then, most disastrously of all, came a 41–0 defeat by Cornell, a team that Penn had previously defeated on three straight occasions. But in Cornell, Penn had confronted the team that would claim the national championship in 1921 by virtue of its 8–0 record.

Heisman's coaching counterpart at Cornell was the dour, pessimistic Gilmour Dobie, who had developed his winning ways at Washington (1908–1916) and Annapolis (1917–1920). During his tour with the Washington Huskies, in fact, he never lost a game while fashioning an amazing 58–0–3 record. At one point, Washington won thirty-nine straight games, the second-longest collegiate winning streak (Oklahoma would have forty-seven consecutive wins in the 1950s). But if Heisman had a habit of harshly criticizing the play of certain players some of the time, Dobie was downright insulting to his players most of the time. Apparently, he incited his men to play harder due to some inner rage that kept his intensely competitive nature fired up. But perhaps "Gloomy Gil," as he was called, knew what he was doing, since the animosity the players felt toward their coach was physically vented on the field against their opponents. In his highly pessimistic manner, Dobie was the prototype of the all-winning coach who always talks as though his team will lose, regardless of the quality of talent he has at his command. Paul "Bear" Bryant was an example of such a coach in more recent times.

At Cornell, Dobie's system continued to pay off handsomely as his teams went undefeated for three straight years. With the great George Pfann at quarterback, the Big Red rolled to twenty-four straight wins in 1921, 1922, and 1923. Like Heisman, Dobie was a dogmatic perfectionist who preached split-second timing as the key to executing a running play. This was particularly true of his version of the single-wing's standard off-tackle play, which, it was said, no team could pull off as well as a Dobie-coached eleven. Unlike Dobie, whose primary concern was how well his players performed on the field, Heisman was a coach whose idealistic approach to the game sought to involve everyone on and off the field in his coaching system—students, faculty, and boosters, as well as the players.

Nevertheless, the game with Cornell in 1921 alerted Heisman to certain of his players' attitudinal problems, which were entirely foreign to his coaching experience. In spite of a rain-soaked, muddy Franklin Field, Cornell's Eddie Kaw had timed his stutter-step to perfection and run for five touchdowns in the Big Red's smashing win. Embarrassed and disgruntled, Heisman was now painfully aware that to help build a winning team his men needed to cultivate other qualities than just those of timing their plays. But because he considered his players as personal extensions of his coaching posture, Heisman had never been one to make excuses for them, especially now that his offensive system was being promoted as the redeeming factor that would help restore Penn to gridiron greatness. What had happened, then? Such a question had to be on the minds of most Quaker supporters during the last four games of the 1921 season, as their team scored but 20 points while their opponents racked up 121. If, as Heisman had declared, "the best defense is a good offense," then something appeared to be terribly lacking in both areas of his team's play.

Immediately following the lopsided loss to Cornell, rumors were rampant that Heisman was on the way out. Such talk was mainly attributable to a faction of students and alumni who were "disgusted with the team . . . , which was not only ground into the mud and ooze of Franklin Field but in the eyes of many, disgraced." Such was the embittered summation of a Philadelphia reporter, who in the journalistic style of the day went on to editorialize about the Penn situation:

The Penn team as it played yesterday is one of the poorest that ever wore the Red and Blue. More than that, it is one of the poorest turned out of a major university in many a year.

After the game one Penn undergrad declared that if the field had been dry the result would have been changed. He didn't say the half of it. The score, if that is what he meant by result, would have been changed in all probability. Cornell would have won by at least two touchdowns more.[11]

In the eyes of the irate reporter there was simply no excuse for this embarrassing loss. But in the eyes of the frustrated Heisman on that miserable, pathetic day, few of Penn's players even came close to his standards of school spirit and cohesive team play. Admittedly he did have some capable, dedicated performers in camp. In addition to Wray, there were Bill Grave, Jack Humes, Poss Miller, and John Thurman—players who had been recruited from the ranks of the Penn student body whose large enrollment guaranteed a high percentage of quality players.

But whereas Heisman had heretofore been able to take disparate abilities, even inferior candidates, and mold them into a harmonious whole, he was now clearly frustrated by the lack of a unified purpose among his players. One of them became so impatient with Heisman's incessant drilling to perfect his shift offense that one day in practice he informed his teammates that he had had enough of Heisman's peremptory, demanding ways. All he wanted, he declared, was someone to "just hand me that pumpkin and let me run!"[12] It was an attitude that was beginning to show up in a number of his players—a defiant stance that challenged Heisman's autocratic rule. So the real coaching problem he now found himself facing was that of trying to cope with a new generation of players who did not take to their coach's old-fashioned way of doing things—his demands of complete loyalty to his ways, his continuous preaching of the gospel of school spirit, and even his traditional manner of issuing his commands on the field through a megaphone. All these things struck some of his players as somewhat quaint, if not antiquated. His patience often tried to the limit, Heisman once burst out in practice: "I have taught you all I know—and still you know nothing!"[13]

By the close of his second season at Penn, then, Heisman was convinced that a major part of his coaching problem was due to a lack of school spirit among both supporters and players. To help resolve his predicament Heisman formed what he called a "Spirit Committee" made up of Penn's undergraduate leaders. Toward the end of his tenure in 1922 he met with this group once a week for a short inspirational talk, but his ultimate purpose was to relay his school spirit message to the entire student body. In a newspaper interview Heisman contended that, in order for his gospel of school spirit to have the support of the students, he needed the help of his committee to reach the thousands who comprised Penn's student body.[14]

But following the 1921 season he became aware of another concern as well—that of administrative indifference. With increased professionalization and the demise of student-controlled athletics, most colleges left the control of athletics to their coaches. But as we have seen, John Heisman wanted every component of the academic scene involved in his coaching system.

One of the Philadelphia papers carried a regular column on its sports page titled "The Old Sport's Musings." By this time sports had grown sufficiently popular to generate daily sports columns with an editorial point of view, and a few months after the close of the 1921 season the column's author commended Heisman for his foresight in inaugurating a policy of winter football to keep his players in shape. Actually, this plan was Heisman's way of reasserting his presence and countering the administrative complacency he had been experiencing during his first two years at Penn. His announcement of winter training helped to revive latent interest among students, too, attracting some 160 candidates in contrast to the regular call for players in the fall that had netted only 85 to 90 men. In sympathizing with his attempt to improve the football situation at Penn, "The Old Sport" viewed Heisman's constructive innovation as one that could "lift the Red and Blue out of the terrible slough into which it has fallen in gridiron matters." In further defense of the Penn coach, the column went on to point out

that college spirit has been dormant and laggard, that the football eleven must be treated by faculty and professors as the gridiron warriors are treated in other universities, that the Provost and his coadjutors must adopt a sympathetic attitude toward football and aid rather than obstruct. . . .

The thing that is appealing at the present time is that Heisman has sensed the utter necessity for urgent changes at Penn, has determined that insofar as he is able he intends to correct pending difficulties and troubles, and that he will return to the University of Pennsylvania next season with the nucleus of a team already known.[15]

Essentially, Heisman's winter training plan was another example of his persistent go-getter nature and demonstrated that he was not going to go down without a fight. But it remained to be seen to what extent his off-season training plan would affect the outcome of Penn's 1922 campaign.

THE NATIONAL GAME (1921)

That football was establishing itself as a truly national game by 1921 was borne out in the season records of some of the leading teams. Iowa, at 7–0, turned in its first unbeaten season, an achievement largely credited to Coach Howard Jones's single-wingback attack that featured an All-American triple-threat back named Aubrey Devine. Highlights of the Iowa Hawkeyes' season were the 10–7 win over Notre Dame that ended the Irish's twenty-game winning streak, and the come-from-behind victory over Purdue on a rain-soaked field, 13–6.

A small southern school that captured Heisman's as well as the nation's admiration at this time was Centre College in Danville, Kentucky. With an enrollment of only around 250 students, the Praying Colonels (so nicknamed because of their devout practice of engaging in prayer before a game) usually went up against much larger and more reputable schools but frequently defeated them. In 1920, they had received national recognition by holding Harvard to a halftime tie before bowing to superior forces. But 1921 gave the Colonels another shot at the Crimson, and this time they came north prepared. Before forty-three thousand fans, Harvard had the better of it in the first half but missed two field goal attempts, and the half ended, 0–0. Then in the second half, Centre finally got the break it had been looking for. After returning a punt to Harvard's 47-yard line, a penalty for piling on gave Centre the ball on the 32. On the next play, quarterback Bo McMillan, with the aid of some well-timed blocking, went all the way for a touchdown. The Colonels then held on to win, 6–0, and claim one of the biggest upsets in football history. The sensational win came as no surprise to Heisman, though, for he recognized in Centre's players, as he had earlier in Sewanee's and Davidson's, the necessary ingredients for successful competition on the gridiron—a strong sense of school spirit and an indomitable will to win.

Another small college team that caught Heisman's attention this year was that fielded by a western Pennsylvania school called Washington and Jefferson (W&J). Coached by Earle "Greasy" Neale (later to become coach of the professional Philadelphia Eagles), the Presidents, despite a solid football tradition, were not as well known as many of the schools they scheduled. Their record was impressive enough for them to be invited to play California in the Rose Bowl, however, although W&J was the smallest school ever to play in the New Year's Day classic. If the Golden Bears thought they had a breather in playing the Presidents, they were sadly mistaken, as this game saw W&J extend its West Coast opponent to the limit. In holding Cal to only two first downs, W&J wound up with a 0–0 tie after the latter had what would have been the winning touchdown called back. But the game was a moral victory, and as an indicator of W&J's quality football program it undoubtedly had a bearing on Heisman's sudden decision to coach there after his final year at Penn.

HEISMAN AND THE 1922 SEASON

If John Heisman ever felt the pressure to produce a winner over the course of his career, he definitely experienced this feeling in the fall of 1922 when he called his squad together to begin training. But bolstered by the positive results of the winter training program, a seven-man coaching staff (the largest of his career), his usual optimistic outlook, and a different approach to drilling his players (showing up well in scrimmage could earn a player time off from two-a-day drills that were conducted in the morning and afternoon), Heisman was certain that the upcoming campaign would be the best since his arrival. And by the last week in September he openly expressed an uncharacteristic preseason satisfaction with the quality of his backfield, a versatile quartet slated to start September 30 against Franklin and Marshall.

Actually, his backfield's versatility was due to the fact that it consisted of three major sport captains at Penn: Jonathan "Poss" Miller of the football team, Al Voegelin of the basketball team, and George Sullivan of the baseball team. In addition, Tex Hamer, the fourth member, was a key member of the track team. Obviously, the strong team leadership Heisman had been looking for was ideally ingrained in this group. Even the Penn line appeared to be much improved, with a number of experienced returnees and capable newcomers on hand. This combination reflected Heisman's work to build the strongest defensive unit Penn had fielded in years, especially since inconsistent defense had been his most formidable problem at Penn. As a result, the Penn line of 1922 would be the heaviest that the Quakers had fielded since the days of Bert Bell.

As he had done in the two previous seasons, Heisman got his team off to a strong start with his usual shutout run, downing Franklin and Marshall, 14–0; Sewanee, 27–0 (the win over this waning southern power was particularly gratifying in light of all the tough games the Purple of Sewanee had given Heisman's past teams); and Maryland, 12–0. Then Swarthmore, which was the first team to score against Penn, was defeated, 14–6. The scoffers were quick to point out the same kind of starts in 1920 and 1921, but when Navy went down, 13–7, leaving the Quakers undefeated at 5–0, everyone began to wonder if Heisman's legendary winning ways were starting to catch on at last.

The game against the Midshipmen of Navy had been as tough as the final score indicated. Played at Franklin Field, this game took on added meaning in that the Middies' coach was Robert C. Folwell, Heisman's predecessor at Penn, who had been more or less forced out of his position as the Quakers' coach. This game also marked the dedication of the newly renovated Franklin Field, which could now seat fifty-five thousand. Completely outplayed in the first half, the Quakers came back from a 7–0 deficit to win, 13–7. Heisman attributed the triumphant result to another of his famous halftime talks, although his actions appear to have contradicted the lesson he had learned at Oberlin about lavishing premature praise on his players:

"Boys," I said, "I'm mighty proud of you. I mean that. Here we've let Navy have the ball almost the entire half and they've scored only one touchdown. As a matter of fact they've run themselves down. . . .

"Now go back there. Take the ball yourself this time. Go get it. Do your stuff this time. It's much better than Navy's. Let them chase you for a while. They'll cave in, this half."[16]

In writing about this game six years after it was played, when he was out of coaching, Heisman had apparently cultivated a more subjective and nostalgic attitude toward the most memorable games in which he had been involved.

However, next came a match with an up-and-coming southern power, Alabama. Like the VMI game of two years before, it had been scheduled as a setup or practice match, as this kind of game against a supposedly inferior foe was then called. Just three years away from making its first trip to the Rose Bowl, the Crimson Tide of Alabama surprised all the experts by knocking off the Red and Blue of Penn, 9–7. As if this narrow loss wasn't a bitter enough pill to swallow, the very next game saw the Quakers lose to cross-state rival Pitt by the slimmest of margins, 7–6. Two such defeats did not do much for Heisman's popularity, and he and his followers must have lost a lot of sleep during the aftermath of these games.

But things began to look more hopeful in the following game when Penn turned the tables on another big in-state foe, Penn State, beating them 7–6. Now with only one game to go, against national champion contender Cornell, Heisman sought to motivate his team to its highest level of performance. But in spite of giving Cornell its toughest game of the 1922 season, the Quakers lost, 9–0, making Heisman's overall record a disappointing 6–3, which was good enough for third place among eastern schools. If better luck had been with him at the right times during this season, he might have produced one of his finest teams.

Heisman was fully prepared to draw on the game statistics of the 1922 season to demonstrate to critics that his men had pulled off a truly superior campaign. As a local newspaper reported Heisman's reaction:

"Most of my energies during 1922 were devoted to building defensively. Our offensive coaches were frankly disgusted because we did not throw everything into the attack. But when you consider everything in a cool mood, you will see that very few of the leaders equaled our record this year of only being held scoreless in one game, and that by Cornell, which I consider the greatest team in the country."[17]

It really didn't matter much now how Heisman rationalized things, for in the wake of the Cornell defeat rumors began to fly again concerning his future at Penn. One of the stories going around had to do with his being courted by two eastern schools and at least four southern institutions. One of the eastern schools eager to land his services was Columbia, which, having banned football during 1906–1914, had compiled a mediocre record since resurrecting its football program in 1915. According to an envoy from New York, who was quoted in a Philadelphia paper, the Columbia alumni and athletic officials had a high opinion of the beleaguered Penn coach: "Heisman has done wonders in arousing not only the student spirit at Penn, but he has worked almost a miracle in causing a re-birth of spirit among the alumni. ... This is just what we need at Columbia more than anything else.[18] Ironically, the visitor from New York recognized much more worth in Heisman's coaching ability than did his disenchanted Philadelphia counterparts. (The coach Columbia would eventually sign in 1923 was Percy Haughton, who decided to try his hand at coaching again after a stint in the business world.)

At this point in early December, 1922, John Heisman's future role at Penn was still up in the air. Then, on December 14, athletic officials announced plans for a "radical change" in Penn's football affairs, a change that if approved would relieve Heisman of his coaching duties and assign him to a newly created position that, for want of a better term, a local newspaper referred to as "football director." The account went on to describe the projected duties of the new position, one for which Heisman seemed admirably qualified at the time: "His task would be to maintain the closest relations and interest between the alumni and undergraduates in a football way. He would be a general co-ordinator to draw together all loose threads of interest and activity, of being in close alliance with faculty, students, graduates and even with future students."[19] In reality, Heisman had been spending a great deal of his time during the year carrying out the duties specified in this description, as his work with the Spirit Committee exemplified. In a sense, then, it was as though the role of football director was being specially created for him, a kind of honorary appointment for a person who had devoted a significant part of his life to Penn football. Then, too, Heisman was a sports personality who had built a national reputation long before he had returned to his alma mater as head coach. (The year 1922 saw the publication of his *Principles of Football*, an event that also greatly enhanced his image as one of the country's foremost gridiron authorities.) Some appropriate recognition for him was in order, it seemed.

However, if Heisman had any knowledge of what was going on within the ranks of the Penn administration at this time, he never admitted it but confessed ignorance. Confined to his apartment in the old Hotel Normandie with a severe cold he had contracted during the Cornell game, he still managed to be his usual candid self in a *Ledger* interview:

"I positively know nothing about these plans," he said. . . . "As for myself, I have no idea of what the thoughts are pertaining to me. If Pennsylvania wants me it has first claim on my services, but I would not lift a finger to retain a position if I was not wanted. I feel that I have put through in large measure the special task for which I was brought here from the South. Conditions were in a chaotic state when I came here, and it was conceded that it would take at least three years to straighten them out. It has, and we really did show results this season."[20]

Respecting the attitudes of the Penn administration, students, and supporters toward Heisman's future role in the school's athletic plans, there was a considerable mix of feelings. While there were some school officials and a strong contingent of alumni who wanted to see him retained as head coach, there were also those who wanted to see him removed from that position, and those who preferred to see him serving in a new post.

Before the month was out, though, Heisman provided everyone an answer when he announced that he would not be a candidate for the head coaching job in 1923, stating that after over thirty years of coaching he felt it was time he took a rest from serving in the role of head coach. (That spring it would be thirty-one years exactly since he set out from Penn for his first coaching job at Oberlin.) His decision appeared to substantiate the belief that he was in line for the position of football director or, more accurately, the director of athletics. In another interview in the Philadelphia *Evening Bulletin*, the thrust of his talk appeared to echo this possibility. In looking to assist the chairman of the Athletic Council that winter, he observed:

> "Already great strides have been made. . . . Whatever else I have accomplished in my three years stay I feel I have developed a permanent spirit of loyalty. This began to be noticeable last season and this year; the students, alumni and faculty cooperated with me splendidly and I greatly appreciate it. They responded quickly to any suggestion I made in the matter of promoting college spirit."[21]

After such a show of loyalty as this, one would have to wonder what it was that suddenly compelled Heisman to leave his alma mater and take the head coaching job at Washington and Jefferson College, the other eastern school that had been courting him. Having been a coach for as long as he had, did he finally realize that missing this part of the game would be too much to bear? Or did he sense an opportunity to relocate at a place where the pressures of coaching would not be nearly as great? Or was it merely the decision of an aging man desirous of returning to his western Pennsylvania roots? Perhaps it was a combination of all these things that helped him make his surprising announcement. But whatever the reason, this dramatic decision was certainly in keeping with the protean personality of the man, one that had always welcomed a challenge of any kind. So following a December 24 visit to Washington, Pennsylvania to meet with W&J officials, Heisman's intentions to remain in coaching were confirmed when the press announced in early January 1923 that he had agreed to a three-year contract.

In spite of his unimpressive 16–10–2 record at Penn, there was considerable press during this period concerning Heisman's positive contributions to the Penn football program, even before it was announced that he would coach at W&J. For example, the Philadelphia *Evening Bulletin* reported:

> Heisman has built up a system which unquestionably is going to lead to great things in football at Pennsylvania.
> When he arrived on Franklin Field to take up his duties in the fall of 1920 things were far from what they should have been. It was a titanic task to get order out of the chaos, but he finally accomplished the feat.
> Next season is sure to find Pennsylvania in the front ranks of American college football. The offensive which has been long a thing unknown on Franklin Field is almost certain to blossom forth, putting Pennsylvania in its proper place in collegiate football.

The article went on to point out a persistent problem that had contributed to the lack of success of Penn's football fortunes: that of not allowing a coach sufficient time to develop a system.[22]

There were other sources that substantiated this outlook. One of them appeared in the University's *Alumni Register* as an editorial entitled "The Football Coach." The piece agreed in effect with Heisman's football philosophy and argued the case for his retention, pointing out a problematic situation that is all too familiar today—the impatience of overly eager alumni and supporters to produce a winner: "One of the essentials of successful football is a continuous system and we do not seem to be patient enough to permit the establishment of this."[23]

While this comment may have reflected the general feeling of those who supported Heisman, the warmest praise of his accomplishments at Penn came from the football captain himself, Jonathan K. "Poss" Miller, in the *Alumni Register*:

This year has been a very successful year for the football team. We came from a last division team to a team which has been rated as a third division team by many critics, with only Cornell and Princeton and West Virginia as our peers. This is an accomplishment we Pennsylvanians should feel proud of and much credit falls upon our coach—Coach Heisman, who played no favorites at any time on or off the field. . . . He has proved that he knows football from start to finish. In fact he has been in active coaching for thirty-one years and has been the author of nearly two-thirds of the present official rulings on football, which alone proves his knowledge of the game. He will go down in Pennsylvania history as the one man who brought Penn's spirit back where it should be and the alumni behind the team to a man.[24]

Yet there were other Penn players who never took to Heisman's dictatorial methods at all. One player (reputed to be guard John Humes) supposedly came across Heisman's little red megaphone following his last day on the field and proceeded to use it as a ball in an impromptu game with some of his teammates. The symbolism of their behavior became quite apparent when, after mimicking their former coach's on-field manner, they conducted a mock funeral service and buried the megaphone.[25]

As far as Heisman himself was concerned, it was now too late for Penn to retain his services, irrespective of any strong feelings toward him, pro or con. The new contract with W&J had irrevocably severed his coaching ties with his alma mater, and as though to dramatize the significance of his new relationship, he spent the month of January 1923 in the then-fledgling winter resort of Miami, Florida, where he did a lot more than just lounge in the sun trying to remedy the lingering cold he had suffered since the Cornell game.

Having worked in real estate during his final years in Atlanta, Heisman realized that fortunes were waiting to be made in Florida, which was then on the verge of a tremendous land boom.[26] It would transform the mangrove swamps between Palm Beach and Miami into a vast coastal stretch of Venetian villages, particularly during the period 1924–1926. So it was that John Heisman was once again in the right place at the right time to transact a lucrative deal for himself.

In 1920, Miami was a city of only about thirty thousand people, but with the establishment of two thousand real estate offices manned by some six thousand agents, all highly motivated to promote and sell property, the city would more than double in population by 1925. As in Heisman's home town of Titusville some sixty years before, stories now circulated about investors becoming rich overnight, for it was not uncommon for a lot purchased for $1,000 to be resold for $200,000. Such an atmosphere surely brought back memories of the fabulous Titusville stories Heisman had heard during his boyhood. At any rate, he realized he was back in a familiar milieu. There was even a Rockefeller connection in the Miami area just as there had been in Titusville, since the oil baron's right-hand man at Standard Oil, Henry M. Flagler, was becoming one of the driving forces in Florida's development through his expanding interests in hotels and the railroad. Although many notable people had previously invested in Palm Beach as a kind of playground for the rich, by the time of Heisman's visit in early 1923 Miami and its beach area were ready to be exploited by a variety of outside investors. Heisman naturally sensed a ripe opportunity to put his go-getter instincts to profitable use. Although the extent of his investment is unknown, it would be wiped out in the financial crash of 1929.

In February, Heisman was back in the Philadelphia area where he was interviewed by a reporter between heats of a track meet at the Camden Armory, where he was a judge. His attitude was at its most positive, almost as though he was pleased and relieved to be rid of the Penn coaching position: "Feeling as fine and fit as a fiddle," said Heisman between heats of the 100-yard dash. "That month in Florida makes me feel like a two-year-old. My cold is all cleared up and from now on I am going to talk football."

He predicted that Penn would be a big winner that fall. By this time, the athletic officials had chosen Lou Young, one of Heisman's top assistants, to be his successor, and Heisman was high on him: "I expect Lou Young to produce a fine team. . . . He has the personality, the spirit is there and there are a number of good players back from last year in addition to the material from an excellent freshman team."[27]

However, his prediction did not prove true, as Young would turn in a mediocre 5–4 season his first time out. Heisman was only a year off in forecasting success, though, for Young's 1924 team went 9–1–1 and won the Eastern championship. (Young's only loss in 1924 was to California, 14–0, at Berkeley.) Young's initial year turned out to be his worst, as during his tenure at Penn (1923–1929) he compiled a 49–15–2 mark, one of the better winning percentages in Penn gridiron annals.

The remaining part of the interview Heisman devoted to discussing his new appointment at Washington and Jefferson. In looking ahead to this fresh challenge, he put forth the optimistic demeanor that had always colored his outlook in taking on a new assignment. Having returned to the campus the preceding week for a short visit where he met with faculty, students, athletes, and the townspeople, he concluded that the place was "excellent for football":

"I talked with the veterans from the last season, and to a man they said that Washington and Jefferson was going to have a great team next fall. I feel the same way myself. I think that we are going to have a winning team out there in the western part of the State. The material is about the best I have looked at in some time. The squad is big, husky and desirous of learning everything about the game. They plied me with questions that showed an eagerness that surprised me.[28]

His new appointment must have nostalgically reminded the aging coach of his successful coaching tenures in the South, making the venture that much more attractive.

THE NATIONAL GAME (1922)

Heisman's final season at Penn was marked by significant developments on other fronts. There was a major rule change, impacting on the point try after touchdown. Theretofore, to gain better position to kick the point after, a punt-out from behind the goal line allowed a team to kick freely from the spot where the ball was caught. From 1922 on, the ball would be placed in front of the goalposts for a scrimmage play in which a team was allowed to run, pass, or kick for the point.

Not surprisingly, Gil Dobie's powerful Cornell team claimed another national championship by going 8–0, maintaining the East's fading dominance at this time. Heisman had good cause to be proud of his Penn team, which had held the national champions to their lowest point total (9) during that season, and for some time after the 1922 campaign he continued to point out how close the Quakers had come to being champions themselves.

Another strong eastern team was Princeton, still coached by Bill Roper. Dubbed as the "Team of Destiny" by the press, the Tigers defied their weekly underdog role by continuing to win, and finished the season with an 8–0 record. The game with Chicago in their first trip to the Midwest exemplified the special kind of grit that characterized this team. Behind in the fourth quarter, 18–7, the Tigers scored a touchdown with six minutes left to make the score 18–14. Then, aided by penalties, they managed to score again on a fourth-and-goal plunge and go ahead, 21–18, with only two minutes left. But Chicago came roaring back, only to be stopped just short of the goal as time ran out. Such big games as the Chicago–Princeton matchup were the stuff of legend, whose dramatic outcome contributed greatly to the growing popularity of football in the 1920s. The press, with its overblown, heroic descriptions of even the most mundane contests, helped convince the public that college football was among the most exciting events in sport.

The top team in the Midwest was again Iowa, which went 7–0 and extended its winning streak to seventeen straight games. With new stadiums popping up all over the country, Ohio State scheduled a game with Michigan to help dedicate its stadium in Columbus. But the Ohio State Buckeyes did not find much to celebrate after the Michigan Wolverines turned Harry Kipke loose. In leading Michigan to a 19–0 victory, the elusive back proved a one-man gang by scoring two touchdowns and kicking a field goal.

On the West Coast the Rose Bowl opened up its new stadium in Pasadena with Penn State's Nittany Lions and Southern Cal's Trojans as opponents. The Trojans won, 14–3. As a coming power, Southern Cal would soon be vying with Andy Smith's California teams for Far West supremacy.

In the South, Vanderbilt also had a stadium to dedicate, the first in the region to be designed only for football. Coach Dan McGugin had invited his alma mater, Michigan, to be his team's opponent, and after stopping the Wolverines' four attempts on the 2-yard line with goal to go, the Commodores managed to hold their Midwest visitors to a 0–0 tie for something of a moral victory.

As Fuzzy Woodruff pointed out, intersectional contests between southern teams and opponents from the East and Midwest continued to abound at this time. However, Woodruff's initial critical stance had now begun to mellow as he observed that these games "gave the southern collegians a chance to see some of the rest of the country, gave them an intimate insight into college traditions the nation over and furthermore taught them a good deal about football, not the least important of these teachings being that the southern game was just about as good as any other game."[29]

One of these intersectional matches that attracted considerable attention at this time was the first meeting between Georgia Tech and Notre Dame in Atlanta on October 28. With Coach Rockne's "Four Horsemen" still a year away from running roughshod over their opponents, Bill Alexander's team was given a fair chance of winning. But the Yellow Jackets, who played tough in the beginning, let the game get away from them and lost, 13–3. Although the Irish would thoroughly dominate the series over the years, the Tech–Irish matchup would always prove to be a headliner no matter who was favored.

However, in 1922 the most significant development in southern football was the transformation of the Southern Intercollegiate Athletic Association into the Southern Conference. Although the SIAA had become a cumbersome organization of thirty members by 1920, the new Southern Conference was almost as unwieldy, with its membership of twenty schools extending from Virginia to Louisiana. Ironically, the large number of members made it possible for some schools to avoid playing each other during the entire life of the conference. But athletic officials of the day recognized that belonging to a conference not only helped to ensure ethical standards among its membership, it was a way to gain national recognition by winning the conference championship.

HEISMAN AT WASHINGTON AND JEFFERSON (1923)

By winning SIAA championships at Clemson and Georgia Tech, Heisman had brought recognition to his teams as well as himself. Even though he had not done as well at Penn in the soon to be dubbed "Ivy League," he quickly realized that in coaching at an independent school like Washington and Jefferson, he was at a competitive disadvantage by not being able to play for a conference championship.

As a venerable, church-related institution with roots dating back to the late 1700s, W&J came into being in 1865 when Jefferson College of Canonsburg, Pennsylvania merged with Washington College of Washington, Pennsylvania, where the new campus was eventually located. Because of its early origins, the college was identified as the oldest institution of higher learning west of the Alleghenies. However, the new college's location in Washington, in an area south of Pittsburgh bordering on West Virginia and Ohio, had become moderately industrialized by 1923. (Incorporated as a city in 1924, Washington's growth over the years had been enhanced by an oil strike in the 1880s and factory expansion in the 1890s.) In this respect it was unlike the small college towns where Heisman had previously coached, but still, something about the close-knit, intimate atmosphere of the college itself was reminiscent of his days at Oberlin, Auburn, and Clemson. As such, it brought out the best of Heisman's natural coaching instincts and at first proved to be a welcome relief from the high-pressured environment he had endured at Penn.

Besides being strong academically, the school had enjoyed a successful reputation in athletics, particularly football. With an administration that was highly supportive of intercollegiate athletics since the 1890s, the W&J president, Dr. J. D. Moffat, envisioned football as one of the most effective ways to publicize a school and increase enrollment. This attitude was not unlike that of many other institutions at this time. As early as 1901, therefore, the college had begun to organize schedules designed to win national acclaim as well as generate revenue. As a result of this all-out effort, W&J fielded some highly competitive teams, among them the 1913 team that went undefeated, beating such teams as Penn State, Pitt, and West Virginia, and tying Yale. The 1914 team was almost as good, with only a last minute, 1-point loss to Harvard to mar its record. But the best was yet to come.

The principal architect of W&J's athletic success and drive for national recognition was Robert M. Murphy, who was appointed as graduate manager (the equivalent of today's athletic director) in 1907. An impressive speaker and successful student recruiter, Murphy was one of the main reasons that many promising athletes signed on at W&J. As we have seen with Centre, Sewanee, and Davidson, this was a day when small schools could hold their own on the gridiron against schools with greater resources. Much of the credit for the small schools' success should go to aggressive, determined athletic managers like W&J's Robert Murphy. To defeat rivals on the order of Pitt and West Virginia would have made a successful season for many schools, but W&J, with Murphy spurring it on, was after even bigger game.

During the period 1917–1919, the school produced one of the game's all-time great players in Wilbur "Pete" Henry, whom Walter Camp rated as the greatest tackle ever to set foot on the gridiron when he named him to his All-America team. Many have since declared that there never has been anyone the equal of Pete Henry in his ability to get through the defense and smother a punt attempt. He was, in fact, the most feared punt blocker of his day.

But if Henry was the greatest player that W&J ever produced, its greatest team was the 1921 squad which, after compiling a 10–0 record, including six shutouts along the way, was invited to play California in the Rose Bowl. This was the era of the California "wonder" teams, and to most football fans the choice of W&J as an opponent for the Golden Bears was nothing more than a setup. But as noted earlier, the Presidents played the highly favored Golden Bears off their collective feet. They even came close to scoring twice (one touchdown was called back) but had to settle for a scoreless tie. Even so, this game would go down as the high point in W&J's football history.

However, after the great Rose Bowl year, the team had fallen to a disappointing 6–3–1 record, and since Coach Greasy Neale had announced his resignation following the 1922 season, the W&J Athletic Council set out to secure the best man available to succeed him. After lengthy review, John Heisman was selected as outstandingly the best man among a score of candidates and a coach of national prominence."[30] At the same time, David C. Morrow, who had twice before been head coach at W&J, was recruited from Bethany College as line coach. Morrow, who could boast of never having had an opponent score more than 14 points on his W&J teams, had built a reputation as one of the nation's premier line coaches. So to those who followed football, it appeared that W&J had pulled off a real coup in obtaining both Morrow and Heisman to head up its team.

Interestingly, Heisman's appointment brought to W&J its third head coach from Penn. Consequently, expectations were high that, like big winners Robert Folwell and Sol Metzger before him, Heisman would "restore the Red and Black prestige lost during the 1922 season." Robert Murphy was highly positive on the appointments: "There naturally is nothing but extreme satisfaction expressed over the securing of [Morrow's] services as our line coach. The same spontaneous acceptance of Heisman as the best man available is also evident among the Wash-Jeff supporters everywhere."[31]

Still very much the self-promoter, on March 15 Heisman published a letter (addressed "Dear New Friends") to the W&J faculty, alumni, and undergraduates in the school newspaper. Not surprisingly, the letter dealt with his philosophy of athletics and what he expected from his "New Friends" in terms of support. Much of it was familiar enough:

> You ask what is my athletics creed. I reply at once that I believe one goes to college primarily to acquire an education; while athletics, important though they be in undergraduate life, must still be considered as secondary in importance. And so I have small use for the chap who never concentrates on anything save athletics. Also, I believe in flawlessly clean play and in conduct of lofty sportsmanship on the field— in practice as well as in match games. It's an excellent thing to be a great athlete, but it's more splendid still to be a fine gentleman. . . .
> If we are to have a winning team next fall we cannot begin too early the work of preparation for a strenuous campaign . . . but what I want and ask right now is that every W.&J. man decide once and for all that he is going to give to the team, the coaches and the management his 100 per cent of moral and practical support through thick and thin. No half-hearted support, no brand of lackadaisical effort will ever do in football. That game is one that calls for the unswerving loyalty, the unquenchable spirit, the absolute best of everybody to the last man."[32]

The words were reminiscent of Heisman in his prime at Georgia Tech, standing forth in their evangelistic intensity as a testimonial to the fact that his disappointing tenure at Penn had not yet undermined his fighting spirit and the will to win.

Opening up the season on September 29 against Bethany College, the W&J team looked ragged, even lackadaisical at times, and in spite of the comfortable 21–0 win over a decidedly inferior team, Heisman knew he had plenty of work ahead in molding the W&J men to his ways. With a notable southern team, Washington and Lee, scheduled to come to campus the following week, he anticipated putting his best foot forward. Unfortunately, though, the game was never played. Instead, one of the early dramas of racial discrimination in sports took center stage.

Like most southern schools of that day, W&L refused to play against any team that had a black player in the lineup. It so happened that one of Heisman's most outstanding players was a hard-running black halfback named Charles "Pruner" West. (West was also a track man who starred in the 1922 and 1923 Penn Relays. After graduating, he went on to a distinguished career in medicine.) Although W&L officials had known West was on the Presidents' squad when the game was scheduled, they had assumed that he would not be allowed to play against their team. But upon their arrival at W&J manager Robert Murphy informed his southern visitors that West would be in the starting lineup. Refusing to play under this condition, the W&L contingent forfeited the game on the spot. In the W&J yearbook, which recorded the athletic results of 1923, the editorial staff sarcastically reported the game as "Not Played. . . . The Washington and Lee squad went back home to attend a Ku Klux Klan meeting that night."

Heisman's views on the game are not known, but because of his reputation for fairness he would surely have sided with Murphy's decision. Even though Heisman had coached in the South for twenty-five years (1895–1919) and was familiar enough with such situations, a story he related later affords us a clue to his personal feelings about breaking the color line. It had to do with the time "El Paso High School played the Tucson [Arizona] High School and won because, among other reasons, Tucson had not played its star fullback, Daniels, a Negro. Colored players were not permitted to play on Texas teams, and rather than offend El Paso and subject Daniels to embarrassment, Tucson had gone on without him." Next year the game was played in Tucson, where the El Paso captain approached the Tucson coach, expressing his team's desire to play against Daniels: "We will play just as clean against him as we would against any white boy. You see, over in El Paso, the public's sort of against colored boys playing and it makes it difficult. Understand?" According to Heisman, "Daniels played one of the best games of his life. El Paso played him hard and clean. His touchdown won for Tucson, and after the game the El Paso lads went to the Tucson dressing room and congratulated him."[33]

An interesting sidelight about Murphy's decision to play Pruner West was revealed much later after his pregame meeting with the W&L officials. It had to do with "the fact that Murphy knew at the time of the conversation in his office that Pruner West had a sprained ankle, and that [Heisman] did not intend to play him at all. Murphy simply would not discredit West by agreeing not to play him."[34]

With the W&L travesty behind him, one of Heisman's biggest career wins came the following week when Brown University came to town. The Bruins were heavily favored, mainly because Walter Camp, as well as other football authorities of the time, had picked them to win the Eastern championship. Big and experienced, the Brown team was expected to take care of the W&J eleven with little difficulty. But Heisman had worked his men especially hard all week to do battle against his first undergraduate school. Consequently, by the end of the game the Bruins found themselves on the short end of a 12–7 score. It was one of the more shocking upsets of the young season.

Another home game followed, this time with area rival Carnegie Tech from Pittsburgh. Carnegie had apparently come to play, as they jumped to a quick 7–0 lead. But with Heisman urging the Red and Black on, his men came from behind to win a defensive struggle, 9–7. So far, his old-fashioned system appeared to be holding up quite well in spite of recurrent injuries to key players.

The following week W&J went on the road for the first time that season to play Detroit. But after failing to take advantage of numerous scoring opportunities, Heisman considered his team fortunate to come away with a 6–0 victory. Perhaps his charges had been looking past the Detroit match to the important contest with Lafayette the ensuing Saturday at the Polo Grounds in New York. But to Heisman it seemed his players' attention to team discipline was woefully lacking, and that this was the real reason for their inconsistent play. At times they performed brilliantly as a concerted unit, and then they would just as suddenly lapse into unexpected periods of uninspired play. Nevertheless, at this halfway point in the season, W&J had compiled an unbeaten 4–0 record. The Heisman early season magic seemed to be working the way it always had.

During this time in the development of college football, a number of eastern teams scheduled at least one of their games in New York, looking to the financial advantage of larger gate receipts than they could ever take in at home. Certainly, schools like W&J and Lafayette, located in small college towns with limited-size stadiums, profited by such a move. As a result, these two schools maintained a running series in New York during the 1920s, generating a rivalry that was among the more heated. The 1923 game, played on November 3, was so intense, in fact, that it ended in a 6–6 tie. Although many Red and Black supporters blamed the disappointing result on the distracting enticements of New York nightlife that beckoned to the players that Saturday evening, the yearbook pointedly declared that in this game "Luck saved the Presidents from defeat." With Lafayette fielding another of its strong teams that year, Heisman must have openly agreed with this observation. But even though he was not pleased with the game's outcome, his team was approaching mid-November still undefeated.

The Presidents came home the following week to smash Waynesburg, 40–0, so prospects were looking good for the big game with Pitt on November 17. But as so often happens in the game of football, things did not come off as planned, and Heisman's team suffered its first defeat of the season, 13–6. The sports editor of the local Washington newspaper candidly explained W&J's collapse in the school yearbook, pointing out that the Presidents had not taken their opponent seriously enough since Pitt had been beaten by both West Virginia and Carnegie Tech: "But Pitt was a much different team against W.&J. than it had been before; played a smart and steady game; while W.&J., undoubtedly over-confident and far from being mentally prepared, failed to display the worth it had shown against Brown and Carnegie Tech, and so lost the game, 13 to 6."[35] To lose to a big rival in a long-standing series always tainted any football season, no matter how successful a team had been in other games. So in facing up to this disheartening development and the fact that the sins of overconfidence and lack of mental preparation had figured in the loss, Heisman still had a chance to soften the sting of public criticism by motivating his team to defeat West Virginia. He immediately started preparing for the big Thanksgiving Day game to be played in Morgantown.

But something had begun to gnaw at him at this point in his coaching career, a distracting problem that would plague him throughout his remaining years as a coach. The players he now had to deal with did not appear to employ or even possess the degree of personal discipline he had always advocated as an essential ingredient for playing the game of football. They certainly lacked the kind of discipline he had had little problem inculcating in his early players—the players of his Auburn, Clemson, and Georgia Tech years. He had already had a taste of this debilitating attitude at Penn, of course, but in the less sophisticated atmosphere of W&J he thought things would have been different. Could it be that northern players, having had more material advantages during their growing-up years, were softer than their southern counterparts?

Actually what Heisman had failed to take into account was that he was now coaching in a different day than in the years before World War I and that the days before the war were as far removed from the 1920s as the days before the Civil War had been from his own growing-up years. In this respect his personal coaching style was no longer right for this newer day. Consequently, the underlying reason for not getting everything from his players that he would have liked was simply that he had failed to adapt his coaching techniques to the changing social environment and attitudes of his players. Little wonder, then, that their game performances were not up to Heisman's persistently demanding standards.

Even so, in the game with West Virginia, which after the Pitt loss and attendant blow to morale could have been a disastrous affair, the W&J players came together, rose to the occasion, and played as well as they had earlier against Brown. As a result, the Mountaineers, though unbeaten in two seasons of play and heavily favored, suffered a shocking 7–2 defeat.

Surprisingly, the win was accomplished "under frightful weather conditions and on a field that was 'skiddy' with mud and water."[36] Fittingly, though, the Washington reporter's assessment of why W&J had won suggested that Heisman's old-fashioned coaching methods could still generate positive results, even at this late point in his career: "A wonderful rejuvenation, coupled with an admirable fighting spirit, that has usually characterized Red and Black teams, and an ability to grasp opportunities, were responsible for this brilliant conclusion to the season."[37] Of course, the "admirable fighting spirit" and "ability to grasp opportunities" were pervasive trademarks of Heisman's coaching. Since there had been numerous injuries to key players throughout the campaign, W&J's 1923 season could have been less than successful had it not been for Heisman's old-fashioned coaching style. Still, to the old coach something had been plainly missing that fall, particularly a wholehearted response from team members to realize his desire for discipline. It was a demand that he thought was also not being supported by the school's administration. So by early 1924, the dissatisfied but still dedicated coach found himself preparing to cast his lot with yet another school—this time, though, his last.

On a personal note, Heisman had now resumed his courtship of Edith Maora Cole, whom he had known at Buchtel. His days as a bachelor coach at Penn had been rather lonely, so renewing his relationship with a woman he had never really fallen out of love with provided him the emotional tie that had been sorely missing since his divorce. As far as his business interests were concerned, Heisman had invested in a sporting goods store in New York City during this time. As the popularity of organized sports had spread, so had the demand for athletic commodities in the support areas of training and individual participation. Coaching for as long as he had, Heisman had learned a great deal about the ins and outs of the sporting goods business. It was also an enterprise that would ultimately determine his decision to locate in New York upon the termination of his coaching career, a significant choice that would set the stage for his final role as a public sports personality.

THE NATIONAL GAME (1923)

At this time, some momentous things were occurring on the national scene. As a sophomore at the University of Illinois in 1923, Harold "Red" Grange made his gridiron debut, one so auspicious it would transform him overnight into an unrivaled star of American sports' Golden Age. In surpassing the outstanding achievements of Willie Heston and Jim Thorpe over three seasons of play, Grange would average 1,212 yards a year from scrimmage and kick returns. Endowed in the main with quickness and speed, he soon became the model halfback whose accomplishments every other back was measured by. As a result, the newspapers and magazines, in recognizing headline copy in whatever this budding star did, made Red Grange their special darling. In leading the Illini to an undefeated season (8–0) and national champion status in 1923, Grange had a remarkable year that featured long runs and spectacular punt returns for touchdowns. Against Northwestern he intercepted a pass and returned it ninety-one yards for a score, but his greatest day was to come in the following year. Overall, Red Grange was college football's dynamic promotional agent who would help turn the game into the glamour sport of the 1920s.

In 1923, Yale also went undefeated at 8–0. Playing before some of the largest crowds of the day (upwards of eighty-thousand people) jammed into the Yale Bowl, the Bulldogs came through with big wins over Army (31–10) and Princeton (27–0). Their biggest scare came in the Maryland game when they had to come from behind to win, 16–14. Because of the Bulldogs' fighting spirit and intense will to win, most followers thought Coach Tad Jones had turned out one of his greatest teams, even though they would wind up having to share the Eastern title with Cornell, which went unbeaten for the third straight year.

This year saw George Woodruff's version of the on-side kick eliminated as a strategic maneuver. Now instead of being able to down the ball and maintain possession after a quick kick, the punting team had to surrender the ball to the receiving team unless the ball was fumbled away.

In the South the twenty teams of the Southern Conference were taking their membership seriously enough to start ignoring intersectional matches in the main and scheduling more games with each other to help determine a clear-cut conference champion. The upshot of all this was increased regional rivalry and growing attendance at games. Georgia Tech led the way by scheduling strong opponents as early as October.

As in the Southeast, football in the Southwest enjoyed a rapid rise to popularity once it got underway. As noted, the Southwest Conference had been formed in 1915, and just four years later in 1919, Texas A&M, coached by Dana X. Bible, came up with the region's first nationally recognized team when the Aggies went undefeated and unscored on in ten games. Only the 1914 Texas Longhorns had posted a comparable mark at 8–0. The major Texas schools, seeking to field highly reputable athletic teams, fell in love with football right from the start. By 1923, the forward pass was both the order of the day and an omen of the future as the Mustangs of Southern Methodist University (SMU) went undefeated on their way to their first conference championship.

HEISMAN GOES TO RICE (1924)

It is interesting that the Southwest Conference took to the passing game when it did, for John Heisman, the coach who had been highly instrumental in implementing the adoption of the forward pass as a permanent feature of the game, would be coaching in this conference the following season. The school that would sign him, Rice Institute, as it was then known, had joined the fledgling conference when LSU dropped out at the close of the 1915 season. Established in 1912, Rice wasted little time getting involved in athletics. Its administration had hired Philip H. Arbuckle of Southwestern University as its director of athletics and charged him with the mission of developing a competitive athletic program. By 1914, the Owls (their unusual nickname was derived from the popular symbol of wisdom on the school seal) played their first full schedule. In 1916 they ran up their biggest score ever in trouncing the team of another new Texas school, SMU, by the improbable score of 146–3.

Even so, during those early years the football teams of Rice experienced rough going, particularly against big rivals Texas and Texas A&M. Part of the reason had to do with the school's unique mission and ambivalent identity. Named after philanthropist William Marsh Rice, who had endowed the school out of his cotton fortune, Rice was initially described as an "Institute of Literature, Science and Art." As basically a liberal arts school, it lacked the more practically attractive missions of its sister institutions. (Not until 1963 would Rice be officially identified as a university.) Consequently, the older, more career-oriented schools in the region always had the advantage in recruiting quality high-school athletes.

Although Arbuckle's 1919 team had taken second place in the conference, the teams of 1920–1923 were mediocre at best, finishing as low as seventh, out of eight teams in the conference, on two occasions. Thus the stage was set for the recruitment of a reputable coach of the stature of John Heisman, someone of "considerable successful experience," as the school newspaper put it. Disenchanted with his Washington and Jefferson appointment, Heisman had been looking around for another coaching job since the close of the 1923 season. Although he had the sporting goods business in New York that demanded his attention, he found it hard to resist any overtures to continue coaching, particularly those that were financially attractive. Because of his many accomplishments in athletics, he knew he was in an advantageous position to bargain,[38] and that was exactly what he did when Rice showed an interest in having him succeed Arbuckle, who had resigned as athletic director in December 1923.

After meeting with Rice officials in February 1924, Heisman set forth his terms. Because of his business interests he wanted to be at Rice only during spring training and the football season. How he expected to administer the other seasonal sports in absentia was evidently something only a person of Heisman's autocratic bent could work out. His audacity in asking for a starting salary of $9,000 and a five-year contract undoubtedly rankled the faculty when they learned of this proposal. (The highest-paid Rice faculty member of that day earned $7,500, and unless tenured all faculty were appointed to annual contracts.) Even so, the trustees ultimately agreed to Heisman's terms and salary demands. Although his contract specified that he be present on campus only from September through December 10 and from March to mid-April each year, Heisman wisely decided to devote himself full-time to Rice athletics right from the start of his appointment. For this change in plans, he had asked for additional compensation, but this request was turned down. At this point in his life, the security-minded Heisman was obviously looking to make the most of any financial opportunity that came his way.

The Houston that John Heisman came to in 1924 was a lot like the Atlanta he had left in 1919—a progressive city of over one hundred thousand in population. With more than one thousand students enrolled in 1923, the Rice campus was beginning to reflect the area's growth. In fact, the school's administration and faculty were having a difficult time accommodating the large influx of students in the limited classroom space available at this time. Along with Rice's emphasis on athletics, however, a new field house had been completed in 1921. Then, with the announcement that Heisman was to be the new athletic director, a wave of optimism seemed to inject new life into both the sports program and the student body. Upon learning of Heisman's appointment the student newspaper (*The Thresher*) scooped all the local papers with a banner front-page story. The newspaper also reprinted a telegram that Heisman had wired: "Greetings to Rice and student body. Everybody roll up sleeves and let's go."

So when John Heisman descended on the Rice campus in the spring of 1924, he brought with him the same infectious enthusiasm he had generated everywhere he had been. Having recently returned from a long-planned European trip with his new wife Maora, he was anxious to get involved with his duties, particularly those related to the football team. But no one was more eager to witness Heisman in action than the Rice students themselves, for his winning reputation had arrived before him, as reported in *The Thresher*: "Contrary to recent newspaper accounts, Heisman did not have a poor season at Washington and Jefferson last year. He lost but one game and that by a single touchdown to the University of Pittsburgh. The Washington and Jefferson team gave the much heralded West Virginia eleven a good beating and at the end of the season was accorded the place of fourth best in America."[39]

Upon assuming his duties as athletic director, then, Heisman's charismatic presence was evident right from the start. When the "R" Association (letterman's club), alumni, and citizens of Houston hosted a banquet at the Rice Hotel to welcome their famous coach officially, Heisman addressed the more-than-one hundred in attendance, and as he spoke the old Heisman oratorical magic pervaded the atmosphere. According to *The Thresher*: "The forcefulness and easiness of his speech held the attention of his listeners throughout and resulted in a storm of applause at the end which lasted for several minutes. The main theme of his talk concerned the five principles which he described as the essentials of football. These were material, coaching, faith, college spirit, and organization."[40]

Realizing that the circumstances surrounding his appointment might not endear him to the faculty, Heisman was tactful enough in his speech to emphasize his traditional stand on academics as of prime importance and athletics as secondary. He maintained, though, that the "ability to think quickly, clearly, and correctly under fire is a valuable product attained in the laboratory of football." In essence his message to the Rice supporters was the same one he had presented everywhere he had gone, and as usual he had his audience in the palm of his hand—particularly when he went on to tell how football could be a unifying force in bringing students, faculty, college, and city together. Harvey Smith, the upcoming football captain, was sufficiently inspired to pledge the squad's wholehearted support, remarking in *The Thresher* "that if loyalty to the coach and hard work mean anything we'll have a winning team next year." After Heisman's trials at

Washington and Jefferson, Smith's pledge must have been like a refreshing spring breeze. Surely, everyone in the audience that evening was convinced that a new era in Rice athletics had begun. As though to symbolize this new beginning, Rice officials gave Heisman free reign to select his coaching assistants.

It did not take long for the new Rice coach to become embroiled in controversy, however. That summer, back east, his recruiting efforts attracted the attention of the National Collegiate Athletic Association, a body that was beginning to take its role in regulating college athletics quite seriously. During this era the recruiting process was not as clearly defined as it is today, especially recruiting conducted in regions beyond the location of a particular college. When a newspaper reporter picked up on Heisman's recruiting efforts in New Jersey, the story gave the impression that he was proselytizing athletes who had already committed to play for eastern colleges.

When Rice administrator William Ward Watkin, who had been instrumental in bringing Heisman to Rice, heard of what had been going on, he demanded an explanation from Heisman. As an individual who in his innovative outlook was always ahead of his time, Heisman responded that he saw nothing wrong with recruiting athletes from another part of the country. Even though he immediately curtailed his activities in New Jersey, it was apparent that his understanding of what constituted amateurism and its relationship to the control of college athletics was in direct conflict with Watkin's stand. In fact, Watkin's obsolescent views on how college athletics should be managed demonstrate just how far apart the athletic world of Rice at this time was from that which Heisman must have envisioned. Watkin contended that

control of athletics should be in the hands of the faculty, without joint committees of alumni, undergraduates, and faculty such as some other schools had. He believed that athletic expenditures should be held to a minimum; there should be no extravagance, wasteful traveling, or undesirable deviation from a student's normal activities when he participated on a team. Scouting and recruiting were unadvisable, as were the scholarships for athletics; and student athletes should not be coddled with special courses or lenient grades.

Although Watkin felt that coaches should be members of the faculty, even though a coach's salary was out of line with a professor's, he reasoned that the operation of the free market would ultimately keep salaries in line.[41]

Fully aware of the growing power and active role that alumni had acquired in influencing the course of college athletics, Heisman recognized that if a truly dedicated coach failed to take an active part in the recruiting process, then a school was leaving itself wide open to a variety of problems. As he would later state his concerns in 1928:

The strict tenets of amateurism will be debauched with fierce abandon as long as alumni take an aggressive pride in their colleges, which pride is usually centered in the college's athletics. . . . There will be professionalism in college athletics as long as high-pressure salesmanship is an important part of increasing college finances, adding buildings to the college plant and fattening the college's prestige and enrollment.

Heisman then went on to describe how go-getter-type alumni participated in the recruiting process at this time. Once he spied a potential superstar, the alumnus merely informed his alma mater of his prize find: "If the authorities back at college have faith in the alumnus' judgment they may tell him to interview the subject of his enthusiasm and arrange to ship him on the moment he is ripe for college."[42] Although this hypothetical situation was written over sixty years ago, it reveals that little has changed since that time, for Heisman's description is remarkably close to what has been going on in more recent times, even though many attempts at reform have been undertaken.[43]

In spite of getting off on the wrong foot with the Rice administration and the fact that he now had a male enrollment only about one-tenth the size of Penn's to draw on, Heisman managed to get his new team off on the right track. In the lingering heat of early October, Rice opened its 1924 season with a 22–6 win over Sam Houston College. A student reporter observed that a "new brand of football for this part of the country was seen," and despite some first-game jitters and mistakes, the Owls had things pretty much under control, displaying "the drive and fight that Coach Heisman asked for."[44]

In the next game, though, Rice found itself behind in the first half to Southwestern University. But after intermission Heisman brought his men back strong as they scored three touchdowns to win, 20–6. Heisman called the game "a step toward getting the fighting tradition, that unyielding, undying spirit that will not be denied."[45]

At this point, prospects for an all-winning season looked good, but in the very next contest a strong LSU team dashed those hopes by shutting out the Owls, 12–0. Even so, the redoubtable Heisman contended that his men had put up a good fight and that LSU's scores had been "acquired through flukes" and were attributable mainly to Rice's lack of experience.

Then in a hard-fought contest against Texas Christian University in Fort Worth, Rice came from behind in the last minute of play to defeat the TCU Horned Frogs, 7–3. Although this was a conference game, Heisman thought that the sluggish play of his team indicated that they might be looking ahead to a bigger conference foe, the University of Texas, their next opponent.

In this, the most important game on the schedule, Heisman recorded one of his and Rice's greatest victories—a 19–6 defeat of the Texas Longhorns. Although several key Rice players were suffering from various ailments prior to this match, the Owls rolled to a surprising 19–0 lead before Texas could manage its only score late in the game. It was only the second time that a Rice team had beaten Texas, and because of this spectacular win Heisman pronounced the season an "undoubted success" no matter what happened the rest of the way.

But with a winning season in sight, Heisman's team soon found itself in the old familiar nosedive that had haunted his Penn teams as three straight losses brought his first season at Rice to a disappointing close. When unheralded Austin College came to town, Heisman saw his worst fears come true: His men had not yet recovered from their great Texas victory and played like it. As a result, Austin scored on a pass play and made the touchdown hold up to win, 6–0. A comic sidelight, at least to the less partisan spectators, saw the Austin quarterback playing in his bare feet, an act of athletic showmanship coming long before the day of the barefoot field-goal kicker.

Rice did manage to give a good account of itself against the two conference opponents remaining on the schedule, but after leading in both games the Owls fell behind to lose to Texas A&M, 13–6, and to eventual conference champion Baylor, 17–9. Untimely penalties and key injuries as well as overall lack of experience accounted in the main for these losses. According to Heisman, "the second string men as a rule were so far behind the first string players that any substitution instantly spelled a decided weakening in the team's offensive and defensive strength."[46]

Nevertheless, the never-say-die coach saw a great deal of promise in his team's 4–4 record:

The Rice Team of 1924 did more to establish Rice fighting traditions than any other team that had gone before them. . . . And at the finish there was not a Rice man anywhere who did not believe that the team had learned a lot of football, had learned the price of success, had learned how to pay that price without whimpering, had learned how to fight to the last gasp for his Alma Mater.[47]

The familiar Heisman rhetoric was still evident, but it would take more than old-fashioned college spirit for Rice to do any better than a 4–4 season during Heisman's regime. His coaching posture still presented an on-field figure that was part martinet, part dramatic actor, but it had now evolved into something of an absurd image that did not come across as true as it once had. William M. McVey, a Clevelander who played tackle on the 1924 team, observed in later years: "On Monday, [Heisman] was like a district attorney— all strategy and discipline—and by the end of the week, he was a Shakespearean actor." McVey recalled one game when Rice was losing, and the situation found Heisman walking up and down the sidelines at halftime talking to himself: "Everyone in the stadium was watching, wondering what was on his mind. Well, he was muttering, 'A team that won't be beat can't be beat' over and over, and then the whistle blew and he suddenly yelled,

'A TEAM THAT WON'T BE BEAT CAN'T BE BEAT' at the top of his lungs."[48] Heisman's faith in what he had always termed college spirit was so much an obsession with him by this time in his career that the emotional side of the game was apparently taking over from his former rational approach to coaching football. He had clearly failed to adjust his approach to the more scientific demands of a new day and time.

THE NATIONAL GAME (1924)

On the national scene, 1924 was the year that Red Grange astonished the sporting world with his sensational football heroics for the University of Illinois. On October 18, Michigan was on hand to help dedicate the new Illinois stadium, but it was the Wolverines' misfortune to run into a one-man gang on that momentous day. All Grange did was run the opening kickoff back ninety-five yards for a touchdown, then score from scrimmage on long runs of sixty-seven, fifty-six, and forty-four yards. Incredibly, he had handled the ball just eight times and scored four touchdowns in the first twelve minutes of the game. In the second half, the Galloping Ghost, as Grange was soon referred to by an admiring press, scored again on a 15-yard dash and then displayed his unique versatility by tossing an 18-yard touchdown pass. Grange's achievement that day resulted in a Big Ten record as Illinois dedicated its stadium with a 39–14 victory.[49]

Heisman wrote emotionally of Grange's overall greatness later in another of his *Collier's* articles: "Do I hear some scoffer belittle Red Grange? Do I hear that advertising made Harold the celebrity he was? Don't be foolish. Any lad with his talent was his own advertising agent. The things he did to fine teams like Michigan and Penn, with both teams laying for him, are the marks of natural greatness."[50]

But the national champion that year was Knute Rockne's Notre Dame team, whose starting backfield was transformed into legend when Grantland Rice wrote the most famous lead in sports journalism in his syndicated column following the Irish's 13–7 win over Army at the Polo Grounds in New York: "Outlined against the blue-gray October sky, the Four Horsemen rode again. In dramatic lore they were known as famine, pestilence, destruction, and death. These are only aliases. Their real names are Stuhldreher, Miller, Crowley, and Layden." In adding to the mythology of college football, such fanfare helped make the 1924 Notre Dame team one of the most famous in the history of football.

Another reason for the Irish's success at this time was the unique offensive system Rockne had installed. Behind a steady dose of up-front blocking (fittingly the linemen were called the "Seven Mules") as well as precisely timed downfield interference, the fast-starting Irish backs wielded a formidable, wide-open style of attack. After lining up in a basic T-formation, they would shift on command into a box-shaped formation and then, following a brief pause, move out in a quick striking play that the defense usually found extremely difficult to halt. As a result, Notre Dame rolled to a 10–0 season, and in the process established a winning, exciting, popular image that has lasted until this day. To be sure, the football legend that is Notre Dame was born during the ballyhoo season of 1924.

Out west, itinerant coach Pop Warner had now taken on the coaching reins at Stanford. The school's big game with the University of California, which was to determine the Coast representative in the Rose Bowl, turned out to be one of the all-time classics. Although the Golden Bears were still undefeated after five years of "wonder" performances under Coach Andy Smith, this year they wound up with two ties on their record. The Stanford game turned out to be one of these.

Before a crowd of over seventy-five thousand at Berkeley, Cal led by 20–6, with ten minutes to play. But then a pass play by Stanford narrowed the gap to 20–13, and in a whirlwind finish the Indians (as Stanford was then known) went eighty-one yards to tie the game at 20–20 with only two seconds left on the clock. Here was another dramatically charged game that helped promote football as America's most exciting spectator sport.

This game also earned Stanford the right to play Notre Dame in the Rose Bowl on New Year's Day, 1925, while national runner-up California invited Eastern champ Penn (9–0–1), now coached by Heisman's successor Lou Young, to its home park where it defeated the Quakers, 14–0. The Notre Dame–Stanford matchup, which featured two of the country's top coaches in Rockne and Warner, was one of the first games to herald the confrontation of superior coaching talent nationally. The game was a natural to showcase such a rivalry in that Warner and Rockne were the leading coaches at this time, both commanding high-powered offensive systems that set the examples for others to emulate. (Warner, who would coach for forty-four years and win 313 games, was named "the greatest football coach of all time" in a 1954 Associated Press poll, mainly because of his inventiveness.) Having perfected his double-wingback formation by this time, Warner sprang it on Rockne in the Rose Bowl. Featuring a baffling combination of reverses and spinners, this formation was further enhanced by the use of a passing fullback—in this case the great Ernie Nevers.

But Stanford's passing efforts backfired when Elmer Layden intercepted a Nevers pass and returned it eighty yards to make the halftime score 13–3, in favor of Notre Dame. Then in the second half, after Stanford had fought back, Layden repeated his first-half heroics by picking off another Nevers pass and running it all the way back, for a final score of 27–10. Although statistics revealed that Stanford had been the superior team on the field, the Indians had simply made too many turnovers at key times to win. Regardless of the outcome, though, the real significance of this matchup is that it contained all the traditional symptoms of bowl-game fever—high-ranking teams, All-American players, and superior coaches competing against each other. It was the advent of an annual madness that would soon envelop the nation.

With football now rising to its highest level of popularity, Percy Haughton had rejoined the coaching ranks in 1923 to help build the gridiron fortunes of Columbia. In courting John Heisman in 1922, the Lions had been looking to shed their lackluster image and assume some of the gridiron glory that many other schools were relishing. But in October 1924, the fourty-eight-year-old Haughton was seized with a fatal heart attack, and one of the formative figures of modern football abruptly departed the intercollegiate scene. Columbia's day in the sun would not come until the arrival of a dynamic coach named Lou Little in 1930.

HEISMAN AND THE 1925 SEASON

The amazing coaching success of the young Knute Rockne and the continuing success of old foe Pop Warner at this time must have aroused a degree of envy in John Heisman, who was experiencing no small amount of frustration in the aftermath of his mediocre first year at Rice. Refusing to admit that his most successful period of coaching was now behind him, he looked forward to the 1925 season in his usual optimistic fashion. Ironically, the very thing that he had always championed—academics—was presenting a real problem to his program, as many of his players were having trouble keeping abreast of Rice's tough curriculum.

To remedy the problem, Heisman proposed setting up an athletic dorm where the players would live and study together—the prototypical living quarters for athletes that we find on many campuses today. Although the plan had the approval of the Rice administration, the establishment of a dormitory reserved for athletes was met with displeasure by the faculty, most of whom felt that athletes should receive no preferential treatment.

However, in being assigned to living quarters in a segregated part of a dormitory in the fall of 1925, Heisman's student athletes were presented with a set of strict rules—there would be no liquor, residents would abide by special study hours, and freshmen as well as those on probation would be restricted to special visiting hours. Proctors and tutors were assigned to see that everything went as planned. Heisman even recruited women students to help athletes develop good study habits and stick to training rules. Undoubtedly the underlying rationale behind Heisman's plan was that, in addition to improving his players' academic standing, having them live together would help build a strong sense of esprit de corps, the kind of team solidarity he had known in the military atmosphere of a school like Clemson. That Heisman was deadly serious about academics was demonstrated when he participated early that spring in a "study rally" designed "to impress upon the athletes the critical condition of Rice athletics" and that the ultimate success of athletics at Rice was dependent on its athletes becoming better students.[51]

Although the new emphasis on academics did manage to help raise the players' grades, it did not do much toward producing a winning season. With a final 4–4–1 mark, in fact, the Owls failed to surpass their previous year's record. By now, though, Heisman was becoming even more adept than he had been at Penn in rationalizing his coaching problems. Summing up the 1925 season, he wrote in the school yearbook that the break-even record was "more than satisfactory to the coaches . . . because the caliber of the material was decidedly below that of the season before, and there was even less of it."[52]

Following shutout wins that season over Austin (32–0) and Sam Houston (6–0), the Owls lost to a strong Trinity team, 13–0, with the scoring all coming in the second half. But in the game against Arkansas, Rice turned the tables in the second half and won, 13–9. According to Heisman, it was in this game that the 1925 Owls "learned to fight."

Nevertheless, in the big game with Texas at Austin, the overconfident Owls wilted in the excessive heat and lost to the Longhorns, 27–6, although Rice had held Texas to a 6–6 halftime score. Besides the heat, Heisman turned to his favorite excuse and blamed the loss on lack of experienced reserves.

Then, playing on a wet, muddy field in their next game against Southwestern University, Rice came through in fine style, 19–0. According to Heisman, his team played "an almost faultless game." In spite of a wet ball, the Owls utilized Heisman's passing strategy to good effect in winning their fourth game of the season.

Now with the possibility of a winning season in store, Heisman took his team to Baton Rouge in early November to face the LSU Tigers. After three scoreless quarters in which both teams battled each other on even terms, LSU pulled off a 50-yard pass play in the last quarter to win, 6–0. It was a heartbreaking loss, and the fact that the LSU pass had even been completed was remarkable since a driving rain storm had suddenly begun. Following this game, intermittent grumbling about Heisman's coaching was beginning to be heard. A reporter in the usually supportive yearbook stated that the reason Rice lost was "due simply to poor team playing and neglect of opportunities."[53]

Against the Texas A&M Aggies, the Owls succeeded in holding the eventual conference champions to a field goal in the first half, but once again yielded to superior forces later on, to make the final score 17–0. Once again, Heisman blamed the loss on lack of reserve strength: "When we had to substitute, then we were bound to lose."[54] With a steady diet of this kind of commentary coming after a painful loss, Rice supporters were beginning to detect a distinctively negative side to their normally positive-thinking coach.

Meeting Baylor in the traditional Thanksgiving Day game, Rice still had a chance to record a winning 5–4 season, but saw this opportunity disappear in a 7–7 tie. It was a symbolic finish to another frustrating season that with the right amount of luck at the right time could have turned into a winning campaign. After leading the Bears 7–0 in the first half (a typical game pattern for Rice in 1925), the Owls allowed a scoring pass in the final quarter for the resulting tie. Statistically and physically, Rice had outplayed its opponent, but it could not come up with the necessary scoring punch to win.

Rice boosters now realized that something was amiss with their football program, and it all pointed to the Heisman coaching system. His implementation of "straight football" was clearly lacking in the imaginative approach at which he was once so adept. He had turned fifty-five that fall, and there were those who believed he was getting too old to perform as a head coach. Expecting solid results from a coach who had a long track record for producing winners, supporters were tired of such defensive editorializing as these comments in the 1926 yearbook: "Probably no coach has ever been faced with such difficulties and problems as has Coach Heisman, and his cheery optimism and doctrine of 'everlasting fight' have won him a deep and abiding place in the hearts of the student body."[55] For those who wanted results on the field of play, Heisman's "cheery optimism" was a poor substitute as the Owls, with only one conference win, wound up in seventh place. If Heisman had an "abiding place in the hearts" of his supporters at this point, it certainly was not attributable to his declining skills as a football coach.

THE NATIONAL GAME (1925)

Nationally, Dartmouth, led by halfback Swede Oberlander, a deadly passer operating out of the single-wingback formation, was considered the nation's best team at 8–0. Among the Big Green's victims in 1925 were Harvard, Brown, Cornell, and Chicago, all by convincing scores.

This year also saw the rise of Alabama to the status of a national power as Deep South football put itself on the map. With nine victories during the regular season, eight of them by shutouts, Coach Wallace Wade's team was invited to play the University of Washington in the Rose Bowl. Sparked by quarterback Pooley Hubert and halfback Johnny Mack Brown, the Crimson Tide, after trailing 12–0 at the half, came back to nip the Huskies, 20–19, in another classic matchup. This game began Alabama's long bowl-game tradition. When Brown, the game's most valuable player, signed a movie contract, a popular Hollywood tradition was instituted as well—that of the star athlete whose athletic fame would help ensure his box-office success.[56]

Another outstanding team of the year was Michigan, which in its game with Illinois held the great Red Grange to just sixty-four rushing yards and won, 3–0. Behind the potent passing combination of Benny Friedman to Benny Oosterbaan, the Michigan Wolverines shut out seven opponents but lost to Northwestern on a muddy field by the narrow margin of 3–2. In facing Penn that fall, Illinois found Franklin Field in a similarly poor condition. But Red Grange had little difficulty in making believers out of the eastern fans who had packed the stands, particularly when they saw him go fifty-six yards through the muck and mire for a touchdown the first time he touched the ball. In the second period his 55-yard run set up another Illini score, and in the second half he scored again off a lateral pass. Grange compiled an astounding, record-setting 363 yards on thirty-six carries in this game for a 24–2 victory.

In 1925 it was proposed that the number-one team be chosen according to a mathematical point system. Devised by an economics professor at the University of Illinois, this plan quickly caught on in certain quarters, especially after Knute Rockne suggested that the system be used to award an annual trophy to the nation's best team. Rockne knew a good thing when he saw it, for his Notre Dame team was primed to be a serious contender for the national championship for the rest of the decade. As the obsession to be ranked number one spread, various rating systems would continue to proliferate until the advent of the Associated Press football writers poll in 1936, which would eventually be recognized as the official championship rating system.

In March, 1925, the death of the highly revered Walter Camp seemed to symbolize both the passing of an era when school spirit was so much a part of coaching philosophy, and the coming of a new age featuring a more professional and systematic style of coaching. This was the kind of system designed to make winning all-important, and its most outstanding practitioner during this transition period was Knute Rockne. It was John Heisman's fate to still be coaching at a time when the older style, with which he was more proficient, was yielding to the new day of a more professionally complex coaching system.

HEISMAN AND THE 1926 SEASON

In looking ahead to the 1926 season, Heisman was fearful that lack of depth, his chronic complaint, would once again present a big problem. While a dearth of reserve strength would plague his entire coaching tenure at Rice, Heisman did command some outstanding players during this time. Among these were his 1924 team captain and fullback Harvey Smith; backs Dick Terrell and Dutchy Wilford; tackles Bill McVey and Joe Heyck; Merle Comstock, who was to be the captain of the 1927 team; and Wash "Heavy" Underwood, the captain of the 1925 and 1926 teams, who was an all-conference center noted for his strong defensive play. Heisman declared Underwood to be one of the game's greatest centers. In his own words, "Wash was a sharpshooter. He could snap the ball on a bee-line 33 yards and so accurately that the receiver could receive it while kneeling without moving his hands more than a couple of inches."[57]

The basic trouble at Rice, as Heisman saw it, was that there weren't enough Wash Underwoods, Harvey Smiths, or Merle Comstocks to go around. In a summation of the 1926 season, Heisman again attributed another mediocre campaign to lack of depth as the Owls came up with a mark identical to the previous season's 4–4–1 record. More specifically, he rationalized that "fully eighty percent of the squad [were] sophomores . . . new to intercollegiate football."[58]

Once again, though, Rice got its new season underway in impressive fashion with shutout wins over Austin (25–0) and Sam Houston (20–0). Before the opening game, prospects for the campaign had been pronounced good, in that "three complete Owl elevens on the field assured Rice supporters that reserve strength would not be lacking this year."[59] But later a disappointing 6–6 tie with Trinity brought the "Heismen" down to earth against a team that had been "much trampled by other conference contenders."[60]

Following a 19–0 win over St. Edwards College the Owls appeared to be back on the offensive track, but then a 20–0 loss to Texas started them on a tailspin of three successive conference defeats by identical shutout scores. According to the yearbook reporter, the loss at the hands of the Longhorns resulted from overconfidence, for Rice had fully expected to beat Texas following a "week of feverish enthusiasm" in preparation for the match. The ensuing 20–0 loss to eventual 1926 conference champion SMU saw Rice playing better on offense but failing to take advantage of scoring opportunities—fumbling on one occasion and then being stopped on the 1-yard line as the first-half clock ran out.

A slim 7–6 victory over Southwestern was to be Rice's final win for the 1926 campaign, as their opponent's missed try for an extra point enabled the Owls to eke out the nonconference win. They were not as fortunate the rest of the way.

Another 20–0 defeat came Heisman's way when his team played their third conference game of the season, this time against the Texas A&M Aggies. Once again the Owls failed to muster enough scoring punch and the necessary defense to counter the Aggies' balanced running and passing attack. Then in the last game of the season against traditional foe Baylor, Rice leading 7–6 in the last quarter, appeared headed for their first conference victory. But the Bears, in a last-ditch effort, drove to the Owl 2-yard line where, after three unsuccessful cracks at the line, they made good on a field goal to win 9–7 and cap another disappointing season for Heisman and his Owls.

In losing all four of its conference games, Rice wound up in the league basement. As a result, the criticism against Heisman started to fly fast and furiously. The school newspaper, his earlier ally, was among the first to get in on the attack with an editorial that raised the pointed question: "What is wrong with Rice and her athletics?" With only a cross-country conference championship for the year, John Heisman, as athletic director, was clearly the object of the article's derision. By this time the words Heisman had written in 1922 were beginning to ring true in his own case: "When a team wins, the coach gets twice as much credit as he deserves; when it loses, he comes in for ten times as much blame as may justly be charged against him."[61]

THE NATIONAL GAME (1926)

While Heisman was agonizing over his coaching problems, some other notable football coaches were experiencing considerable success in 1926. Pop Warner, for example, brought Stanford to national championship prominence with a team that went 10–0–1. Its toughest game had been a 13–12 matchup with Southern Cal before meeting Alabama in the Rose Bowl.

Played on January 1, 1927, this game was the first to be broadcast on national radio. With pioneer radio sportscaster Graham McNamee at the microphone, this event represented the most significant breakthrough in sports communications up to that time, contributing to the air of immediacy that television would eventually expand upon to create a national family of sports spectators. The game, though, was not nearly as exciting as the previous year's between Alabama and Washington had been, and the most dramatic moment didn't come until near the end. After Alabama had blocked a punt in Stanford territory, the Crimson Tide rolled to a quick score, and with time growing short made good on an extra point try for a game-ending 7–7 tie.

Navy's new coach, Bill Ingram, piloted the Midshipmen to an undefeated season at 9–0–1, with the tie coming against Army in a game played at Chicago's Soldier Field. It marked the first time that this game had been scheduled anywhere other than the East Coast, and it also attracted the largest crowd ever to watch a football game up to that time—110,000. The spectators were amply rewarded, too, as the game turned out to be among the more thrilling of the year. It ended in a 21–21 tie, but only after both teams kept trading leads during the course of the action.

In 1926, Tennessee's new coach was Bob Neyland, who proceeded to inaugurate a winning dynasty at the Knoxville campus. In so doing, he accomplished for southern football what Vanderbilt, Georgia Tech, and Alabama, each in its own way, had done before him. In fact, it didn't take long for Neyland to see to it that big intrastate rival Vanderbilt and its long-time coach, Dan McGugin, never reigned supreme in the area again. At heart, there was nothing really fancy about Neyland's winning system. A West Point graduate who achieved the rank of general, Neyland took a distinctly military approach to coaching the game, but one based mainly on the fundamentals of defense rather than offense. Like John Heisman, Neyland was a stickler for details who spent lengthy sessions on the most basic football tactics, particularly the kicking game and pass defense. Like Heisman, too, he had a penchant for maxims that captured and projected the essence of his coaching philosophy. He took care to post his pithy sayings on the walls of his players' locker room. The inspirational rhetoric of the southern football coach, which equated results on the field with fiery orations in the locker room, was a tradition begun by John Heisman and embellished on by coaches like Bob Neyland. His teams would continue to bask in the national limelight throughout the 1930s.

HEISMAN AND THE 1927 SEASON

Although the outlook for the 1927 season at Rice was optimistic, at least from the viewpoint of loyal supporters who felt that "the Owls should enjoy a good conference season,"[62] such was not to be. In fact, the season of 1927 was to be the worst in John Heisman's entire coaching career. As it turned out, this season, his only losing one, would also be the final one of his long career as a football coach. During that ominous fall, it must have dawned on Heisman that for himself as a coach things would never be as grand and glorious as they had been, and he would acknowledge this realization for the first time in his illustrious career. The yearbook summed up his final season: "Players themselves gave their best, but the going was hard and the eleven the coach had fashioned had failed to weather the storm. The team showed power at times, but it was not sustained throughout the four quarters of play, and it was during these lapses that the opposition put over telling blows."[63]

The "telling blows" metaphor was aptly chosen, not only for the agonies that the football team endured during the 1927 season but for those of John Heisman as well. Over the course of the campaign, criticism came at him from all sides. In a way his situation was worse than it had been at Penn because much of the criticism was unjustified. At Rice he simply did not have the same material to work with that he had had at Penn. Nevertheless, he never completely gave up during the 1927 season. To shore up his line after the graduation of Wash Underwood, Heisman switched three-year backfield star Merle Comstock to a line position. Although Comstock gave a good account of himself at center, this maneuver was simply not enough to turn Rice into a winner. Accordingly, Rice, in its first game, which was something of an omen, lost to Loyola of New Orleans, 13–0. This match revealed that the Owls were desperately lacking in offensive force.

The next game saw them come through with just enough offense to edge Sam Houston, 13–7. But the following week a surprising St. Edwards team held the Owls to a 0–0 tie in a dully fought game that seemed to epitomize the frustrations of Heisman's career at this time.

Next, in the season's first conference game with SMU, the Mustangs continued their two-year dominance of the Owls and rolled to a 34–13 victory,

mainly on the strength of their solid passing attack. In the following conference matchup with Texas, Heisman's charges held the Longhorns to just
one touchdown after three quarters of play, only to lose eventually by
27–0.

For Heisman, it was now becoming increasingly difficult to get his team
motivated to face an opponent. It was even more difficult to get himself
motivated sufficiently to face his players. He was even accused of favoritism
as some players contended that his coaching system would not allow backs
he did not like to carry the ball. As Edwin Pope analyzed Heisman's situation,
"At the tail end of his career, he simply could not gear tactics to personalities."[64] The sad truth of the matter was that for Heisman, unaccustomed to
a loser's role, the challenge of coaching was no longer the exciting adventure
it used to be. Now any win would be considered cause for special celebration.

But another loss followed, this time a terribly disappointing match to the
usually tame Southwestern team, 14–12. With a little luck the Owls could
have pulled this one out, but the ball was simply not bouncing their way, a
plight of which Heisman had been made painfully aware. In fact, his predicament became even more obvious when he had to face Centenary College
with four of his regulars out of the lineup due to injuries. As though to
underscore Heisman's problems even more emphatically, the unheralded
Louisiana team ran roughshod over the Owls, 33–7.

Although Rice managed to stop Texas A&M's fine quarterback, Joel Hunt,
in the next game, Heisman's men could not keep Dana X. Bible's Aggies
from scoring two touchdowns and, as a result, the Owls wound up losing,
14–0. They had played well overall against the eventual conference champions and national championship contenders, however, and the yearbook
reporter commented that "it was the first time in the season that the team
had shown sustained fight."[65] The Owls' erratic play over the season was
undoubtedly indicative of the wavering situation in which Heisman found
himself.

He had never been a quitter, of course, and the thought of having to resign
under fire went against the very grain of his go-getter nature. But with
criticism starting to mount to an unbearable degree, he now realized he had
no other choice except to tender his resignation. His record now stood at 1–
6–1, with his team having been outscored 148 to 52. Out of thirty-four games
played during his four-year tenure at Rice, Heisman had won only thirteen.
Enduring his first losing season was the lowest emotional point in his entire
coaching career, and even though he still had the Thanksgiving game with
Baylor to go, Heisman had now made up his mind to resign. Although he
had performed as a Shakespearean actor on stage he was not going to be a
tragic figure in real life, for he had endured all the "slings and arrows of
outrageous fortune" he cared to. So right before the start of the Baylor game
he presented his terms of resignation to the Rice board of trustees.

Nevertheless, John Heisman did close out his career as a winner, for in the game with Baylor, Rice played one of its finest games under Heisman to defeat the Bears, 19–12. It was the Owls' first conference win in two years, and the yearbook reporter fairly glowed: "Throughout the entire game, the team played as it had never played in previous games and climaxed an otherwise poor season with a well-deserved and glorious victory."[66] If the players had known of their coach's intention to resign, it could have been that they were playing their hearts out either in jubilation or in tribute to his departure. More than likely, though, it was the special Heisman touch that was still capable of bringing his men together for one last concerted effort.

Summarily, the Rice trustees accepted Heisman's resignation, effective December 1 of that year, and his termination was announced at the annual football banquet after the season's close. Although the board had cancelled his contract, the rest of his salary was paid for the year and part of the next. A dejected but still-proud Heisman refused to discuss publicly the reasons for his resignation. After thirty-six years he had coached his last athletic team. He was fifty-seven years old but not too old, he was sure, to look around for something else to do—something unique to challenge his go-getter instincts, which were still alive and well.

THE NATIONAL GAME (1927)

The Southwest Conference had come into the national picture this year with Texas A&M as a championship contender, as noted. But TCU held the Aggies and the great Joel Hunt to a scoreless tie when, late in the game, Hunt was tackled on the 1-yard line on a fourth-down play. It was a tackle that was more than a game-saver, though, for it halted the Aggies' quest for a national title.

The Rose Bowl game on January 1, 1928, saw Coach Jock Sutherland's Pitt Panthers (8–0–1) take on Stanford, only to lose in a hard-fought contest, 7–6. It was the exciting hoopla and aura generated by intersectional games like this one and those that had preceded it that would ensure the success of the Rose Bowl and other bowl-game spinoffs soon to follow.

In 1927 there were some significant rule changes designed to improve play. The goal posts, looming ever-dangerous as a formidable barrier to offensive players, were moved back from the goal line to the end line of the end zone. This change had considerable impact on the kicking game. As Heisman would observe in 1928, "Drop and place kicking were regarded as quite valuable scoring devices from 1910 to 1920; but somehow they've fallen off in popularity. Particularly since last year when the rules made field goal kicking all the more difficult by retiring the goal posts ten yards back of each goal line."[67] (The professional game, which did not realize significant popularity until the 1940s, would revive interest in the field goal as an offensive weapon in 1933 by moving the goal posts up to the goal line, affording a better shot for the now-popular place kick. Other rule changes instituted in 1927 included putting the ball into play within thirty seconds of the start of official playing time to prevent unnecessary delay, and not allowing the kicking team to advance a fumbled punt beyond the point where the ball was recovered.

In contrast to the progress of college football during the 1920s, professional football had been struggling to make a name for itself. Recognizing the fabulous name appeal that Red Grange had projected throughout his college career, the Chicago Bears, who along with the New York Giants were the only successful franchises at this time, signed the Illinois halfback to a professional contract soon after the 1925 season. On a grueling thirty-game barnstorming tour against teams all over the country, Grange was paid thousands of dollars per contest, a venture that lost much of its appeal when he became too beat up to play at his best. His professional career would fade in a few years, but the real significance of Red Grange's defection to the professional ranks is that it opened the gates for a host of college players to follow. Although the nucleus for the National Football League had been established by the mid-1920s, professional football, even with collegiate stars in its ranks, still had a long way to go to realize its destiny as a highly appealing spectator sport. Meanwhile, college football was enjoying undreamed-of popularity.

THE NATIONAL SCENE (1927)

Like the decade of the 1920s, which started out so full of promise and great expectations, only to encounter a number of unexpected political and economic pitfalls toward the end of the decade, so the coaching career of John Heisman developed along similar lines. Heisman's life had spanned the days from a predominantly rural America to a time when it was a more capitalistic, industrialized, and urban society. Many of the positive and negative developments of the day that affected the social, political, and economic life of the American people also had profound effects on organized sports and its managers. Toward the close of the 1920s, the times were accelerating at a rapid rate, and with this acceleration came an attendant fascination with sport as spectacle. The mass appeal of professional baseball and college football was, in a sense, the result of these sports' capacity to transport their viewers and followers back to a more innocent time far removed from the encroaching complexities of urban life, providing a kind of escape from the harsh realities of everyday living. Nevertheless, significant technological breakthroughs during this decade helped enhance the social quality of urban life.

With the advances in mass transportation that had been made by the mid-1920s, particularly in the automobile industry, the increasing mobility of the American people made sporting events and other opportunities for leisure and recreation much more accessible. Because of the ready availability of such activities, city life became much more attractive to a rising middle class who now had more money and time to devote to sporting and leisure avocations. During the 1920s John Heisman, too, became a thoroughly indoctrinated city man, living in growing urban centers like Philadelphia and Houston, so that by the close of the decade he would readily elect to dwell in that American mecca of urban life, New York City. In the city one could now be as close as possible to the pulse of the sporting life.

Although Heisman had espoused an urban, cosmopolitan view of the world, even during his coaching tenures in the predominantly rural areas of Auburn and Clemson, the dizzying transformation of a rural mindset into a more urbanized one through the rapid revolution in the mass media must have given him reason to pause and reassess his essentially conservative values in light of all these new developments. Motivated in the main to entertain rather than inform, the mass media (newspapers, magazines, radio, and movies), in promoting fashions, behavior fads, celebrities, and consumer products, had contributed to a homogenized way of viewing things and events. Consequently, this situation in sports conditioned the American people to become one big family as they were presented heroic images for celebrity worship. Radio, which was becoming an important force at this time in helping mythologize the sports figures popularized by the press, demanded that listeners use their imaginations in the process of absorbing and visualizing an event. Radio announcers of sporting events enhanced this process with their overly dramatic descriptions of game action. The result was a big parade of larger-than-life heroes in all the major sports of the era, commonly referred to today as the Golden Age of American sports. And whether Heisman realized it or not, spectator sports, particularly college football, had become an integral part of the mass entertainment craze. It was a psychologically essential part, which provided Americans with both a sense of national identity and a welcome escape from the humdrum routine of daily life. Leading sports figures, who were being promoted as celebrities by newspapers and popular magazines such as the *Saturday Evening Post* and *Collier's*, as well as by movie-house newsreels, unwittingly contributed to a fantasized interpretation of sports experience that was mirrored in popular fiction and Hollywood feature films.[68]

It was in such an atmosphere that John and Maora Heisman headed for New York toward the end of 1927. Thirty-six years of coaching lay behind him, and other than his sporting-goods business he had no idea what lay ahead. But his past accomplishments and his go-getter traits would qualify him for playing yet another role in the continually expanding world of big-time sports, particularly as this world was being expressed through the unparalleled success of intercollegiate football.

NOTES

1. "Tech Mourns Loss of Heisman," Philadelphia *Evening Ledger*, February 9, 1920.

2. Ibid.

3. "Report Heisman Is Picked as New Penn Football Coach," Philadelphia *Evening Bulletin*, January 1920, 22.

4. "Penn's New Gridiron Coach Has Appearance of a Scholar," Philadelphia *Evening Bulletin*, February 9, 1920, 22.

5. Ibid.

6. Ibid.

7. L. F. "Fuzzy" Woodruff, *History of Southern Football*, vol. 2 (Atlanta, Ga.: Georgia Southern, 1928), 107.

8. Ibid., 142.

9. "Heisman Plans to Alter Shift Play," Philadelphia *Evening Bulletin*, April 9, 1921.

10. Ibid.

11. "Will Release Coach Heisman," Philadelphia *Evening Ledger*, November 25, 1921.

12. Edwin Pope, *Football's Greatest Coaches* (Atlanta, Ga.: Tupper and Love, 1956), 127.

13. Ibid.

14. "Heisman Predicts Penn's 1923 Football Team Will Be Winner," Philadelphia *Evening Bulletin*, December 1922.

15. "The Old Sport's Musings," Philadelphia *Evening Ledger*, January 6, 1922, 14.

16. John W. Heisman, "Between Halves," *Collier's*, November 17, 1928, 53.

17. "Plan Radical Change in Penn Grid Affairs," Philadelphia *Evening Ledger*, December 14, 1922.

18. "Heisman May Coach Columbia Gridmen," Philadelphia *Evening Bulletin*, December 6, 1922.

19. "Plan Radical Change" Philadelphia *Evening Ledger*.

20. Ibid.

21. "Heisman Predicts," Philadelphia *Evening Bulletin*.

22. Ibid.

23. "The Football Coach," The University of Pennsylvania *Alumni Register* (December 1922).

24. Jonathan K. Miller, editorial in The University of Pennsylvania *Alumni Register* (January 1923).

25. Pope, *Football's Greatest Coaches*, 127.

26. In this frontier Eden, Heisman could never have dreamed of the significant role that the state of Florida would come to play in the future of intercollegiate football, or that the university established in the Miami area during the 1930s would go on to win a series of national championships.

27. "Heisman Predicts Winner for Penn," Philadelphia *Record*, February 2, 1923.

28. Ibid.

29. Woodruff, *History of Southern Football*, vol. 2, 185.

30. "Heisman of Penn Elected Head Coach" *The Red and Black* (Washington and Jefferson student newspaper), January 18, 1923.

31. "Heisman to Coach at W&J 3 Years," Philadelphia *Evening Ledger*, January 4, 1923, 18.

32. "Coach Heisman States His Creed," *The Red and Black*, March 15, 1923.

33. John W. Heisman, "Here Are Men," *Collier's*, November 16, 1929, 25.

34. Quote is from a letter by the W&J student manager, cited in David Scarborough's doctoral dissertation, "Intercollegiate Athletics at Washington and Jefferson College: The Building of a Tradition" (University of Pittsburgh, 1979), 84.

35. Lawrence R. Stewart, "A Resume of the 1923 Football Season," *Pandora* (W&J yearbook), vol. 40 (1925), 105–6.

36. Ibid., 105.

37. Ibid., 105.

38. In 1923 and 1924, Heisman served as president of the American Football Coaches Association, an organization he helped found. It was a role that undoubtedly enhanced his bargaining power.

39. "Heisman to Arrive for Practice Soon," *The Thresher*, February 23, 1924.

40. "Heisman, Character Builder, Is Accorded Enthusiastic Welcome to Owl School," *The Thresher*, March 28, 1924.

41. Frederika Meiners, *A History of Rice University: The Institute Years, 1907–63* (Houston, Tex.: Rice University Studies, 1982), 105.

42. John W. Heisman, "Their Weight in Gold," *Collier's*, November 24, 1928, 28.

43. The most recent recruiting reform attempt is the 1991 report of the Knight Foundation Commission. Acknowledging that "big-time revenue sports are out of control," the report recommended that university presidents exercise administrative control of athletic programs, that universities undergo annual certification reviews by outside auditors to determine if their athletic programs are honest, and that athletic departments reflect the university's educational values.

44. "Athletics," *The Campanile* (Rice Institute yearbook), vol. 10, 1925.

45. Ibid.

46. Ibid.

47. Ibid.

48. Helen Cullinan, "Heisman Bronze Is Sculptor's 'Dream,' " *Cleveland Plain Dealer*, December 15, 1986, 1-c, 5-c. In this article, William McVey, who became a noted sculptor, also tells of his commission to do an eight-foot bronze of Heisman for the Georgia Tech campus.

49. In this game, Coach Bob Zuppke of Illinois reinstituted the huddle to combat crowd noise. It was thought that Zuppke had been the first to employ this innovation outdoors, but Glenn Warner had introduced it in 1896 at Georgia, as noted [previously] in chapter 1. Although the Rules Committee had threatened to abolish it, after this widely publicized game the huddle started to become a permanent feature of football strategy.

50. John W. Heisman, "Fast and Loose," *Collier's*, October 20, 1928, 54.

51. See "Athletics" in *The Campanile*, vol. 11, 1926.

52. Ibid.

53. Ibid.

54. Ibid.

55. Ibid.

56. For further discussion of this tradition, see Wiley Lee Umphlett, *The Movies Go to College: Hollywood and the World of the College-Life Film* (Madison, N.J.: Fairleigh Dickinson University Press, 1984), 27–31.

57. Heisman, "Fast and Loose," 54.

58. See "Athletics" in *The Campanile*, vol. 12, 1927.

59. Ibid.

60. Ibid.

61. John W. Heisman, *Principles of Football* (St. Louis: Sports Publishing Bureau, 1922), 337.

62. *The Campanile*, vol. 12, 1927.

63. See "Athletics" in *The Campanile*, vol. 13, 1928.

64. Pope, *Football's Greatest Coaches*, 118.

65. *The Campanile*, vol. 13, 1928.

66. Ibid.

67. John W. Heisman, "Look Sharp Now!" *Collier's*, November 3, 1928, 19.

68. See Umphlett, *The Movies Go to College*, 15–44.

$$6$$

The Inception of the Heisman Trophy: Memorializing the Coach, the Player, and Their Game (1928–1936)

No one player or coach or team or college ever knew or will know all there is to know about football.

—John W. Heisman,
Principles of Football (1922)

While the Heisman Trophy is given to but one man, it serves, too, as a symbol of the general excellence of college football. . . . The Heisman, in its broadest and best sense, is an award presented annually which honors the greatness of college football as it is embodied in one man.

—John T. Brady,
The Heisman: A Symbol of Excellence (1984)

HEISMAN, ADVOCATE OF THE GAME (1928–1929)

Although the 1920s came to be known as the Golden Age of American sports, the times were not so golden for John Heisman, as we have seen. Of his three coaching appointments during the decade, only his one-year stint at Washington and Jefferson resulted in any degree of success. Had he stayed on at Penn, he might have achieved the winning reputation that was the lot of his successor, Lou Young; when Heisman departed, it was clear that the University of Pennsylvania Quakers were on the brink of regaining their earlier gridiron glory. As his many supporters contended, Heisman had played an instrumental role in Penn's football revival. So it would have been fitting for him to have closed out his career as a big winner at his alma mater.

In spite of his decline as a coach in the 1920s, though, Heisman did manage to retain a high degree of prestige and respect, due primarily to the coaching reputation he had achieved earlier. With his 190 victories on the football field, his career record would ultimately be ranked among the all-time best. (Although Heisman's official coaching record stands at 185 wins, this author's research has uncovered five additional victories for which he never received recognition. See Appendix.) And even though his retirement would give Alonzo Stagg a clearcut claim to the title "dean of college coaches," other laurels would come to Heisman during the late 1920s and on throughout his remaining years. In twice serving as president of the American Football Coaches Association, he had sought to impress upon its members his standards of coaching excellence as well as the need to lead an exemplary life for their players, the kind of lifestyle that had characterized his entire career in athletics. Additionally, his outstanding book on football strategy and coaching leadership ably demonstrated his intuitive feel for the game, and enhanced his reputation as a football scholar.

Because of his extensive knowledge of football's complex history and development, soon after his retirement Heisman was invited by *Collier's* weekly to write a series of articles dealing with the evolution of the game and his own role in this process. As competitors, both *Collier's* and the *Saturday Evening Post* had begun to devote a significant amount of space to sports, to capitalize on their widespread popularity. If any journal reflected the popular tastes of the American people during the 1920s, particularly their interest in sports, it was the *Saturday Evening Post*.[1]

Considering the solid reputation of the *Post*, then, it was a real scoop for *Collier's* to publish Heisman's well-received series of eleven articles during the football seasons of 1928 and 1929. These pieces, all of which are quoted from throughout this book, are remarkable for their balanced air of seriousness and humor, particularly since many writers of the day adopted an overly heroic and occasionally mawkish style when writing about sports. The humorous cast to Heisman's writing is all the more remarkable when we consider that he was not very far removed from the unpleasant circumstances that had closed out his coaching career. Clearly his love of the game transcended any feelings of bitterness or animosity he might have harbored. Then, too, as one observer has noted, "Once he escaped from the pressures of having to win, the more congenial side of his personality reasserted itself."[2]

So in a sense, the *Collier's* pieces were a kind of emotional purge—in large part a distillation of highly emotional moments recollected in tranquillity—and the memories came forth in a torrent. The result was some of the era's most open, honest, and straightforward writing about the humorous and serious sides of a major American sport, an outstanding achievement in spite of Heisman's occasionally overwrought style.

On the humorous side, the naiveté of certain football fans was among his favorite topics. In an article informing readers about the finer points of watching football, Heisman related an incident concerning a faithful fan who had called him about securing seats on the goal line in order to see "all the good playing and the knockdowns." Heisman replied:

"You mean touchdowns?"

"Yes," I guess that's it. Anyway, can I have them?"

"Of course, but you know the touchdowns might be made at the other end of the field," I reminded her.

"At which end do you think they'll make the most?" she inquired anxiously.

"I wish I knew."

"Well," she said after a pause, "I'll try the east end of the field, but I do think you should arrange to have some at both ends."[3]

In a similar vein, Heisman tells of the unwanted advice he often received from self-appointed "experts" on the game's finer points—for example, a letter from a Georgia Tech alumnus who proposed a "bit of passing strategy" that "would revolutionize the game":

All the passer had to do [Heisman summarized] was to flip the ball to one of the ends, who would then throw the ball to a halfback in a slightly advanced position. Then the halfback would hurl the ball to the other end, who, by this time, would be well down the field. And it followed that this end would then keep up the good work by passing to the other halfback who would have but a step to go for a touchdown.

Heisman wrote that when he ignored this illegal scheme for advancing the ball, he was "unmercifully lambasted . . . by this grand-stand tactician as a 'swell-headed guy who knew it all.' "[4]

Heisman also liked to tell stories about football converts—those who at first were bitterly opposed to the game (his father, for example), mainly because of its brutality, but who after attending a match were suddenly transformed into emotionally intense fans of the game. One such incident he recounted involved the president of a southern college who finally consented to watch a game after years of criticizing those who preoccupied themselves with football, whether player, coach, or spectator. The team coaches, in order to impress their boss as much as possible, invited the dignified gentleman to sit with the players on the bench. But after three quarters of play, he still appeared to be unmoved and entirely lacking in the spirit of the game. Then, as Heisman tells it, "things happened," for, with the score 0–0, one of the opponent's backs broke loose on what appeared to be a big touchdown run. But the safety man caught him by the ankle:

Down they came, twenty feet from where Prexy [the president] stood. Prexy had risen with the rest of them and unconsciously was yelling with the multitude. His voice was high, strident, roar-piercing.

"Kill him, kill him," the old boy screamed.

And then, catching himself, he added, a trifle less savagely:

"But don't hurt him, don't hurt him—any more than you have to."[5]

But for humor that even smacked of slapstick, Heisman seemed to relish stories about black football players. As he remarked, "If you like a bit of humor in your football you ought to cultivate the game as it is played by Negroes. I should like to say, too, that for earnest football you need to go no further. The colored boy takes it seriously."[6]

His stories about how blacks played the game also reveal a patronizing viewpoint, however, particularly in the manner of their telling. In these stories Heisman showed a condescending side that mirrors the prevailing attitude toward blacks participating in athletics at this time. For example, he wrote about two black teams in Nashville who had to play on a field only 65 yards long when it was supposed to be officially 110 yards in length. Prior to the start of play, the captains of the teams had "agreed that the side scoring a touchdown should keep the ball and from a point 45 yards from the opponent's goal go at it again." Upon scoring from this distance, they would get credit for a "whole" touchdown. One of the teams soon scored what the opposing captain termed "half a touchdown." The other captain did not see the logic of this situation, contending that there was no such thing as half a touchdown. The other captain countered:

"Who says so? Half a touchdown, half a dollah, half a hour, halfback—"

"Yeah? Well, listen, half-witted, I know sompin' you ain't half of?"

"Say it."

"You ain't half a liah, you's two liahs."

About a half hour later the police had the situation well in hand.[7]

Heisman could even be humorous about a topic he took quite seriously— the ill-advised use of what he euphemistically termed "vivid profanity" or "badly tainted epithets" by players and coaches on the football field. In *Principles of Football* he especially warned against the coach's reliance on profanity: "It is a great temptation, but it does no good. . . . Cut it out and your players will turn out to be finer sportsmen."[8] As though to support this admonition, Heisman told the following anecdote on himself. It concerned the father of one of his men who had asked his son if Coach Heisman ever cursed at the team:

"No, Dad," said the boy, "but he can give you hell without mentioning the word once."

"Well," said the gratified father, "at least that's better than swearing."

"Like hell it is," replied the lad. "It hurts a damned sight worse."[9]

The serious side of Heisman's pieces for *Collier's* was reserved to expound on major developments of the game, particularly those in which his own contributions figured, and to relate stories and incidents that supported his faith in football as a builder of character and teacher of sportsmanship. In this latter category he surprisingly confessed to being a "frank sentimentalist in football": "But why not? I've seen it in all its phases. I've seen rough stuff, intentional and unintentional, and rejoice that the dirty player, like the weakling, hasn't lasted. . . . I've seen moral courage in football as often as physical. I've seen football make men out of condemned material."[10] Accordingly, John Heisman was among the foremost of those early college coaches who espoused a character-building philosophy of athletics, one that equated a player's dedicated performance on the athletic field with his potential for success in later life.

With regard to significant breakthroughs that affected football's ultimate destiny, there was no more serious topic for Heisman than his personal role in the legalization of the forward pass. So he was naturally inspired to refer to it over the course of his *Collier's* series. To convey his special feel for the impact of the forward pass on the game as we have come to know it, Heisman gave his most dramatic description in a 1928 article. To set the stage, he depicted a hypothetical on-field situation in which a player is fading back to deliver a forward pass to a designated receiver down field. Once the ball is in the air, said Heisman,

We are caught hard in the wildest thrill in modern football: The forward pass. There may be a variety of reasons why football, today, has become the greatest of outdoor attractions, why it is necessary in these modern times to secure tickets for the great game weeks in advance if you hope at all to be there, why even the high-school game will fetch thousands to the stands.

But perhaps the opening up of football has had most to do with it. And then there is nothing to the open game but the passing. There are no other moments in sport and few in life, however you play it, which grip you so hard as do those during which the ball speeds through the air above the heads of two well-trained teams. Your heart rides on that ball. It rises and falls with that ball.[11]

Although Heisman was writing his *Collier's* articles at a time when college football was at a peak of popularity (as the enthusiastic reception of his writings attested), serious problems had developed nationally in the management area of the game. Recognizing that most institutions of higher learning were going their separate ways in managing their athletic programs, the National Collegiate Athletic Association had issued a call for an independent agency to examine the condition of college sports as early as 1916. The challenge was finally undertaken in 1926 by the Carnegie Foundation for the Advancement of Teaching. College athletics, having started out under the governance of students, who in turn were supervised at most institutions by faculty committees, had become so professionalized over the years that students and faculty no longer had much say-so in their control. Even the administrative leaders of these colleges, from the president on down, now felt obligated to support the production of winning teams in order to maintain the financial support of alumni and win over public loyalty.

Concerned about the deleterious effects that must-win athletic programs were having on American education, in particular on the student athletes, the foundation's commission visited 112 American and Canadian universities, colleges, and schools, over a three and a half-year period. The commission then issued its findings as a fact-finding rather than a fault-finding report about education, but the defects in the management system of American college athletics were glaringly evident. If athletic programs existed to benefit students, then according to the report, the system had neglected its primary mission in three main ways: (1) "Due to the dominance of 'older persons' supplanting student leaders in the coaching echelon of sports management, not all students were being involved in sports; (2) hypocritical postures had been implemented under the guise of 'faculty control' and 'athletics for all'; and (3) intercollegiate sports had become overly commercialized."[12]

The thing that most concerned the commission was the third charge concerning the commercialism that had infiltrated intercollegiate athletic programs, resulting in increased professionalism in the recruitment and training of athletes and sometimes overshadowing the academic mission and intellectual life of many educational institutions. In the preface to the report, the commission's major concern was summed up: "The question is not so much whether athletics in their present form should be fostered by the university but how fully can a university that fosters professional athletics discharge its primary function." If all this has a familiar ring to it, it is mainly because in over sixty years since the report's appearance, not much has been done to carry out its recommendations.

Ironically, Heisman's piece dealing with the eligibility problems that football recruiting had created ("Their Weight in Gold") had appeared in *Collier's* just the year before the release of the Carnegie Commission report. As we have seen, Heisman was never reluctant to voice his opinions about what he felt was wrong with this perennially problematic area of college football.

Yet, in this same article, Heisman contended that considerable improvement in the eligibility process had taken place since the 1890s when intercollegiate football was "full of repeaters and ringers and boilermakers." He cited the examples of Walter Camp who played for Yale as a postgraduate, George Woodruff, Amos Alonzo Stagg, Leonard Wood, and even himself—all of whom played at schools while they were coaching. The problem in the early days was compounded by the fact that players who were both talented and academically qualified were hard to come by:

> Therefore [coaches] hunted the logging camps, the docks, the iron foundries, the local police force, the boiler factories and the truck drivers' union.

In those days, if 200 pounds of fine football material were able merely to read and write a little, his chances of winning a job on a big college eleven were bright. They took their entrance exams on the gymnasium scales. Today a coach will not look at a prospect who hasn't at least five admission units. And the standard set by the Carnegie Foundation—that 15 units be demanded of the would-be entrant to first-line colleges—has just about ruined the business for the tramp athlete.[13]

John Heisman surely took offense upon hearing the commission's indictment of "older persons" having taken over coaching responsibilities in college athletics. As he had always justified the role of athletics in the total educational mission, Heisman could surely defend the professional role of older persons as necessary leaders for college teams. As a longtime champion of both academics and athletics, Heisman had subscribed to the traditional Greek synthesis of mind and body, stressing the importance of each side's complementary relationship in the educational process. In this process, Heisman always gave equal ranking to both student athletes and student backers.

In spite of the Carnegie report's findings and the resultant outcry from self-appointed critics of college athletics, Heisman maintained that the immense popularity of football decreed that it would endure no matter what a university administration felt mandated to do to curtail it. He also asserted that the students themselves, whom the report cited as being neglected by the existing system, were actually desirous of intercollegiate football being implemented on a highly competitive level since their school was a reflection of their own vested interests. In fact, there were students who intended to have a winning team even if it meant paying out of their own pockets to see to it. In his article on recruiting ills, Heisman dramatized this point:

"Love will find a way," said a football-mad alumnus one evening after several hours of ineffectual work on a non-athletic prexy.

Whereat the undergraduates assembled in the gymnasium, where each class pledged itself as a body to support one athlete. And in consequence of that mass patriotism four of the finest ball carriers this country has ever seen on a single team were assembled and maintained in luxury.[14]

But Heisman, realizing that his outspoken manner might offend those directly involved in football's management system, closed out his exposé in a typically optimistic manner:

I would not have you believe that these ringers and boilermakers dominate the game nor that they are even a considerable portion of the great mass of players. The contrary is true. The legitimate student today is hugely in the majority. And gradually, with the entrance examinations becoming more exacting and the scholastic requirements growing taller, the undesirables are vanishing. And football is more popular with the public than ever.[15]

Although Heisman's viewpoint was somewhat myopic in its pronouncement that "the undesirables are vanishing," his declaration that college football was "more popular with the public than ever" was borne out by the accomplishments of the two top-rated teams of the year in which Heisman was writing (1928), one from the West Coast (the University of Southern California) and the other from the Southeast (Georgia Tech).

THE NATIONAL GAME (1928–1929)

Coach Howard Jones, who had enjoyed highly successful tenures at Yale and Iowa, led his University of Southern California team to a 9–0–1 record and national championship contention. During the year his squad had been good enough to overcome Stanford University and the deception of Pop Warner's double-wingback formation by the score of 10–0. Although Warner's tactics stirred up considerable interest in the East, Jones's more conservative style of play had spelled the end of Warner's supremacy in the West.[16] After defeating Notre Dame 27–14, the USC Trojans were slated to face undefeated Georgia Tech (13–0 winners over the Irish of Notre Dame) in the Rose Bowl, but a disagreement with bowl authorities resulted in the Golden Bears of the University of California being selected instead.

Ever since Heisman's departure from Georgia Tech, Coach Bill Alexander had kept the Tech Yellow Jackets on the edge of greatness, so the Rose Bowl invitation offered him an excellent opportunity to show the country just how good a team he really had. By this time, the South had come on strong as an area of established gridiron powers, and during the period 1925–1931, five southern schools lay claim to national championships. Although Georgia Tech, which was among these contenders, would go on to beat California in the Rose Bowl on January 1, 1929, the narrow victory would turn on one of the most bizarre and legendary plays in football history.

During the first half, after Cal had blown several scoring chances, a Golden Bear running back fumbled the ball, which Cal center and captain Roy Riegels retrieved on the bounce at his own 34-yard line. But somehow he got his sense of direction mixed up and headed pell-mell toward the wrong goal sixty-six yards away. As the huge crowd looked on in disbelief, one of Riegels's teammates finally caught up to tackle him before he could cross the goal line for a safety. But on the ensuing California punt, Tech blocked it for a safety anyway when the ball rolled back out of the end zone, and Tech led at the half, 2–0. The second half saw the Yellow Jackets score a touchdown to stretch the score to 8–0. The frustrated Cal team finally got a drive underway that resulted in 7 points, but it was not enough as Tech went on to win, 8–7. Although the "Wrong Way" moniker would haunt Riegels for the rest of his life, his mistake did result in an important rule change in 1929, stipulating that a recovered fumble was to be ruled dead at the point of recovery and therefore could not be advanced.

Led by All-American center Peter Pund, the Yellow Jackets were named national champions by the Helms Hall of Fame Foundation, an achievement that naturally pleased Heisman when he heard about his old team's good fortune. Although he sorely missed coaching during his first year of retirement, Heisman was clearly in the right place to keep up with the game. In choosing to live in New York City, he enjoyed the opportunity to witness quality football first hand as a number of big-game matchups were being scheduled there. The Army–Notre Dame clash, for example, which was played in Yankee Stadium that year, was the game in which Knute Rockne supposedly carried out George Gipp's death-bed wish when he exhorted his men at halftime to go back on the field and win the game for the Irish great. After falling behind 6–0, Rockne's team, as though truly inspired, did come back to win in a thriller, 12–6, while the Army Cadets, sparked by Chris Cagle, wound up on the 1-yard line as time ran out.

New York University, under Coach Chick Meehan, turned out superior teams during Heisman's initial years in New York. Heisman was highly impressed with Meehan's military approach to the game—having his team break huddle and approach the line in called cadence, often catching the defense off guard as they did so. The showmanlike Meehan even had a cannon fired when his team scored a touchdown, an event that took place rather frequently with All-American fullback Ken Strong in the lineup.

In the Midwest, Minnesota's Bronko Nagurski, a future professional star, was making his presence felt, particularly in the big Wisconsin game. He not only scored the game's only touchdown but he also helped preserve victory with a superb defensive game in which he recovered a fumble, batted down a pass on the goal line, made a touchdown-saving tackle on the 10-yard line and intercepted a pass on the game's final play. In his day, Nagurski hardly had an equal as a defensive player.

In the resurgent South, the Tennessee Volunteers stood next to Georgia Tech in prominence, as the Volunteers turned back the Alabama Crimson Tide, 15–13. After two straight trips to the Rose Bowl, Alabama relinquished the long train ride to the coast to Georgia Tech, who had beaten the Tide decisively that year, 33–13.

In 1929, Knute Rockne, having endured his worst season the previous year with four losses, led Notre Dame to an undefeated mark (9–0), even though every game that year had to be played on the road as the construction of the Irish's new stadium continued. Rockne was also suffering from a phlebitis condition in one of his legs, a situation that compelled him to delegate much of the on-field coaching to an assistant.

In spite of the stock market crash in late October of that year, fans continued to flock to football games. When Notre Dame defeated Southern Cal at Chicago's Soldier Field, 112,000 people were in attendance, while at Yankee Stadium, 79,000 showed up to watch Navy edge Army. Notre Dame and the service academies would be instrumental in perpetuating the popularity of football during the trying economic times ahead. Finishing second to Notre Dame, Purdue at 8–0 won the Big Ten championship for the first time. Highlights of the Purdue Boilermakers' season included wins over Michigan (30–16), who had led at one point 16–6, and Iowa (7–0). Mounting a devastating ground attack along with a tough defense, Purdue produced its first All-American player in tackle Red Sleight.

In the South, Bob Neyland's Tennessee Volunteers finished another undefeated but once-tied season. Led by triple-threat Bobby Dodd, a future Georgia Tech coach, and ferocious guard Herman Hickman, who also had coaching in his future, the Volunteers brought their single-wing attack to near perfection. At Tulane, Coach Bernie Bierman started the Green Wave on a three-year victorious run with a 9–0 record, foreshadowing even greater accomplishments ahead for this outstanding coach.

Although tied by Southern Methodist University, Texas Christian University was good enough at 9–0–1 to win the Southwest title. Slighted by the Rose Bowl, this area of the country was beginning to think about a bowl game of its own, one that would materialize in a few years as the Cotton Bowl.

One of the year's top players, and as a little man whom John Heisman idolized, was Yale's Albie Booth.[17] In front of eighty thousand spectators against Army in the Yale Bowl, the 144-pound, 5-feet 6-inch halfback put on a one-man show that turned him into a football legend. Army, behind the heroics of All-American halfback Chris Cagle, had built up a 13–0 lead before the Bulldogs of Yale began to fight back. By halftime Booth had scored and kicked an extra point to make the score 13–7. But the second half belonged to Booth. He scored two more touchdowns, one on a 65-yard punt return for the game breaker, and drop-kicked two more extra points for a final score of 21–13. By scoring all of the Bulldog points, Albie Booth had joined the ranks of Yale's gridiron immortals.

HEISMAN AND THE DOWNTOWN ATHLETIC CLUB (1929)

A significant event of 1929, at least as far as John Heisman's immediate future was concerned, was the laying of the cornerstone of the Downtown Athletic Club on November 19 in the heart of Manhattan's financial district. Ironically, just several weeks earlier the Wall Street area had been the scene of the stock-market crash that would set the stage for an economic depression of such dire consequences that it would put millions out of work and create mass poverty that would last until the 1940s.

Until this time, the go-getter side of John Heisman's life had directly parallelled the ever-increasing profitability of the American economy. Spurred on by continued expansion of the manufacturing, construction, and automobile industries, the business boom peaked in the 1920s at about the time, paradoxically enough, that Heisman's career as a football coach was on the wane. By the end of the decade, sales in business and industry had begun to decline and stock prices were falling off. The decade-long process of unrestrained investing, both large and small, which had built a pyramid of paper profits based on the certainty that the market would keep rising, had set the stage for an economic collapse of unimaginable proportions. Yet hardly anyone could recognize the telltale signs of economic malaise that had been building up over the decade. Consequently, what transpired on October 29 was so sudden that it was practically an overnight event, resulting in an economic disaster that would have worldwide impact. The businessman-industrialist, who had become something of a popular hero, was now retreating in disgrace as frauds and schemes of every kind were revealed and fortunes were lost overnight.

Heisman himself, in losing his investment in the Florida land boom, was now compelled to cut back on his lifestyle. Accustomed to a fairly high standard of living, he and his wife soon moved from their Park Avenue apartment to more modest quarters in the Roosevelt Hotel. In spite of the pervasive hard times, though, he continued to be active in the sporting-goods business. He parlayed it into a fairly prosperous enterprise, mainly through recommending athletic equipment and supplies to coaches and athletic directors, reflecting the continued popularity of sports during these bleak times. Fortunately for those engaged in the sporting-goods industry, the need for its products and services kept expanding. In the establishment of the Downtown Athletic Club, therefore, Heisman must have recognized an excellent opportunity to branch out in still another direction and perhaps even further his business interests.

When the club's governing body conducted a search for the person to head up their athletic program, John Heisman was among the leading candidates, having been highly recommended by one of his former players and Georgia Tech athletic board chairman, Chip Robert. The day the search committee came to interview the old coach in his suite at the Roosevelt, they found him alert and vigorous, ready to field any question that came his way. But what impressed the committee the most was his response to their question of what he would do if he got the job. "The first thing I'll do," he confidently replied, "will be to see what other people in the field are doing." He got the job, and, true to his word, one of the first things he did was to travel to Detroit and Chicago to study the organization and mission of the clubs there.

The New York club opened its doors on October 1, 1930, not the best of times to get an enterprise of such magnitude off and running. But, bolstered by the core members of the original organization established in 1926, it soon began to build an even more solid membership. The varied attractions the club afforded must have been the main reason for its recruiting success. At thirty-six stories the building was certainly large enough, and at a cost of $4,700,000 (an astronomical sum for that day), it was costly enough as well. There were 120 individual rooms along with three sitting rooms, a sun roof, an Olympic-sized swimming pool, and racquet courts. In the austere times of the 1930s, the DAC had indeed a palatial layout. Today the DAC boasts

135 guest rooms, the most up-to-date fitness and athletic facilities for both men and women, meeting and banquet facilities (there is even a Heisman Room Restaurant), and a membership of more than three thousand. Needless to say, the annual Heisman Trophy award has had a lot to do with the club's continued popularity.

THE ATHLETIC CLUB IN AMERICA

The tradition of the athletic club in America dates back to the late 1860s when organized sporting activities began to establish themselves after the Civil War. During this time every team sport that sprang up seemed to generate its own club of participants and supporters. In anticipating the day of organized intercollegiate athletics, this trend had begun with the inception of rowing as a competitive sport. Other sports would soon follow, not only in the colleges but also in urban areas. Here, population growth would enhance the popularity of professional team sports like baseball and the establishment of leagues in which intercity club members would compete with each other for league championship honors.

The model for athletic clubs with social leanings was set with the founding of the New York Athletic Club in 1866, which other metropolitan areas around the country would begin to emulate during the 1870s. Although the New York club was originated to further the cause of track and field competition, it was not long before it began to cater to other sports that appealed primarily to the society set, such as tennis and golf. In turn, the formal club concept ultimately inspired the more democratic clubs that would spring up in city neighborhoods and in institutions like the YMCA, so that by the late 1880s there were several thousand of these clubs in existence. As noted in chapter 1, John Heisman himself played on a club football team when he was at Brown, and many of the school's opponents were so-called city/town or neighborhood clubs. Some of the city/town clubs were competitive enough to be included on the schedules of colleges that had varsity teams. In looking back over the football schedules of the 1890s and on into the early years of the new century, we can see that such clubs played a significant role in the scheduling of a college team's early season matches.

Impressed with the club sports concept, the military services also began to take an active interest in organized athletics. Recognizing the value of sports, not only in physical conditioning but in building morale as well, the military bureaucracy made organized athletics an integral part of their training missions. Football, the most military of all team sports, had become a varsity sport of the service academies in the 1890s. By World War I, sports were deemed important enough by the Navy Department for it to hire Walter Camp as athletic advisor. But if athletics could impact on the military system, so too the military way affected athletic training in the colleges—as Heisman had learned firsthand when he was coaching at Clemson at the turn of the century. In fact, Heisman once observed: "The first duty of a soldier is to obey orders. It so happens it's the first duty of a football player as well."[18]

Club sports even helped spread the popularity of athletics among high schools during the early part of this century, particularly football. It wouldn't be long before the local high schools would become training grounds and important recruiting sources for area colleges looking to produce competitive football teams. During his Georgia Tech days, John Heisman had first discovered the worth of high-school athletic programs as a reliable recruiting source.

The competitive spirit that American sports had inspired demanded management control in all areas and at all levels. In their organizational zeal the athletic clubs of the 1860–1890s era reflected the growing preoccupation with the sports that had made a strong impact on the American people. In particular, the young college graduate beginning to make his way in the world looked to athletic club membership as a way to enhance business opportunities and social prestige as well as to perpetuate the memories of his college days, as either an athlete or a supporter. He hoped his membership would ultimately qualify him to be among the so-called insiders of American sport. These were mainly the wealthy and well-to-do who had sufficient leisure time to devote to the more individualized sports of tennis, cricket, and golf. To engage in such patrician sporting endeavors was looked upon as a kind of privileged exercise that spoke to one's personal achievement. In looking ahead to an organization like the Downtown Athletic Club, the elite membership of the late nineteenth-century athletic clubs would have a significant influence on American sports by emphasizing a club's social aspects as either a complement or an alternative to athletic participation for its own sake.

But after the 1890s, a number of clubs in metropolitan areas began to fade, due mainly to financial pressures resulting from overbuilding. With such a dubious precedent, then, it is a wonder that the New York Downtown Athletic Club ever got off the ground, much less survived the bleak years of the country's worst depression. Contributing to the club's success was a combination of solid management (the appointment of John Heisman was a brilliant move) and the realization that sport promoted itself as a natural antidote to the terrible times of the 1930s.

THE GAME IN THE EARLY 1930s

What, then, were the social and economic effects of the Depression on college football during the 1930s? According to a 1932 article in the student newspaper at Washington and Jefferson College where Heisman had coached, both local and national interest in football fell off at this time, at least from the student point of view. Claiming that this attitude was also prevalent at larger institutions like Michigan, NYU, and Princeton, the W&J report contended that football was no longer the glamorous sport it had been: "With the so-called 'traditional school spirit' gone the way of corduroy pants and pennants, the spectacular has lost a great deal of its glamour. . . . Gone are the 'pep' meetings, the mad cheering, the do-or-die-for-alma-mater spirit of yesterday. And, consequently, gone are the huge mobs that once filled the stadium and the coffers of the Athletic Association."[19]

Although what probably triggered this negative outlook was the reaction of a more sober-minded student generation to the meaningless frivolity of the 1920s, there were clear signs throughout the country that college football was undergoing severe economic setbacks. Indeed, in the early 1930s it was reported that gate receipts had declined by 30 to 40 percent. As a result, athletic directors at a number of major colleges were forced to retrench, mainly by restricting scholarships and cutting back on equipment expenditures and other spending. Some colleges even gave up their football programs altogether.

Regardless, the game was now too solidly established to roll over and die, especially during a time when football's naturally aggressive and determined style of play seemed to symbolize the kind of psychological attitude that the American people needed to endure the economic tribulations brought on by the Depression. And while rising operational costs threatened many athletic programs, the drive to win and build revenues grew even more imperative, with the paradoxical result that intercollegiate football in the 1930s became increasingly influential as an adjunct to the collegiate scene. Unfortunately, the businesslike control that the game demanded often became an end in itself, resulting in win-at-all-cost programs and ever-widening digression from the collective standards of ethical behavior that the NCAA expected institutions to abide by.

Overall, though, the 1930s would see the game that Heisman helped invent become accepted as a truly national sport, with champions being crowned from coast to coast. The Midwest's Big Ten would dominate the decade with four national championships and one runnerup, and the Southwest would produce three national titles. Concurrently, the East with one championship and a runnerup, the Far West with a championship and two runnerups, and the South with six runnerups would demonstrate the truly national character that college football had assumed during this time.

Leading off the decade, Knute Rockne's 1930 Notre Dame team, which was to be his last, was perhaps his greatest. On their way to an undefeated season (10–0) and the national championship, the Irish showed the mark of a true champion by coming back to win on a number of occasions, particularly in two down-to-the-wire contests. Although in the Northwestern game the Wildcats' overwhelming offense outgained Notre Dame's for practically the entire game, the Irish managed to bounce back in the final five minutes behind the precision punting of Frank Carideo to set up two quick touchdowns for a 14–0 win. Against Army, Rockne's charges came from behind in the last three and a half minutes on a 55-yard touchdown run and Carideo's extra point to edge the Cadets, 7–6. Of such heroics the spirit of Notre Dame was born, the never-say-die attitude that Heisman himself had always tried to instill in his men throughout his coaching career.

At 10–0, Alabama also had an undefeated season, mainly because Coach Wallace Wade now had the quality players needed to deliver. Leading examples of this kind of talent were triple-threat Johnny "Sugar" Cain at tailback and All-American Frank Sington at tackle. Chosen to play the undefeated Washington State Cougars (9–0) in the Rose Bowl, the Crimson Tide continued its winning ways by stunning the Cougars, 24–0.

In the spring of 1931, the nation was shocked by the tragic death of Knute Rockne in an airplane crash in Kansas. But his passing made Irish supporters even more determined to carry on the winning tradition that their beloved coach had begun. On the larger scene, Rockne's death could not have come at a bleaker time, especially in a psychological sense. Yet it helped football fans everywhere realize the debt they owed to leaders such as Rockne. Like Heisman, these were men who had faith in the game's worth and who, because of their intense dedication, would be memorialized wherever football would continue to be played.

Under new coach Hunk Anderson the Irish made a valiant go of it. Nevertheless, they saw their twenty-six-game unbeaten string come to an end against Southern Cal in the next-to-last game of the 1931 season. Played before over fifty thousand fans in probably the grimmest year of the Depression, the game turned out to be one of the most exciting in the annals of the Notre Dame–Southern Cal series. By the third quarter the Irish had built up a 14–0 lead, and at that point it appeared that they would surely add another victory to their long streak. But suddenly Coach Howard Jones's version of the single-wing, which depended on a variety of reverses and deceptive maneuvers, began to work against the stubborn Irish defense, resulting in a score that made it 14–6. (The extra-point try was blocked.) When the Trojans scored again, the score stood at 14–13, and then with about a minute left they kicked a field goal to win, 16–14. It was only the second time the Irish had lost at home since 1905. Having previously won titles at Yale and Iowa, Howard Jones was now assured of another national championship. In fact, Jones would be the only coach ever to accomplish this feat at three different colleges.

To test Southern Cal's championship quality, Coach Bernie Bierman's unbeaten Tulane team, which had kept the South in the title picture, was invited to play the Trojans in the Rose Bowl. At 11–0, the Green Wave of Tulane came in as the favored team, but, by capitalizing on several key fumbles Southern Cal wound up on top, 21–12, to cement its title claim. Nevertheless, Bierman, in winning twenty-eight games and losing only two during 1929–1931 (including the 1932 Rose Bowl), had made a real power out of heretofore unrecognized Tulane. His brightest days in the sun were yet to be, though, when he went north to coach the University of Minnesota.

Actually, the dominant teams of the decade were Minnesota and Michigan of the Big Ten Conference, a clear indication as to where the nation's gridiron power had now shifted. The Michigan Wolverines won championships in 1932 and 1933 while the Minnesota Golden Gophers claimed titles in 1934, 1935, and 1936. During the period 1934–1936, Minnesota lost only one game under Coach Bierman.

Michigan's venerable football tradition came to championship fruition during the 1932 and 1933 campaigns. By now, Fielding Yost had assumed the role of athletic director, while one of his former players, Harry Kipke, performed as head football coach. But coaching leadership was the only organizational change for the Wolverines, for Kipke carried on Yost's strategy of utilizing the punt as a defensive weapon to keep the opposition pinned down while drilling his men in the art of blocking their opponents' punts. Kipke's coaching paid off with consecutive 8–0 seasons and national championships. In fact, Kipke's overall tenure at Michigan would result in a remarkable thirty-one wins (seventeen by shutouts), only one loss, and three ties.

Other noteworthy gridiron happenings during this time included the end of Southern Cal's twenty-seven-game unbeaten streak at the hands of Stanford's "Vow Boys" in 1933. Having lost five straight times to the Trojans, the Stanford team took an oath that they would not lose another. That year they made their word good as they defeated USC and its great back, Cotton Warburton, 13–7. At 5-feet 6-inches and 145 pounds, Warburton was another player in the mold of John Heisman's tiny giants. That college football was a team game of intense emotion was dramatically borne out in Stanford's commitment to winning a game of this stature.

In the South, Tennessee continued its rise to dominance as Coach Bob Neyland's 1931 team, which many viewed as his greatest, set the pace for later Volunteer teams of the decade. (In his first seven years of coaching the Vols, Neyland produced a phenomenal 61–2–5 mark.) Stressing defense and flawless play ("The team that makes the fewer mistakes wins," said Neyland), the 1931 team gave up just 15 points over the season. Highlights of the Vols' season included wins over such strong teams as Alabama (25–0), Vanderbilt (21–7), and NYU (13–0). Guard Herman Hickman became part of gridiron legend in this latter game when the NYU team aimed four straight goal-line strikes at Hickman's position and ultimately wound up losing ten yards! The year 1932 saw the Volunteers fashion another 9–0–1 season. However, in the national championship race, the best Tennessee could come up with during the 1930s was runnerup finishes in 1938 and 1939. Other southern teams that came close were Alabama in 1930 and 1934, Tulane in 1931, as noted, and LSU in 1936. Since John Heisman's Golden Tornado national champions at Georgia Tech in 1917, the South as a region of football powers had been building a national image. By the 1930s it had arrived in full force.

The Southwest Conference also rose to the fore in the 1930s with SMU and TCU in the running for the national title in 1935, TCU winning in 1938, and Texas A&M winning in 1939. The 1935 Southwest championship was decided in a big game between SMU and TCU, both teams coming into the season-ending contest with perfect records. Led by "Slingin' " Sammy Baugh, the TCU Horned Frogs made a real contest of it before losing out to the SMU Mustangs, 20–14. With a Rose Bowl invitation riding on the outcome, this game commanded enough attention to be the first game broadcast nationally from the Southwest, and a large cadre of notable sportswriters came to Fort Worth to cover the game. In representing its conference in the Rose Bowl, SMU, as the only Southwest team ever to play there, lost a close one to Stanford, 7–0. Appropriately, though, teams from this part of the country had begun to get the recognition they deserved. In 1934, Texas would edge Notre Dame in South Bend, 7–6, to command even more respect. During the years he coached in the region, John Heisman had come to recognize Southwest teams as a tough, up-and-coming breed that practiced a brand of rock 'em, sock 'em, wide-open football. The real glory days of Southwest football lay just around the corner.

By this time the East had finally faded from national dominance, although Princeton was runnerup to Michigan in 1933 and Columbia was a surprise winner in the 1934 Rose Bowl. Nevertheless, one of the most outstanding, though somewhat unheralded, eastern teams was Andy Kerr's 1932 Lehigh team. Having learned his football as an assistant to Pop Warner, Kerr came to Lehigh University in 1929 and immediately turned out a winner. In fact, his teams would wind up 25–3 in the first three years of his tenure. The influence of Pop Warner on Lehigh's offense was obvious, as Kerr implemented wingback reverses, buck laterals, the hook-and-lateral, and something he called the downfield lateral. This play was so successful that it was copied by teams all over the country for a number of years. Although his great 1932 team was unbeaten, untied, and unscored on, it was jokingly referred to as the "4-U" team since it was also uninvited to play in the Rose Bowl. The University of Pittsburgh got the honor instead.

In 1933, Princeton and Columbia upheld the honor of the Ivy League as the Princeton Tigers finished second to the Michigan Wolverines, while the Columbia Lions went on to pull off a major upset in the Rose Bowl. With new coach Herbert "Fritz" Crisler at the helm, Princeton fashioned a 9–0 season, giving up a total of only 8 points, and these points were not scored until the final two games against Rutgers and Yale.

Although they had lost to Princeton, 20–0, Lou Little's Columbia team was invited to play Stanford in the Rose Bowl, January 1, 1934. Lacking in quality reserves, the Lions combined deception and the advantage of a wet field to outplay the heavily favored Stanford team. On a perfectly executed naked reverse play that Coach Little had cryptically designated as KF–79, Columbia scored the only points of the game to win, 7–0. Little's systematic approach to labeling and deploying his offense was a sign of how technical football was becoming.

The year 1931 saw Amos Alonzo Stagg, who had coached at the University of Chicago for forty-one years, reach the mandatory retirement age of seventy. Still not ready to hang up his cleats, the following year would find the grand old man of football coaching at the College of the Pacific. He would coach for another twenty-eight years and live to be 102. Because of the large membership of the Southern Conference (now twenty-three schools) and the difficulty in making travel arrangements and scheduling opponents to determine a champion, the larger schools of the unwieldy organization broke off in 1932 to form the Southeastern Conference. It would eventually become one of the strongest in the nation. In 1953, the Southern Conference would again break up, with the larger schools forming the Atlantic Coast Conference.

One major rule change approved in 1932 was designed to prevent a ball carrier from crawling with the ball and subjecting himself to injury. Under the new rule, the ball was to be declared dead when any part of the body except the hands and feet touched the ground.

HEISMAN AND THE DOWNTOWN ATHLETIC CLUB IN THE EARLY 1930s

Meanwhile, during the early years of the 1930s, John Heisman was adapting to his athletic director duties at the brand-new Downtown Athletic Club. He found his new role a challenging job, but he naturally missed the coaching life after all those years out on the field. Nevertheless, Heisman's innovative side was still evident as he kept coming up with fresh ideas to attract more club members. One in particular proved to be very popular: the Touchdown Club of New York, a brotherhood of football aficionados who came together periodically to profess their mutual interest in the game and to honor those who had helped advance its cause. It was first organized under Heisman's supervision in 1933. He also conducted a Friday luncheon series during the football season at which the alumni of schools that had lost on the gridiron the previous week had to explain the reasons for their team's downfall. Only Heisman could have come up with a unique twist like this.

Because of his knowledge of football history, Heisman was frequently called on by outside sources seeking to capitalize on his expertise and background about the game's early development. In 1932 he was asked by the editors of *Illustrated Football Annual* (a magazine in the vein of the later Street and Smith annual preview) to select an all-time football team, a difficult task due to all the excellent players he had coached, played against, and heard about over the years. The criteria he used to make his selections are open to conjecture. But in 1902, while he was coaching at Clemson, he had been requested to pick an All-Heisman team, and his thoughts in making that selection give us a probable clue as to how he might have gone about carrying out the later assignment. At that time in his coaching career there were four teams (Oberlin, Buchtel, Auburn, and Clemson) he could choose from, and according to Heisman:

No two of these teams were coached in exactly similar systems. The changes of play from year to year were frequently startlingly marked, and players who did exceptionally good work under one system might not have been so fortunate under the system of a different season; but as I invariably make my plays conform to the needs and abilities of the players I have on hand (not the players to the plays), I would anticipate no difficulty in evolving a system to suit the eleven best men.[20]

He went on to name a first and a second team. Auburn clearly conformed best to Heisman's selection system, for his teams there were represented by six players on the first team and five on the second. (One wonders, though, if his selections were influenced more by his system or by the fond memories he had of his days at the Alabama school.)

Similarly, in selecting his all-time team in 1932, Heisman's criteria may have been determined by how these men would have measured up to a "system to suit the eleven best men." By 1932 he was far enough removed from his early coaching days to command a more objective attitude in naming the following all-time eleven, although his personal prejudices still shone through:

Ends: Harold "Brick" Muller, California; Huntington "Tack" Hardwick, Harvard

Tackles: Hector Cowan, Princeton; Wilbur "Pete" Henry, Washington and Jefferson

Guards: William "Pudge" Heffelfinger, Yale; Truxton Hare, Penn

Center: Adolph "Germany" Schultz, Michigan

Quarterback: Walter Eckersall, Chicago

Halfbacks: Harold "Red" Grange, Illinois; Edward Mahan, Harvard

Fullback: Edward "Ted" Coy, Yale

Although "Heisman never claimed a monopoly of virtues for the good old days," as sportswriter Joe Williams reminds us, he apparently thought enough of the old-time players to include six of them on his all-time list, that is, those players who had completed their eligibility before 1912, the year that marked the beginning of the so-called modern era of the game. Of this list, Heisman had played against Cowan and Heffelfinger—and, of course, we know his lofty opinion of these stalwarts. But of all the players he had named, his all-time personal favorite was Chicago's Walter Eckersall (1904–1906). Williams tells us why:

One of the persuasive reasons, of course, was that the Chicago star never weighed more than 140 pounds. Of him he once wrote:—"So rounded and polished was "Eckie" in the execution of every detail of play of every department of the game, it would be hard to say in which he most excelled. Built like a steel bullet, darting like a swallow in flight, he constantly electrified beholders with the brazen audacity of his tactics and the tenacity of his purpose."[21]

As we have seen with numerous players he coached and with Yale's great back Albie Booth, Heisman identified with small men because he himself as a player had been small. In his "enthusiastic failing for football runts," Williams remarked that Heisman had a "theory that spirit, not power, made football stars." In "generating more spirit than the giants," the little players exercised what Heisman called "physical compensation." To support his theory, "Heisman had a list of All-America stars dating 'way back, none of whom weighed more than 150 pounds, and he challenged all and sundry to match the list with giants. And for a fact it was a list that could not be easily matched."[22]

In spite of the huge average size of today's football players, Heisman's theory continues to hold up respecting the number of relatively small players who still dare to play the game, both collegiate and professional. Nevertheless, Heisman did express reservations in comparing the "good big man" and the "good little man":

The smaller man is generally faster and nimbler, he has better use of himself, he co-ordinates better, he is often more aggressive than the bigger man, and he is frequently clearer headed and quicker witted. When, however, the big fellows have all these attributes in high degree and throw them into the game they become the really great players—the Heffelfingers, Hares, Hestons, DeWitts, Coys, and Thorpes.[23]

FOOTBALL IN THE MID-1930s

By the mid–1930s, college football was regaining the economic status it had enjoyed in the 1920s. Near the end of the decade *Liberty* magazine assessed the intercollegiate game as a $50,000,000-a-year business—a lot of money for the Depression years, to be sure.[24] On the heels of growing financial stability came the founding of three more big bowl games to compete with the prestigious Rose Bowl: the Orange Bowl (1933), the Sugar Bowl (1935), and the Cotton Bowl (1937). Primarily showcasing the achievements of host teams from the South and the Southwest, these bowls were auspicious monuments to the enduring popularity and success of intercollegiate football. On January 1, 1933, the first game of the new Orange Bowl (the second-oldest of all bowl games) was played between the University of Miami and Manhattan College. Miami won, 7–0. They would go on to greater things, and during the 1980s and 1990s were perennial national championship contenders. By this time, too, the acceptance of big-time athletics was graphically reflected in the pages of magazines like the *Saturday Evening Post*, where "sports now dominated, with scores of articles each year on baseball, football, and boxing."[25]

The most dominant team at this time was Coach Bernie Bierman's Minnesota Golden Gophers, who during the period 1934–1936 captured three national championships. In 1936, Minnesota became the first team to be chosen national champion by the brand new Associated Press poll. Although it competed with a number of other top-team rankings, the AP poll was eventually accepted as the official top-team poll through its nationwide network of reputable sportswriters who voted each week for the nation's top-ranked teams until an official champion was named at the end of the season.

In losing only one game in three years, Bierman built his dynasty at Minnesota around a strong running game and the fundamentals of blocking and tackling, the trademarks of a Bierman-coached team. Feeling that these basics of the game would never go out of style, Bierman declared in the 1970s, long after his retirement: "A good running game behind good blocking is the smartest game. . . . Passing is a gambler's game, played by fools. I could take a team today, teach it to take the ball away from the other team on defense, control the ball on offense and beat the best of them with their new-fangled, fancy aerial attacks."[26]

Heisman would have vehemently disagreed with Bierman's opinion about the forward pass in that the offensive threat of the pass is really what made the modern game more balanced and infinitely more exciting, simply because there is an element of gambling in attempting a pass play. (Ironically, Minnesota won the 1934 contest against Pitt, 13–7, on a pass in the final minutes.) Like many old-time coaches, Bernie Bierman naturally adhered to the system with which he had been most successful.

In 1935, Bierman reloaded to finish as national champion again. Among his players was a future coaching great, Bud Wilkinson, whom Bierman contended was one of his smartest players ever. Wilkinson had to be well versed in the game, being one of the few players of the more specialized modern era to perform both as a lineman and as a back during his collegiate career. Although the Gophers' unbeaten string of twenty-eight games was stopped in 1936 by Northwestern, 6–0, in a rain-drenched contest, the AP poll created something of a controversy by selecting Minnesota as national champion over a number of other claimants with comparable records. However, the arguments of 1936 would pale in comparison to the way future poll rankings would embroil the football public.

Heisman would probably have placed little stock in the validity of the AP ranking system, in view of the comments he made after Georgia Tech's runaway game with Cumberland in 1916, as discussed in chapter 4. To him, statistics were the machinations of sportswriters and really meaningless in making team comparisons and determining national rankings. He believed that the way a team truly qualified for a national championship was through head-to-head meetings with the strongest teams around.

In 1934, there were many who thought that Alabama should have been named national champion instead of Minnesota. Some polls, in fact, did choose the Crimson Tide because of the following accomplishments: They won all nine of their regular season games, averaging nearly 32 points a game; they defeated tough Tennessee, 13–6, Georgia Tech, 40–0, and Vanderbilt, 34–0 (old Heisman foe Dan McGugin coached his last game in this one); and then soundly trounced Stanford in the Rose Bowl, 29–13.

Coached by former Notre Dame player Frank Thomas, the Tide featured the play at the ends of two future greats: Paul Bryant, who would wind up coaching at his alma mater and setting the mark for career coaching wins in Division I-A at 323, and Don Hutson, who would become one of the all-time professional football pass receivers. Against Stanford in the 1935 Rose Bowl, Hutson scored two key touchdowns on passes and gained a total of 164 yards. He would go on to become a star for the Green Bay Packers.

In the first Sugar Bowl game, played on January 1, 1935, Tulane defeated Temple, 20–14. The Owls of Temple were coached by Pop Warner, who had shocked the football world by leaving Stanford to return to the East. The other Owls, Heisman's last team, Rice, finally captured a Southwest Conference crown with a 20–9 win over Texas. Heisman must have been pleased to see the long-suffering Rice fans finally claim a championship.

Having first been modified in 1912, the shape of the ball underwent its final transformation in 1934—the most significant step toward enhancing the passing game. The result was a ball measuring twenty-eight inches around the ends and twenty-one and one-half inches around the circumference, weighing approximately one pound. This move paved the way for the T-formation quarterback who would come into his own in the 1940s and revolutionize the passing game.

If any one game of this era can be singled out to exemplify the worth of the forward pass and just how far college football had evolved since that November day in 1869 when Princeton first met Rutgers, it would have to be the 1935 contest between Notre Dame and Ohio State. As a Big Game matchup whose outcome was not decided until the final seconds, it contained all the dramatic elements that football could generate. The prominent role that passing played in this game's outcome demonstrates just how integral an offensive weapon the forward pass had become.

Played before over eighty thousand spectators at Columbus, Ohio, the game had begun to look like a sure win for the Ohio State Buckeyes when after three quarters of play they found themselves ahead 13–0. But then the seemingly impossible began to transpire as Coach Elmer Layden's charges finally started to fight back. Andy Pilney ran a punt back to the OSU 13-yard line, and following a pass to the 1-yard line the Irish scored but missed the extra point, to trail by 13–6. Upon getting the ball back, they then marched to the OSU 1-yard line, only to fumble the ball away. There were only three minutes left on the clock when Notre Dame started out again from its 22-yard line. Then, on four consecutive pass completions, the Irish tallied again but again missed the extra point to find themselves behind by 13–12. Two minutes remained when Notre Dame tried an on-side kick that failed as the Buckeyes recovered the ball at midfield. Clearly all they had to do now to win was run the clock out. But an end run resulted in disaster when the ball was knocked loose, and was last touched by Notre Dame before going out of bounds. Consequently, on a rule that had been adopted in 1930, the Irish were awarded the ball at their own 49. With only ninety seconds now left, Pilney tried another pass but, finding his receiver covered, sped for the goal line. Knocked out of bounds at the 19, he lay still where he had fallen. Concerned Irish rooters would eventually see him carried off the field on a stretcher. With fifty seconds still remaining, Layden sent in a substitute back named Bill Shakespeare, clearly a classic name for this classic game. After throwing one pass that was nearly intercepted, he connected on his next one to the Irish left end for a touchdown and an improbable 18–13 victory as bedlam broke loose in the stands. After all was said and done, though, it was the forward pass that had made victory possible for Notre Dame. For it was its timely utilization on that memorable day that turned this game into legend—a game, in fact, that would be talked about for years to come.

THE INCEPTION OF THE DOWNTOWN ATHLETIC CLUB (HEISMAN) TROPHY

Being the keen observer of the game that he was, John Heisman undoubtedly relished hearing and reading about classic matchups like the Notre Dame–Ohio State confrontation. Such encounters clearly bore out what he had maintained all along—that the adoption of the forward pass would not only open up the game of football but turn it into the most exciting spectacle in modern sport. Although by this time in the game's development football's image as a nationally recognized game was solidly established, many more dramatically intense, emotion-packed matchups would take place as a result of the ongoing refinement of the game's rules and the impact of significant off-field events affecting its public reception. One of these momentous events was soon destined to make the Heisman name a synonym for excellence in measuring the college football player's performance on the field.

Although by 1935 he was approaching retirement age, Heisman had become so involved in his role at the Downtown Athletic Club that the notion of retiring probably never once crossed his mind. Joe Williams would later write at the time of Heisman's passing that he never thought the old coach was "particularly happy in his executive labors at the Downtown A.C., but it was something to do and he had grown too old for coaching." Heisman undoubtedly missed being involved in coaching, envying his contemporaries Warner and Stagg for still being active. They were notable exceptions, however, and he had at least cast his lot with an organization that kept him very close to athletics, particularly the game he had held so dear practically all of his life.

In his private life Heisman practiced his usual retiring lifestyle, one that always starkly contrasted with the go-getter image he had projected throughout his public life. Even in his coaching days he had preferred the pursuits of the quiet life when he was not actively engaged in producing winning teams. The New York years were no different as he and Maora took in the wealth of cultural events that the city had to offer, in particular dramatic and operatic productions. At this time he had also begun to make plans for a new book, a project he referred to as a history of the human side of football.

To satisfy his strong competitive nature and to stay physically active and fit, Heisman had taken up golf, mainly at the urging of Atlanta's golfing great, Bobby Jones, whom he had known since his Georgia Tech days. (Jones had presented him with a set of clubs and taught him some of the finer points of playing the game.) Initially labeling the game a sissy sport, Heisman grew to take on its special challenges sufficiently to shoot in the high 70s and low 80s. Golf soon became another of the many goal-oriented activities he identified with throughout his life, and during summer vacations spent in his wife's hometown of Rhinelander, Wisconsin, he particularly enjoyed testing his playing skills.

By this time in his life, then, Heisman had naturally mellowed, both philosophically and physically. But in early 1935 when Willard B. Prince, founder and editor of the Downtown Athletic Club's newsletter, the *DAC Journal*, first proposed that its membership sponsor an annual trophy to honor the most outstanding college football player east of the Mississippi, Heisman was compelled to assume his authoritative coaching posture once again. To Coach Heisman, football was strictly a team game in which individual recognition and achievement were subservient to overall team performance. How, then, could one player be singled out as better than his peers? How could an offensive specialist be looked upon as more valuable than a defensive man? How could a halfback be more essential than a lineman who made it possible for the back to gain yardage? To the old coach, Prince's proposal seemed somewhat absurd.

But then at a luncheon attended by New York area sports reporters, Heisman, in mentioning Prince's proposal to the gathering, was surprised at the enthusiastic reception it received. Soon even Heisman himself joined in the move to make the trophy a reality. Never in the wildest stretch of his imagination, though, could he have foreseen the kind of lasting impact that the realization of Prince's idea would have on his name.

After agreeing to award the first DAC Trophy at the close of the 1935 season, the club's administration appointed a committee that immediately set out to identify a qualified sculptor to construct a unique trophy appearance that would convey more meaning than a cup or a bowl. The committee had concluded, in fact, that the most appropriate symbol would be a replica in bronze of an idealized, though realistically portrayed, player in the act of running with the ball. Little did the committee realize at the time that their concept would evolve into the most familiar image and coveted individual award in college sports.

The search soon turned up a young, talented sculptor named Frank Eliscu, a graduate of Pratt Institute and a National Academy prize winner. In setting out to get the job done, Eliscu selected one of the top players on the previous year's New York University football team as his model—a former high-school classmate named Ed Smith. Eliscu came up with a rough clay model of his project, which the DAC committee approved contingent upon former Notre Dame player and now Fordham coach Jim Crowley's inspection. However, it was Crowley's players whose critique provided Eliscu with the final verification he needed to carry out his commission. In modeling the various running positions from different angles, the players helped Eliscu come up with the trophy's finished, lifelike appearance of a driving, side-stepping runner cradling a ball in his left arm while thrusting his right arm at an imaginary opponent.

The final inspection came on November 16, 1935, when Notre Dame coach Elmer Layden came to town. Having played a 6–6 tie with Army that day, he and his team were invited to view the new trophy after a dinner at the McAlpin Hotel. Highly impressed with Eliscu's work, the team members proclaimed the finished product an artistic as well as an athletic triumph. After its refinement and final endorsement by qualified representatives of two well-known collegiate institutions, the trophy was ready for casting in bronze.[27] Meanwhile, the club prepared to elect a worthy recipient.

Actually, the club itself had no voice in the voting, and in that first year the election was confined to sports-oriented representatives in the East. (The balloting went national in 1936 when, after John Heisman's death, the trophy's name was changed to the Heisman Memorial Trophy.) Today there are five sectional representatives across the land who recommend the various state appointments within their districts. The state representatives maintain updated files on all eligible electors in their states, most of whom are sportswriters, sportscasters, and telecasters. Around mid-November each elector receives a ballot with which to vote for three players on a 3–2–1 point scale designed to eliminate sectional favoritism. The player receiving the greatest number of points is named the winner.

Although he did not play for a winning team, the initial recipient of what was then called the DAC Trophy was highly qualified. He was Jay Berwanger, whose Chicago Maroons had a mediocre 11–11–2 record during his three varsity seasons. But Berwanger himself was something of a one-man gang: He not only called his team's plays, he also ran, passed, punted, blocked, played defense, kicked extra points, kicked off, returned punts and kickoffs, and, of course, was expected to play sixty minutes of football to get all his chores done. It was truly fitting that such an all-around player was chosen as the trophy's first recipient, for Berwanger obviously met John Heisman's high standards of team play.

At the time, though, winning the DAC Trophy made little impression on Berwanger. He had been more impressed with being selected Big Ten player of the year by the *Chicago Tribune*, for which honor he received a silver football replica. However, he was quite excited about the free trip to New York that he and his coach, Clark Shaughnessy, got for receiving the DAC award. But at the time he had no idea of the trophy's future import. In fact, the significance of the New York award didn't

hit Berwanger until another fifteen years had passed, by which time Heisman Memorial Trophy winners were regularly turning their collegiate honors into lucrative professional contracts. "I never dreamed the Heisman would ever be so important," he said. "Nobody talked about it for twenty-five years. Then television came on the scene, giving college football more exposure, and it became a big deal that I had won the first one."[28]

As a super athlete at a tough academic school, Berwanger was an average student who worked hard for his degree and after graduation made his way in the business world on his own merits. In this respect, he was a student-athlete molded after the go-getter ideal, and this was certainly another reason Heisman himself approved of his selection.

Another distinction of Jay Berwanger's athletic career is that he became the first player to be drafted in the newly established player selection system of the National Football League, designed by Bert Bell, one of Heisman's former coaching assistants at Penn and now owner of the Philadelphia Eagles. After Berwanger turned down the Eagles' offer in 1936, George Halas, looking for a hometown draw for his Chicago Bears, attempted to sign him. At the time, professional football teams could not offer the kind of money they do in today's lucrative TV market. Consequently, Berwanger turned down Halas's offer to opt for a career in business.[29]

PORTENTS OF THE GAME IN THE 1930s

Professional football in the 1930s, reflecting the precarious state of the American economy, was striving to build a popular base that would put it on firmer financial ground. To make for a more exciting contest and attract more fans, club owners sought to open up the game even more than the colleges had. Goalposts had been moved up from the end line to the goal line to encourage more scoring opportunities by field goals; forward passes were now allowed from any point behind the scrimmage line; so that a team would have sufficient room to run a play near the sidelines, a 10-yard zone was created along either sideline to which point the ball was brought back when it carried within this area or out of bounds (the colleges had also adopted this same ruling, and in 1938 the zone was extended to fifteen yards); but most significantly, the National Football League realigned itself into two divisions to create a championship playoff between the Eastern and Western leaders at season's end and, of course, retain fan interest to the end of the season.

But there was another area of more immediate concern. As a sporting goods entrepreneur, John Heisman was attuned to the players' protective needs as the game had evolved. Due to the technological breakthroughs that began occurring in the 1930s with the development of new fibers, plastics, and production techniques, protective padding became sturdier, more comfortable, and safer. The major sporting goods manufacturers that sprang up, such as McGregor, Rawlings, Wilson, and Spalding, were quick to respond to the game's special needs as they continued to change.

Knute Rockne always contended that the shoe was the most important item of support in playing the game. In developing from the modified baseball shoe of the late nineteenth century, the high-topped shoe with interchangeable cone-shaped cleats that came into being in the 1930s underscored Rockne's assessment.

Although some professional players refused to wear helmets as late as the 1930s, the more comfortable leather helmet introduced in the latter part of that decade eventually won all players over. With its sponge rubber padding that incorporated a suspension system, the helmet of that day looked ahead to the plastic model that appeared after World War II and ultimately the face mask of the 1950s.

The uniform itself, as a team identifier, was growing stylishly sleeker and more colorful, with bold designs that featured stripes, inserts, and striking logos. Sensitive to the psychological need for strong visual identity among its followers, the professional game pioneered the eye-catching designs and distinctive colors of uniforms and supporting equipment. The more conservative college game would start to emulate these developments over the years. A sign of things to come occurred in the 1931 Rose Bowl game, when the Washington State Cougars came on the field attired from head to toe in bright red uniforms.

In spite of the advances made by the pros, the college game was still king at this time. So the surest way for professional owners to attract fans to the stands was to recruit big-name college players such as Ernie Nevers, Don Hutson, Bronco Nagurski, and Sammy Baugh. To capitalize even more on the popularity of college football, sportswriter Arch Ward of the *Chicago Tribune* organized an annual game for charity in which a college all-star team was assembled to square off against the preceding year's professional champions. For the first five years of the series, the collegians held their own, but after World War II the pro teams came to the fore as more and more college players were lured into the professional ranks due to increasingly lucrative contract offers. Beginning in the 1960s, multimillion dollar contracts with network television would result in undreamed-of player salaries.

Clark Shaughnessy, the University of Chicago coach, was instrumental in revolutionizing both the professional and the collegiate game by resurrecting the prototypical T-formation offense that had been invented by Walter Camp, expanded upon by Amos Alonzo Stagg in the 1890s, and later modified by Glenn Warner and Knute Rockne. Shaughnessy, in fact, helped George Halas install the T in the Chicago Bear offense, and the result was a devastating 73–0 win over the Washington Redskins in the 1940 professional championship game. As primarily a passing formation, the T offense proved once and for all that the forward pass was here to stay. It also proved what Walter Camp had asserted back in the beginning: that football was a game of unlimited offensive possibilities, as strategic variations such as the split-T, the wing-T, the slot-T, the veer-T, the wishbone, and variations of the I-formation sprang up over the ensuing years.

Shaughnessy had become head football coach at Chicago when Stagg had departed the scene in 1932. The Chicago program had been established in 1892, the same year that Heisman had started out on his coaching career at Oberlin. Under Stagg, it had begun modestly enough, as noted in chapter 2, but the Maroons soon grew into a national power. By the time of Stagg's departure, though, Chicago football was clearly on the wane as the school's emphasis on academics left little room in the minds of Chicago officials for compromise. Even though the Maroon football team was no longer a power in the Big Ten, no one was quite prepared for the shock that came in late 1939 when university president Robert M. Hutchins announced that the school was cancelling its football program.

There were many who thought that Chicago could have maintained its program by deemphasizing football in the manner that the Ivy League schools and other former gridiron powers around the country had been doing. But, having won Big Ten championships in 1899, 1905, 1907, 1908, 1913, and 1924, the Maroons had not captured a title in fifteen years. So in now lagging behind the other conference members, Chicago had already, in effect, deemphasized football. Perhaps no one stated the belief that football should have been retained at Chicago more forcefully than Cleveland sports columnist Gordon Cobbledick, who termed Chicago's "football suicide" to be "an unnecessarily drastic step":

Dr. Hutchins has made it clear that he did not approve of modern high pressure football. In this he was not unique among college presidents. Probably a majority of them, if they were freed of their fear of alumni pressure long enough to state their true feelings, would take the same stand. For football has become a Frankenstein in many colleges. It has got beyond the control of educators. . . . But, instead of abolishing football, Chicago could have done what many a college before it has done. It could have dropped out of a class in which it demonstrably could not compete, and it would have been welcomed as a worthy addition to the company of colleges in which football is not big business, but a game for and by students.[30]

Because football had become such an integral part of the collegiate scene, it seemed inconceivable to students of the game like Cobbledick that a long-time program like Chicago's could be irrevocably dismantled. This is why, of course, he felt that the Chicago administration should have followed in the steps of the programs like Washington and Jefferson that had decided to deemphasize. Perhaps, then, the Chicago decision really was an admission of its inability to control the football program, as Cobbledick went on to say. This was not just a problem at Chicago but was being experienced at many other private schools at the time, in particular Carnegie Tech, Georgetown, and Villanova.

Actually, the Chicago situation epitomized the ongoing dilemma that every college and university involved in big-time football at the time had to face—whether to maintain a high level of competition or deemphasize it. Coaches like Stagg and Heisman, whose careers bridged the evolution of the game from its earliest days to its most recent stage of development, symbolized the ironic relationship that football had come to have with the institutions who felt compelled to sponsor a sport that was now more of a business than a game. Stagg surely experienced this feeling during his final days at Chicago, and as we have seen, Heisman had begun to speculate about the coach's changing relationship with the game during his tenures at Penn and Rice.

It would be exactly thirty years after the demise of football at Chicago that the game was reinstated there, in the same image that Cobbledick had originally envisioned—at the more deemphasized Division III level with a schedule that included schools like Beloit, Ripon, Lake Forest, Coe, and Knox. As it turned out, this reintroduction clearly demonstrated that football *can* be played in an atmosphere where academics come first and school spirit is the main ingredient in putting together a winning team. Here were the coaching philosophy of John Heisman and the spirit of Amos Alonzo Stagg reincarnated in a day of big-time athletics, the magnitude of which neither of them could ever have imagined.

So despite its uncertain relationship with the academic side of the collegiate experience, by 1936 the game of American football had firmly established itself as an annual ritual in the national sporting scene. The advent of the football season each autumn saw the general public, college communities, and alumni anticipating yet another opportunity for their respective teams to get in the running for a national championship—or perhaps just to win the Big Game on their schedule. John Heisman, who had lived long enough to see his cherished game achieve the national acceptance he always knew it could, would feel the same promise and anticipation he always had at the beginning of each gridiron season. But unfortunately 1936 would be his last; in fact, he would not even live through the season.

The results of the 1936 campaign continued to reflect the nationalization of the game, as Minnesota, the power of the Midwest, would once again wind up at the top. LSU was the Southern Conference contender but lost 21–14 to Santa Clara in the Sugar Bowl. Although Arkansas won its first Southwest title, future professional great Sammy Baugh took TCU to the first Cotton Bowl game on January 1, 1937 in Dallas where the Horned Frogs of TCU defeated the then Hilltoppers of Marquette, 16–6. In the East, Coach Jim Crowley had built the Fordham Rams into a national power. One of his "Seven Blocks of Granite," as the Rams line was referred to, was future coaching great Vince Lombardi, who would play a key role in professional football's rise to prominence in the 1960s.

Toward the end of the decade another sign of things to come appeared in the persons of two talented black halfbacks on the UCLA squad: Kenny Washington and Jackie Robinson. While a multitude of rule changes, innovations, and ethical problems would characterize football's future (such as two-platoon substitution, free substitution, the 2-point conversion, player specialization, recruiting infractions, and drug abuse) none of them would have quite the impact that black players would have on the game.

THE PASSING OF JOHN HEISMAN (1936)

The most momentous off-field event of the 1936 season, at least as far as its future impact on college football was concerned, was the unexpected death of John Heisman, just after the season had gotten underway. With the sudden chill of an eastern autumn his illness had started out as nothing more than an annoying head cold, but the old coach soon found himself confined to bed at home under his doctor's care and his wife's attentive eye as his situation worsened into what was diagnosed as bronchial pneumonia. In a little over a week he quietly passed away on October 3, just a few days before his sixty-seventh birthday. His body was transported to his wife's hometown of Rhinelander, Wisconsin, where a brief, simple funeral service was conducted at St. Augustine's Episcopal Church, the kind of ceremony Heisman would have approved. From the playing fields and go-getter ambiance of Titusville, Pennsylvania, he had passed through the often uncertain but intrinsically appealing challenges of a long coaching career, to find his final resting place in a town whose name was reminiscent of his own Germanic origins.

The nationwide reaction to Heisman's death was relatively subdued, probably because he had been inactive in coaching for nearly ten years. According to Joe Williams, "In the hoopla and hurrah of the World Series the passing of John Heisman didn't receive much attention. And certainly not the attention it warranted." Williams then went on to compose a fitting tribute to

Heisman's achievements, concluding that "his contributions were many and vital, and the game has good reasons for remembering him and his work."[31]

The *New York Times* hailed him as an "all-around authority on athletics" and "the inventor of many methods used in modern football."[32] *The New York American* called him a "grid pioneer" and the "first to introduce the forward pass,"[33] while the *Philadelphia Record* identified him as the "father of the forward pass."[34]

The most effusive eulogies were those carried by the *Houston Post* and the University of Pennsylvania alumni magazine, now called the *Gazette*. If Heisman had been criticized during his career for deceptive play, then these pieces saw to it that his reputation was exonerated. The *Houston Post* editorialized:

Houston remembers John W. Heisman, former football coach at Rice Institute, as a man who not only advocated good sportsmanship and clean living but followed his own precepts.

In his daily life he exemplified the spirit of clean rivalry he instilled into his players on the practice field and in the locker rooms of the gymnasium.

He was a man . . . who placed his reliance in the old-fashioned belief that the best team deserved to win and set out to produce the best team.[35]

That Heisman's legacy still persisted at his alma mater was attested to by the following excerpt from the *Gazette*: "John Heisman was a profound student of the game of football. He was a gentleman and a scholar and sought to introduce these characteristics in his coaching and contacts with boys. He was decidedly an influence for good."[36]

But the longest lasting honor for Heisman came in the form of the trophy that perpetuates his name (even though it would have the paradoxical effect of subsuming his persona in the broader context of the trophy's award significance). Shortly after Heisman's death, Downtown Athletic Club officials elected to rename the year-old award the John W. Heisman Memorial Trophy. (In spite of such a high honor, it would not be until 1954 that Heisman was elected to the National Football Hall of Fame along with the other coaching greats of the game.) Heisman's wife, Maora, who would live on until 1964, was honored, too, as the DAC sent flowers to her every December at award time.

The first Heisman Trophy was awarded on December 10, 1936, to Larry Kelley, an all-around Yale athlete who had run away with the voting that year. As a pass-catching end and the first of only two linemen ever to win the award, Kelley had figured in many of the Bulldogs' gridiron victories during his career. Because of his outstanding record as a pass receiver and in light of Heisman's role in the legalization of the forward pass, Kelley's selection seemed highly appropriate. It was as though Heisman himself had had a vote in choosing such a player, especially one who, in addition to his athletic ability, had played at a school where the traditions of the game of football ran deep. Kelley would later turn down professional football and baseball contracts and even a movie role about his athletic career at Yale.

In a recent interview, Kelley, now in his late seventies, echoed the thoughts of Jay Berwanger concerning the importance of winning the trophy. "The Heisman Trophy is a million-dollar thing now," he said, which is particularly ironic in view of the fact that his professional football offer was for only $11,000. Kelley's sense of accomplishment is derived from belonging to what he calls the "fraternity" of Heisman winners—a feeling of belonging to a great tradition.[37]

By the time of John Heisman's passing, then, it appeared that the game that was as old as he was had come full circle. As Stanley Woodward would report in the New York *Herald Tribune* in 1940 on the impact of the modern T-formation:

> By successive stages football had progressed from the dull, unimaginative push-and-pull game of those early years to the punting game of Yost's Michigan teams of the early 1900s, to the accelerated, more open style burgeoning with the forward pass, to the power and deception of the Warner wingback attack, with the overshifted line, and linemen pulling out as blockers; to the shifting offenses of Stagg, Heisman, Dr. Williams, Harper, and Rockne, most spectacularly exploited by Notre Dame until the rule makers took the momentum out of it, and now, finally, back to the T with its modern, streamlined embellishments.[38]

Truly, the basic elements had always been there for a game of unlimited strategic possibilities. John Heisman had recognized these things all along. What it had taken was the imagination of a visionary to look far enough ahead to what had to happen and the determination of a go-getter to see that what had to happen did happen. Fortunately, John Heisman had both the vision and the determination to see that his beloved game would realize its full potential.

NOTES

1. See Jan Cohn, *Creating America: George Horace Lorimer and the Saturday Evening Post* (Pittsburgh, Pa.: University of Pittsburgh Press, 1989), 32.

2. S. Fred Roach, Jr., "John William Heisman" in *Dictionary of Georgia Biography*, vol. 1, eds. Kenneth Coleman and Charles Stephen Gurr (Athens, Ga.: University of Georgia Press, 1983), 434.

3. John W. Heisman, "Look Sharp Now," *Collier's*, November 3, 1928, 18.

4. Ibid., 19.

5. John W. Heisman, "Rough Humor," *Collier's*, November 9, 1929, 48.

6. Ibid., 47.

7. Ibid.

8. John W. Heisman, *Principles of Football* (St. Louis, Mo.: Sports Publishing Bureau, 1922), 358.

9. John W. Heisman, "Between Halves," *Collier's*, November 17, 1928, 18.

10. John W. Heisman, "Here Are Men," *Collier's*, November 16, 1929, 25.

11. John W. Heisman, "Fast and Loose," *Collier's*, October 20, 1928, 14.

12. See David Scarborough, "Intercollegiate Athletics at Washington and Jefferson College: The Building of a Tradition." (Ph.D. diss., University of Pittsburgh, 1979), 109.

13. John W. Heisman, "Their Weight in Gold," *Collier's*, November 24, 1928, 55.

14. Heisman, "Their Weight in Gold," 56.

15. Ibid., 57.

16. Stanford had come east to play Army in 1928, and with Warner's double-wingback attack functioning at its best, the Cadets eventually found themselves on the short end of a 26–0 score. Many eastern coaches who saw and heard about the game's outcome were so impressed that they soon started implementing the double-wing system.

17. According to sportswriter Joe Williams, Heisman was incensed when Booth wasn't unanimously picked for All-America honors, demanding, "What does a ball carrier have to do to please you fellows in the press box?"

18. Heisman, *Principles of Football*, 236.

19. *The Red and Black* (Washington and Jefferson College student newspaper), October 20, 1932.

20. Joe Sherman, *Clemson Tigers: A History of Clemson Football* (Columbia, S.C.: R. L. Bryan Co., 1976), 10–11.

21. Joe Williams, "Heisman Knew Football," Column in *New York World Telegram*, October 1936.

22. Ibid.

23. Heisman, *Principles of Football*, 333.

24. Yankee Stade, "Football—A $50,000,000 Business," *Liberty*, October 2, 1938, 11–12.

25. Cohn, *Creating America*, 246.

26. Bill Libby, *Champions of College Football* (New York: Hawthorn Books, 1975), 91.

27. The original, mounted on a black onyx base set on an Italian marble pedestal, is fourteen inches long and thirteen and one-half inches high and weighs twenty-five pounds. It is on permanent display in the lobby of the Downtown Athletic Club.

28. Dave Newhouse, "Breakaway Jay and the First Heisman," *University of Chicago Magazine* (Winter 1986): 3.

29. In capitalizing on the highly dramatic ingredients of college football, Hollywood recruited Berwanger and other gridiron stars of the day for a 1936 movie entitled, appropriately enough, *The Big Game*.

30. Gordon Cobbledick, "Chicago's Football Suicide Too Drastic," *Cleveland Plain Dealer*, December 24, 1939.

31. Williams, "Heisman Knew Football" (October 1936).

32. "Obituary," *New York Times*, October 4, 1936.

33. "Obituary," *New York American*, October 4, 1936.

34. "Obituary," *Philadelphia Record*, October 4, 1936.

35. "Obituary," *Houston Post*, October 4, 1936.

36. "Obituary," *University of Pennsylvania Gazette*, November 15, 1936.

37. Nathan Dominitz, "Heisman Hero: Kelley in 'Fraternity'," Pensacola *News-Journal*, November 12, 1991, 1C, 3C.

38. Quoted in Alison Danzig, *Oh, How They Played the Game* (New York: Macmillan, 1971), 403.

Conclusion
The Heisman Legacy

Had the New York Downtown Athletic Club begun awarding its trophy earlier in the 1930s, it most likely would have been called the Knute Rockne Memorial Trophy, considering the emotional impact that the Notre Dame coach's tragic death had throughout the country in 1931. Yet in retrospect the DAC's decision five years later to name the new trophy in honor of its recently deceased athletic director appears to have been an appropriate move for a number of reasons.

In contrast to his practical, business-oriented manner, the scholarly side of John Heisman demonstrated how a man of cultured tastes and learned pursuits could also succeed as a college football coach. Despite the stories that circulated charging him with devious on-field tactics, Heisman's personal philosophy and overall career achievements belied the general conception of the professional coach as an uncouth ruffian more obsessed with winning than with the welfare of his players. Others during his time, such as George Woodruff, Dr. Henry Williams, Amos Alonzo Stagg, Knute Rockne, and Dr. Jock Sutherland, also exemplified how coaches of a scholarly bent could lend respectability to the image of the football coach. But because of his natural feel for public relations and his tenures at various schools around the country over a thirty-six-year period, Heisman did more to refine the football coach's public image than any other individual of his day.

Then, too, in authoring the reputable book *Principles of Football*, which presented his own highly personal yet tradition-oriented approach to coaching the game, Heisman displayed still another side of the cultured coach. This facet prompted sportswriter Joe Williams to comment: "Probably no man in America knew more about the history of football or knew more of the so-called immortals of the game than Heisman. A few months before he died he told me that he was getting ready to write what he called a human history of the sport."[1] The *Collier's* pieces referred to throughout this book attest to Coach Heisman's human interpretation of his game as well as his bountiful knowledge of its development. Because of his intimate feel for intercollegiate football and its role as an inspirational adjunct to the spread of higher education in America, it is unfortunate that Heisman's human history project was never realized. We can only speculate in the context of Heisman's *Collier's* series just how meaningful his proposed book would have been in helping us to comprehend more fully the development of the indigenous American sport of football. Even so, the positive image of the professional football coach as a dedicated, highly intelligent student of the game remains an integral part of the Heisman legacy.

Ironically, Heisman's human approach to the game stemmed, in part, from the objective relationship he maintained with his players and his realization of the special power he held over them as a coach. This understanding of the coach's powerful influence undoubtedly explains why he kept a social distance from his players off the field and also points out why many coaches have found it necessary to follow suit. According to Heisman, the football coach "has the undoubted power to make or mar the lives and whole future careers of something like a hundred young men every year that he is in charge of football at this, that or the other institution."

Because of this extraordinary and dangerous power, the coach is heir to a "tremendous responsibility":

> If the coach is a worthless, reprehensible fellow, a man of bad character or none, he is bound to do the boys enormous harm. If, however, he is a high type of man with lofty ideals and firm principles of right and truth, one who recognizes his power and his responsibilities, then it's well he coaches football and it's well for the boys that play football under him that they went to that school. Such a man will do more downright character building for the boys than can nineteen ministers out of twenty, or ninety-nine fathers out of a hundred.[2]

The fact that Heisman could generate productive performances from even the most mediocre of his football candidates, particularly during his years in the South, bears out his personal conviction that anyone, regardless of his physical size, can play the game of football, provided he is able to summon forth the necessary fighting spirit. Appropriately, Heisman's greatest contribution to opening up the game—his unrelenting fight to legalize the forward pass—made it possible for many undersized players to participate in football who might never otherwise have been able to play. Because of his unique ability to produce a winning combination by bringing out the best qualities in himself and his individual players, Heisman was essentially a coach's coach—one whose successful coaching manner was certainly worthy of emulation. Not until the waning years of his career did his coaching philosophy begin to falter, and that was primarily because of his inability to adapt his methods to changing times.

However, due to his professional emphasis on always playing to win in a milieu traditionally thought to be governed by an amateur code, Heisman's traditional coaching style has always come under fire. The most recent attacks have come from liberal factions who contend that the overemphasis on winning and widespread promotion of the character-building myth in team sports have dehumanized them and contributed a great deal to the myriad problems of contemporary sports. Right or wrong, though, the Heisman coaching posture is still very much with us. In fact, its conservative teachings have developed into an ingrained socialization process within the American sports establishment—from grade school on to the professional ranks. As Heisman himself reminds us in *Principles of Football*, "the athletic field is about the best laboratory known" for a young man to develop the qualities necessary for success in life: will power, self-control, and clear thinking, as well as the formation of good habits designed to mold a young man into a "sportsman and a gentleman," at least according to the high-minded character-building standards of an earlier day. To Heisman, the football player's best habits resulted from dedicated attention to self-discipline and his venerable college spirit, an inspired mindset that "teaches the meaning of the words loyalty, fidelity, love of country, patriotism."[3]

In this sense, Heisman thought of words as psychological tools to teach his philosophy of football, and, as we have seen, he made the most of them in both his coaching rhetoric and public relations. In Heisman's heyday most sports fans would have agreed that in teaching the abstract virtues he extolled, athletics served a very important role in reminding not only athletes but all citizens of the teamwork qualities that are essential to the success of any organization. For as we have seen throughout Heisman's coaching career, his college spirit concept was not confined to the boundaries of the athletic field:

A member of the football team has others to whom he is answerable in his conduct besides himself. If he is derelict in his duty he harms others as well. He is liable to undo the whole season's work of the coaches, to nullify completely the herculean efforts that a hundred men have been making for months to turn out a flawless machine that shall bring fame and honor to themselves and undying glory to Alma Mater. More, he is risking blasting the high hopes and breaking the hearts of thousands of alumni and undergraduates, of trustees, of faculty members, of friends and well-wishers throughout the length and breadth of the land.[4]

The paradoxical thing about Heisman's role in spreading his college spirit gospel is that while his own old-fashioned system would break down in the 1920s, his basic approach to coaching athletics in general and football in particular would live on in later coaches' special interpretation of sport as a molder of character and builder of men. In fact, the Heisman coaching philosophy, as a form of virile Christianity best exemplified in the precepts of his day's Young Men's Christian Association, is still apparent in today's Christian athlete organizations. In these groups the college spirit code of cooperation among players and supporters has been extended even further to include personal loyalty to Jesus Christ and his teachings.

When we consider how the football coach's reputation as popular hero came about, particularly in the kind of charismatic image that a coach like Knute Rockne projected, we have to acknowledge that John Heisman played a key role in helping establish and perpetuate this heroic image. As the *Houston Post* commented upon Heisman's death:

> The immense popularity of football has made the modern coach more than a mere instructor. Frequently he becomes the idol of thousands of youthful followers of the sport. Knute Rockne became one of the outstanding youth leaders of the country. John Heisman throughout his career set a fine example for the young Americans who look upon the football coach as a hero.[5]

Helping to memorialize the image of the football coach as a popular cultural figure of heroic dimensions, then, is certainly another aspect of the Heisman legacy.

John Heisman intuitively realized, too, that athletics, particularly the dramatically intense and emotionally charged game of football, can have a unifying effect on the college campus—that athletics function symbolically as the spiritual center of the school, drawing all its diverse components together in one common cause. This was clearly why he made such a big point of indoctrinating the student body in his personal philosophy of school spirit everywhere he coached. Serving at eight schools of distinctively different missions all over the country made him especially aware that, regardless of the diversity of college students' backgrounds, they were all essentially alike with respect to their extracurricular interests, and that school spirit was the one common thread that held them all together. This was also why Heisman thought a strong show of school spirit was the major inspirational force behind the quality performance of his teams and the psychological key to whether or not they developed into winners. Accordingly, he considered not just the student body but every component of the collegiate scene to be highly instrumental toward this end:

> A winning football team is never turned out by the coach and players alone. . . . It's spirit, in the last analysis, that wins in football, and much the greater part of that spirit must be infused into the squad by the rest of the college—the president, trustees, faculty, alumni, undergraduates, friends, and so on down even to the very janitors of the buildings.[6]

The reason for the decline of Heisman's peculiar brand of school spirit is likely that somehow it just doesn't seem right for our more cynical and less innocent day. This decline is in its way a telling comment on the decadent condition of intercollegiate athletics today. Indeed, old-fashioned school spirit has now been supplanted by a predominantly personalized mood that might be referred to as "school arrogance," a visibly aggressive pose held by students, alumni, and boosters—one clearly mandated by a win-at-all-costs outlook. How college athletics took on such an attitude has been astutely analyzed by Allen Guttmann in his stimulating survey of contemporary sport, *A Whole New Ball Game*:

Once the tradition was established that athletes—football, basketball, and baseball players; swimmers, runners, and wrestlers—*represent* the university and provide models for students and alumni to admire and emulate, the juggernaut of intercollegiate athletics was set in motion. The psychological mechanisms of identification were (and are) such that victory or defeat of a football team was (and is) felt as a personal triumph or humiliation by thousands and tens of thousands of students. To obtain psychic satisfaction and avoid vicarious humiliation, administrations are ready to pay coaches salaries that are far beyond the limited imaginations of mere professors.[7]

Paradoxically, John Heisman, in promoting the athlete as the visible representative of his school's best traditions, was in the vanguard of this movement. However, not until he began coaching at Penn, after all his earlier success, did he start to realize the sociological as well as psychological significance of the "juggernaut" he had helped set in motion. At Penn it had been the alumni-booster group's growing disenchantment with his less-than-successful coaching methods that sensitized him to the precarious position that can devolve on the coach who fails to produce a winner. Heisman's final years of coaching at Rice served as a reminder of how painful the losing experience can be to a successful coach.

When Heisman commented in 1903 that superior football coaches could "command salaries practically without limit," he surely never dreamed that a big-time coach's annual salary would rise to the astronomical level it has today. Yet contemporary football coaches, spurred on by the lucrative financial opportunities afforded them through television contracts and endorsements of commercial products to supplement the base salary paid them, are actually the heirs to the enterprising, even mercenary position that Heisman himself promulgated once he discovered that successful football coaches were in high demand.

Although the munificent salaries of many of today's coaches may appear way out of line to most observers, meeting the demands of numerous community service and public appearance commitments, in addition to enduring the pressures of having to win on the gridiron, has surely enhanced the public relations role that most coaches play in proving their overall worth. In this respect Heisman pioneered the reputation of the coach as "P.R." man, especially during his years at Georgia Tech. As pointed out in chapters 3 and

4, Heisman was a recognized community leader in Atlanta during the years 1904–1919, an era that saw his off-campus involvement expand in proportion to the growth and success of Georgia Tech athletics. Accordingly, the high point of this relationship came when the football team captured a national championship in 1917.

Not only was Heisman highly visible as a public figure during this time, he also formulated a public voice through his writings that appeared in a variety of publications. Naturally sensitive to the power of the printed word, he used the subject of sports as an emotional springboard to demonstrate how people could become better citizens, advocating everyone's involvement in sports as either participants or spectators. Actually, John Heisman assumed so many public roles that he became one of the first of our modern coaches to realize that there simply are not enough hours in the day for the totally dedicated coach to fulfill all the responsibilities that may be expected of him.

As opinionated as he was about the concerns of his own day, John Heisman surely would not hesitate to express his personal feelings about the myriad problems that confront intercollegiate athletics today. Then, too, as academically oriented as he was, Heisman would surely agree with a major recommendation of the 1991 Knight Foundation Commission's report that student athletes be declared ineligible if they are not on course to complete work toward a degree. But Heisman would likely view many present-day problems and concerns as going deeper than academics and as being attributable to a lack of dedication on the part of the highly pampered college athletes who are more committed to their own selfish career interests than to the overall good of their team. It is an attitude completely contrary to the code of self-sacrifice and team play that Heisman always held up as an essential part of his coaching philosophy.

In assessing the accomplishments of recent recipients of the trophy named in Heisman's honor, one has to wonder to what degree Heisman's personal philosophical standards of quality performance might have been considered in the process of choosing the most outstanding football player in the country. Perhaps Princeton's Dick Kazmaier, the 1951 trophy winner, who ignored the professional ranks to become a successful businessman, summed up the Heisman legacy more aptly than any other player before or since when he remarked: "Football gave me values that were essential to a career in business. How to handle losses as well as wins. How to commit yourself to a goal . . . with dedication and discipline and the recognition of something bigger and deeper than one's self."[8]

As the quintessential team man, though, Heisman would naturally disapprove of the fact that the award has been presented mainly to running backs and quarterbacks. He would undoubtedly view the trophy as essentially a symbol of the character-building qualities that the game inculcates in those who participate in it, in reality the kind of values that are impossible to measure or evaluate. To Heisman a mere trophy could never suffice as the ultimate reward for playing the game of football anyway, for he always contended that every player, no matter what the level of his abilities, is directly rewarded through the personal satisfaction derived from actually participating in the game. From Heisman's highly personalized point of view as both player and coach, then, the sacredness of the game itself and what it might teach a participant about himself were the truly important things. His belief in this outlook was dramatically expressed through a classic on-field confrontation he described in the last piece he produced for *Collier's* in 1929. As much as anything else that John Heisman wrote, its typically inspirational if old-fashioned message seems to sum up all the reasons why he held the game of football in such high esteem:

It happened in 1922. Ohio State and the University of Illinois were fighting in desperation. A bad feeling had sprung up between the teams and not only the play became rough but the language. The lads were well on the way to completely forgetting themselves when Pixley, captain of Ohio State, called, "Time out!"

Looking at his own backfield but obviously addressing both teams, he said:

"The relations between Ohio State and Illinois have always been fine and clean. I wonder if we want to ruin them today. I don't think so. Neither do you fellows. This is a wow of a game. Why spoil it? Let's try to be men."

The spirit of those two teams changed instantly. There was a loud shout of approval from both sides. Hard, fast football ensued—clean, good-natured and good-tempered. Ohio State won.

Football? A great game—a great game.[9]

If intercollegiate football is truly to remain a great game then perhaps a reconsideration of the old-fashioned values that the legacy of John Heisman has bequeathed to us would not be so far-fetched after all.

NOTES

1. Joe Williams, "Heisman Knew Football," *New York World-Telegram* (October 1936).

2. John W. Heisman, *Principles of Football* (St. Louis, Mo.: Sports Publishing Bureau, 1922), 17–18.

3. Ibid., 1–7.

4. Ibid., 8–9.

5. "Obituary," *Houston Post*, October 4, 1936.

6. Heisman, *Principles of Football*, 336–37.

7. Allen Guttmann, *A Whole New Ball Game* (Chapel Hill: University of North Carolina Press, 1989), 106–7.

8. Quoted in George Allen, *Strategies for Winning: A Top Coach's Game Plan for Winning in Football and in Life* (New York: McGraw-Hill, 1990), 77.

9. John W. Heisman, "Here Are Men," *Collier's*, November 16, 1929, 46.

Appendix: John W. Heisman's Coaching Record, 1892–1927 (190 Wins, 70 Losses, 16 Ties)

There is some confusion as to how many football games John Heisman actually won during his thirty-six-year coaching career. The author's research has revealed that Heisman should be credited with 190 wins, based on the following summary of total games won at the various institutions where he coached.

1892—Oberlin College (7–0)

1893—Buchtel College (5–2)

> Heisman recorded that he also coached a two-game road trip for Oberlin this same year, winning at Chicago and at Illinois, thus making his overall 1893 record 7–2. These two wins were never officially credited. (See chapter 2.)

1894—Oberlin College (4–3–1)

> Heisman recorded that he also coached Buchtel's only game this same year, a win over Ohio State, thus making his overall 1894 record 5–3–1. He was never officially credited for this win. (See chapter 2.)

1895–1899—Alabama Polytechnic Institute (Auburn) (13–4–1)

> With only thirty seconds left to play and Auburn leading 11–6 over Georgia, the referee called this game on "account of darkness" and declared the final score a 0–0 tie. Heisman appealed to the Southern Intercollegiate Athletic Association, and a year later the Auburn team was recognized as the winner of the contest by the original score. Somehow the win was never officially recognized; this is yet another Heisman victory that got away. (See chapter 2.)

1900–1903—Clemson College (19–3–2)

1904–1919—Georgia School of Technology (Georgia Tech) (102–29–6)

1920–1922—University of Pennsylvania (16–10–2)

1923—Washington and Jefferson College (6–1–1)

> The game with Washington and Lee was forfeited to W&J because the former team refused to play against a team that fielded a black player. Thus Heisman's overall 1923 record should be 7–1–1. (See chapter 5.)

1924–1927—Rice Institute (14–18–3)

Bibliography

BOOKS

Allen, George. *Strategies for Winning: A Top Coach's Game Plan for Winning in Football and in Life.* New York: McGraw-Hill, 1990.

Baker, William J. *Sports in the Western World.* Totawa, N.J.: Rowman and Littlefield, 1982.

Boorstin, Daniel J. *The Americans: The Democratic Experience.* New York: Vintage, 1974.

Bourget, Charles J. P. "Poet Beyond the Sea." In *This Was America,* edited by Oscar Handlin. New York: Harper and Row, 1964.

Brady, John T. *The Heisman: A Symbol of Excellence.* New York: Atheneum, 1984.

Bronson, Walter C. *The History of Brown University, 1764–1914.* Providence, R.I.: Brown University Press, 1914.

Bryan, Wright. *Clemson: An Informal History of the University, 1889–1979.* Columbia, S.C.: R. L. Bryan Co., 1979.

Calhoun, Donald W. *Sport, Culture, and Personality.* 2nd ed. Champaign, Ill.: Human Kinetics, 1987.

Caton, Lewis H., Jr. "Washington and Jefferson College: In Pursuit of the Uncommon Man." Ph.D. diss., University of Pittsburgh, 1972.

Clark, J. Stanley. *The Oil Century: From the Drake Well to the Conservation Era.* Norman: University of Oklahoma Press, 1958.

Cohn, Jan. *Creating America: George Horace Lorimer and the Saturday Evening Post.* Pittsburgh, Pa.: University of Pittsburgh Press, 1989.

Danzig, Allison. *Oh, How They Played the Game.* New York: Macmillan, 1971.

Durant, John, and Les Etter. *Highlights of College Football.* New York: Hastings House, 1970.

Gutkowski, Bob, ed. *The College Game.* Indianapolis: Bobbs-Merrill, 1974.

Guttman, Allen. *A Whole New Ball Game.* Chapel Hill: University of North Carolina Press, 1989.

Heisman, John W. *Principles of Football.* St. Louis, Mo.: Sports Publishing Bureau, 1922.

Jensen, Oliver, ed. *The Nineties.* New York: American Heritage, 1967.

Knepper, George W. *New Lamps for Old.* Akron, Ohio: University of Akron Centennial, 1970.

Lewis, Guy. "Enterprise on the Campus: Developments in Intercollegiate Sport and Higher Education, 1875–1939." In *History of Physical Education and Sport,* edited by Bruce L. Bennett. Chicago: Athletic Institute, 1972.

Libby, Bill. *Champions of College Football.* New York: Hawthorn Books, 1975.

McCallum, John. *Ivy League Football Since 1872.* New York: Stein and Day, 1977.

————. *Southeastern Conference Football.* New York: Scribners, 1980.

Meiners, Frederika. *A History of Rice University: The Institute Years, 1907–63.* Houston, Tex.: Rice University Studies, 1982.

Menke, Frank. *Encyclopedia of Sports.* New York: A. S. Barnes, 1953.

Novak, Michael. *The Joy of Sports.* New York: Basic Books, 1976.

Perrin, Tom. *Football: A College History.* Jefferson, N.C.: McFarland, 1987.

Pope, Edwin. *Football's Greatest Coaches.* Atlanta, Ga.: Tupper and Love, 1956.

Powel, Harford, Jr. *Walter Camp: An Authorized Biography.* Freeport, N.Y.: Books for Libraries, 1970, reprint of 1926 ed.

Roach, Fred, Jr. "John William Heisman." In *Dictionary of Georgia Biography* vol. I, edited by Kenneth Coleman and Charles Stephen Gurr. Athens, Ga.: University of Georgia Press, 1983: 433–34.

Scarborough, David. "Intercollegiate Athletics at Washington and Jefferson College: The Building of a Tradition." Ph.D. diss., University of Pittsburgh, 1979.

Sherman, Joe. *Clemson Tigers: A History of Clemson Football.* Columbia, S.C.: R. L. Bryan Co., 1976.

Smith, Ronald A. *Sports and Freedom: The Rise of Big-Time College Athletics.* New York: Oxford University Press, 1988.

Spanton, A. I., ed. *Fifty Years of Buchtel, 1870–1920.* Akron, Ohio: Buchtel Alumni Association, 1922.

Storr, Richard J. *Harper's University: The Beginnings.* Chicago: University of Chicago Press, 1966.

Thomy, Al. *The Ramblin' Wreck: A Story of Georgia Tech Football.* Huntsville, Ala.: Strode Publishers, 1973.

Umphlett, Wiley Lee. *The Movies Go to College: Hollywood and the World of the College-Life Film.* Madison, N.J.: Fairleigh Dickinson University Press, 1984.

Wallace, Robert B. *Dress Her in White and Gold: A Biography of Georgia Tech.* Atlanta, Ga.: Georgia Tech Foundation, 1969.

Woodruff, L. F. "Fuzzy." *History of Southern Football.* 2 vols. Atlanta, Ga.: Georgia Southern, 1928.

ARTICLES

"Athletics." *The Campanile* (Rice Institute yearbook). Vols. 10 (1925), 11 (1926), 12 (1927), 13 (1928).

"The Football Coach." The University of Pennsylvania *Alumni Register,* December 1922.

Griessman, Gene. "The Coach." In *The Heisman, A Symbol of Excellence* by John T. Brady. New York: Atheneum, 1984.

Heisman, John W. "All Aboard for the Class Games." *The Yellow Jacket* (Georgia Tech student magazine), December 1911, 13–16.

———. "Are You Coming Out for Football? If Not, Why Not?" *The Yellow Jacket*, November 1911, 11–14.

———. "Athletic Odds and Ends." *The Yellow Jacket*, February 1913, 366–74.

———. "Athletics." *The Yellow Jacket*, February 1916, 259–63.

———. "Between Halves." *Collier's*, November 17, 1928: 18, 53–55.

———. "Fast and Loose." *Collier's*, October 20, 1928, 14–15, 54–55.

———. "Football Again." *The Yellow Jacket*, October 1915, 33–38.

———. "For Athletes During the Off-Season." *The Yellow Jacket*, January 1913: 296–306.

———. "Here Are Men." *Collier's*, November 16, 1929, 25, 44, 46.

———. "Hero Stuff." *Collier's*, November 2, 1929, 18–19, 72–73.

———. "Hold 'em." *Collier's*, October 27, 1928, 12–13, 50–51.

———. "Inventions in Football." *The Baseball Magazine* 1, no. 6 (October 1908): 40–42.

———. "Look Sharp Now!" *Collier's*, November 3, 1928, 18–19, 32.

———. "More About College Spirit." *The Yellow Jacket*, October 1911, 19–22.

———. "Our Athletic Outlook." *The Yellow Jacket*, October 1912, 72–87.

———. "Our Athletic Outlook for 1913." *The Yellow Jacket*, October 1913, 50–56.

———. "Our Baseball Team." *The Yellow Jacket*, May 1913, 565–76.

———. "Our Football Team and Others." *The Yellow Jacket*, November 1912, 172–83.

———. "Review of the Baseball Season." *The Yellow Jacket*, June 1914, 468–74.

———. "Review of the Football Season." *The Yellow Jacket*, December 1913, 166–74.

———. "Rough Humor." *Collier's*, November 9, 1929, 21, 47–48.

———. "Rules Rush In." *Collier's* November 10, 1928, 12, 13, 38, 42.

———. "Signals." *Collier's*, October 6, 1928, 12–13, 31–32.

———. "Suggestions As to Football Rule Changes for 1910." 2-page pamphlet (undated).

———. "Tech's Baseball Outlook." *The Yellow Jacket*, March 1915, 258–66.

———. "Their Weight in Gold." *Collier's*, November 24, 1928, 28, 55–57.

———. "The Thundering Herd." *Collier's*, October 13, 1928, 12–13, 59–60.

———. "Why Tech Beat Cumberland 222–0." *Georgia Tech Alumnus Magazine*, Spring 1985, 23–25. (Reprinted from *The Blue Print*, 1917 Georgia Tech yearbook.)

Moore, John Hammond. "Football's Ugly Decades, 1893–1913." *The Smithsonian Journal of History* 2 (Fall 1967): 49–68.

Miller, Jonathan K. Editorial, The University of Pennsylvania *Alumni Register*, January 1923.

Newhouse, Dave. "Breakaway Jay and the First Heisman." *University of Chicago Magazine*, Winter 1986, 2–9.

Nichols, J. H. "50 Years of Football." *Oberlin Alumni Magazine*, 1941.

Oriard, Michael. "On the Current Status of Sports Fiction." *Arete: The Journal of Sport Literature* 1 (Fall 1983): 7–20.

Sack, Allen L. "Yale 29—Harvard 4: The Professionalization of College Football." *Quest* 19 (January 1973): 24–34.

Simpson, David P. "Historical Sketches of Athletics at Oberlin." *Oberlin Alumni Magazine* 10, no. 6 (March 1914): 161–62.

Stade, Yankee. "Football—A $50,000,000 Business." *Liberty*, 2 October 1938, 11–12.

Stewart, Lawrence R. "A Resume of the 1923 Football Season." *Pandora* (Washington and Jefferson yearbook). Vol. 40 (1925).

Watterson, John S. "Inventing Modern Football." *American Heritage* 39, no. 6 (September-October 1988): 103–13.

"Who's He and Why?" *The Yellow Jacket*, March 1913, 418–21.

NEWSPAPERS AND PAMPHLETS

"Announcement of Mr. John W. Heisman, Football and Baseball Coach." Privately printed seven-page promotional pamphlet, published early 1900s.

"Coach Heisman States His Creed." *The Red and Black*, March 15, 1923.

Cobbledick, Gordon. "Chicago's Football Suicide Too Drastic," *Cleveland Plain Dealer*, December 24, 1939: 2C.

Cullinan, Helen. "Heisman Bronze Is Sculptor's Dream." *Cleveland Plain Dealer*, December 15, 1986: 1C, 5C.

Dominitz, Nathan. "Heisman Hero: Kelley in 'Fraternity'." Pensacola *News Journal*, November 12, 1991: 1C, 3C.

"Heisman, Character Builder, Is Accorded Enthusiastic Welcome to Owl School." *The Thresher* (Rice Institute student newspaper), March 28, 1924: 1.

"Heisman May Coach Columbia Gridmen." Philadelphia *Evening Bulletin*, December 6, 1922.

"Heisman of Penn Elected Head Coach." *The Red and Black* (Washington and Jefferson student newspaper), January 18, 1923.

"Heisman Plans to Alter Shift Play." Philadelphia *Evening Bulletin*, April 9, 1921.

"Heisman Predicts Penn's 1923 Football Team Will Be Winner." Philadelphia *Evening Bulletin*, December 1922.

"Heisman Predicts Winner for Penn." Philadelphia *Record*, February 2, 1923.

"Heisman to Arrive for Practice Soon." *The Thresher* (Rice Institute student newspaper), February 23, 1924: 1.

"Heisman to Coach at W&J 3 Years." Philadelphia *Evening Ledger*, January 4, 1923: 18.

"J. W. Heisman New Coach." *The Thresher* (Rice Institute student newspaper), February 19, 1924: 1.

"Penn's New Gridiron Coach Has Appearance of a Scholar." Philadelphia *Evening Bulletin*, February 9, 1920: 22.

"Plan Radical Change in Penn Grid Affairs." Philadelphia *Evening Ledger*, December 14, 1922.

"Report Heisman Is Picked as New Penn Football Coach." Philadelphia *Evening Bulletin*, January 1920: 22.

Sherman, Jon, "Titusville Pays Tribute to John Heisman." *The Titusville Herald*, September 1, 1984: 3, 10.

"Tech Mourns Loss of Heisman." Philadelphia *Evening Ledger*, February 9, 1920.

"The Old Sport's Musings." Column in Philadelphia *Evening Ledger*, January 6, 1922: 14.

"Titusville's Tribute to John W. Heisman." Occasional pamphlet, dated July 18, 1984.

"Will Release Coach Heisman." Philadelphia *Evening Ledger*, November 25, 1921.

Williams, Joe. "Heisman Knew Football." Column in *New York World-Telegram*, October 1936.

Index

Alexander, Canty (Georgia Tech), 132, 138, 156, 156 n.24

Alexander, William A. (Georgia Tech), 113, 131, 135, 151, 153, 167, 182, 220

American Football Coaches Association. *See* Heisman, John W., American Football Coaches Association

American Intercollegiate Football Association, 9, 10

Associated Press poll, 7, 197, 201

Athletic Club in America, 224–25

Baker, Eugene (Yale), 8, 9

Barrett, Charley (Cornell), 133

Barron, Red (Georgia Tech), 147, 148, 149, 151

Baugh, Sammy (TCU), 229, 239, 242

Bell, Bert (Penn), 140, 144, 169, 175, 238

Berwanger, Jay (Chicago), 237–38, 244, 245 n.29

Bezdek, Hugo (Penn State), 115

Bierman, Bernie (Tulane, Minnesota), 227–28, 233

Big game traditions: intersectional game, 47, 55, 97, 167–68, 182; intrastate rivalries, 47, 65, 152; Little Brown Jug, 74; Thanksgiving Day game, 9, 47, 73; weekend revelry, 168

Black players: emergence, 134–35; impact, 242; racism problems, 71, 185–86

Blake, Morgan (Georgia Tech), 125, 144, 160

Booth, Albie (Yale), 47, 222, 232, 245 n.17

Bowl game tradition: Cotton Bowl, 232, 242; Orange Bowl, 232; popularity, 197–98; radio, first football broadcast, 203; Rose Bowl, first official (1916), 15, 134; Rose Bowl, prototype (1902), 74; Sugar Bowl, 232, 234

Brickley, Charley (Harvard), 122, 126

British sporting influence on football, 8

Brown, Johnny Mack (Alabama), 200

Brown, W. S. "Lobster" (Georgia Tech), 92

Brutality in football, 11, 14, 36–37, 86, 87, 99, 104–5

Bryant, Paul "Bear" (Alabama), 171, 234

Burks, Auxford (Alabama), 84

Cagle, Chris (Army), 221–22
Cain, Johnny "Sugar" (Alabama), 227
Camp, Walter (Yale): coaching
    philosophy/role, 9, 10–12, 26 n.15,
    218; contributions to the game, 10–
    12, 26 nn.16, 17, 18, 60, 240;
    forward pass posture, 52, 53, 60, 71,
    86, 88, 89, 90, 100, 105; reputation,
    9–10, 142, 201, 224
Capitalist influence on football, 7–8
Carideo, Frank (Notre Dame), 226
Carnegie Commission report (1929),
    217–20
Carpenter, Bill "Big Six" (Georgia
    Tech), 141, 142, 145
Centre College, 173–74, 184
Chamberlain, Guy (Nebraska), 133
Club football, 16, 38, 224, 225
Cobbledick, Gordon (Chicago), 240,
    241
Cochems, Eddie (Clemson, St. Louis),
    88, 91, 94
Conferences. See under geographical area
Corporate nature of football, 4–5, 25
    n.8, 131
Cowan, Hector (Princeton), 19, 231
Cox, Carlisle (Georgia Tech), 80, 147
Coy, Ted (Yale), 104, 231, 232
Crisler, Herbert "Fritz" (Princeton),
    229
Crowley, Jim (Notre Dame, Fordham),
    196, 237, 242

DeLand, Lorin (Harvard), 12
Depression. See Great Depression
Devine, Aubrey (Iowa), 173
Dobie, Gil (Washington, Navy,
    Cornell), 111, 134, 148, 166, 170–71,
    181
Dodd, Bobby (Georgia Tech), 82, 113,
    131, 144
Donahue, Mike (Auburn), 83–84, 95,
    99, 111, 113, 124–25
Donnelly, Sport (Princeton), 23–24
Dorais, Gus (Notre Dame), 127
Douglas, Toots (Tennessee), 64–65
Downtown Athletic Club of New York
    City, 101, 222–24, 225, 247

Downtown Athletic Club Trophy,
    236–38, 245 n.27
Dudley, William L. (Vanderbilt), 48

Early years of football: faculty
    opposition to, 38, 43, 75 n.24;
    Harvard/Yale influence on, 6–9;
    history (1869–1890s), 5–13;
    officiating, 23–24; scoring system, 11,
    26 n.14, 56; signal systems, 37–38;
    student role, 8–9, 25 n.11; style of
    play, 21–23; tactics, 11–12, 13, 41;
    uniform/equipment, 21–22, 28 n.38
Eastern football: 1869–1890s, 5–13;
    1890s, 40–41, 60; 1900–1919, 73, 85,
    86, 94–95, 99–101, 104, 110–11, 121–
    22, 126, 128, 129, 133, 139, 148,
    154–55; 1920s, 166, 174, 181, 189–
    90, 197, 198, 200, 201, 203, 221,
    222; 1930s, 229, 242; "Ivy League,"
    183, 240; New York City scheduling,
    73, 187. See also Heisman, John W.:
    Penn tenure; Washington and
    Jefferson tenure
Eckersall, Walter (Chicago), 231–32
Eligibility of players, 31, 41, 47, 48,
    50, 96–98, 101, 140, 148
Eliot, Charles W. (Harvard), 87
Eliscu, Frank, 237
Engle, Rip (Brown), 15

Far West football (Pacific Coast, PAC
    Ten): 1890s, 13; 1909–1911, 104,
    111, 114, 139–40; 1920s, 166, 197,
    220; 1930s, 226, 227, 228, 242; Rose
    Bowl, 15, 74, 134, 146, 149, 174,
    186, 197, 200, 203, 206, 220, 227,
    229–30, 234
Fincher, Bill (Georgia Tech), 141, 144,
    145, 151
Flowers, Buck (Davidson, Georgia
    Tech), 144, 147, 148, 151, 152,
    153
Folwell, Robert C. (Penn, Navy), 155,
    160, 161, 175, 184
Forsythe, J. A. "Pee Wee" (Clemson),
    67
Forward pass, 51–52, 88–89, 90–91,

93–94, 233; Notre Dame–Army game
(1913), 126–27; Notre Dame–Ohio
State game (1935), 234–35;
supporters of, 88, 91, 94, 105, 106,
115 n.9

Gipp, George (Notre Dame), 149, 155,
166–67, 221
Grange, Harold "Red" (Illinois), 115
n.21, 129, 189, 196, 200, 201, 207,
231
Grant, John W. (Georgia Tech), 131,
151
Great Depression, impact on football
(1930s), 225–26, 227, 232
Griessman, Gene, 5
Guttmann, Allen, 251
Guyon, "Indian" Joe (Georgia Tech),
141, 142, 145, 144, 147, 148, 150

Halas, George, 149–50, 238, 240
Hall, Lyman (Georgia Tech), 69, 70
Hare, T. Truxton (Penn), 9, 231,
232
Harlan, Judy (Georgia Tech), 141, 142,
144, 148, 151, 152
Harley, Chic (Ohio State), 139, 145,
155
Harper, Jesse (Notre Dame), 129,
244
Harper, William Rainey (Chicago),
43
Harris, Nathaniel (Georgia Tech),
80
Haughton, Percy (Harvard, Columbia),
99–100, 105, 106, 121, 126, 129, 131,
141, 154, 166, 169, 176, 198
Hauser, Pete (Georgia Tech), 111
Heffelfinger, William "Pudge" (Yale),
19, 32, 41, 60, 231, 232
Heisman, John W.: academic
standards, 3, 38, 122, 192, 198–99,
252; acting career, 59, 66, 79; all-
time team selections, 230–31;
American Football Coaches
Association, 210 n.38, 214; attraction
to football, 3–4, 24, 253; Auburn
tenure, 48–59; baseball coach, 82,
123, 127; basketball coach, 119, 121,
122; Brown student, 14–16, 27 n.27;
Buchtel tenure, 35–39; business
ventures, 179–80, 189, 191, 208, 223,
239; Clemson tenure, 61–70;
coaching innovations/methods, 11–13,
28 n.38, 32–33, 34–35, 36, 37, 39,
44, 45, 50–51, 53, 63–64, 67, 75
n.24, 76 n.38, 82–83, 84, 86, 92–93,
100, 103–4, 111, 113–14, 120–21,
130, 131, 149, 152–53, 162, 172, 175,
188, 198, 203–4, 244; coaching
philosophy, 68, 69, 96, 118–19, 121,
123–24, 145, 162, 163, 169, 171, 172,
185, 186, 188, 192, 195, 201, 204,
217, 219, 224–25, 233–34, 241, 248–
51, 252–53; coaching record, 160,
214, 255–56; coaching reputation, 40,
51, 57–59, 62, 68–69, 76 n.27, 160,
161, 177, 188, 195–96, 200, 205,
213–14; "college spirit" posture, 111–
12, 114, 172–73, 178, 196, 249, 250–
51; Downtown Athletic Club, 222–
24, 230, 235–37; "football axioms,"
118–19; forward pass role, 51–52,
88–89, 105–6, 127, 190, 217, 248;
Georgia Tech tenure, 79–154; go-
getter influence/nature, 3–5, 20, 45,
159–60, 173, 206, 208, 222; high
school years, 3–4, 14; jump shift, 92–
93, 107, 128, 142–45, 168–69; law
career ambition, 17, 24; marital/
courtship relationships, 39, 65, 66,
125, 147, 151, 154, 189, 192, 208,
236, 243; Oberlin tenure, 30–35;
officiating problems, 51, 54, 55, 56,
57, 58, 132; parentage, 3, 24 n.3;
Penn student, 16–24, 29; Penn
tenure, 159–81; personality, 16, 19–
20, 49, 59, 125–26, 149, 160–61, 162,
178, 214, 236, 247; physical
appearance, 18, 27 n.29, 102, 162;
political leanings, 72; press
relationship, 40, 62, 161, 173, 178–
79; public figure, 101–2, 251–52;
racism posture, 134, 186; recruiting
eligibility views, 97–98, 130, 193–94,
218–19; Rice tenure, 190–206; soccer

impact, 14; Titusville influence, 2–5;
tributes at death, 242–43;
Washington and Jefferson tenure,
183–89; writing ambition/
accomplishments, 40, 79, 108–9,
214–18, 230–31, 248, 252, 253
Heisman, William Lee, 3, 4, 39
Heisman Trophy, 235–38, 243–44, 245
n.27
Helms Hall of Fame Foundation, 7,
139, 220
Henry, Wilbur "Pete" (Washington and
Jefferson), 139, 145, 155, 231
Hershberger, Clarence (Chicago), 60
Heston, Willie (Michigan), 74, 85, 86,
115 n.21, 189, 232
Hickman, Herman (Tennessee), 228
Higher education and football: alumni
influence/support, 73, 76 n.28, 110,
167, 218; black institutions, 71;
Brown University, 14–15, 27 n.27;
Buchtel College, 38; business/
industry influence on, 4–5, 7–8;
Carlisle Indian School, 94; Carnegie
Commission report (1929), 217–19;
Chicago, University of, 42–43, 240–
41; Clemson College, 59, 61–62;
Franklin, Benjamin (educational
views), 17; Georgia Tech, 80–81;
Knight Commission report (1991),
210 n.43; Morrill Act of 1862 (land
grant institutions), 25 n.10, 49, 61,
62; Oberlin College, 31; Rice
Institute, 190–91, 193–94; rule
change meetings (1905–1906), 86–90,
115 n.9, 115 n.10; student social
behavior (1920s), 164; Washington
and Jefferson College, 183; World
War I impact, 140–41. See also
Heisman, John W.: Auburn tenure;
Penn tenure
Hinkey, Frank (Yale), 41, 60
Hollenbeck, Bill (Penn), 164
Howard, Frank (Clemson), 62
Huguley, Ed (Auburn), 55, 56, 57
Hutchins, Robert M. (Chicago), 240
Hutson, Don (Alabama), 239

Intersectional game. See Big Game
traditions

Jones, Bobby, 101, 236
Jones, Howard (Yale, Iowa, USC),
104, 173, 220, 227
Jones, Tad (Yale), 139, 189

Kaw, Eddie (Cornell), 171
Kazmaier, Dick (Princeton), 252
Kelley, Larry (Yale), 243–44
Kerr, Andy (Lehigh), 229
Kipke, Harry (Michigan), 182,
228
Knight Foundation Commission report
(1991), 210 n.43, 252

LaFitte, Ed (Georgia Tech), 82
Layden, Elmer (Notre Dame), 196,
197, 234, 237
Lewis, William Henry (Amherst,
Harvard), 71, 91, 134
Little, Lou (Columbia), 140, 198, 229,
230
Loeb, Al (Georgia Tech), 21, 51, 104,
120, 126

McCallum, John, 47
McGugin, Dan (Vanderbilt), 83–84, 97,
137, 143, 144, 182, 203, 234
Mackey, Harry (Penn), 21
McLaughry, Tuss (Brown), 15
McMillan, Bo (Centre), 174
McNamee, Graham, 203
McVey, William (Rice), 195, 201, 210
n.48
McWhorter, Bob (Georgia), 110, 113,
121, 125, 151
Mahan, Eddie (Harvard), 126, 133,
231
Meehan, Chick (NYU), 221
Merriwell, Frank (Gilbert Patten), 9,
86
Midwest football (Western Conference,
Big Ten); 1870s–1880s, 13, 31, 32;
1890s, 45–46, 60, 61 (see also
Heisman, John W.: Buchtel tenure;
Oberlin tenure); 1900–1919, 73–74,

86, 93, 104, 111, 122, 126, 128–29, 133, 139, 146, 148, 155; 1920s, 166, 173, 181–82, 189, 196–97, 200–201, 221–22; 1930s, 226–27, 228, 233, 242

Miller, Jonathan K. "Poss" (Penn), 172, 175, 179

Missionary coaches, 31, 46, 75 n.5

Modern football, advent of (1912), 117–18

Modern uniform/equipment, 239

Moffat, Alex (Princeton), 60–61

Morrow, David C. (Washington and Jefferson), 184

Muckrakers' criticism of football: Godkin, Edward L., 86; Needham, Henry Beech, 87

Muller, Brick (California), 166, 231

Murphy, Robert M. (Washington and Jefferson), 183–84, 185, 186

Nagurski, Bronko (Minnesota), 221, 239

Naismith, James, 76 n.28

National Collegiate Athletic Association (NCAA), 89, 98, 100, 105, 106, 193, 217, 226

Neale, Earle "Greasy" (Washington and Jefferson), 174, 184

Nevers, Ernie (Stanford), 197, 239

Neyland, Bob (Tennessee), 128, 203–4, 228

Notre Dame, University of: impact on football, 149, 196–97; Rockne tenure, 148 n.49, 155, 166–67, 182, 196–97, 201, 221, 226–27

Numbered jersey, advent of, 128

O'Dea, Pat (Wisconsin), 61

Oliphant, Elmer (Purdue, Army), 139

Paterno, Joe (Brown), 15

Pfann, George (Cornell), 171

Poe brothers (Princeton), 60

Pollard, Fritz (Brown), 15, 134, 139

Popularity of football, 13, 39, 60, 73, 86, 110, 114, 126, 127, 164–65, 167–68, 196, 214, 219, 220, 221, 226, 241–42

Press coverage, of football, 39–40, 108–9, 120, 126, 136–37, 173, 181–82, 189, 214, 233

Prince, Willard B. (Downtown Athletic Club), 231

Principles of Football (1922), 38, 109, 118, 130, 177, 216, 247, 249

Professional football, 206–7, 238–40, 242

Professionalization of college football, 8, 25 n.13, 73, 96, 97, 98, 105, 130, 131, 154, 172, 201, 217, 218

Pund, Peter (Georgia Tech), 220

Radio, impact of, 164, 203, 208, 229

Regional pride/rivalry, 86, 111, 167–68, 190

Religion, and football, 4, 45, 250, 256

Rice, Grantland, 26 n.18, 98, 108, 196

Riegels, Roy "Wrong-Way," 220

Riggs, Walter Merritt (Clemson), 59–60, 68, 69

"Ringer" problem, 50, 96–97, 98

Robert, Chip (Georgia Tech), 84, 92, 96, 98, 141, 223

Robinson, Jackie (UCLA), 242

Rockefeller, John D., 2–3, 4, 43, 180

Rockne, Knute (Notre Dame), 40, 66, 127, 129, 148–49, 155, 166, 182, 196, 197, 198, 201, 221, 226, 227, 239, 244, 247, 250

Roosevelt, Theodore, 71–72, 81, 87–88, 89, 108, 115 n.9, 150

Roper, Bill (Princeton), 111, 181

Rugby-soccer influence, 5–7, 25 n.12

Rule changes/concerns: 1870s, 7, 9; 1880s, 10, 11–12; 1890s, 12, 18, 20, 41; 1900–1916, 72–73, 83, 85, 86, 87–88, 89, 90, 92, 105–7, 109–10,

114, 117–18, 125, 140; 1920s, 181, 190, 206, 207; 1930s, 230, 239

Savage, C. W. "Fred" (Oberlin), 32, 33
Schultz, Adolf "Germany" (Michigan), 85, 231
Shaughnessy, Clark (Chicago), 238, 240
Shift (glide, jump, quick), 92–93, 106–7, 128, 129, 138, 142–43, 162, 168–69, 170, 172, 196–97
Sington, Frank (Alabama), 227
Sitton, Vedder (Clemson), 68
Smith, Andy (California), 166, 182, 197
Smith, Ed (NYU), 237
Smith, Harvey (Rice), 192, 193, 201, 202
Socialization process in football, 45, 71
Sociocultural background: 1890s, 41–43; 1900–1903, 70–72; 1910, 80, 107–10; 1914–1919, 128, 150–51; 1920, 163–64; 1927, 207–8; 1929, 180, 220–23; 1930, 225–26, 232–33
Southern football (Southern Intercollegiate Athletic Association-SIAA, Southern Conference): 1890s, 46–48, 52, 54–55 (see also Heisman, John W., Auburn tenure); 1900–1919 (see Heisman, John W.: Clemson tenure; Georgia Tech tenure; 1920s, 165, 167–68, 173–74, 176, 182, 185–86, 190, 200, 203–4, 209 n.26, 220–n21; 1930s, 227–29, 230, 234
Southwest football (Southwest Conference): 1914–1919, 129, 133, 146, 155; 1920s, 167, 190, 206, 222 (see also Heisman, John W., Rice tenure); 1930s, 229, 232, 234, 242
Stagg, Amos Alonzo, 19, 26–27, 36, 43–45, 71, 74, 85–86, 88, 93, 94, 106, 107, 126, 129, 160, 214, 218, 230, 240, 241, 244, 247
Strong, Ken (NYU), 221
Strupper, Everett (Georgia Tech), 131–

32, 133, 135, 137, 141, 142, 144, 145, 153
Sutherland, Jock (Lafayette, Pitt), 170, 206, 247

T-formation, 18, 26 n.17, 44, 129, 142, 234, 240, 244
Thayer, Harry "Pop" (Penn), 22
Thomas, Frank (Alabama), 234
Thomy, Al (Georgia Tech), 51, 56, 66, 148, 151, 152
Thornton, Harry (Penn), 46
Thorpe, Jim (Carlisle), 100–101, 114, 115 n.21, 122, 150, 189, 232
Tichenor, Reynolds (Auburn), 50, 51
Titusville, Penn., 2–3, 4–5, 48, 101, 180
Torrey, Bob (Penn), 85
Turner, Frank (Georgia Tech), 69, 70, 82

Underwood, Wash (Rice), 204

Vandergraaf, Bully (Alabama), 132

Wade, Wallace (Brown, Alabama), 15, 134, 200, 227
Wagenhurst, Elwood O. (Penn), 21, 38, 161
Wallace, Robert B. (Georgia Tech), 16, 69
Warburton, Cotton (USC), 228
Ward, Arch (College All-Star game), 239
Warner, Glenn "Pop," 43, 44, 51, 52–53, 61, 76 n.38, 86, 94–95, 97, 103, 107, 122, 133, 139, 145, 147–48, 197, 198, 203, 210 n.49, 220, 229, 234, 244, 245 n.16
Washington, Kenny (UCLA), 242
Watkin, William Ward (Rice), 193
West, Charles "Pruner" (Washington and Jefferson), 185, 186
Wilkinson, Bud (Minnesota), 233

Williams, Carl (Oberlin, Penn), 18, 33, 85

Williams, C. R. "Bob" (Clemson), 63

Williams, Henry (Minnesota), 73, 86, 106–7, 129, 244, 247

Williams, Joe, 68, 231, 232, 235, 242–43, 245 n.17, 247

Wood, Leonard (Georgia Tech), 81, 218

Woodruff, George (Penn), 13, 18–19, 41, 60, 73, 85, 160, 161, 166, 190, 218, 247

Woodruff, L. F. "Fuzzy," 62, 66, 92, 96, 146, 165, 167–68, 182

World War I, impact on football, 140–41, 146, 147, 150–51

Yost, Fielding (Michigan), 74, 83, 85, 136, 166, 228, 244

Young, Lou (Penn), 180, 213

Zuppke, Bob (Illinois), 128–29, 139, 210 n.49

About the Author

WILEY LEE UMPHLETT is Associate Professor of Sociology at the University of West Florida. He is the author of numerous publications and books on sports and popular culture.

Recent Titles in
Contributions to the Study of Popular Culture

Hibernian Green on the Silver Screen: The Irish and American Movies
Joseph M. Curran

Film Directors on Directing
John Andrew Gallagher

Seeking the Perfect Game: Baseball in American Literature
Cordelia Candelaria

Take One: The Control Room Insights of Ten TV Directors
Jack Kuney

A "Brand" New Language: Commercial Influences in Literature and Culture
Monroe Friedman

Out of the Woodpile: Black Characters in Crime and Detective Fiction
Frankie Y. Bailey

Freaks of Genius
Daniel Shealy, editor
Madeleine B. Stern and Joel Myerson, associate editors

Encounters with Filmmakers: Eight Career Studies
Jon Tuska

Master Space: Film Images of Capra, Lubitsch, Sternberg, and Wyler
Barbara Bowman

The Cosby Show: Audiences, Impact, and Implications
Linda K. Fuller

America's Musical Pulse: Popular Music in Twentieth-Century Society
Kenneth J. Bindas, editor

Not Just for Children: The Mexican Comic Book in the Late 1960s and 1970s
Harold E. Hinds, Jr., and Charles M. Tatum

DEMCO